HENRY CLAY FRICK

Henry Clay Frick

The Life of the
Perfect Capitalist

Quentin R. Skrabec, Jr.

McFarland & Company, Inc., Publishers
Jefferson, North Carolina, and London

Library of Congress Cataloguing-in-Publication Data

Skrabec, Quentin R.
Henry Clay Frick : the life of the perfect capitalist /
Quentin R. Skrabec, Jr.
p.   cm.
Includes bibliographical references and index.

ISBN 978-0-7864-4383-3
softcover : 50# alkaline paper ∞

1. Frick, Henry Clay, 1849–1919.   2. Businesspeople—
United States—Biography.   3. Capitalists and financiers—
United States—Biography.   I. Title.
HC102.5.F75S55   2010   338.092—dc22 [B]   2009051570

British Library cataloguing data are available

Front cover: Henry Clay Frick (Library of Congress);
background Pittsburgh, Pennsylvania (Pictures Now)

Manufactured in the United States of America

McFarland & Company, Inc., Publishers
Box 611, Jefferson, North Carolina 28640
www.mcfarlandpub.com

To Henry Clay Frick,
the quintessential capitalist.

Also to Our Lady of Victory,
and my wife and editor, Barbara.

Table of Contents

Acknowledgments

Any research is based on the quality and skill of many archivists and tour guides. I was blessed to have some of the best. So much inspiration and knowledge were gained from endless tours of Clayton and tour guides such as Cassie Wright. I would like to especially thank Alesha Shumar, archivist at the University of Pittsburgh; Wendy Pfleg of the University of Pittsburgh; and Barry Ched and Gil Pietrzak of the Carnegie Library of Oakland. The Carnegie Library was the first library I ever entered, and it remains my first stop to research a book Thanks also to Julie Ludwig, associate archivist of the Frick Collection (New York), and Greg Langel of the Frick Center. It is impossible to write Pittsburgh history without the help of the excellent staff of the Heinz History Center. The History Center is a true treasure both for its archives and its inspiration.

I owe much to many who are gone, including my grandfather, Louis Skrabec, who spent years showing me the mills of Pittsburgh and relating their history.

Prologue

The research for this book has taken me many places, but in many ways this god-in-my-literary pantheon has been a walk down memory lane. I grew up literally in Frick's backyard. I played and learned in Frick Park for days on end in my youth. My home in Swisshelm Park was built on the location where troops camped during the Homestead Strike. Across the street from my home on a steep cliff was a panoramic view of Homestead, where my grandfather worked. My grandfather also worked for Frick's Union Railway. I owe my education to the generosity of "robber barons" such as Carnegie and Frick.

My inspiration for writing this book was rooted in my first trips to the Carnegie Library. My grandparents lived in Swissvale near where the Frick family often picnicked. I know the very footsteps of Henry Clay Frick well. I collected fossils from the same rock formations as Childs Frick. My family had many steelworkers, and I followed my love of steel with a metallurgical engineering degree from the University of Michigan. I worked for years as a manager of a steel melt shop. I loved the night glow of the steel city of Pittsburgh. I have seen and felt steel strikes from both sides of the issue.

Preface

Over the years I have been working on a biographic pantheon of American capitalism and exceptionalism. Men like George Westinghouse, H.J. Heinz, and Michael Owens offered me the safety of writing about business icons who were well liked and often even loved by their employees. I had focused on the famous and populist members of that pantheon, however; possibly the greatest American capitalist was its most infamous. Certainly in any such pantheon, Henry Clay Frick would have to be a candidate for the seat of Jupiter were it not for his poor reputation with labor. Frick, however, like the Roman gods, had shortcomings; yet a pantheon of American capitalism without Frick would be made of paper, not marble. Frick, of course, represents some of the problems of capitalism. It would take other gods, such as William McKinley in government and William McGuffey in education, to help limit the blind pursuit of money that is possible with capitalism.

Frick was extremely generous, however, and saw giving as personal, not a requirement of a capitalist. Frick saw it as a basic right to accumulate wealth; yet on a percentage basis, few people give as much to charity as Frick did. In this respect he was a pure capitalist, seeing capitalism as a freedom, a right, and the preferred economic system of democratic societies. Frick's excesses represent not so much evil as the blindness that comes with success. Frick was human, not evil, and his life demonstrates many shortcomings found in all of us. His notoriety and wealth, of course, magnified his shortcomings. Never have I written a book that required such effort to see the human side of a man and find good. Still, to fully build a literary pantheon of capitalism, I felt it necessary to understand men like Frick to fully see the advantages and disadvantages of American capitalism.

Henry Clay Frick has touched my life in many ways. I grew up in Pittsburgh a few miles from his beautiful mansion, and I spent most of my youthful days in Frick Park, which was a direct path from my home to the mansion. I remember well as I grew up venturing more miles into Frick Park with my maturity until finally one day reaching the far gate at the Frick mansion. I never fully understood who Henry Clay Frick was. I do remember vaguely in my teens that many considered him a true devil of the past, but I never really asked anyone. I only knew he had built my favorite playground, in which I spent almost every day playing. To my ignorant mind, Henry Clay Frick was a Santa Claus, a man who gave me this great park in my backyard. I felt the same way about Andrew Carnegie. It was a real treat when my dad took me to the Carnegie Museum and Library in the Oakland section of Pittsburgh. When I was old enough to ride the streetcar, we went often to the Carnegie Museum after waiting outside the wall of old Forbes Field for baseballs hit out of the park. The great thing was that the museum was completely free.

As I studied history, the picture of Henry Clay Frick changed. Frick seemed marked for the ages by the Homestead Strike of 1892. This was the reason that even in his hometown, there is no tribute to him. Recent documentaries on the Homestead Strike show bitterness passed on to new generations. I gave a talk at the John Heinz Historical Center in 2007, and the mere mention of Frick brought boos from the audience. Jack the Ripper seemed to have a better image among Pittsburghers. Henry Clay Frick's reputation would in many ways taint the work of others such as H.J. Heinz and George Westinghouse. More recently, historians have started again to strip away years of bias. Oxford historian Kenneth Warren even suggested in 1989: "It was an heroic age; it does not seem too fanciful to claim that Henry Clay Frick should be ranked with the highest in its business pantheon."

I don't believe history is ready to place Frick in that position. History itself has been bipolar in its approach to Frick. Family-sponsored biographies have been favorable, but most others have seen him as the anti–Christ, a Hitler figure of the business world. Carnegie apologists have used Frick as the scapegoat to improve Carnegie's own legacy. In fact, Carnegie and his associates had launched a thirty-year effort to rewrite the relationship of Frick and Carnegie. A further problem is that Homestead was more than a strike; it was a political rupture in the fabric of American society.

Frick had both saintly and evil attributes. While labeled a "robber baron," he believed in playing fair to amass his millions. Contemporaries admired Frick for his ethical and straightforward business dealings. Enemies and friends preferred to deal with Frick because he was trustworthy. He enjoyed using his money to fulfill his passion for art collecting, but was he any more extreme than many of us who are passionate about a hobby? Yes, we can spend too much on it in both money and time, but that is a sin common to most of us. Hopefully it is possible to admire his good traits, while deploring his negative attributes. Hopefully we can see the man in the legend of the press as having characteristics similar to our own. There is no question that his daughter saw a much different man from the one described by the press. My many years as a manager in the steel industry with an office not far from Homestead gives me another perspective at times into Frick the manager. Frick's handling of Homestead is often characterized as Frick unleashing an army of Pinkerton Guards on innocent poor immigrant workers. We shall see that the facts are much different.

I have spent decades studying the Homestead Strike and it too has become a battle of mythology. This doesn't excuse some bad decisions by Frick that caused Homestead, but neither was Homestead the epic battle of good versus evil. It really was a battle between the well-paid trade unionists against the extremely overpaid owners. The average poorly paid laborer was left in the middle and unrepresented. Frick's behavior represented the norm, perhaps that of the majority of managers of the period. My own experience in the steel industry showed that strikes often take men to the worst of their emotions.

I have often wondered what I might have done if I had been in Frick's shoes. Many managers, including myself, might well have taken similar steps but would have lacked the anti-union passion. To a great degree, the Homestead Strike was a predetermined political event. The union, the strikers, Frick, Carnegie, the press and the politicians created an environment that led to deaths. The union, for example, consisted of a small group of the highest-paid workers. Both the union and management left the immigrant day laborers, who represented the majority of the workforce, out of the negotiations. Homestead cannot be reduced to bullet points. Like Frick, union struggles of the period are complex, not the black and white they are often reduced to in history books. It was a time of struggle over the means of production. Socialists claimed ownership of the means and property of production that had been built by the capitalists. The American citizen of the period was obsessed with property rights that had routinely been denied or abused in Europe. Public opinion changed with events or press stories. The union-management model of today is much different from the view of 1892. Today there is an acceptance of union and management struggles as part of the normal process of business. Property rights are still defended today in any strike.

The final challenge of this biography was to blend the personal and business aspects of his life, matters that are often treated separately. On one end there is an outstanding intimate portrait by Martha Frick Symington Sanger, and on the business end there is Kenneth Warren's business biography. Frick's personal and business lives were in many ways a dichotomy. I wanted to see Frick through my eyes as an operations manager in the steel industry. I knew the struggles of good people on both sides of strikes resulting in civil breakdown. I had experienced the tension at the mill during a strike and understood how easy it is to get backed into strong stands. I have experienced violence during a strike where I saw rational men lose their temper. As a Pittsburgh youth, I learned the impact of strikes on workers and their families.

Later I came to understand the view of a steel manager. I knew and made some of the same mistakes as Frick. I could relate to Frick the manager and executive, and it is in this view I could offer a different look at Frick. I knew well the pain and struggle of managing a steel mill and going home from that environment. I knew the challenge of managing an operation that runs 24/7 and demands much of its managers. Frick had managed family and mill better than I had. I knew well the mills and towns of the Monongahela River Valley, and many times followed Frick in his own footsteps. I knew the dust and dark days of industrial Pittsburgh. I could personally relate to Childs Frick, who found a love for science in Frick Park and the Carnegie Institute of Pittsburgh. From my youth, I knew the other side of the union issue. Now as a business professor, I can also see the organizational genius of Frick as well. There were also many surprises in the research, such as his anonymous generosity, his love of children, and his patriotism. Frick proved to be as complex and as average as all of us.

A Technical Note

It would be impossible to detach the historical technology from Henry Clay Frick's life. Homestead and the steel industry of Frick's time represented a struggle between industrialization and crafts manufacture. It was a revolutionary change in how men worked and lived. The complexities of the technology can often confuse the reader's ability to fully understand the success of men like Frick. This technology can be just as confusing to the modern engineer because these processes have long been dropped from textbooks. Every effort is made to explain the processes simply throughout the biography; however, this technical note can help and can be used as a reference for the reader.

Iron was a kingmaker in ancient times. The Hittites had an iron monopoly until about 1000 B.C. The Hittites had discovered that the mixing of charcoal, ore, and limestone with heat result in reducing iron from its oxide, known as iron ore. The Hittites also tapped the power of bellows to generate the high heat needed. A wood fire can reach 1,650 F; with blown air, it can reach the 2,300 F needed for iron smelting. Iron was made in very limited amounts until the seventeenth century, when high stack charcoal furnaces started to be built. These stacks ranged from 10 feet to 50 feet high. They were top-fed with alternating layers of charcoal, iron ore, and limestone. These charcoal furnaces were common in the United States from 1700 to the end of the Civil War.

As a boy, Frick would have been familiar with the many charcoal furnaces of his home county of Westmoreland. From 1790 to 1850, Westmoreland County was the heart of the charcoal iron furnace industry. It was in Westmoreland that a group of capitalists known as the Pig Iron Aristocracy commercialized the west. Many of Pittsburgh's old banking families had ties to the charcoal iron furnaces of Westmoreland.

Old charcoal iron stacks can still be found in western Pennsylvania, the Hocking Hills of Ohio, western Maryland, and northern Michigan. Working and fully restored furnaces can also be seen in Pennsylvania, Ohio, and Massachusetts. Some were even pressed back into service during World War I. Amazingly, some charcoal furnaces are still used today in the wood-rich areas of South America and China. Henry Clay Frick made his fortune from the switch of iron smelting furnaces from wood charcoal to coke and coal. Coke was produced by burning oils, tars, and volatile materials out of coal, resulting in a lump of high-energy carbon. Coke was revolutionary because it had enough energy to enable making the furnace stack higher than could be fueled by soft, low-strength charcoal. Coal before coking lacked the strength and the high-energy value of coke. A higher stack of iron ore and fuel meant more iron production. Today's huge blast furnaces of coke, iron ore, and limestone are used to continuously produce pig iron. Being a derivative of coal and having a higher strength and energy, coke made it possible to built higher stacks and develop higher heat. The resultant blast furnace iron product, as noted, was high in residual carbon, which we call pig iron, blast furnace, or cast iron. Iron with about three percent carbon in it is known as pig iron or cast iron. Coke, however, was also a versatile fuel used to fire iron reheating, puddling, glass furnaces, and rolling mill furnaces. The making of iron and steel products in the nineteenth century required a series of working operations that required reheating the iron. The "Connellsville coke" of Frick's Westmoreland County was the highest quality coking coal in the world. It was low in volatiles, producing the highest energy coke possible, and low in elements such as sulfur, which was detrimental to blast furnace iron.

The term pig iron has been used throughout this book to refer to blast furnace iron. As a liquid, it flows readily and can be cast into shapes. You can still see cast iron products in wood-burning stoves, lawn furniture, old toy banks, and Grandma's iron skillet. Pig iron was high-strength but it is not flexible and can be brittle. If charcoal furnaces or blast furnaces did not cast directly into products such as stoves, they casted an immediate product into "pigs." Pig iron "pigs" were 50-pound bars that were then sold to rolling mills, foundries, wrought iron makers, and steel makers. When Frick was born in 1849, pig iron commonly went to foundries that remelted it and poured it into shapes such as parts for steam engines. The foundry used a special reheating furnace fueled by coke, known as a cupola. In the 1850s, Pittsburgh had many foundries producing steam engines and cast cannon and cannonballs. The biggest use of pig was the production of wrought iron, which required the reheating of the pig iron in a puddling furnace. Wrought iron could also be produced by the ancient swordmaker's way of heating pig iron and hammering it to burn out carbon. Burning out carbon produced a product close to elemental iron, which was soft and flexible. Hammering forges, or in some cases rolling mills, produced this product. In Frick's youth there were many rolling mills in Pittsburgh that produced wrought-iron nails, bands, structural beams for bridges, and wagon wheels.

The fastest way at the time to reheat pig iron was in a puddling furnace, which allowed hot paste of pig iron to have the carbon worked out. A single puddling furnace was seven feet by seven feet, a batch or heat was around 600 pounds. The heat would require 800 pounds of coal or coke to bring the furnace up to temperature. A puddler using a hook would turn this pasty ball over and over in the heat. The ball might weigh as much as 200 pounds. Then the puddler hammered the paste over and over. The process was repeated until a metallurgical metamorphosis turned the mass into steel or wrought iron. The puddler in Frick's boyhood was highly crafts-oriented, but it was hard work. Jules Verne described it best in an 1885 novel:

> Teams of half-naked giants, armed with long hooks, were working with great activity.... In the immensity of this monstrous forge, there was a constant motion, torrents of endless belts, dull blows against the roar of continuous throbbing, continuous fireworks of red sparks, and the glare of kilns raised to white heat.... And yet they were tough fellows, these puddlers! Kneading at arm's length a metal paste of two hundred kilos in torrid heat while staring at this blinding, incandescent steel is dreadful work which wears a man out in ten years.[1]

Today, low-carbon steel has replaced wrought iron in applications like nails. The skin on your car is probably the closest thing to wrought iron we use today. Puddlers were true craftsmen serving years of apprenticeship as assistants.

The puddler could also produce steel as a product. The removal of less carbon from pig iron or control of carbon results in steel, a stronger and tougher material than wrought iron, and more flexible that cast iron. Like iron, steel changed the political maps because of its superior strength and workability. The processing of high quality steel remained tightly held secrets in places like Damascus, Toledo, and Sheffield. Early in history, steel had been the product of a smith beating hot "iron" on an anvil to remove carbon to the proper level. The heat-and-beat method was great for farriers, blacksmiths, and swordmakers, but could not support the needs of an Industrial Revolution. The puddling method of making steel had come into wide use in Frick's youth (1849 to 1870), but it still was very limited in its ability to produce large amounts of steel. Henry Bessemer "invented" a high-volume process and Andrew Carnegie commercialized it. By the 1880s, Bessemer steel was quickly replacing wrought iron in tonnage usages such as railroad and bridge building. A single Bessemer converter could produce as much as twenty times the output of a full day's work of the puddler in 40 minutes. Furthermore, the Bessemer steel operating crew required much less skill than the puddler and his crew. In fact, most of the Bessemer furnace crew was considered unskilled labor. The Age of Steel represents the end of the Industrial Revolution, but as a material it still reigns supreme. The ability to mass-produce steel in a Bessemer converter required higher and larger blast furnaces, which created a boom for coke and a path for Henry Clay Frick to make a fortune. Sheffield, Toledo, and Damascus had been the ancient steel centers, but the rise of the Industrial Revolution gave rise to new cities of steel, like Essen, Pittsburgh, and Youngstown. For interested readers, a Bessemer converter can be seen in Pittsburgh's Station Square.

Until Carnegie managers worked out the process flow and Frick integrated mills with company railroads, there was a lot of remelting and reheating in steelmaking. In the 1870s, the Bessemer converter got its liquid pig iron from solid "pigs" remelted in a cupola air furnace. For Carnegie's first steel mill at Braddock, the pigs were made eight miles downriver, then shipped as solid pigs to the Braddock cupola furnaces to remelt it for the Bessemers. Cupola furnaces used air and coke to remelt pig iron quickly. Even when Carnegie added pig iron blast furnaces to the mill at Braddock, liquid pig often could not go directly to the Bessemer because of timing. It took Bill Jones, Braddock's plant manager of Edgar Thomson Works, to invent a mobile holding (refractory brick-lined) tank to hold and mix liquid pig iron in 1879. This "Jones mixer" allowed blast furnace operations to feed Bessemer converters direct with huge fuel savings by eliminating the cupola furnaces. Today foundries that lack large blast furnaces and buy solid pig still use the coke-fired cupola. Frick more than anyone realized the value of the Jones mixer, and was at Jones's widow's door to ensure he had the rights to it when Jones was killed in a furnace explosion. By 1885, a single day's production of steel at Edgar Thomson Works was more than all the world's puddlers could produce in a day. The puddling process would hang on at small specialty steel manufacturers, but the puddler's craft by 1885 had gone the way of horseshoe farriers after the introduction of the Model T.

Steel production of Frick's middle years produced liquid pig iron in huge blast furnaces, consuming huge amounts of coke. The high carbon liquid pig iron was then taken to a Bessemer converter (via the Jones Mixer on railroad tracks), where air was blown through the molten pig iron, burning out the carbon. A Bessemer converter held between 15 to 20 tons of liquid iron. The length of the air blow controlled the amount of carbon in the steel and thus the properties desired for its end use. Today pure oxygen replaces air in a process known as the basic oxygen process. Steel became a cheap engineering material in the 1870s with the Bessemer process that was better at making material for railroad rails and nails than wrought iron. For a period between 1890 and 1950, the Bessemer process was replaced with the open hearth furnace, which made higher quality steel. The open hearth furnace still required liquid or solid pig iron from coke-fired blast furnaces. In the early days of Homestead's open hearth, a cupola furnace melted solid pig iron to feed the open hearths. Additional heat to the open hearth was supplied by coke (or natural gas) as well and could liquefy solid pig iron or steel scrap. The solid pig iron originally came from furnaces across river from Homestead, but Frick's Union Railroad system put hot liquid pig iron to be transported across the river from Carrie Furnaces to Homestead. The open-hearth process took more time and energy, but it produced a much higher quality steel than the Bessemer process. An open hearth furnace can be seen at Youngstown's Museum of Industrial History.

Open hearth or Bessemer furnaces were poured (tapped) into large refractory brick ladles. The liquid steel was then poured into molds, producing a typical 18-inch to 36-inch square ingot. A typical ingot for the period weighed 7,000 pounds. It then had to go through a series of reheats and rolling processes. The first rolling mill was the blooming mill, which reduced the product to a 12-inch by 12-inch square "bloom." The blooms would be reheated and rolled at a billet mill, producing a 4-inch by 4-inch square. These billets could be sold to nail, wire, rod, structural, or sheet mills to produce a specific end product. One of Frick's overlooked contributions was his in-house railroad which allowed immediate movement of rolled product directly to reheating furnaces, saving enormous amounts of energy. Frick's United States Steel plants offered some of the first fully integrated mills, moving from raw materials to finished product. The rolling process became less labor-intensive with automated handling systems. The rolling process had been improved, but not to the extent of the revolutionary change of the Bessemer process, and the roller and his crew remained crafts-oriented. The Bessemer equivalent of a technology revolution in rolling didn't come until 1970, with the advent of continuous casting, which eliminated the blooming mill. The roller still required years of experience to achieve the processing knowledge needed.

Introduction

Henry Clay Frick's reputation has suffered from his own reticence, and from the myths which by now others have implanted firmly into the folk memory of students of American industrialization. Labour relations and above all the adverse publicity associated with his typically unyielding attitude during the Homestead strike, the accounts of his conflicts with Carnegie, written by those acting as apologists for the latter, and Carnegie's own extraordinary autobiography—all these have managed to blacken his reputation.

— Kenneth Warren, 1989
Historical Society of Western Pennsylvania

In 1907, when the Pittsburgh Chamber of Commerce honored 28 of its distinguished sons, Henry Clay Frick's listed profession was "capitalist." The term capitalist brings mixed feelings even today, and that is the root issue in brushing a portrait of Henry Clay Frick. Kenneth Warren clearly portrays the problem with obtaining a true picture of America's greatest capitalist. Henry Clay Frick was the quintessential capitalist, unabashed his belief in the pursuit of wealth as a basic right. He learned to love capitalism's rewards and became its most ardent philosopher. He was a capitalist to the end, a capitalist who attached no social requirements or strings to how his money had to be spent. He had no larger worldview of capitalism, unlike his former partner, Andrew Carnegie. He gave much to the community but was not a well-known philanthropist. He believed that giving should be personal and anonymous. He viewed himself as a type of financial gladiator going to the arena each day. In that arena, victory was the only goal and it dominated his focus. He did, however, believe in strict rules as to the nature of the fight. His friends were nonexistent once he entered the arena, where Frick was a cold and calculating fighter. Once he left the arena, he was a caring family man, unlike most of his "robber baron" associates. His heart softened as he left the arena's gate, and he exhibited a tender love of children and of giving to help poor children. Yet Frick is an enigma who left little in the way of records in his defense. The incomplete picture raises questions like: Was Frick a tough and hardheaded manager or one that had "a stoic acceptance of the shedding of blood"?[1]

In America's rust belt there is a pantheon of bronze and iron. This pantheon remains today overlooked at the McKinley Memorial in Niles, Ohio. While lost to the travel guides and tourist trails, it embodies an American spirit of greatness and a time of industrial superiority. It is here that an ironmaster of the nineteenth century, Joseph Butler, built an architectural monument to a fallen friend and supporter of the industry: his beloved President William McKinley. The financial support for such a project came from another admirer of McKinley: America's bad boy, Henry Clay Frick. It is the bust of Henry Clay Frick that fills the prominent place of America's Jupiter at the memorial. Frick, a Pittsburgher, has found no such honor in his hometown or in any other American town. In the last October of his life, Henry Clay Frick visited this Niles Memorial, as he had done often in the years prior, and was brought to tears. Those tears surely were not for McKinley alone but for golden times now past. It is in Niles, Ohio, alone that Frick finds such a place of honor.

This is the man that unions to this day believe to have been the ancient devil known as

Mammon,[2] blamed in part for building a dam for a fishing lodge that caused the infamous Johnstown Flood, which killed over 2,200. Considered the man behind the bloody Homestead Strike of 1892, Frick would never find rest in his hometown. Even old friends such as Andrew Carnegie shunned him. Remembering him more as a monster that put the pursuit of art ahead of his laborers, labor historians hold him up as "Capitalism's Devil." But was Frick really the devil of American lore, or its best example of American capitalism's two faces? The Homestead Strike more than anything created a historical black hole sucking almost any of Frick's good attributes into its vortex. Many historians have looked at Frick and his times as a period of greed gone wild. Frick has become a poster boy for the great evils that some believe inherent to capitalism. However, take the Homestead Strike out of the record, and the view of Frick is much different.

Henry Clay Frick represents historical extremes and contradictions. Few have supported the early hagiographic family biographies, while most have supported the image of the evil union-hating Hun that has become known as Henry Clay Frick. Recently, the view of Henry Clay Frick has become one in which he represents the true evil of capitalism. Frick's role in the Homestead Strike of 1892 seemed to have marked him for history, yet his views on unions were no different from those of his saintly neighbors, H.J. Heinz and George Westinghouse. Frick, a loving husband and father, is more often pictured as a brute willing to break the poor immigrant worker at any cost. Yet Frick often helped poor children without much fanfare, giving millions to children's organizations and hospitals. He formed a national organization to help retarded children.[3] He created a Pittsburgh educational fund to improve grade school education. In December of 1915, when the bankruptcy of Pittsburgh Savings caused 40,000 schoolchildren to lose $130,000 (about $1.5 million today) of their school's dime savings plan, Frick repaid them all in time for Christmas, wiring the money from New York. Frick was not the Nero of the Gilded Age, promoting wild parties of excess, but a good father and family man. The fact is Frick was neither a saint nor a devil, but a complex product of a struggling America. In the end, Frick gave much to the city that disowned him. Frick also gave much to the children of the very workers who vilified him. It is that side of the man that is lost to history.

Frick's dislike of unions was shared by the best of the capitalists and even many laborers. His error was in his approach to the issue. Unlike Westinghouse and Heinz, or even Bismarck and Krupp in Germany, he refused to address the problems of labor in the workplace as the best alternative to unionization. He linked unions with socialism, which was the belief of most at the time. Unions to most Americans were a foreign idea, being imported from Europe. German-American craftsmen refused to join them, as did many laborers. Even Samuel Gompers, the father of American unions, opposed the European style of unionization, which included politics and street protests. Frick refused to deal with the union, and unfortunately, with most of the underlying problems in the workplace. He took a hard line with unions, refusing to accept them or their grievances, which often took both sides to the brink. Like Carnegie, Frick lost his sense of the workplace from which he had come. His world had become the boardrooms, theater, art museums, and clubrooms of the capitalists. To some degree, philanthropy offered a way to excuse his approach and maybe ease his conscience. Stoic, yes; cold, yes; but not bloodthirsty: He was more lost in a parallel world of Victorian times. He was a man lost in himself, but a man with a heart. While many men of similar temperament but of lesser means live their life in obscurity, Frick was a public figure. The press of the day, lacking movie stars and sports heroes, looked for news in the rich and wealthy. To the public, the average worker had the right to oppose unions, but the wealthy had no right to oppose any worker organization.

Frick's destiny may well have been modeled by the gods and augured by his namesake.

Henry Clay of Kentucky had ruled a divided Congress for decades. At one point, Congress had been under weeks of stress and infighting. Neither party was willing to cross the aisle. The president watched powerlessly. The farm representatives and the opposition of industrial states had battled to a standoff. One Midwest congressman rose to share his observations of the industrial belt and forge an alliance:

> In passing along the highway one frequently sees large and spacious buildings, with the glass broken out the windows, the shutters hanging in ruinous disorder, without any appearance of activity and enveloped in solitary gloom. Upon inquiry into what they are, you are almost always informed that they were some cotton or other factory, which their proprietors could no longer keep in motion against overwhelming pressure of foreign competition.[4]

This may well have been spoken this year, but it was not. This was the defense of the tariffs by Henry Clay in 1820. With the tariff of 1816, Clay inaugurated the "American System" of focused, protective, and selective tariffs for the good of the nation. He had joined a national debate on capitalism's role and destiny in America. The debate had started with Jefferson's agrarian view versus the manufacturing philosophy of Alexander Hamilton. The rebirth of industry brought on from Clay's "American System" would enable America to achieve economic freedom from the British in 1825. Henry Clay would find many followers in the early German-American families of Pennsylvania. Henry Clay's popularity in the coal regions of Pennsylvania would lead to the naming of Frick and augur a new standard bearer of capitalism. It would be the "American System" of Henry Clay that Frick would also champion.

The American System of Henry Clay was capitalism, but it was *American capitalism*. It was not the global capitalism of Adam Smith, Andrew Carnegie or even J.P. Morgan. It was assumed that only the purity of American democracy could assure the long-range success of capitalism. This American capitalism was shameless nationalistic; it was not philosophic or idealistic capitalism. Democracy was the American political philosophy; capitalism was merely a means to economically strengthen America. America was destined to be a beacon of democracy, not capitalism. It had no interest in the free trade of Britain, which was considered a nation of merchants. America realized, as the colonists did, that economic independence had to precede political independence. It realized that economic warfare was at the heart of America's success. It had learned the hard lessons of manufacturing weaknesses translating into battlefield defeats. It realized that the right to bear arms meant nothing if you could not manufacture arms or gunpowder.

Henry Clay saw manufacturing as the soul of a country. He predicted correctly the decline of the British Empire as it switched to a "nation of merchants." Even Jefferson, before his death, would acknowledge the manufacturing soul of the nation. Henry Clay fought for the manufacturing soul until the 1850s when a young Abe Lincoln took up the cause with his advisor Matthew Carey. Lincoln is remembered for freeing the slaves, but another of his accomplishments was American protectionism. It wasn't until Ohio Congressman William McKinley took up the cause in the 1880s that America achieved the true independence that had been strived for since 1776. America boomed as Britain declined, in its application of Adam Smith's theory. McKinley had found a simple truth in the necessity of man as a maker and producer. Man's soul is in making and using tools; it is what distinguishes him from the animals. It is the level and nature of manufacture that defines the level of civilization. McKinley's ancestors had been charcoal iron makers in the same district in Pennsylvania as the Frick family. Bankers and merchants were ancillary to McKinley's vision, and were not the heart of an economy. It was McKinley's roots in a middle class iron-making family that formed his view, and this view forged an alliance with labor and capital for a common goal. For McKinley, his greatest award would be a gavel given to him earlier as Chairman of the Ways and Means Committee. The gavel was made of wood from the plantation of Henry Clay and hailed him as the "Napoleon of the American System." Americans came to love the patriotic capitalist, and Henry Clay was a common birth name in the 1840s, but none would achieve the fame of Henry Clay Frick. It would be Henry Clay Frick that would rally the resources to bring McKinley to the presidency.

The McKinley presidency was the industrial Camelot of America. It was a presidency that Henry Clay Frick was initially reluctant to support but came to admire. Personally quite different, Frick and McKinley shared a common belief in capitalism. In the five years of the McKinley presidency, America rose to world leadership in economic might and Frick to national prominence. America led in the manufacture of steel, iron, coal, oil, electrical equipment, tools, and machinery. The boom spurred a massive influx of immigrants as jobs went unfilled in a massive economic boom. The government's biggest issue was what to do with the surplus. The government coffers overflowed, not from taxes (there was no income tax!), but from tariffs on incoming imports! America had created a manufacturing utopia. Some might argue that many problems would follow, but the manufacturing success also covered many evils and fed many immigrants and their families.

This manufacturing boom of the 1800s evolved out of eastern Ohio and western Pennsylvania. Driven by residents of Scots-Irish and German stock, it united American values and capitalism into a new approach to industrialism. It was an economic manifest destiny that replaced the closing of the west as the new frontier. It represented a rare alliance of labor and capital. It supplied the fuel for the world's torch of liberty. It was an era of great American pride ushered in with the Columbian Exposition of 1893 in Chicago. It created a mindset that America's factories, buildings, ships, and technology had to be the biggest and best. For industry, it was a golden era of great capitalists such as Henry Clay Frick, Andrew Carnegie, George Westinghouse, H.J. Heinz, J.P. Morgan, Charles Schwab, and John Rockefeller. True, the slums of the paramount cities of the period such as Pittsburgh offered dismal habitats for new immigrants, but the average stay in the slums of the period was a little more than a generation. The economic boom pulled many up the ladder to the middle class. Unfortunately, it is a period hidden in the shadow of the progressive era and the larger-than-life Teddy Roosevelt.

The period of 1865 to 1910 was one of America's greatest expansions. It was a time of struggle as well. It had the ambiguity of the French Revolution, as America struggled to define the roles of capital and labor. The robber barons of the period such as Henry Clay Frick are often considered legendary in their greed and evil. They, however, were not old world aristocrats but first-generation American wealth. Many had lived in the very slums they were said to have created. Wealth was rarely their passion, though they were happier making money than spending it. They were often seduced more by power than money. They gave most of their money away in the end, improving the lives of millions; yet their workers could hardly feed their families. They believed in the capitalistic principle of unlimited business returns yet felt worker pay had to be controlled for greater profits. They are hard to categorize as devils, angels, or fallen angels. Their image has been too often defined by extremes of hagiographic biographies or angry labor historians. The reality is far different. The capitalist and worker are more similar than different, and no capitalist better represents that dichotomy than Henry Clay Frick.

Prior to the Homestead Strike, Frick lived a simple, although wealthy life, often riding the streetcar to his office at the mill. Frick's Pittsburgh suburb was the nation's richest, home of the Carnegies, Mellons, George Westinghouse, and H.J. Heinz. He stood in the shadow of his partner Andrew Carnegie. The Homestead Strike changed Frick and all around him. The strike is also colored in lore and bias. The usual portrait is that of the evil capitalist Frick trying to crush the fledging union of poor immigrants. Frick's position is as much exaggerated as that of the union. The real struggle was against the union of skilled workers. The union did not represent or want to represent the $1.00-a-day slum-dwelling unskilled immigrant laborer. The skilled workers discriminated based on race as well. Hungarians and Slavs were barely better than the blacks in their thinking. Eventually, with no other place to go, the immigrant laborers joined. Frick's hardheadedness allowed the strike to escalate to violence. Fear on both sides rode the standoff too far. The Homestead Strike has been long remembered for its violence, but it paled in comparison to the violence and destruction of the great Railroad Strike of 1877 in Pittsburgh. At the time, many still remembered the violence, fires, and city riots that gangs joined in 1877, but today the nationwide violence and loss of life in 1877 are lost in the political shadow of the Homestead Strike. History has crowned Homestead the honor of America's most notorious strike. Carnegie's control of the media and managers helped frame Frick as the villain. This does not excuse Frick in any way, but to better understand him, the whole man must be looked at.

Not that Frick had a pristine reputation prior to Homestead. He had been tough in negotiating with the coal unions. He had been a founding member in an exclusive club in the mountains around Johnstown, Pennsylvania. The organization was known as the South Fork Fishing and Hunting Club, which would be mired in scandal following the famous Johnstown Flood of 1889. Frick had been a founding member of this rich man's resort. A dam on a small mountaintop created a lake for fishing and sailing. It became known by Carnegie as the "glorious mountain," and reporters talked of sailboats on a mountain. The faulty dam would burst in May of 1889, creating one of America's worst disasters. Even by today's standards, the Johnstown Flood has statistics on the level with the collapse of the Twin Towers on 9-11. The official death count was 2,209, with hundreds missing. Wherever the blame belonged, the press pinned it on the wealthy members of the club, and the name of Frick was the most prominent in the newspapers. Of the club members, Frick gave $5,000, Andrew Mellon gave $1,000 and Carnegie $10,000 to help the victims, while most of the club members gave nothing.

Frick was a man of many contradictions. Because he is demonized for his opulent spending on art, his charity is often lost. A man known as an oppressor of workers was a devout family man who gave much to the education of Pittsburgh's youth and poor, as well as one of the city's largest parks. In his earliest days of managing the coal mines, a local newspaper said he was known "for his fair treatment of workmen and generosity in supplying the wants of the needy." Frick gave freely; yet unlike his rival, Andrew Carnegie, Frick put his name on little. He lived between two industrial saints, H.J. Heinz and George Westinghouse. These saints were not all that different in their hatred of unions, yet Frick is called a devil by unionists to this day. Frick had many saintly attributes as well. He was a family man in an age of capitalist scandal, parties, and sexual excess. The day after Frick's death, the radical socialist Alexander Berkman, who had shot Frick after the Homestead Strike, was captured in Chicago. On hearing of Frick's death, Berkman said: "It's too bad he cannot take the millions amassed by exploiting labor with him." Frick, however, would leave his millions to organizations like the Home for the Friendless, the Children's Hospital, the Pittsburgh Free Dispensary, and countless educational organizations and hospitals in the steel and coal towns of Pennsylvania. Unfortunately, in business, Frick could be overly tough. He believed in survival of the fittest as the operative rule in business. Like many self-made men of the period, Frick could distance himself from the realities at the mill, clinging to a philosophical high road.

Frick's giving went far beyond his will. Frick's living record of charity is deep, extensive, and often personal. He gave extensively to education throughout his life. He often donated to children's causes. He gave liberally to Pittsburgh and Westmoreland hospitals such as Braddock Hospital, Homestead Hospital, Beverly Hospital, Infants Hospital, Lakeside Hospital, Children's Hospital, and many others. He gave millions to colleges such as Princeton, University of Pittsburgh, and Wooster College. He gave extensively, as did his daughter, to help wounded soldiers. He gave often to help the poor and to settlement projects such as Kingsley House. He was also fond of organizations such as the YWCA, Children's Aid Association, and YMCA. Frick gave anonymously, so it is difficult to make a full list; but he gave on a level near Carnegie, with no memorials to his giving. In fact, in most cases he demanded anonymity as part of the gift.

Frick's patriotism is another attribute that has been overlooked. He believed in a fair playing field for capitalism as well. He once wrote a personal letter to William McKinley, arguing that the steel industry did not need any increases in tariffs. He gave millions of his own money to the military and soldiers. In many ways making money was an intellectual game for him. Having money was simply a result of playing the game well. Stealing money or winning the lottery would be without meaning for him, and his quest for money had meaning. Inherited money had no meaning to him, and he hated the inherited wealth of many in New York. Money earned without effort, skill, and gamesmanship had no value to him. He would have little to do with the great parties and balls of the old rich. As a board member of Equitable Insurance, Frick led a management reform of wasteful partying on corporate money.

In the end, Frick became more and more isolated, scorned by unions and laborers. He was disliked in his hometown of Pittsburgh, where there were no tributes to him. He had shown his belief in capitalism to be greater than friendship with neighbors like George Westinghouse. He stood by in the war room of J.P. Morgan in 1907 as highly profitable Westinghouse Electric went bankrupt in a brief money crisis. Hated by his former partner Andrew Carnegie, he was despised by the many business followers of Carnegie. Yet these very critics found him more trustworthy than Carnegie in personal dealings. Many pointed to him as the "butcher of Homestead," but there was plenty of blame to go around. Even the many poor children he helped in Pittsburgh would grow up to despise his name. Yet he had a great love of children that is rarely noted. Frick had experienced many personal setbacks prior to and immediately after the Homestead Strike. He lost his beloved seven-year-old daughter Martha, who died from swallowing a pin. A few weeks after the strike, he lost his newborn son. Martha would haunt him to his death. For years Frick left the newborn son's and Martha's graves unmarked, as if unable to accept death or the pain of dealing with it. Fresh flowers were maintained at the picture of Martha in his bedroom, and he kept a lock of her hair in the room as well. He died looking at a picture he purchased to remind him of his lost daughter.

Unlike his old partner Carnegie, Frick hated to talk to the press and left his legacy to history and providence. He was a private man who lived by a strict rule of confidentiality in his private and business dealings. Carnegie, on the other hand, spent the better part of his life building a legacy, much of which came at Frick's expense. Furthermore, Carnegie had a loyal following of wealthy managers that met into the 1940s to praise the "Carnegie System." This group, known as the Carnegie Veterans Association, despised Frick and continued to frame the legacy of Carnegie. Historian David McCullough noted Frick's approach to the press:

> He simply did not talk to the press ever, at any time. It was his standing policy. He was a highly uncommunicative sort anyway and, by nature, abhorred forms of notoriety. He had no trust in newspapers, no liking for reporters, and talking to them, he was convinced, was bad for business. Only once in his life did he break his rule and speak freely to a reporter, but it was with the understanding that he could edit the copy, which he did, reducing a full column to exactly ten lines.[5]

Carnegie used the press to build a legacy, while Frick left his legacy to the press he abhorred.

Carnegie was also blessed by the Carnegie Veterans Association, which consisted of 32 ex–Carnegie managers. The group had started when many of the Carnegie boys found themselves as the top managers in United States Steel New York headquarters. In 1902 these men, known as the "Boys of Braddock," including Alva Dinkey, Charles Schwab, William Dickson, William Corey, and James Gayley, started to meet for lunch at New York's Lawyers Club. By the end of 1902, the group expanded and would meet annually at Carnegie's New York mansion at Fifth Avenue and Ninety-First Street. Carnegie and his wife hosted an annual dinner for them. Frick would never be invited to either the informal or formal meetings of the group. The group would meet into the 1930s. At one point the group had presidents of the three largest steel companies and controlled 40 percent of America's assets. Dickson was a gifted writer and was able to have a major impact on history's view of Carnegie, which also biased the view of the Carnegie-Frick feud of later years. The veterans moved Carnegie (and themselves) to the level of mythology.

Frick's personal legacy seemed to be his belief in capitalism. Certainly this belief helped Frick find peace with some of his questionable actions. Before his death, Frick contributed much to the building of the McKinley Presidential Library at Niles, Ohio. It is in this marble pantheon that America's greatest industrialists are honored. Honoring men filled with contradictions like Frick but bound by a belief in capitalism, this pantheon was filled with bronze busts representing the zenith of American capitalists. Its torch remains ready to be taken up by some future generation. Interestingly, even as Carnegie hesitated on donations to the Memorial, the Carnegie Foundation collected funds to assure that Carnegie's bust would be included. Built as a shrine to America's great manufacturing past, it was a place that an older Frick visited often, and he was known to cry in these peaceful visits.

In death, Frick has fared no better. At best, he has been forgotten in his hometown, and at worst, he still invokes a passionate hatred, seen as symbolic of the evil of capitalism. While his partner Carnegie is remembered for the best, Frick more than anyone made Pittsburgh the greatest industrial center in the world and America's fifth largest city; however, his employees built no memorial to him, as did those of George Westinghouse and H.J. Heinz. Few associate the large and beautiful Frick Park of Pittsburgh with the legacy of the industrialist. There is no bronze statue tribute to him in Pittsburgh. Yet his beautiful daughter, Helen Clay Frick, would spend her life dedicated to the positive memory of the loving father she had known. She lived alone in the old Pittsburgh mansion until 1984, maintaining it and defending the memory of her father. While passionate and extreme, Helen Clay Frick was right that most written about him is decisively biased from both sides, but that was the very nature of Frick.

Helen Clay Frick for years prevented any balanced view of Frick through harassment: If even the slightest personal weaknesses were noted in a biographic effort, Helen made life difficult on the biographer. Although the negative slant was overwhelming, it required some positive slant. While there has been no definitive biography, recent books have started to deal more fairly with this notable American icon. Carnegie biographers tend to play down any role of Frick in the rise of American industrial greatness. Martha Frick Symington Sanger, in her *An Intimate Portrait of Henry Clay Frick*, said: "Although my great-grandfather, Henry Clay Frick, died in 1919, he has remained a living presence within our family. Because he was renowned as an art collector, respected as an industrial genius, and despised as an oppressor of labor, the combination of his memory and reputation makes him a difficult ancestor to understand and embrace."[6] In his extremes and contradictions we will see ourselves. Looking at Frick through the eyes of a Pittsburgh steel manager may add another perspective and dimension to this American icon.

1. A Heritage of Capitalism

Henry Clay Frick was born in Westmoreland County in southwestern Pennsylvania on December 19, 1849, on top of the world's richest coal seam. He was the son of John W. Frick and Elizabeth Overholt, a fourth-generation American on both sides of his family tree. The Frick family was Swiss and the Overholts were German, from the Palatine area in the Rhine Valley. In many ways, the journey of both families to western Pennsylvania was similar. It was a quest for economic and religious freedom and a better future. Western Pennsylvania was the heart of the Whig Party of Henry Clay, and it had become a fortress of the new and emerging concept of American capitalism. It was an ethnic blend of Scotch-Irish and German that saw the soul of freedom in property rights. It supplied the nation its iron and whiskey. Western Pennsylvania had become famous in the 1790s for its resistance to federal taxes in the Whiskey Rebellion.

The Frick family came from the Celtic-Burgundian ancestry of the village Sisseln-Thal. Today the village of Frick is there. The Frick family has Swiss records traceable to A.D. 1113.[1] Henry Clay Frick's great-great-grandfather left Switzerland in 1732. The Frick family was one of the early followers of Menno Simons (1496–1561), who formed a group of Anabaptists (rebaptizers) in 1525 known as Mennonites. The group was really a schism of Lutheranism. They believed in adult baptism, which the Swiss government declared illegal, forcing many to flee to Germany. The Mennonites created independent economic villages, learning to prosper in isolation. Early Mennonites were known for farming, weaving, and alcoholic beverages (mainly beer and wine). Many in the Frick family were master weavers, including Frick's great-great-grandfather, Johann Nicholas Frick. Weavers had been the first craftsmen to be affected by automation and the Industrial Revolution. Johann Nicholas Frick came to America in 1767 to the Germantown section of Philadelphia. Germantown had been a magnet for Swiss, German, and Dutch Mennonites fleeing persecution and looking for a better economic future.

The Frick family found a welcoming Swiss Mennonite community at Germantown. Mennonite Francis Daniel Pastorius, with the help of William Penn, had founded Germantown in 1683. The initial families were linen weavers, and the farmers took to growing flax to support the linen production. The town's seal included the inscription "Vinum, Linum et Textrinum," which means "grapes, flax, and trade." Germantown residents brought with them the idea of capitalistic trade fairs, and the Germantown Fair first held in 1701 was the first such fair for American craftsmen. Germantown production of stockings was said to be 60,000 pairs in 1760.[2] The Mennonites proved expert in building looms and spinning wheels. Mennonites built roads and spread the product of their work to the west. They developed the nation's first turnpike of commerce with the central Pennsylvania German community of Lancaster. Another technology that these Mennonites quickly adapted was the use of grist and grain mills. These Mennonites became known as the "Pennsylvania Dutch."

On Henry Clay Frick's mother's side, the Overholt (originally Oberholtzer) family had come earlier, with the first wave of German immigration. One of the earliest of the non–British immigrations was that of the Germans, which was sometimes for needed skills. One of the earliest was in the 1720s; Alexander Spotswood brought seventy Palatinate Germans to Virginia to start ironworks at Spotsylvania and Germania. Spotswood added one hundred African slaves to cut wood for blast furnace fuel. Germans were also recruited for blacksmithing, glassmaking, and gun making. There was a slow and steady immigration of German Protestants during the eighteenth century. One cause of German immigration was the invasion of the German region of Palatine on the French border by the French army during Queen Anne's War (1702–1713). The first wave of these Pennsylvania Palatinates settled in Germantown and Lancaster. By the end of the eighteenth century, nearly 100,000 Palatinate Germans came through Philadelphia. Germantown represented the first stopping point for both Palatinate Germans and the Swiss and augured the future mixing of Swiss and Germans in America.

Palatinate Germany of the Oberholtzer family and the Swiss corridor of the Frick family were the core of the Protestant Reformation. This European area was heavily populated with Lutherans or deviating sects such as the Mennonites and Moravians. In the 1500s, Palatinate Germany became a place of refuge for Protestants from Switzerland, Holland, and Germany. This may explain why some Overholts claim some Swiss lineage. The Mennonites originated in Switzerland but came under religious persecution. In 1671, Prince Karl Ludwig offered the Mennonites religious freedom. The Palatinate area in the early 1700s became a battleground for Europe. In 1709, Queen Anne offered help for immigrants wanting to leave to help resettle Protestant Ireland, and William Penn offered land in America as well. Crop failures in the 1710s spurred even more immigrants. The plague also hit many of the area's cities as refugees flooded in. Martin Overholt, an ancestor of Henry Clay Frick, was born near Frankfort-on-the-Main in 1709 in the midst of the turmoil. Interestingly, Frankfort-on-the-Main was the location of the first European trade fairs in the 1100s that gave birth to the concept of capitalism.

Martin Overholt (1709–1744) came to America in early 1730 as a result of this Franco-German warfare and the economic downturn, which continued in the Palatinate Rhine area on a local level into the 1730s. Martin Overholt, Henry Clay Frick's great-great-grandfather, sailed from Rotterdam to Philadelphia, as would Johann Nicholas Frick (Henry Clay Frick's other great-great-grandfather) a few years later. By the Revolutionary War, over 100,000 Germans had come to America. Most of these were new variations of the German Lutherans and separatists like Dunkers, Mennonites, and Moravians. Martin Overholt was a Mennonite. These Germans who went to Pennsylvania were a mix of farmers and craftsmen. The Overholts were farmers. What some call the first wave of real immigration into New York was the largest single immigration in the colonial period. There was also a very small Catholic group that appeared to have made it to America from the Palatinate region. Most of these Germans settled in coastal New York. Many of these early Germans died of typhus fever, but some established a stretch of German farms 12 miles long along the banks of the Mohawk River. The Germans and the Swiss aggressively moved west, setting up a string of outposts for future migrations to western Pennsylvania. With family ties along this western movement, they set up an extensive trade network. Martin Overholt eventually settled on a large farm at Point Pleasant on the Delaware River in Bucks County. Like most Mennonite farms, the Overholt farm became a commercial operation selling surplus to Philadelphia and Lancaster.

German and Swiss families set up a transportation network between Philadelphia and Lancaster to support the extensive trade. This first turnpike allowed German farmers to become wealthy by supplying both Philadelphia and Lancaster. A large variety of German and Swiss religious groups participated in this first "Pennsylvania Dutch" commercial network. The Old Order Amish and various Lutheran sects that settled Lancaster, Pennsylvania, were a mixture of Swiss and German. The Moravians and the Mennonites, in particular, can be credited with the spread of civilization in Pennsylvania and Ohio. Families and communities split between the turnpike nodes of Germantown and Lancaster. A large branch of the Mennonite Frick family settled in Lancaster and remains there today. The Moravians first came to Georgia in the 1730s and followed the southern Scotch-Irish north through the Allegheny mountain valleys in the 1740s to Pennsylvania. They had a missionary goal to baptize and Christianize the native Indians and further stretched the Pennsylvanian turnpike and commercial ties to western Pennsylvania. The Moravians mixed on the frontier with the Scotch-Irish and Indians, turning small frontier outposts into villages and cities. In Pennsylvania, towns like Bethlehem, Lancaster, and Nazareth were early German towns and Moravian settlements. Often there was tension with the Moravian anti-drinking stance and love of the Indians, but they were city builders. The Germans built log cabins, churches, schoolhouses, and gardens in former outposts. German building was often the sign for the wilder Scotch-Irish to move on. Still, some stayed and became part of the first melting pots of America. Often the separatist views of the first German groups were lost by the second generation, especially on the Pennsylvania frontier, where they mixed with the Scotch-Irish and Swiss. The German population in Pennsylvania reached 20,000 as early as 1727 and topped 25,000 by 1745.

These early German immigrants advanced farming, transportation, trade, banking, and industry. They were the first to bring crops such as cauliflower and asparagus to America. They built some of America's first barns, modernized the production of cabbage, horseradish, and turnips, and pioneered food preserving in America. The Germans were the trailblazers for the American agricultural revolution. As their crop productivity and yield increased beyond their needs, they started to supply eastern Pennsylvania, New Jersey, and cities such as Philadelphia. The Mennonites from Germantown came and built looms, spinning wheels, and grain mills. Lacking banks and even a common currency, they backed notes on family name and personal relationships. The Swiss and German Mennonites expanded American capitalism as they moved west. In the 1730s, they developed one of America's first highways, known as the "Great Philadelphia Wagon Road." At the western terminus of the road, German craftsmen developed the "Conestoga wagon," also called the prairie schooner. These giant freight wagons were named after Conestoga Creek at Lancaster. These wagons were watertight and used iron belts around the wooden wheels. Six- to eight-horse teams pulled these freight wagons. They moved in convoys of up to a hundred wagons. By the 1740s, there were around ten thousand Conestoga wagons in use. The road branched into Virginia and the Carolinas. Benjamin Franklin's mail system was extended through these wagon trains. In the 1750s, it was said that German Lancaster employed thirteen blacksmiths (one of whom was a Frick relative), five wheelwrights, twenty joiners, and seven turners in the production of these manufactured wagons.[3] The Germans went into breeding "Conestoga" horses to further improve the overall transportation system.

Lancaster not only moved farm products to Philadelphia, but gathered furs and whiskey from the western frontier for shipments to Philadelphia. Lancaster was a western outpost for Germans, Swiss, and the Scotch-Irish, which fostered the development of manufacturing. Lancaster played a key role in the development of western Pennsylvania in whiskey production. Some of the Frick family had come to Lancaster in the 1730s, starting a family network that would ultimately bring them to western Pennsylvania. More importantly, it got the Frick family involved in commerce. Lancaster became a key part of a trading network between western Pennsylvania and Philadelphia. The German and Scotch-Irish connection and network strengthened through the 1730s as wagons ventured west. The Lancaster-Philadelphia turnpike and the German/Swiss network was really the beginning of American capitalism and commerce.

Trade brought manufacture to Lancaster, such as saddle making and gun making to supply the frontier. As a growing center of manufacturing, Lancaster started to attract not only German gunsmiths but also Swiss and Scotch-Irish. In the 1730s, Swiss gunsmith Peter Leman started to develop the "Pennsylvania rifle" at his Lancaster shop. European smoothbore muskets were not suited for hunting in the American backwoods. Leman's new rifle had a longer barrel, improved sights, reduced bore, and better balance. It quickly became popular on the American frontier. By 1740, Lancaster was the capital of American gun manufacture and the home of our greatest gunsmiths. In 1752, General Braddock made a Lancaster Scotch-Irish gunsmith master armorer to his army. In the 1770s, Lancaster was critical in supplying the colonial army with guns. Lancaster's population passed 10,000 with leather and clothing trades growing as well. The city in 1773 had fifteen master weavers, nine master stocking weavers, thirty shoemakers, ten tanners, seven saddlers, five skinners, and two boot makers. The Lancaster branch of the Frick family were mainly weavers and blacksmiths. German-American farmers often took up the growing craft of blacksmithing. German farmers had ancillary blacksmithing skills, and blacksmithing was in high demand in the growing nation of America. All of these master craftsmen had numerous journeymen and apprentices working for them. Lancaster emerged from a trade center to manufacturing center, showing a more efficient concentration of manufacturing than the plantation system had produced. As America's first manufacturing town, Lancaster foreshadowed Pittsburgh, Cleveland, and Chicago.

From the capitalistic manufacturing center of Lancaster, many Germans, Swiss, and Scotch-Irish looked for more manufacturing opportunities in the hills of southwestern Pennsylvania. The Frick and Overholt families converged on the boom county of Westmoreland (a neighbor to the Pittsburgh area). Johann Nicholas Frick and his family came first in 1780 from Germantown. Johann had heard much of this rich land from his brother in Lancaster and on the frontier of western Pennsylvania. Cornwallis and his British officers had hoped to have plantations in this rich country had the British defeated the Colonials. One of Johann's sons, George, served in the War of 1812. The Fricks were farmers who came to Westmoreland County via Lancaster and the old Forbes road over the mountains. After the Revolutionary War, the cheap land being offered motivated them. It was Johann Nicholas and his family, including son George Frick, who came to Westmoreland County around 1785. Johann purchased a farm at Port Royal while the others settled around Irwin and Adamsburg. George was a farmer, a blacksmith and an entrepreneur. George built a small gristmill to process grain for the surrounding farmers. George Frick often moved grain from his farm by flatboat to New Orleans, where he died from scarlet fever on one of the trips. Henry Clay Frick's grandfather, Daniel Frick, had a small farm and blacksmith shop in Westmoreland County. Daniel Frick had nine children by his first wife in Westmoreland County: Mary, John, George, Lucinda, Delilah, David, Jacob, Abraham, and Henry Clay Frick's grandfather Daniel Jr. The eldest son of Daniel Frick, Jr., was John W. Frick (Henry Clay's father), who was born in 1822 in Adamsburg.

The Overholt family (Frick's mother's side) came to Westmoreland County in 1800. One of Martin Overholt's sons, also named Martin, had settled in western Pennsylvania in the 1790s, and he encouraged his father Abraham and his brother Henry to bring the family west. It was Henry Overholt, a wealthy Bucks County farmer, who packed up his family in a string of Conestoga wagons. The Overholt family came by way of the Cumberland gap route known as Braddock's Road. The Overholt clan consisted of Henry and his wife Anna, five sons, six daughters, five sons-in-law, two daughters-in-law, and thirteen grandchildren. Henry's son Abraham (Frick's grandfather) was twelve years old when he arrived in Westmoreland. Westmoreland was considered to be a Garden of Eden. It was rich farmland connected by a river system that could take products to New Orleans and the world beyond. New Orleans had a large German population involved in river and international trade via the city's port. Whiskey and iron bar were manufactured in Westmoreland and shipped to Europe via the

Monongahela-Ohio-Mississippi River system. Westmoreland County also had a major charcoal iron industry by the time of the arrival of the Frick and Overholt families.

Westmoreland County had been the crossroads of the American frontier since ancient times. In the 1600s, two major Indian paths, Glades Path and Nemacolin's Path, brought hunting parties to this neutral Indian territory. Nemacolin's Path had been used in the 1750s by George Washington to survey the frontier. A few years later a young George Washington and a British force was forced to surrender to the French at Fort Necessity, Westmoreland. In 1755, General Braddock, along with George Washington, built Braddock's Road, following Nemacolin's Path on their way to defeat near Fort Duquesne (Pittsburgh). In 1758, General Forbes built Forbes Road, following Glades Path on his way to revenge Braddock's defeat and capture Fort Duquesne. Both of these roads opened Westmoreland County up to settlement. In 1821, German settlers built the Somerset and Mount Pleasant Turnpike (present-day State Highway 31), which became an important transportation route for whiskey and coal for Pittsburgh.

The Scotch-Irish came to the area in the 1740s and were followed by the German settlers. Westmoreland County offered rich farming land and abundant game. Bear, deer, wood buffalo, and turkey were abundant, and passenger pigeon flocks darkened the skies. Western Pennsylvania was defined by the confluence of the Monongahela River (through Westmoreland County) and Allegheny River to form the Ohio River at Pittsburgh. The rich soil of these river flood plains had been used for corn planting by the Indians in the early 1700s. The Scotch-Irish found this soil ideal for rye and whiskey making. By the 1780s, "Monongahela Rye" was world famous, having a large market in Europe. The Scotch-Irish stills produced rye whiskey, then moved it by river boats to New Orleans and then by ship to New York and Europe. These whiskey-producing settlers would be the first to rebel against government taxation. The settlers were characterized by the observation: "Every cabin contained a Bible, a rifle, and a whiskey jug."

The "Whiskey Rebellion" of the western Pennsylvania Scotch-Irish in the 1790s would be the root of American domestic politics. George Frick (Henry Clay's great-grandfather), as a gristmill owner, was an integral part of whiskey production in the 1790s. The Monongahela Valley was filled with the smoke of whiskey stills in the 1790s. Rye whiskey was a mainstay of the area's Scotch-Irish distilleries and the German gristmills, and a huge small business initiative. Grain sold for a few cents a bushel, but whiskey sold for $1 a gallon, which made turning grain into whiskey very profitable. It was more cost-effective to move whiskey down river as well. As a British colony, the whiskey production had been controlled and taxed, but the remoteness of the Monongahela Valley made it almost inaccessible to British tax collectors. President Washington and Secretary of the Treasury Alexander Hamilton imposed an excise tax on whiskey in 1794. As a tax collector in western Pennsylvania, Scotch-Irish General Neville was chosen even though he had initially opposed the tax. The tax schedule varied, but it was around six to ten cents a gallon. The valley Scotch-Irish mustered a militia and burnt the estate of General Neville. It was the first test of the federal government. A few days later, the federal leader, General James MacFarlane, was killed. For weeks Scotch-Irish militia roamed the area. Hamilton persuaded Washington to send 13,000 troops to western Pennsylvania to put down the rebellion. Before the militia had reached Pittsburgh, the uprising was diffused as the Presbyterian Church preached enforcement of the law. The Scotch-Irish, however, moved into Kentucky and Tennessee to produce their whiskey. The new frontier was out of the reach of the federal tax collectors. These Pennsylvania emigrants would form the Kentucky and Tennessee bourbon and whiskey families of today. The migration of the Scotch-Irish whiskey makers created an opening for the western Pennsylvania German settlers to move into the business. The loss of some of the larger whiskey makers offered opportunity to new settlers with capital, such as the Overholts.

It was Henry Overholt (Henry's grandfather) who seized this opportunity. The Mennonite Church opposed Henry Overholt, but he moved forward in 1810 with a distillery, which was a small homemade still. He had started with farming and then opened a gristmill to be a processor of grain for the Scotch-Irish whiskey makers. It became clear that he could make ten times the money selling grain processed to whiskey than selling it as grain. In 1812, he purchased an old Scotch-Irish 150-acre farm with a small log distillery for $7,500 (nearly a quarter of a million today). In the late 1830s, Abraham and Christian Overholt upgraded to a commercial stone distillery. After a few years, Abraham bought out Christian, who then opened a general store. Abraham originally marketed his whiskey as "Old Farm Whiskey," then built a second distillery to produce "Old Overholt," which is still produced today in Kentucky. The flavor of the "Old Overholt" whiskey is said to be "richer than Jim Beam rye with a tinge of sweetness which contrasts with the heat of the Wild Turkey Rye." In the 1840s, the Overholts produced "Old Monongahela," the favorite of naturalist John Audubon and noted in Melville's novel *Moby-Dick*. Abraham Overholt built an industrial village around his distillery with a cooper and blacksmith shop. In the 1840s, he added a brick mill as well. He let nothing go to waste, feeding the used distillery mash to a herd of over two thousand hogs. His meat business became substantial, and Abraham was shipping hogs to Pittsburgh and points west by 1847.

The Overholt home was a substantial two-story brick house. The Overholt homestead and distillery were located on Jacob's Creek. The creek had deep pools, which were popular for swimming, as it flowed in to the Youghiogheny River. The creek was popular for fishing as well, and a young Frick developed a lifelong interest in fishing there. The creek supplied the power for the Overholt grain mill. Clay was abundant for brick making in the area. The surrounding rolling hills were covered with oak, locust trees, and chestnut for building and charcoal making. Most of the hardwood of the area had been lumbered out by the late 1840s due to the booming charcoal iron industry in Westmoreland County. Area farmers grew rye and raised pigs, hogs, and cattle. All of the German farmers had substantial vegetable gardens. Cabbage, horseradish, and potatoes were popular, and the area's Germans were some of the earliest to grow tomatoes in the North. Since coal outcroppings were common, most farmers in the area used coal for home heating.

On October 9, 1847, John W. Frick married Elizabeth Overholt, bringing these families together. Initially, the Overholt family was not thrilled with the poor farmer John Frick. The problem was twofold. First, John W. Frick's father, Daniel Frick, was a Swiss Mennonite, but his mother, Catherine Miller, was Irish. The Irish were considered to be the lowest class of citizen. Daniel Frick and particularly John W. Frick were also loosely associated with the Lutheran Church, as the Frick family had moved away from the stricter tradition of the Mennonites. Maybe more infuriating to the Overholts was that Elizabeth was three months pregnant at the time of the wedding. In addition, John W. Frick had lost interest in farming early on. As if things weren't bad enough, John W. Frick had a job at the distillery but was interested in becoming an artist, though he showed little talent for it. One steel historian described John and Elizabeth as trying to "make the least possible amount of money by doing the greatest possible amount of work."[4] John W. Frick, always a bit of a nonconformist in this rigid community, would become the black sheep of the Overholt family.

The German and Scotch-Irish land of western Pennsylvania had a strong influence on Frick. The first wave of Germans came because of both religious persecution and a government takeover of the crafts. The revolutionary 1840s in Europe had caused the crafts guilds to be banned and be replaced with a type of trade union. In addition, socialism was evolving in Germany. German crafts guilds, in order to protect crafts jobs, formed a policy which banned automatic looms. In 1847, there were 2,262 automated looms versus 116,832 hand-looms. The crafts system to a large degree was institutionalized. The problem was that cheaper cloth, made on automated looms, flooded Germany, crushing the overall industry. In the 1840s, many German craftsmen had gone to France to learn their trades, but France followed the German approach to free trade in the late 1840s, and German manufacturing and crafts all but disappeared. German craftsmen looked next to the United States to establish their old trades. German locksmiths, tailors, shoemakers, cigar makers, brewers, bakers, brick makers, and others headed for America. In America, these craftsmen tried to merger crafts with union protection again. The crafts union would become the future target of Henry Clay Frick's focus to automate and apply management control. These pre–1850 Germans were known as "Grays," and were fiercely opposed to trade unionism but also dreamed of a labor republic based on the crafts system.

These western Pennsylvania Germans mixed with the Scotch-Irish to take on a strong belief in property rights. The area had become part of a political belt that went through Pennsylvania, Ohio, Kentucky, and Indiana, where the Whig Party would morph into the Republican Party. It was western Pennsylvania that supplied the votes for Abraham Lincoln, the first Republican president. It was this combination of Whig/Republican protectionism and Scotch-Irish industry in which we can find the roots of capitalism. When the Scotch-Irish Mellon family first came to Westmoreland from Ireland in 1818, Andrew Mellon (father of Judge Thomas Mellon) became close friends with Abraham Overholt.

2. Boyhood, 1849 to 1860

Even with their somewhat rocky start, John and Elizabeth Frick set up their home at the "Spring House" behind the Overholt mansion and barn. The Overholt mansion at West Overton, Pennsylvania (a bit north of Connellsville in Westmoreland County), was a beautiful three-story house surrounded by farmland. The springhouse, on the other hand, had been a small cottage built around the water pump, which had earlier functioned as a smokehouse and summer kitchen. George Harvey described the Spring House:

> It was an unique abode, solidly built of stone, comprising three snug rooms; protected from gales in Winter by walls eighteen inches thick, and warmed by a huge fireplace containing serviceable ovens; cooled in the Summer by pipes of running water, and furnished with bright red carpets for the floors, blue china and steel knives and forks for the table; a small book case for a living room, a grandfather's clock, with works of wood, from Connecticut, and other paraphernalia of the period.[1]

The house was a mere 25 feet by 18 feet with two small windows on each side. It reportedly had pictures of George Washington and John Adams. A short distance away was the huge six-story brick distillery and flour mill of Abraham Overholt. At the time of Henry Clay Frick's birth, the distillery was producing over 150 gallons of whiskey per week. Since the 1810s, wealthy farmers were producing more because of the dreaded whiskey tax for small producers.

The Overholts would slowly warm up to the new Frick family in their backyard. Their first child, Maria Overholt Frick, was named after her grandmother and was born in 1847. Henry Clay Frick was born on December 19, 1849. Henry Clay was named after the leader of the Whig Party, to which both families belonged. Zachary Taylor, a Whig, was in the White House. Abraham Overholt was a local leader of the Whig Party, which supported high tariffs to protect American industry, property rights, and federal projects such as road building, and opposed slavery. As a boy, Henry Clay Frick would be known as "Clay" by friends and family. Helen Clay Frick, Henry Clay's daughter, described Abraham and Maria Overholt's influence:

> ... the Overholt stamp was left on Henry Clay Frick in another and more personal way. Tall, courtly Abraham Overholt, a staunch Mennonite, was an industrious man of strong principle and tremendous energy in his black broadcloth suit and wide-brimmed silk hat; he was a distinguished figure who commanded the respect and admiration of the community. Equally imposing was Abraham's wife, Maria Stauffer, dressed exquisitely in her black ashes of cashmere and her cap of bobbinet lace, her velvet-trimmed silk capes.[2]

Henry Clay himself would be a stylish and dapper dresser throughout his life.

Westmoreland County in 1849 was in a recession, and all of the coke furnaces and most of the iron furnaces were cold, but whiskey had proven recession-proof. Fayette and Westmoreland Counties in 1849 were still in a rural area of farms with the occasional home industry such as a distillery, iron furnace, or textile mill. Most of the area was rolling farmland on the western plain of Chestnut Ridge. The area was predominantly Scotch-Irish, with German enclaves such as West Overton (on PA 819 between the towns of Mount Pleasant and Scottsdale). The farms produced wheat, rye, oats, corn, and barley. The forest of black walnuts, hickory, beechnut, buckeye, and butternut showed signs of some deforestation by the old iron operations. There were abundant fish in the rivers and creeks, although some creeks had been polluted by the numerous charcoal iron furnaces. Charcoal furnaces were being built on creeks for waterpower to drive the air blast needed. Game such as deer, bear, turkey, and passenger pigeon was still abundant. Foxes and squirrels were also common, but wolves had been exterminated by hunting and a wave of hydrophobia. Rattlesnakes continued to be a problem. The area had abundant deposits of iron ore and coal as well as fireclay for bricks. There were also good deposits of sand for glassmaking. In 1849, the area had river navigation and good roads connecting to the growing industrial city of Pittsburgh, some fifty miles away.

At the time of Frick's birth, Pittsburgh had a population of 47,000. Across the river, Allegheny City (now Pittsburgh's north side) had another 26,000, and the nearby river valleys had an additional 49,000. Most of Pittsburgh's population was Scotch-Irish Presbyterians and German Protestants, but German and Irish Catholics had started to come to Pittsburgh to fill the industrial job openings. Politically, the Whig Party had taken hold of the great manufacturers and tradesmen of Pittsburgh. Western Pennsylvania in 1849 was on the eve of an industrial boom that would change it forever. Iron puddlers formed a union known as the Sons of Vulcan. The Baltimore & Ohio Railroad and the Pennsylvania Railroad were making slow progress towards western Pennsylvania. At the time of Henry's birth, these two railroads were in competition to reach Pittsburgh first, which would be achieved in 1852 with the Pennsylvania Railroad arriving first.

A year before Henry's birth, a poor twelve-year-old Andrew Carnegie had arrived with his immigrant family from Scotland. On the day of Henry Clay Frick's birth, Andrew Carnegie was working as a bobbin boy in a Pittsburgh cotton mill for $1.20 a week, which consisted of six 12-hour days. Also in 1849, a 35-year-old Pittsburgh lawyer, Thomas Mellon, formerly of Westmoreland, made his first investment of a coalfield north of Pittsburgh on the Pennsylvania Canal. It would prove highly profitable by supplying fuel to the city. Pittsburgh in 1849 produced no pig iron or steel, but its forges and nail mills were the major consumers of pig iron from Westmoreland County. It had already earned the name of the "Smoky City" due to its use of coal to power industry and heat homes. Pittsburgh, which burned more coal than any other American city at the time, was starting to come out of a nationwide recession.

Frick was considered "delicate," "frail" and "sickly" from birth. In 1852, when Henry Clay was going on three, a third child, Elizabeth Frick, was born to the family. The relationship between the Fricks and the Overholts seemed to be strained, probably because of the less than auspicious start. The story is told that Abraham Overholt saw Henry let a wagon hand fall on Maria, the oldest child, and became worried for the health of the children. Abraham had little Maria moved to the mansion house to raise her there. Some have noted the possible psychological impact of the loss of his sister, but the moving of his sister to the mansion house when he was not quite age three would not seem enough to be overly traumatic. It may have also been a simple matter of space in the Spring House. The Fricks would have three more children: Aaron in 1855, J. Edgar in 1859, and Sallie in 1862. The family moved to a small nearby farm after the birth of Aaron. The strain between the families probably did affect Henry. The Fricks never overcame John's stigma as the black sheep. For whatever reason, Henry Clay was not one of the popular grandsons of Abraham Overholt, but his grandmother Maria was actively involved in his early care, and Henry remained close to her throughout her life. The Fricks seem to have been ostracized by the local Mennonite Church and switched to the more liberal German Lutheran Church, although it is doubtful that they were churchgoers.

Henry Clay's childhood was marred by his lack of physical strength. The first problem occurred when Henry Clay was six years old. His father took him to visit his grandfather

Daniel Frick in Van Buren, Ohio. Daniel Frick had moved to Ohio with the family from West-moreland after the death of his first wife. Daniel Frick was a farmer, gristmill operator, and blacksmith in the small Ohio community. (Interestingly, the Frick family would open up their own distillery in Van Buren in 1859.) In 1855, Daniel Frick became deathly sick, and a young Henry and his father went to see him. In those days, it was a three-day trip by horse and buggy. It appears that Henry Clay Frick contracted scarlet fever upon his arrival.

Scarlet fever at the time was a major killer of young children. Henry Clay survived, but with long-term consequences. He collapsed into rheumatic fever and inflammatory rheuma-tism, which would plague him all of his life. The rapid progression of medical problems required Henry to remain in Van Buren for several months. It appears likely he suffered some heart damage as well. Henry's father returned to Westmoreland for the birth of the fourth child, Aaron, who was mentally retarded. It took Henry over a year to recover, and he was unable to walk the mile necessary to get to school. The problem remained sporadic through-out his youth, often causing him to miss school or having to make special arrangements to transport him. Later in life, after a long day of work, he was forced to take a nap or take med-ication for the muscle pain and headaches. His lack of physical strength restricted him from playing in popular ball games, but Henry still participated as a scorer. Henry never let the cruelty of the playground defeat him, but only made him more determined to succeed. Lim-ited in physical ability, Henry Clay developed his mental skills to advance. Clay became an excellent chess player and enjoyed the game throughout his life. Henry was also very com-petitive and excelled at the less physical lawn games of horseshoe pitching and quoits (loop tossing). Henry was known as one of the best players in horseshoes. In fact, whatever the endeavor, Henry could be overly competitive. Early on he developed a dream to achieve the wealth and riches of his grandfather.

His grandfather Overholt was active in business, the Whig Party, the Republican Party, and the school board. It was in the election of the school board and in the school board meet-ings that Americans got their first real taste of democracy in action. German immigrants and the Scotch-Irish of Westmoreland put education and schools on a high plane. Grandfather Overholt was a community force in the improvement of schools and a member of the school board. A school board member functioned as part principal, part superintendent, part pur-chasing clerk, and part maintenance man. It was at the school board meeting that heated debates determined teachers' salaries and money was allotted for repairs or building a new school. It was in dealing with these frontier school boards that western Pennsylvanian William McGuffey found the inspiration for his series of readers. It may well have been that Over-holt's work to improve local education was the root of Frick's later generous support of schools.

Henry Clay Frick was a solid student who excelled in mathematics. He also showed a flair for the popular Spenserian style of fancy handwriting. Like his father, Henry enjoyed a bit of drawing and painting as well. He was raised on the *McGuffey Readers*, which preached both capitalism and philanthropy. He would be one of many great industrialists and leaders to come from America's one-room schoolhouses. The *McGuffey Readers* taught him to love good literature, and Frick developed a love for reading early in life. Henry often missed school due to sickness, but when he could, he attended the local public school in 1857 and 1858. He also attended West Overton School in 1861 and 1862 when the family rented a house in the town of West Overton. In addition, he spent several terms in high school level grades at Westmoreland College, Mount Pleasant Institute, and Otterbein College through the age of seventeen in 1866. Henry often was behind and struggled to keep up became of his missed school. He seems to have enjoyed the classics and even took some Latin. Descriptions of the young boy vary widely from "sensitive" to "strong willed." He clearly was a hard worker and wanted to achieve, but at times his fellow students ridiculed him. Some friends noted he had a temper, but he appears to have learned to control it, channeling his anger into achievement.

The person who most influenced him was his grandfather Abraham Overholt. Early family biographers believed that Henry was "ashamed" of his father's low ambition, but his attitude was more admiration of his grandfather than a resentment of his father. Henry clearly emulated his grandfather's style and dignity, and with age, his grandfather grew closer to Henry. Still, grandfather Overholt was a stern and difficult man to get close to, and he had many children and grandchildren competing for his attention. Henry was well dressed, serious, and disciplined. Politically, he quickly adopted the Whig Party of his grandfather and namesake. It was said that fourteen-year-old Clay was determined not to dress like a "poor farmer" but in the style of his well-dressed grandfather. The poor surroundings of his home were in stark contrast to the opalescence of his grandparents' mansion. He started as a clerk in 1863 at his uncle Christian Overholt's (1824–1898) West Overton store to earn money for clothes. This was a general store or "emporium" that was owned by Christian Overholt and Barney Schallenberger. Christian Overholt was also president of the Mt. Pleasant First National Bank. Henry's mother had her sixth child, Sallie, in 1862, and money was short within the family. Henry's wages at the store were three dollars a week, which was typical for such a job held by a young boy. Henry's father never owned a farm but leased houses as the family grew; in 1863 they were renting a home in West Overton across from the Overholt store. With the birth of Sallie, the family leased a somewhat larger home. Henry started work at his uncle Martin Overholt's general emporium in Mt. Pleasant at a wage of six dollars a week and moved in with his uncle. He seemed extremely proud of being the grandson of Abraham Overholt and dreamed of accomplishing similar achievements in life.

Things greatly improved for Henry in Mt. Pleasant as he briefly attended a type of college known as the Classical and Scientific Institute and later Westmoreland College. He again excelled in math and took over bookkeeping at his uncle's store. Bookkeeping opened the world of cost accounting to Henry, which would be his strength throughout his career. Henry was particularly fond of the fancy and artistic chirography of accountants of the period. This artistic fascination with the account book offers an important insight for Werner Sombart in his *The Quintessence of Capitalism*. He saw the accounting book as the very symbol of capitalism.[3] It is in these entries that one learns the economy of acquisition.

It was during this period that Henry became interested in reading. Like many boys of the time, he was introduced to Napoleon in the *McGuffey Reader*, which led him to read a borrowed copy of *The Life of Napoleon Bonaparte*. He would share his love of Napoleon with many capitalists of the period such as Andrew Carnegie and Charles Schwab. He also shared a passion with many students of the period for the works of Sir Walter Scott. He joined a type of literary fraternity known as the Philo Union. Henry became bookkeeper and treasurer and also led several book drives to improve the Philo Union library. Frick also became involved in civic activities, joining the Independent Order of Good Templars of Mt. Pleasant. He would become treasurer of this organization as well.

His religious development seemed to be one of searching during the period. He seemed closer to his father in rejecting the strict beliefs and behavior of the Mennonites. The area Mennonite church was in West Overton, surrounded by opportunities to explore other traditions. The local Mennonites were becoming more assimilated into the bigger community. The Mennonites lacked the large community that had existed in Bucks County and eastern Pennsylvania. Much of the Overholt family in later years joined the Lutheran Church, which was close in many traditions to the German Mennonites. While in Mt. Pleasant, Henry attended the Baptist and Methodist churches but never fully committed to any particular church. He found some acceptance in Thomas Jefferson's Deist approach to religion. Jefferson's *Life and Morals of Jesus Christ* (also known as *The Jefferson Bible*) was his favorite religious reading throughout his life. Jefferson prepared *The Jefferson Bible* by eliminating the references to miracles and focusing on the moral teachings of Jesus. This approach was popular with the Unitarian movement of Frick's youth and was consistent with the Freemason philosophy. It was said that Henry would hand out copies to his friends throughout his life. In 1868, Henry chose to become a Baptist, as did his parents. The Baptist ranks exploded in this period of religious awakening.

While at Mt. Pleasant, Henry took up card playing, something the Mennonite Church saw as the work of the Devil. Still, Henry would remain fond of cards throughout his life. Tradition has it that while working at his uncle's store in 1868, Henry had a "difference of opinion" with his uncle's partner, Barney Schallenberger. Whatever the issue, the problem resulted in his grandfather's asking Abraham Tinstman to give Henry a job at the Broadford Distillery. Abraham Tinstman was Henry's cousin, the son of Elizabeth Overholt, and at thirty-five, was the manager of the operation. At the age of nineteen, Henry was made an office boy with a salary of $25 a month. Henry worked hard and improved his skills at bookkeeping, but he still dreamed of bigger things. Family legend had it that he had a goal to make a million dollars as a young man. Certainly, such a goal would have been consistent with the competitive nature of Henry Clay, and the goal of becoming a millionaire was often talked about in pop culture of the time. Pittsburgh was rapidly becoming a magnet for young men in the hills surrounding it. While Henry became an outstanding bookkeeper, he saw sales as a better avenue to riches. Within the year, he asked his Uncle Christian to help him find a sales job in Pittsburgh. His uncle secured him a position at Eaton's Department Store at a salary of $6 a week.

Henry borrowed fifty dollars for a suit from his Uncle Christian and took the fifty-mile train trip to Pittsburgh. He rented an apartment on Anderson Street in the German section of Allegheny City (Pittsburgh's north side) across the Allegheny River from Pittsburgh. Allegheny City was a growing transportation and industrial hub. Frick would arrive in Allegheny City the same year that a young George Westinghouse arrived there to start his air brake company, and H.J. Heinz opened his business selling garden vegetables and horseradish in Allegheny City that year. Allegheny City, which had also been the port of entry for a young Andrew Carnegie, was the real boom town. Allegheny City was fueled by coal, and homes and factories poured out smoke and coal dust. Allegheny also was the home of the area's wealthy and the German middle class. The working class comprised ethnic Germans looking for upward mobility. The Republican-controlled city of Allegheny was a required stop for every candidate for president. Men like William Thaw, Benjamin Jones, James Laughlin, and Henry Buhl, the great capitalists of Pittsburgh, lived in Allegheny City. In the 1850s, the original "Millionaire's Row" was Allegheny City's Ridge Avenue. No city in America had such wealth concentrated in one row of mansions. Allegheny City soon became the classy suburb of Pittsburgh industrialists.

The great manufacturing expansion of the Civil War had created a retailing boom in the late 1860s, with Pittsburgh's most famous department store, Boggs and Buhl, opening in 1869. In addition, Isaac Kaufman opened a small Pittsburgh store. Frick would have also observed the opening of a new bank in Pittsburgh by Thomas Mellon, another Pittsburgh capitalist who would shortly become a business associate of Frick. After a few months Frick searched for a better salary. He found a position at Macrum and Carlisle, a department store in Pittsburgh, at a salary of $8 a week plus some commissions for sales. The store specialized in women's apparel and necessities. He walked across the bridge from Allegheny to Pittsburgh each day to Macrum and Carlisle. He was an aggressive salesman, challenging the pecking order on the floor. Of the twenty salesmen employed at Macrum and Carlisle, one by the name of William Blair claimed the right to service the best customers based on his sales record. Frick challenged the privilege as unfair but was required to prove himself. Frick made himself popular with the lady clientele and soon overtook Blair in sales and received an increase in salary. Still, within a few months, he again switched jobs for higher pay. This time it was at Copper's, a very fashionable dealer of black-tie goods, for which he received a salary of $12 a week, which was an outstanding wage for the period. His good looks and smart dress played in his favor to improve his lot as a salesman. His aggressiveness and sense of fair play and competition would augur those of his business career.

His schedule was as ambitious as his dreams. He rose and dressed for breakfast at seven at the boarding house on every weekday. He had over a mile to walk across the Ninth Street Bridge to reach the store at

Henry Clay Frick in his teens (courtesy Carnegie Library of Pittsburgh).

eight. He worked at the store until six and then crossed the river again to have dinner at the boarding house. He crossed back to attend night school at Iron City Commercial College to study accounting till nine-thirty, finally returning home around ten. On Sundays he attended Fourth Avenue Baptist Church. It is believed his interest in art continued along with the opportunities to become more involved in the city of Pittsburgh. One story even suggests that he continued to draw and paint as a hobby, but his schedule didn't seem to leave much time for such pursuits. Allegheny City was, however, the cultural center of Pennsylvania. Allegheny millionaires such as B.F. Jones and Benjamin Thaw of the "Pig Iron Aristocracy" had built several cultural centers, including converting the second floor of the City Hall into an art gallery.

Allegheny City, with a population of 60,000 when Frick arrived, was a city of beautiful parks, while its cross-river rival Pittsburgh had none. Men like William Thaw, Harry K. Thaw (son of William), Benjamin Thaw (son of William), Benjamin Jones, James Laughlin, John Shoenberger, E. Stevens, Henry Phipps,[4] Henry Oliver, and Henry Buhl, the Pig Iron Aristocrats of Pittsburgh, lived in fashionable Allegheny City. Frick drew inspiration from his viewing of "Millionaire's Row." It would be a group with whom Frick would find acceptance later in life. (Andrew Carnegie had spent his youth in the only small ghetto of Allegheny City, near where Frick was now renting.) Within 20 years, Frick would be lunching daily with these men at the Duquesne Club. Originally a Whig Party stronghold, it converted to the new Republican Party in the 1850s and would bring the first Republican Party convention to Pittsburgh in 1855. Allegheny City had more Republicans per square foot than any city in the nation; and in the tight election of 1860, the city delivered 10,000 votes for Lincoln. Lincoln would even make a brief stop there prior to going to his hotel in Pittsburgh on his way to the White House. While Frick was renting there, President U.S. Grant visited Allegheny to open a city park. President Rutherford B. Hayes would also visit this aristocratic city of Allegheny of pig iron manufacturers; actually, every president from Lincoln to Taft would visit Pittsburgh's north side.

Allegheny City and its twin neighbor Pittsburgh were in a postwar boom when Frick arrived. Pittsburgh was then known as the "Glass City," being the largest producer of the nation's glass. Pittsburgh was also the center of the oil industry, with 52 refineries processing Pennsylvania oil from north of the city. Westinghouse would open up his first railroad air brake plant in 1869. Pittsburgh was the largest producer and user of coal-fired steam engines. The Pennsylvania Railroad and most of the nation's railroads were expanding west out of the gateway of Pittsburgh. The railroads had taken a poor immigrant, Andrew Carnegie, and made him an investor and industrialist. Andrew Carnegie had teamed up with Pennsylvania Railroad executives, Edgar Thomson and Thomas Scott, to form Keystone Bridge Company. A rich young Andrew Carnegie dreamed of building hundreds of bridges across America's great rivers, as well as replacing thousands of old wooden bridges with his superior iron structures. The Pittsburgh papers were filled with the story of how Keystone built the longest span bridge (the Eads Bridge) at St. Louis. Carnegie also had a share of Union Iron Mills, Iron City Forge, and Cyclops Iron Mills. Railroads were the major users of iron in 1850; and by 1870, railroad iron made up over 50 percent of the production of iron. Carnegie was making iron axles for railroad cars. Carnegie's companies were some of the largest users of pig iron to make wrought iron products via the puddling process. Puddling required the reheating of pig iron into a hot pasty mix to be worked to wrought iron and rolled or forges into beams, rails, and axles. At the time, Carnegie had no blast furnaces and had to purchase pig iron, mainly from Westmoreland charcoal furnaces. There were only a handful of blast furnaces in Pittsburgh producing 70,000 tons of pig iron a year at $40 a ton. Carnegie couldn't get enough pig iron locally and was buying pig iron from Youngstown blast furnaces and Pennsylvania charcoal furnaces. A great industrial boom was underway, causing shortages in labor and pig iron, which would create a much different world. Young boys in Westmoreland County dreamed of going to Pittsburgh to make their fortunes.

Frick would have been witness, in his short stay in Allegheny, to the beginning of a major change in Pittsburgh and America's Industrial Revolution. The newspapers of the times were filled with little else. His German neighborhood was being overrun in 1868 and 1869 by an influx of new German immigrants, but these German immigrants were different. They were poor Catholic Germans who had been recruited to take unskilled labor jobs in the Union Iron Mills of a young Andrew Carnegie. In 1867, the failing Union Iron Works had cut the wages of the steel furnace men known as puddlers. The men formed one of the first ironworker unions, calling themselves the "Sons of Vulcan." At the time, such high-level workers were forming trade unions. They restricted entry into the craft and kept their methods secret. Welsh and English puddlers controlled these "forges" or shop unions. These trade unions did not protect the lowest and most mistreated the laborers. These puddlers were paid by the amount of steel produced. The wage was around $9 a ton, which for ten hours of work might translate to $15 to $20 a week. This was better pay than most front-line managers and fore-men. Puddlers and iron rollers were considered the "worker aristocracy" of Pittsburgh. Most of the unskilled laborers not in the Sons of Vulcan were paid around 70 cents a day. These mill laborers did not belong to tonnage production crews and made up the majority of the mill workers. Actually, the puddler was the master craftsman and received the $9 per ton; he in turn paid a handful of men on his crew. A crew worked five "heats" of about a half-ton each per ten-hour day. The lowest man on the puddler's crew made around $4 for the week. The ten-hour day became the standard of the puddlers' union.

What happened next would augur an event 25 years later that would change both Frick's and Carnegie's legacies forever. In this case, a young Carnegie in 1867 locked out the union at the mills in hopes of breaking the union and its strike. The strike spread to other Pittsburgh iron and steel mills. In late 1867, the producers raised a fund to recruit poor Germans in Europe to bring in to work. The next two years would bring a wave of cheap German laborers, who were trained as puddlers. At the same time, they were used to lower wages and to replace the bottom of the labor force. The combination of cheap labor, the breaking of trade and crafts unions, and a booming iron market made Carnegie a millionaire by 1869. Although the replacement of the highly skilled puddlers was the least successful of Carnegie's and the manufacturers' strategies, the replacement of the day laborer with a cheaply paid immigrant laborer proved extremely profitable. Actually, the wages of the puddlers increased too, as they hired some of this cheaper labor for their crew!

Pittsburgh of 1869 was a gray world of coal burning, iron manufactures, cast iron foundries, and steelmaking. This great industrial city, whose smoke often limited daylight to a few hours a day, had one of the nation's highest incidences of disease. Pittsburgh alone had the highest incidence of typhoid fever because of its polluted water; and its sewage system was no better than that of a medieval village. Often typhoid fever in Pittsburgh was a death sentence, since it led to air-related complications such as pneumonia. In late summer of 1869, an overambitious and rundown Frick contracted typhoid fever and was taken back to his grandmother's West Overton home to recover. There his grandmother and sister Maria nursed him. His hard work and drive had impressed his grandfather. The year before a sick Henry Clay Frick returned to his grandmother's mansion to be nursed to health, a young Andrew Carnegie (33 years old) "retired" to New York. Carnegie had reached an income of $50,000 per year from his investments (about a million dollars today), of which $20,000 a year came from his Union Iron Mills alone. Young men like Carnegie were fast becoming idols of ambitious younger men like Henry Clay Frick.

Frick, however, had more immediate concerns with his battle with typhoid. The air at West Overton was still fresh and clean, though in a few years it would be filled with coal dust and carbon dioxide. Frick improved by late September. Frick had failed to make his millions, but he had once again impressed grandfather Overholt. Frick was given an opportunity to do some tasks for his grandfather at the distillery. It was probably an easy way to get Frick to be accepted by the family managers and give him a chance to build back his strength. There is always resistance in a family business to the dividing of assets and authority among family. There is good evidence that the distillery business was losing money in 1869. Frick seemed to have won over his older cousin, Abraham Tinstman, and other family members. Abraham Overholt then directed Abraham Tinstman to give Frick a bookkeeping position at the Broad Ford distillery, so at age twenty Henry became chief bookkeeper for A. Overholt & Company. His salary was $1,000 a year, which at the time was a considerable sum. Obviously, grandfather Overholt wanted the young Frick to stay home this time. Like he had always done, Frick put all he had into the position and expanded into other areas.

On January 15, 1870, Frick's world would again be turned upside down by the death of his grandfather, Abraham Overholt. Frick had now lost his biggest backer. More problematic was the condition and distribution of the estate. Abraham proved not be a master of personal finance. The estate consisted of $395,000, or about seven million in today's dollars. Abraham Overholt left six major shares to his widow, his sons' widows, his two surviving sons, and his daughter and Frick's mother, Elizabeth. A small stipend was left to Frick's sister Maria, who had been raised by Overholt. Frick, who had assumed he would be left a large amount, got nothing. Even worse, Overholt's businesses were near bankruptcy due to the need to settle accounts. Both the West Overton Distillery and Broad Ford Distillery were already bankrupt. Abraham's sons, Martin and Christian, were personally near bankruptcy. Interestingly, the struggling Elizabeth Overholt Frick was probably the soundest financially of the children. Frick's fortunes in a few months had changed dramatically, but Frick would soon tap into the growing fortunes of Connellsville coke.

3. Connellsville Coke: Gray Gold

The coal is very unlike that in the adjacent basins. The cost of producing Connellsville coke is therefore at least fifty cents per ton less than that of neighboring regions.
— Connellsville Coke and Iron Company
Annual Report, 1881

George Washington had noted the seams of coal in the Pittsburgh area back in the 1750s. This so-called Pittsburgh Seam followed the Monongahela River to Westmoreland County. At places this seam was nine feet thick. During the Revolutionary War, coal dug in the hills was used to heat Fort Pitt. By the 1790s, the Ohio and Monongahela River valleys were using coal to heat houses because of its regional abundance. By 1810, Pittsburgh had become known as the "Smoky City" from home heating alone! Coal sold at six cents a bushel and burned better than charcoal made from walnut. The farmers of the region started to operate small mines to make money down river in markets like Pittsburgh. These part-time miners were known as "winter diggers," "pumpkin rollers," "wheats," and "greenies." The abundance of coal in western Pennsylvania led to experimenting in many applications for the use of coal. One earlier use was in the production of salt, in which it supplied heat to dry liquid brine pumped from wells, and was also used to drive the steam engine pumps. Abraham Overholt was an early experimenter and a "winter digger."

Abraham Overholt was a thrifty farmer who, as early as 1820, was experimenting with the coal found in the area to heat his home and fuel his distillery. Many farmers were using the coal for heat by the 1830s, but they lacked good transportation to the booming Pittsburgh market. The Monongahela and Youghiogheny Rivers were navigable only in late winter to early summer and a few weeks in the autumn rainy season. Connellsville farmers could use the Pike, but that put their coal at a price disadvantage in the Pittsburgh market. Farmers continued to favor whiskey production over coal in the 1830s. Whiskey at $1 a gallon offered profitability by land transport that coal did not. Still, farmers like Overholt continued to make a small profit on small loads.

One could make a quick dollar by shipping a barge load of coal to Pittsburgh during high water periods or even down river to Cincinnati. Pittsburghers such as H.J. Heinz and Thomas Mellon had been known to turn a quick profit by shipping coal on the rivers. Overholt could take it by wagon to a loading dock at Broad Ford on the Youghiogheny River, or he could dig up the coal right at Broad Ford. The Broad Ford coal seam was another that had been noted in George Washington's journal in 1753 when he visited William Cawford's farm on the Youghiogheny. In the 1850s, Overholt would build another distillery at Broad Ford, using coal for fuel, along with wood. From the Youghiogheny River dock at Broad Ford, a riverboat of coal could be taken to New Orleans, as Abraham Overholt's brother did in the 1830s. Overholt utilized the German trade network along the rivers to set up the coal shipments. German traders, utilizing family ties in Cincinnati and New Orleans, were a key part of this commerce. Coal heating was the preferred method in the cities like Pittsburgh as nearby forests had been lumbered out. Coal cooking failed because of the odor, but blacksmith shops used it for a number of industrial applications, and forge shops were booming in Pittsburgh in the 1820s. Pittsburgh was the first to use coal in glassmaking in the 1790s, which for centuries had been based on wood. Pittsburgh was consuming 10,000 bushels a day by 1833, and a row of coke ovens stayed busy at the base of Coal Hill. By 1837, the Pittsburgh glass industry was the largest in America and consumed 1.5 million bushels a year, while Pittsburgh's iron industry consumed about 100,000 bushels a year. The total consumption in Pittsburgh was about 500 tons a day (about 12,500 bushels) in 1837 at a selling price of 38 cents a bushel.

Mining in Europe was considered a craft and followed the crafts system of management. The mining master craftsman set up his crew of apprentices and helpers, and he was paid by the bushel. He then paid the members of his crew, which is how it was done initially in American mines. The Welsh, Scotch, and Cornish were known for their mining skills and were attracted to the better pay of American mines. An 1819 British miner compared American opportunities:

> ... coal cost 3 cents per bushel to be gotten out of the mines. This price, as nearly as I can calculate enables the American collier to earn upon average, double the number of cents for the same labor that the collier in England can earn; so that as the American collier can, upon an average buy his flour for one third the price that the English collier pays for his flour, he receives six times the quantity of flour for the same labor.[1]

In Western Pennsylvania a lot of farmers mined the open surface seams with no expertise because miners were in short supply, and the demand for coal far exceeded supply. Westmoreland mines were outcroppings that could be mined with limited deep-mining expertise.

Pittsburgh's appetite for coal grew exponentially from 1810 to 1850. Most of the early coal mines were on the Monongahela River in towns like Braddock and Turtle Creek. In addition, down-river demand from Pittsburgh mushroomed. In 1836, the Monongahela Navigation Company was incorporated to build a series and dams and locks to allow coal barges all year on the Monongahela River. By 1844, the Monongahela was navigable 55 miles from Brownsville to Pittsburgh. The success of the Monongahela River shipping inspired the Youghiogheny Navigation Company to incorporate in the 1840s. The Youghiogheny and Monongahela River navigation opened up the market for coal in the counties of Fayette, Westmoreland, and Washington. Coal was moved in 75-foot flatboats known as "joe boats," which made one-way trips down river. Shipping was limited to high water periods prior to river locks in the 1850s. Shipments from that region went from 750,000 bushels in 1844 to 12,400,000 in 1850, and to 37,400,000 in 1860. Pittsburgh adopted the use of steamboats to move coal in the 1850s. Steamboat companies "pooled" coal shipments by towing twelve barges at a time, with each barge carrying about 12,000 bushels, or roughly 450 ton, of coal. Companies charged fifty dollars a barge or about four cents a bushel. The German trade network had key trade nodes in Cincinnati, St. Louis, and New Orleans, allowing Westmoreland farmers to make a quick profit on a barge of coal. Most of this coal was being used for heating in the West and fueling the iron industry of Pittsburgh. The Allegheny Mountains prevented the shipments to the central and eastern Pennsylvania iron industry, which was supplied by eastern Pennsylvania anthracite coal. The mining of coal in Westmoreland created a land boom, with prices tripling from thirty-five dollars per acre to over a hundred dollars per acre. Westmoreland farmers were becoming wealthy.

In the east and in western Pennsylvania, coupled with the industrial boom of Pittsburgh, the need for coal created demand for more transportation systems. Another factor in the opening of the bituminous coal fields was the improved river navigation, roads, and canals. The National Road supported by national politicians such as Henry Clay helped, but the National Road bypassed Pittsburgh in favor of Wheeling; however, it did pass through the Fayette County coal towns of Uniontown and Brownsville. Pennsylvania politicians and Pittsburgh industrialists started to develop other routes to Pittsburgh's industries. The Pennsylvania Turnpike, which crossed the state, was fully developed in the 1830s. The turnpike was augmented in western Pennsylvania with "plank" roads, which used wooden planks over dirt or macadam. Pittsburgh investors also poured money into the Pennsylvania Canal in the 1830s. This canal from Philadelphia to Pittsburgh was really a combination of canal, road, and mountain railroad inclines. The Pig Iron Aristocrats of Pittsburgh like William Thaw and Benjamin Jones financed the canal. Canal boats were actually loaded on the railroad inclines to take them over the Allegheny Mountains. The canal went through northern Westmoreland County and moved coal to Pittsburgh, albeit at a high cost. It also allowed anthracite coal from eastern Pennsylvania to be used by Pittsburgh industries and even supplied anthracite coal for iron-making furnaces in Westmoreland and Fayette Counties. Anthracite hard coal was being pioneered in western Pennsylvania iron fur-

Henry Clay Frick at age 20 (courtesy Carnegie Library of Pittsburgh).

naces to replace charcoal. The local bituminous coal of Westmoreland County had initially proved too soft for iron making.

Coal in Pennsylvania was of two basic types. A hard, high-energy coal found in eastern Pennsylvania, known as anthracite, could be used directly to smelt iron ore. While anthracite was high energy, its high ignition temperature of 950 F did not make it a good substitute for wood-burning stoves for heating. The western Pennsylvania type of coal found near the Overholt farm was bituminous coal. Bituminous "soft" coal is high in volatile matter, which burns as gases. Bituminous coal burns at a lower temperature and gives a lower level of heat. Bituminous coal can be converted to a denser type of fuel known as coke. Coke can then be used to fuel iron-making furnaces.

There were several coke districts in western Pennsylvania, but the richest and most productive was the Connellsville district, which ran through Westmoreland and Fayette counties. Connellsville in Westmoreland County would become the "Capital of Coke." The Connellsville district is part of the rich "Pittsburgh seam" that is open on the Monongahela and Youghiogheny River banks. The district is 42 miles long and 3.5 miles in width, and covers all of Westmoreland and Fayette counties. The richest strip of this coal deposit ran from Latrobe, Pennsylvania, south through Scottsdale, Connellsville, and Uniontown to the Fairchance-Smithfield area. The richest three-mile strip, from eight to eleven feet thick, ran by the Overholt farm in today's Westmoreland County.

Burning bituminous coal directly was dirty and inefficient. Coke, however, was a hard, high-temperature fuel that could be used in salt making, steel puddling furnaces, glass furnaces, forge shops, foundries, and iron making. The earliest way of making coke was a simple pile of wood and coal. The pile was ignited and then covered to burn slowly for days. The process was similar to charcoal making. The main drive to coke was caused by the lumbering out of hardwood to make charcoal for area iron furnaces. Westmoreland and Fayette counties gave rise to the first charcoal iron furnaces west of the Alleghenies in the 1790s, attracting German and Scotch-Irish iron makers from all over America. By 1810, Westmoreland and Fayette counties had over 15 charcoal iron furnaces with associated forges and rolling mills.

The real boon for the Connellsville coke district was coke's use as a blast furnace fuel. The county had been the center of American iron making from the 1790s, but the fuel had been charcoal, not coal. The burning of hardwood incompletely in a large pile produced charcoal, which is pure carbon (volatiles removed) and an excellent fuel. Workers known as "colliers" managed the process; "collier" derived from "coal," meaning the wood was supposedly turned to "coal." A large charcoal operation would require as many as 12 colliers and a master collier. A collier could make $1.50 a day, and the master could make $3.00 a day. A collier piled burning wood and covered it, so it would convert to charcoal through incomplete combustion. It took ten days for a smoldering wood pile to be converted to charcoal, and the process required constant tending by colliers. The collier was considered a type of craftsman, and early furnaces had an apprentice system.

A typical charcoal iron furnace was a 30-foot-high stack made of limestone blocks. By 1820, western Pennsylvania had hundreds of these charcoal iron furnaces in operation. A charcoal furnace required huge amounts of wood to operate. Larger eighteenth-century furnaces could consume 840 bushels or 22 cords of wood in a 24-hour period. That translated into almost an acre of wood! A rough estimate for a charcoal furnace was a half-acre of wood per ton of iron produced. The average furnace turned out twenty to twenty-five tons of iron a week. Western Pennsylvania started to experience wood shortages in the 1840s, but Britain had made the switch to coal decades earlier. With the amazing charcoal consumption of iron furnaces, by the start of the eighteenth century, Britain's hardwood had been lumbered out by iron production. Britain had to pass laws to restrict the use of oak, in particular because it was a strategic material for the shipbuilding industry. Hickory was considered the best for charcoal, but oak, chestnut, and walnut were commonly used. America's huge hardwood forests kept furnaces on wood into the mid–1800s, while England had been forced to switch to coal one hundred years prior. (Even today Brazil still uses charcoal, and its use is creating a lumbering out of wood in the rain forests there.) Abundant wood gave America a significant cost advantage over British iron.

The problem by the end of the 1820s was that western Pennsylvania charcoal furnaces were stripping hardwood at an unsustainable rate. Charcoal prices were rising rapidly with the hardwood shortage. The Pennsylvania legislature passed an act to encourage companies to move into coke production. On June 16, 1836 the act stated: "To encourage the manufacture of iron with coke or mineral coke."[2] Additionally, the Franklin Institute offered a monetary prize for "the person who shall manufacture in the United States the greatest quantity of iron from the ore during the year, using no other fuel than bituminous coal or coke, the quantity to be not less than 20 tons." Some eastern Pennsylvania iron furnaces were finding the use of anthracite coal a good substitute for charcoal, but western Pennsylvania bituminous coal used directly in iron furnaces proved too soft and low in energy. Coking of bituminous coal to improve strength and energy content had been developed in England in the late 1700s.

The great western Pennsylvanian ironmaster and iron plantation manager Isaac Meason seems to have been the first in America to push the use of coke in his Westmoreland and Fayette County furnaces. Meason's furnaces operated but a few miles from the Overholt farm. Meason was aware of the coal and coking technology of Scotland, and saw its future in a number of industries. Meason's charcoal furnaces were stripping an acre of woodland a day (800 bushels of charcoal). Charcoal was extremely labor intensive, with dozens of woodchoppers and colliers assigned to a single furnace. Meason started to experiment with coke as early as the 1790s. He appears to have had hired English ironmasters in 1800 to help him make the conversion. His Fayette and Westmoreland furnaces were ideally located on the Connellsville bituminous deposits of coal. By 1812, Meason had built coke piles and was using coke throughout the operation. Meason proved to be a metallurgical wizard, improving many processes related to the manufacture of iron and iron implements.

The wrought-iron industry had been growing with another technological breakthrough by Scotch-Irish ironmaster Isaac Meason, the iron baron of Pennsylvania's Fayette County. Meason invented a new type of puddling process to convert pig iron into wrought iron needed for nails. Iron nails were the tonnage product in the 1820s and 1830s of Pittsburgh manufacturers. The switch from log cabins to frame housing had caused a super boom in nail demand. Actually it was more of a codependency, as volume nail production made frame building economical. Nails prior to 1800 were made through painstakingly long operations by blacksmiths on anvils. As volume increased, blacksmith shops grew into small factories and then into naileries. Nails made Pittsburgh the "Iron City" because of its natural and man-made strategic advantages. Pittsburgh had three nail factories by 1806, but most of these were extended blacksmith operations of southern Scotch-Irish immigrants. Coke and coal were both used in these puddling furnaces, which came from demand for nails. By 1820, Pittsburgh had numerous nail mills for the ever-growing demand of the west. By 1830, nail production boomed, creating the demand for coal and coke. The puddling furnaces required massive deliveries of coke from Fayette and surrounding counties.

In 1833, Meason built the first beehive coke furnaces at Connellsville. Two area farmers, Lester Norton and a Mr. Nichols, built the first U.S. beehive furnace out of cut stone to supply area iron furnaces. These earlier plantation blast furnaces could easily double or triple daily production of the charcoal furnace. Meason's coke-fueled furnaces were some of the most profitable, and exceeded the British quality. His castings, such as stoves and sugar-, and salt-making kettles, went all over the country. Meason's pig iron also dominated in the Pittsburgh market in price and quality. His technology would put him in the lead over western Pennsylvania iron furnaces and make him a fortune. Meason's coke led Abraham Overholt to experiment with coke as a clean fuel for his distillery. Other farmers and carpenters started to build riverboats to move the coke to Pittsburgh to fuel-hungry industries. In 1840s, coke was regularly being shipped to steam engine plants and foundries in Cincinnati. Coke's hardness allowed it to ship well, while bituminous coal powdered on transport.

The real boon in the use of pig iron came with the opening of a puddling furnace in 1819 by Union Rolling Mill and later the Union Iron Mill. Puddling furnaces required high energy, like coke or anthracite coal. Englishman Henry Cort had invented puddling in 1784 and Meason had improved it in the 1790s, but it took another fifty years for it to be widely used in America. Again it was Isaac Meason who pioneered the use of coke in puddling furnaces. Puddlers were the top-paid craftsmen in the country, making as much as $25.00 a week when laborers made 60 cents a day. Puddling made wrought iron production many times more efficient, and puddling could produce a wide range of material properties by controlling the carbon content. Puddling could also be used to make steel, which grew in demand during the Civil War. The Union Rolling Mill of Pittsburgh would become America's largest consumer of pig iron until the arrival of Carnegie's steel mills in the 1870s. The puddling furnaces of Pittsburgh would make the transition into steel mills in the 1860s.

Another part of the growth of coke use was brought about by the mushrooming in the foundry business, which cast steam engines, cannons, stoves, and machinery. Pittsburgh foundries remelted pig iron in furnaces called cupolas. Pig iron was purchased from Ohio or Pennsylvania charcoal iron furnaces and brought to foundries in Pittsburgh, since Pittsburgh at the time had no charcoal iron-making furnaces. Pittsburgh's appetite for coke in the late 1840s and 1850s could not be supplied by Connellsville coal and coke until river navigation and the railroads opened the flow in the mid–1850s. In the meantime, coal mines started to be opened a few miles up the Monongahela River at Braddock. Judge Thomas Mellon, the future banking mogul, would team up with the Corey family of Braddock in developing these mines. Thomas Mellon had invested very successfully in a small mine in 1849. In 1856, He became a silent partner in J.B. Corey & Company. Corey was the true expert in mining the rich Pittsburgh coal seam. Corey had brought in expert Welsh miners to mine the coal. Over 2,000 British miners immigrated to the United States in the 1850s, and over 35,000 in the 1850s. The technique used small man tunnels and "ravine dogs" to pull out small cars of coal. The family of Thomas Dickson opened mines in nearby Swissvale and Braddock Hills. Mellon would become one of Pittsburgh's wealthiest citizens because of these early coal investments. The Coreys, Dicksons, and Mellons were on the verge of the biggest coal demand boom ever with the development of the iron-making blast furnace.

It would be the combination of coke furnaces, steel puddling furnaces, foundry cupolas, and the evolution of the modern blast furnace that turned coal into gold. The development of the blast furnace would become the economic engine of the coal energy. Pittsburgh would not have its first blast furnace until 1859. By the 1850s, river transportation had opened up the Connellsville coal for Pittsburgh use. The Mahoning Valley of Ohio, however, produced most of the pig iron used in Pittsburgh finishing mills. Pittsburgh was merely a user, not an iron producer. Coal competition was brisk, however. Mahoning Valley had one advantage over the Pittsburgh area. It had a very special coal deposit, which allowed for the rise of the modern blast furnace. The coal deposits in the area possessed some rare blast furnace qualities. Only the coal deposits around Glasgow, Scotland, had similar properties. This "splint" coal was a semi-anthracite coal capable of firing a blast furnace directly. Charcoal furnace stacks were limited to about 40 feet, but the strength of coal allowed stacks to go much higher to 70 or 80 feet. The higher stacks allowed more furnace output. The additional heat coupled with stack height allowed these coal blast furnaces to double the output of a charcoal furnace. Most higher stack blast furnaces in Pittsburgh and West Virginia used coke made from coal at a higher cost. The immediate cost of coking and transporting coke was eliminated with the use of Mahoning Valley hard coal. In the late 1850s, Youngtown blast furnaces were leading the world. Mahoning Valley pig iron was supplying the rolling mills of Pittsburgh and Wheeling, as well as enabling the creation of new rolling mills in eastern Ohio. While the use of Connellsville coal and coke in the Pittsburgh finishing mills was a large market, it was small compared to blast furnace usage.

The early blast furnaces of the 1850s were built to produce pig iron for other iron operations. The blast furnace could stand on its own, supplying many different foundries and rolling mills at points distant from the operation. The story of the next blast furnace in Pittsburgh is the story of Jones and Laughlin Steel. That story begins with the world's first oil baron, Samuel Kier, and Kier's young bank manager Benjamin Franklin Jones. Both men had invested earlier in canals. In 1850, Kier focused his energy on oil, while Jones invested in puddling furnaces and rolling mills on Pittsburgh's south side (known as Brownstown). Another Pittsburgh iron investor, William Thaw, teamed up with Kier to extend canals to connect Pittsburgh and Youngstown. Benjamin Jones was Scotch-Irish from a modest background, but as a young boy showed an attitude for business. Jones had been manager of the Pennsylvania Canal prior to this move in 1850, but in the 1840s he was a partner of a charcoal furnace and forge in Pennsylvania's Indiana County. The furnace failed when a change in national tariffs allowed more imports. Jones and Thaw would, however, become the first Pittsburgh millionaires, and years later they and their families would be Frick friends and associates.

Pig Iron Aristocrat Jones never got his south-side works running, but in 1853 he teamed up with two German ironmasters, Bernard and John Lauth. Samuel Kier was also an investor in the company known as Jones, Lauth, and Company. The 1853 partnership agreement of B.F. Jones would augur that of the future steel king, Andrew Carnegie. The agreement called for all profits to be reinvested in the operation. Furthermore, the partnership was the first to apply the idea of vertical integration in the pig iron industry. Vertical integration meant owning the full manufacturing chain from raw materials to distribution. B.F. Jones looked to use Connellsville coke to run his Pittsburgh furnaces. Good metallurgical coke strength would allow Jones to increase stack height and furnace output beyond those of Mahoning Valley. Jones focused in particular on the needs of the booming 1850s railroad industry. The partnership opened a rolling mill in 1855, known as the American Iron Works, and got its pig iron from the Falcon Furnaces of Youngstown, Ohio. The plant rolled bar and rails. The Lauth brothers were brilliant engineers and the American Iron Works became the most productive rolling mill in the country. The American Iron Works soon became a major consumer of pig iron, and the partnership looked to open its own Pittsburgh blast furnaces.

The accelerating use of coke in Pittsburgh and the opening of the Pennsylvania Railroad created the first commercial coal mines in Westmoreland County. The first mine was established in 1854 by Thomas Scott, who later became president of the Pennsylvania Railroad. A few months later, Westmoreland Coal Company opened a nearby mine. The larger and more accessible seams of Westmoreland and Fayette Counties allowed for larger operations than those of the Monongahela Valley. These mine operations used about fifty miners per mine. These were slope mines dug into hillsides that could remove coal in wheeled carts pulled by mules in place of Welsh dogs. By 1857, shaft mines were developed, in which the shaft went down vertically to the seam and coal was brought out in hoists. The new mines attracted Welsh, Cornish, and Scottish coal miners who could earn three cents a bushel, which translated into six to eight dollars a day, far above the two dollars a day earned in Europe. These miners were considered craftsmen and specialists, having served long and arduous apprenticeships in Europe. They were also independent operators being paid for their level of production and hiring their own laborers to load coal. These early miners were piece-rate and were free to determine their own working hours. They were responsible for their own equipment, such as candles, shovels, picks, and "lard" lamps. Most of the larger Westmoreland mines in the 1850s shipped coal to Pittsburgh to be converted to coke there. Many of the German farmers utilized the German river trade network, which allowed them to ship coal to Cincinnati for heating.

B.F. Jones took vertical integration to new heights, while some Youngstown pig iron makers had combined coal, coke, and ironmaking in late 1859. Jones partnered with Connellsville coal operations and river transporters to bring coal to his beehive coke furnaces. The commercial coal mines at Connellsville could readily outproduce the Monongahela mines of Braddock and Swissvale. He owned several of the Pennsylvania coal mines, such as Vesta Mines in the Connellsville coal district. Jones built his coke ovens on the Monongahela River docks. The coke ovens fed his Eliza Blast Furnaces at his American Iron Works. He purchased iron ore mines in Michigan and Minnesota, investing in canals and railroads to transport ore. The works had puddling furnaces and rolling mills to produce iron products. Benjamin F. Jones and his brother took to "forward" integration as well. They built warehouses in Chicago and Pittsburgh, initiating the idea of iron and steel processing centers for the end user. Coke production could not keep up with demand by 1859, when there were thirty cupolas making iron for foundries in Pittsburgh.

In 1859 another partner, Scotch-Irish Pittsburgh banker James Laughlin, came into the partnership. The pig iron requirements for the rolling mills were soon outstripping the abil-

Bank of coke ovens in Westmoreland County (courtesy Carnegie Library of Pittsburgh).

ity of Pennsylvania and Ohio furnaces to supply them. As part of Jones's vertical integration, he set up two blast furnaces (Eliza furnaces) on the north side of the Monongahela River. (Naming blast furnaces after women was a tradition in the early days of the industry.) These furnaces were 45 feet high and had a 12-foot bosh. Additional integration included the building of coke beehive furnaces. Coal was brought down the river from Connellsville. Iron ore was brought in from Missouri and the Great Lakes. The Pennsylvania Railroad connected the huge coal fields of Westmoreland by 1855, cutting the cost and increasing the availability of coal and coke. Vertical integration allowed Jones and Laughlin to become the low-cost producer, a lesson that a young Andrew Carnegie and later a young Frick would note and study. The basic layout of the operations at Jones and Laughlin would remain intact until 1980! B.F. Jones and Thomas Mellon, both Whigs, helped form the new protectionist party of the 1850s. This would be today's Republican Party, which held its first convention in 1856 in Pittsburgh, now known as the birthplace of the Republican Party. Both Jones and Laughlin worked behind the scenes with the pig iron lobby to assure Lincoln's protectionist policies. Their support was a key reason why Lincoln carried Allegheny County by a huge majority.

The Civil War would create a huge expansion in the number of blast furnaces to make pig iron, cupolas to cast cannon, and puddling furnaces to make wrought iron and steel. The beehive furnace, which had been invented in Connellsville, became the standard for the production of coke. The beehive looks like a brick igloo with a hole in the roof, having a 12-foot diameter base. The lining was fireclay brick, which was also abundant locally. The coal was added through the hole on the top. The beehive coking process was perfected by Frick and Company and consisted of five steps: charging, leveling, quenching, drawing, and loading. These huge beehive coke ovens took a standard load of five tons of coal for burning. The coking time varied from 72 hours for puddling or foundry coke to 48 hours for blast furnace coke. The quenching and drawing steps were hot, dirty, and physical. When the coke was ready, the oven man pulled the coke out through a side door, quenching it with a spray of water to stop the burning. It took a coke drawer three hours to get the coke out of an oven and another three hours to charge it. The layout of Frick's earlier works allowed the coke to be directly loaded into railroad cars. One coke drawer was responsible for drawing and loading two ovens a day. Five tons of coal produced about 3.1 tons of coke, along with an endless stream of noxious smoke and dirt. A coke-oven worker made about $1 a day. Coke sold for around 80 cents a ton in the 1860s, about double the price of a ton of coal. It took 9.58 tons of coke to produce 1.78 tons of pig iron in a blast furnace. From 1845 to 1880, Westmoreland coal and coke shipments were increasing at a rate of 2.5 million bushels every year. Miners at the time got four to five cents a bushel (96 pounds). A bushel of coal sold for about forty cents. A miner by hand could do about 100 bushels for $5.00 a day, and with the help of a "ravine dog," about 160 bushels for $8.00 dollars a day. This was in a time when a laborer made about $1.00 a day, a carpenter about $2.50 a day, and a blacksmith about $3.00 a day.

During the Civil War, western Pennsylvania became the forge and armorer of the nation. Coal requirements for Pittsburgh for the five years prior to the war were 423,000 tons, versus 5,500,000 tons during the war. The Connellsville district boomed and coke ovens began to be opened. The biggest coal dealer in the area was B. Corey and Company, with Judge Thomas Mellon as the majority stockholder. B. Corey and Company had a fleet of barges to move coal down the Ohio River to other industrial cities such as Cincinnati and St. Louis. Pittsburgh, however, produced as much as 25 percent of the Union's artillery, 15 percent at Fort Pitt Foundry alone. At least 80 percent of the Union's naval iron plate for ships and most of the Union's armor plate was rolled in Pittsburgh. All of the artillery carriage axles and most railroad axles were forged in Pittsburgh. But most of the raw pig iron came from Ohio and from Westmoreland and Fayette counties, as Pittsburgh had only three blast furnaces, though it added two more large ones at the end of the war. All of these blast furnaces were using Connellsville coke. The coke boom created the Pittsburgh and Connellsville Railroad, which followed the Monongahela River to Pittsburgh for about forty miles.

Coke fueled the Union's great cannon foundries of the Civil War. The greatest producer of mammoth cannon was the Fort Pitt Foundry in Pittsburgh. Fort Pitt Foundry was the direct descendant of the Joseph McClurg works of 1804. This foundry would produce 60 percent of the Union's heavy artillery and 15 percent of all Union artillery. The Fort Pitt Foundry became famous throughout the war across Europe, as reporters marveled at the huge guns cast there. Fort Pitt Foundry had led the country in the development of heavy cast iron guns and cannons in the 1850s. The real advance in heavy artillery came from the work of army Major Thomas Jefferson Rodman. Major Rodman was the superintendent of the Watertown Arsenal in Massachusetts. Large cast cannons had become problematic, since these hot-cast cannon developed internal strains as the metal cooled. The strains would cause the cast cannon to break on cooling, split during transport, or burst on firing. Rodman had worked out a revolutionary process of cooling the cannon from the inside core. This allowed for a hollow tube to be cast. Prior to this, large cannon in America and at Germany's Krupp Works were cast solid and bored out. Rodman had received a patent in 1847, but the army was unimpressed. He moved to Pittsburgh and started a series of production experiments that made news around the world. Over the next ten years Rodman perfected his process of hollow-cast cannon. In 1860 the Fort Pitt Foundry cast a pair of 15-inch Rodman "Columbiads," the largest guns in the world. The casting of the great Columbiad became the basis for Jules Verne's 1886 novel *From the Earth to the Moon*. The Pig Iron Aristocrats were now the pride of the country and heroes worldwide. The foundry had stockpiled a smaller 10-inch version to supply the army.

Pittsburgh was truly the forge of the Union, and Connellsville was the nation's coal mine. Pittsburgh had over 400 puddling furnaces in operation during the war. Its rolling mills had an annual capacity of over 150,000 tons annually, and its foundries had an annual capacity of over 34,000 tons. At the same time, Pittsburgh was experimenting with a new iron product known as steel. Steel was being made by the "German method," a "high" volume variation of crucible steel. This required pig iron to be heated in crucibles in coke and coal-fired furnaces for days. Then carbon was re-added to produce steel. One crucible might only hold 200 to

1,000 pounds of steel. Larger castings required a simultaneous pouring and mixing of the liquid steel. Several Pittsburgh foundries such as Singer, Nimick, & Company were casting small (three-inch) rifled steel cannons to compete with German and British guns. By 1864, Pittsburgh's Hussey, Wells and Company, using the crucible and German method, could produce 20 tons of cast steel a day (when most steel companies were casting about a ton a day). Pittsburgh's Schoenberger and Company started making the steel horseshoes to replace wrought-iron shoes in 1867. Steel would never be a factor during the Civil War, but would bring the Pig Iron Aristocrats much wealth. Ultimately, however, steel would spell the end of the Pig Iron Aristocracy and the beginning of Pittsburgh's steel titans and Connellsville's coke titans.

The Pig Iron Aristocrats and the coal barons of Pittsburgh were not only the ones who won the war but also the ones who profited the most. The Republican tariffs assured a boom in national production. The great iron triangle of Ohio, West Virginia, and Pennsylvania saw growth as never before and became the consuming market for Connellsville coke. In Connellsville, farmers (like Frick's relations) and a new breed of coal miners were making fortunes. The war would also stimulate huge leaps in pig iron technology. The huge profit margins in the pig iron-related businesses were poured back into the businesses. Equally as important, the pig iron end users such as the railroads experienced similar growth. The expansion of the iron and coal industry during the war would be the infrastructure in place to make America the premier industrial nation.

The postwar iron and steel boom would make Connellsville the coke capital of the world. The railroad expansion of the postwar era was creating millionaires and new companies. Railroad track grew from 22,000 miles in 1860 to 52,922 in 1870. Men like Andrew Carnegie, Henry Phipps, Henry Oliver, Thomas Scott, and Edgar Thomson were making fortunes supplying iron bridges, rails, and axles to the booming railroad industry. Pittsburgh was kept so busy it was constantly short on pig iron, coke, and laborers. Nor was Pittsburgh alone: A great iron works had sprung up in Connellsville's backyard of Johnstown, Pennsylvania. Cambria Iron Works was making wrought iron rails for the railroad industry in 1853. More importantly, a young Irishman, William Kelly, was experimenting in the 1850s at Cambria in a new volume steel-making process, which would become known as the Bessemer process. A creative group of Cambria Iron managers saw a new future in steel rails replacing wrought-iron rails. In 1867, Cambria Iron Company rolled the first steel railroad rails, opening up the Age of Steel. In western Pennsylvania, Cambria Iron built a complex of blast furnaces and Bessemer converters in 1871. Bessemer Steel production would go from a mere 3,000 tons in 1867 to over a million tons a year by 1880. The manufacture of steel via the blast furnace and Bessemer converter would make hundreds of new western Pennsylvania millionaires. Connellsville coke would fuel the new steel industry. By the 1890s, Connellsville would have more millionaires per capita than any other place in the country, maybe in the world.

4. The Prince of Coke

It has been stated that the future millionaires of America will be found among the iron and coal mines of Pennsylvania. That they will be found among the rolling mills, the foundries, the machine shops and the coal companies of Pittsburgh, there can be no doubt.
— Pittsburgh As It Is (1857)

The Overholts had not overlooked the changing environment created by the coke boom of the war. Connellsville was being talked about as a future boom town as major railroads looked to partner with coke and coal operations, and farmers made fortunes selling coal rights. Overholt's grandson, Abraham Overholt Tinstman, had worked his way up in the distillery organization and had formed the partnership of A. Overholt & Co. This company was listed as "Manufacturers of Flour and Youghiogheny Whiskey." Abraham Tinstman also purchased six acres of coking land in 1865 with Joseph Rist. Shortly after, they sold half the land to Col. A.S. Morgan of Pittsburgh, who built the area's first major battery of coke ovens. In 1868 Abraham Overholt lent Abraham Tinstman money to purchase part of Morgan Mines in the Broad Ford Run Valley near the distillery. The Westmoreland coal boom was just beginning in 1868, with shipments moving to St. Louis and New Orleans with the support of Mellon family money. The Morgan Mines had been a key coal producer and coke maker during the later part of the war. Morgan Mines built a battery of over hundred small coke ovens that were supplying smaller foundries and rolling mills throughout Western Pennsylvania. They built a mile of railroad to connect with the Mt. Pleasant and Broad Ford Railroad, which allowed Pittsburgh shipments. Tinstman and Morgan had full control of the Connellsville coke production, but many Pittsburgh iron makers such as Jones and Laughlin were buying Connellsville coal and shipping it to Pittsburgh to be coked.

The Morgan Mines was the first major commercial mining operation. The original mines were slant mines into the hills, which could be mined using mules and wagons. While the miners were subcontractors paid by the bushel, the mine operation required a new group of employees. Supervisors were hired at $3 to $4 a day to oversee mining, coke, and river operations. Laborers were hired at $2 a day, a high wage for the time, because labor was short in this farming county. Coke oven workers were paid a $1 a day. Initially, the only labor available was young farmers or temporary farm labor. Farmer labor was utilized at $20 to $25 a month with room and board. Morgan Mines was one of the first to start importing badly needed labor, the shortage of which was restricting expansion. The mine also required the work of blacksmiths and carpenters. The company store was a natural evolution in a farming district where dry goods and equipment were not readily available.

After the death of their grandfather Abraham Overholt in January of 1871, thirty-seven-year-old Tinstman and Henry Clay Frick played chess late one night, discussing the boom market for coke. Frick had seen the boom of the iron and steel mills firsthand, and Tinstman's main source of income was from his small coke operations and his investment in Morgan Mines. Frick had also done business as a clerk at his grandfather's sawmill with "Little Jim" Cochran, farmer and carpenter turned miner, who had made a fortune selling coal and coke. Cochran mined by the bushel and shipped coal by river to Pittsburgh and Cincinnati.

Cochran made the first shipment of Connellsville coke to Cincinnati in 1843. Little Jim perfected the design and use of the beehive coke oven. He had built a fleet of wooden barges for transportation. He had experimented with coke, developing a market with small Pennsylvania furnaces and building the first commercial bank of ovens in the 1850s. The locals called Cochran the "King of Coke," a title that Frick would someday take. Frick was always eager to listen to coal miners like Cochran, and it was from this informal education that Frick learned about coal and coke. Morgan Mines was supplying A.O. Tinstman with the amazing sum of $110,000 per year, and that was the type of income that could fulfill Frick's dreams. Tinstman wanted to expand, but he was personally overextended in numerous business endeavors.

Still, the Morgan Coke Works could not produce enough to supply the new large blast furnaces of Pittsburgh. Frick proved a true visionary following the success of the two great Eliza Furnaces of Jones and Laughlin in Pittsburgh, which had major coal mines in the Connellsville district, but had to make coke in Pittsburgh. There were rumors that Jones and Laughlin were looking to expand into Connellsville coke and coal. Both Frick and Tinstman were aware that the Baltimore & Ohio Railroad and the Pennsylvania Railroad planned connecting branches in the next year. In 1870, the Mahoning Valley had twenty-one blast furnaces, more than any other district. Most of these furnaces were merchant pig iron stand-alone furnaces that supplied a number of pig iron users. These furnaces had used a hard local coal for fuel but were experimenting with coke. The Clinton Furnace in Pittsburgh had been using Connellsville coke since 1859. In addition, two separate groups of Pittsburgh Pig Iron Aristocrats were looking to bring on new blast furnaces. Also, a young outsider, Andrew Carnegie, was looking at building a huge furnace complex to feed his many rolling mills. Carnegie's Union Iron Mills and Keystone Bridge had become the nation's biggest consumers of pig iron, and Carnegie had no pig iron furnaces to supply them. Frick had seen the endless buzz in the

An engraving of a Pennsylvania beehive coke oven in 1875 (courtesy Carnegie Library of Pittsburgh).

Pittsburgh papers about the pig iron boom and furnace and mill projects. It was also becoming common knowledge that Connellsville coal made the world's best coke, and furnaces in Ohio, Pennsylvania, Maryland, New York, New Jersey, and even Connecticut were experimenting with Connellsville coke. Frick saw a future where coke would soon be gold. The market was extremely short on coke to supply this pig iron boom, and Frick wanted badly to get in on the coal project.

Tinstman needed money to buy and expand the Morgan Coke Works so it could become more profitable and supply the iron and steel market. This would include the cost of additional coal lands and the building of fifty large coke ovens. Tinstman had already invested in and been elected president of the Mount Pleasant and Broad Ford Railroad, which serviced the Morgan mines, but Tinstman was already highly leveraged and needed capital. He needed partners. The partnership would include Joseph Rist, who was a friend of Tinstman and from a coal land family. Henry Clay Frick brought in his distant cousin John S. Overholt, who was courting his sister Maria at the time. Joseph Rist was to be a two-fifths partner, while Frick, Tinstman, and Overholt would have a fifth each. Their first purchase was twenty acres of coal land near Broad Ford. They purchased the land from John Rist in December 1870 for a price of $52,995. Frick required a loan backed by his father and mother (and maybe his grandmother) for his share of $10,599. The other partners were fully engaged in other operations and investments, so as part of the agreement, Frick would manage the mine while remaining the chief bookkeeper for the distillery with its $1,000-a-year salary. He would take no salary for managing the coal mines.

Joseph Rist and Tinstman were, in effect, silent partners, while management fell to Overholt and Frick. John S. Overholt had a fear of underground mining and wanted only limited involvement in the management of the mines. Things got worse as the mine experienced a near deadly cave-in. John S. Overholt agreed to limit his involvement to a year. Frick, on the other hand, let his ambition rule in going into the mines. Frick wanted to learn to make coke, developing his expertise as his grandfather had done with whiskey distilling. He took readily to managing men and seemed to enjoy the power despite the lack of salary. The arrangement allowed for the new firm to operate under the name of H.C. Frick and Company. Coal was being sold to other companies to coke, but Frick believed coke was the most profitable product. Shipping soft coal to Pittsburgh to coke was wasteful and inefficient because it powdered during handling and transportation. Coke ovens did not pay for "fines," or dust, but only usable coal. This gave the advantage to Connellsville over building coke ovens in Pittsburgh. At the time, the Connellsville and Pittsburgh area had about 250 coke ovens, and the market was expanding beyond the industry's capacity to supply the blast furnaces, foundry cupolas, rolling mill furnaces, and puddling furnaces. The improved river navigation and rail connections gave Broad Ford a direct route to the great new blast furnaces of Pittsburgh, which would supply the future steel industry. Both river and rail improvements were under way to further support Connellsville coke making. Frick started to buy up coal lands from farmers using a skillful system of personal loans backed by his father and the Overholt name. He realized that in this old German Mennonite community the Frick and Overholt names went back to the days of the Whiskey Rebellion of the 1790s. Frick realized the economic value of what today we call "goodwill." Frick also had proven financial skills. No matter what the organization, whether the distillery, Masonic Lodge, or church, Frick became its treasurer and bookkeeper. He clearly made his brief education in accounting pay, and his financial skills the cornerstones of his success.

Next came the plan to build a battery of fifty beehive coke ovens in March of 1871. Frick was the most aggressive of the partners, wanting to bring up capacity quickly to establish the company as a supplier to the new Pittsburgh blast furnaces. Frick needed an additional $10,000 to finance the beehive coke ovens, and he approached Judge Thomas Mellon of the banking firm of T. Mellon & Sons of Pittsburgh. Thomas Mellon had originally come from Westmoreland County and knew both Frick's grandfather Overholt and Frick's mother Elizabeth Overholt Frick. That tie at least got him in the door, but Frick and his company lacked the experience for such a loan. Mellon, however, was a well-informed businessman and was in the middle of the pig iron boom in Pittsburgh. Furthermore, Mellon had made his first real money in the coal business and that success continued through the Civil War. What Frick lacked in experience, he made up for in hope and enough business sense to persuade Mellon for the loan. Mellon recognized Frick as "determined, persuasive, and audacious entrepreneur after his own heart."[1] Mellon also had several investments in coal mines, which had been highly profitable since the 1850s. In a letter to his son in the 1850s, Thomas Mellon called the coal industry "one of the best" and "highly respectable." Mellon went on to call coal "the most important article in productive manufacture."[2] The nation in 1871 was experiencing a major business expansion that seemed to have no end, and the future for iron, steel, and coke seemed extremely bright. For these reasons, Henry Clay Frick got his first bank loan.

What raised the old judge's eyebrows was when the twenty-one-year-old Frick returned in a couple of months asking for another $10,000 to build another fifty beehive ovens! Mellon now called in his friend and partner James Corey of Braddock to take a closer look at Frick's operations. Mellon had partnered with Corey and Thomas Dickson in the 1850s, and had a number of mines in Braddock, North Braddock, Braddock Hills, and Swissvale. While they were some of the highest producing mines of the time, most of the coal was used directly in heating and fuel for stream power. Corey was himself starting to explore the idea of coke production, but the Braddock area mines were small slant tunnels, which did not lend themselves to high-volume operations. Furthermore, the Braddock coal was not of the coking quality of the Connellsville area, so it was with great interest that Corey went to look at Frick's operations. Corey would give Mellon a glowing report: "Lands good, ovens well built, manager on the job all day, keeps books evenings, maybe a little too enthusiastic about pictures, but not enough to hurt; knows business down to the ground; advise making loan."[3] Frick got the loan with a 10 percent interest rate.

By 1871, Frick was an important Connellsville businessman, approaching the status of his grandfather. Frick, however, was far more obsessed with work and reaching his goal of making a million. He showed an amazing ability to work long hours in difficult environments. He did take time to socialize and he enjoyed getting dressed up for a social event. He never fully embraced a particular religious creed, but he did readily adopt the vision of God as a universal creator as defined by the Freemasons. He became the treasurer of the King Solomon Lodge No. 346 in Connellsville. A year later he joined the Urania Chapter No. 192 at Greensburg. By 1880 he would achieve the highest orders of the York Rite — the Orders of the Knights of the Rose Croix, the Knights of the Malta, and Knights Templar. He was very comfortable with this universal approach to religion that had first drawn him to the *Jefferson Bible*. The Freemasons of the Pittsburgh area had deep roots in the founding Scotch-Irish industrial community of the area. After the Presbyterian Church, no organization had the influence of the Freemasons, including men like Thomas Mellon.

Frick's second loan would be the start of a lifetime relationship with the Mellon family and bank. Just as interesting in Corey's report to Mellon were his notes on Frick's living quarters, which Corey called a "shack." Actually, the shack was a small two-room cabin. The shack was further described as having a portion for "prints and sketches" in his "half-office and half-living room in a clapboard shack." It is amazing that a struggling businessman living in a shack was then collecting and drawing pictures. Clearly, it would augur his future of art collecting with the sons of Thomas Mellon. With the loan, he built a hundred new beehive coke ovens at Broad Ford along the Youghiogheny River, which could soon be connected by the new branch of the Baltimore & Ohio Railroad. These new ovens would become known as the "Henry Clay Works." The other, older beehive ovens were on the Mt. Pleasant and Broad Ford Railroad and then were known as "Novelty Works" (later known as "Frick Works"). In 1871 Frick had 200 out of 550 coke ovens in the Connellsville area and about 1200 nation-wide. By 1872, Frick was the major investor in the partnership, and the company was the largest coke works in the Connellsville area and the largest separate coke works in America. But this would be shorted-lived, as over twenty competitors were entering the business and expanding quickly. Still, Frick had not tapped into the blast furnace market successfully.

The old Pittsburgh aristocrats looked first to their old coal fields near Pittsburgh. These fields were at locations on the Monongahela River such as Braddock, Pennsylvania, and others northeast of Pittsburgh near the Pennsylvania Railroad, such as Irwin, Pennsylvania. These were fields of bituminous coal, not of the metallurgical high quality of the Connellsville seam. Even William Coleman, a partner of Carnegie, had gotten Carnegie money for fifty coke ovens to be built at Latrobe, Pennsylvania, in 1871. This "Monastery Works" was to supply Carnegie's first blast furnace project in Pittsburgh. This company had been supplying Carnegie and had also advanced money for fifty coke ovens at Turtle Creek, Pennsylvania, on the Pennsylvania Railroad just up the Monongahela River from Pittsburgh. This location became known as Larimer Station and was managed by Carnegie's cousin, Dodd Lauder.[4] This Turtle Creek operation at Larimer Station did not have the high quality of Connellsville coke and was barely profitable. Carnegie also contracted with Westmoreland Coal Company of Irwin to supply his furnaces in 1871. Westmoreland Company had been supplying the coal gas market. Carnegie was determined to control his own sources of coal and coke, which was part of his overall strategy of vertical integration. Carnegie's trip to Europe in the 1870s to study the steel industry convinced him: "One vital lesson in iron and steel that I learned in Britain was the necessity for owning raw materials and finishing the completed article ready of its purpose."[5] Still, demand for coke was growing faster than even the optimistic forecasts of Frick had suggested, and Carnegie was in no position to control his supply of coke.

As Frick had envisioned the business was booming, supplying coke to rolling mills, foundries, and forge shops in Pittsburgh, Chicago, Wheeling, St. Louis, and Cincinnati. The real boom for coke, however, was just beginning in Pittsburgh. Two rival groups of Pittsburgh Pig Iron Aristocrats started large pig iron blast furnaces to supply their rolling mills. Prior to this, the majority of pig iron coming into Pittsburgh was from the charcoal iron furnaces of Hocking Hills, Ohio, and the hard-coal-fired furnaces of Ohio's Mahoning Valley. Mahoning Valley had a type of hard coal known as splint coal that could be used directly in blast furnaces. In 1872, Pittsburgh would start two new coke-fueled blast furnaces to meet these requirements for pig iron. These furnaces would require 2.3 tons of coke for every ton of pig iron produced. Both of these projected furnace projects were designed to produce 50 tons of pig iron every day from each of the furnaces. The first project was the twin Isabella Furnaces, which was backed by a consortium of Pittsburgh pig iron users, including Lewis Dalzell & Co.; J. Painter & Sons; Graff Bennett & Co.; Sprang, Chalfant & Co.; and Oliver Brothers & Phillips. At the same time Andrew Carnegie organized a furnace company with Henry Phipps, Tom Carnegie, and Andrew Kloman (Kloman, Carnegie & Co.) to build Lucy Furnace. Both of these furnace projects were going to use Lake Superior Ore and Connellsville coke to maximize productivity.

Both these furnace projects came on stream in early 1872. These furnaces started producing about 250 tons a week each; then in the summer, one of America's greatest industrial competitive battles started between the two companies. The newspapers followed the daily and weekly tonnage production as sports scores are followed today. The furnace managers made personal bets, and the local saloons became betting parlors for the workers and public. These furnaces battled back and forth, breaking new world records weekly. By the end of 1872, the furnaces were averaging 500 tons a week. In August of 1872, Isabella No. 1 overtook Lucy at a rate of 612 tons per week. In October 1873, Lucy took the record back at 653 tons per week. The battle created experiments which proved that Connellsville coke was the best for furnace productivity. Carnegie's partner Henry Phipps was an amateur chemist and met-allurgist whose furnace experiments demonstrated the superiority of Connellsville coke. The battle went back and forth for years until, at the end of 1873, they were averaging 775 tons per week. At this rate, Lucy Furnace was using 100,000 tons of coke annually. A single bee-hive furnace could make about 450 tons of coke a year, so Lucy would require a battery of 222 coke ovens to keep it running. Carnegie's partners wanted an assured and unified sup-ply of Connellsville coke.

Such increases in furnace production put a strain on Connellsville coke production and drove the price of coke up. Being a bean-counter by trade and disposition, Frick poured his profits into paying off debt and expanding carefully. Bankers and new investors rushed to Connellsville to bring more coke competition on line. Still, the coke market consisted of over 40 individual operations with many shared investors. The number of Connellsville coke works went from five in 1871 to over thirty by 1873. There were a little over a thousand coke ovens in the Connellsville area in 1873. The region lacked the capacity to supply the ten Pittsburgh blast furnaces, let alone the other furnaces in western Pennsylvania and the huge mill require-ments and other furnaces in other states. While Frick only had a small part of the Pittsburgh blast furnace business, he was the low-cost producer of Connellsville, and profits soared as the price of coke increased. Frick was in the best position to ride the new steel boom. Frick had built his advantage by the use of cheap immigrant miners, replacing the old Welsh and English model of miners as craftsmen. In addition, his two coke works and mines were directly on railroads. Finally, unlike the other coke producers, Frick was a hands-on manager with debt and credit training. Frick realized early on that the long-term winner would be the most cost-efficient operation.

The idea that Frick paid the lowest wages and used coal police in the 1800s has been reported over the years as fact without evidence. The accusation again surfaced in 1964. Daughter Helen Clay quickly sued to prevent publication. While throwing the case out, the judge did note, based on his research, that "wages paid at the Frick Works were higher than those paid elsewhere."[6] Certainly, Frick in the 1870s was not in a position to pay lower than the competition because he needed skilled miners, which were in short supply. Frick was one of the first to bring in eastern European laborers, which he paid higher than European min-ers and laborers but less than American. There is no evidence of any abuse in these early years. Frick was competing for labor and capital, and he was one of over forty operators in the Connellsville district alone. The violent mining strikes were isolated in eastern Pennsyl-vania and in the western mines in the Monongahela Valley closer to Pittsburgh.

Frick tried to replace the basic laborers with immigrant workers, but initially the min-ers remained "operators" paid for product. Still, Frick was able to bring in some low-cost labor. Frick had learned from watching Carnegie's use of immigrant labor in the puddling opera-tions at Union Iron Mills. Both Carnegie and Frick had limited education except for a few business courses at Pittsburgh accounting schools. The focus of these courses was a type of cost accounting, which would dominate the successful companies of both men. Frick proved a tough boss in dealing with the Welsh and English "operator"-type miners. Miners were paid by the bushel and heaped a bushel with coal. For coke production, round or chunk coal was needed. Miners put small pieces, fines, and "slack" in the bushel, which would yield no salable coke. Owners and managers like Frick installed screens to pay the miners for only solid product. The bushel system had assumed a weight per bushel of 96 pounds, but Frick installed weight scales to pay on an actual weight system. One crafts miner described the operation before 1880: "We were paid so much a ton, about seventy-cents, we be in the chamber filling carts with coal. We didn't work in gangs together, we worked each one alone. I had a pick and I had a shovel and I had an auger to drill a hole — the auger could drill six feet in the face. There were eight hundred and some workers and each of them had their own room."

Frick resisted the very early union movements in the coal fields. The bituminous mines of western Pennsylvania were newcomers compared to the anthracite mines of eastern Pennsylvania where unions were having some success. Unlike mining, coke making was a new process and not controlled by craftsmen. The heat and fumes made it the type of work that few of the local stock of farmers were interested in. This allowed Frick to use cheap immigrant labor, and he became a leader in hiring immigrant coke operators. Frick, like Carnegie a few years before, actually sent agents to western Europe to recruit cheap labor. Frick was able to recruit some freed ex-slaves in search of labor as well. Frick avoided the crafts system in the coke works by developing a supervisory system which allowed unskilled labor. Frick resisted any union or organized efforts to control the operation in the earliest days of the company. His toughness in these early days would position him to survive the hard economic times looming on the horizon in 1873.

The first part of 1873 had been extremely robust with railroads expanding rapidly and new steel mills coming on line. Andrew Carnegie was proceeding with his plans for a monster steel mill at Braddock, Pennsylvania, to produce railroad rails. Carnegie, McCandless, and Company had been formed to build this Braddock mill at what would be the world's biggest industrial plant. Ground was broken on April 13, 1873, at Braddock. Railroads were expanding tracks almost without reason all over the United States. Railroad stocks were soaring on the New York Stock Exchange. The first signs of trouble occurred thousands of miles away, as a financial panic hit London, Berlin, and Vienna in May of 1873. The undercapitalized and heavily indebted American railroads were dependent on selling bonds in Europe. Even Carnegie had gone to Europe to sell bonds for his iron and steel companies. The financial crisis of Europe started to create problems in the American stock market by August 1873. The final stock market crash came on Black Friday, September 18, 1873, with the railroad stocks leading the crash. Mellon Bank was the first in Pittsburgh to feel the pain, finding on September 19 that they had lost $60,000 in deposits in New York and Philadelphia. Mellon, however, remained strong financially. In Pittsburgh, however, the banks showed no panic and business remained normal. The thick black smoke of prosperity blanketed the city, restricting sunlight to the hours between noon and three o'clock. The stock crash did not immediately affect the industrial manufacturing plants until December.

Interestingly, the effect of the stock crash was almost immediate in Connellsville. One of Frick's notes and several of Abraham Tinstman's were being called in. Many of the Overholt family were overextended, and it would be John W. Frick's signature that saved his son, not the Overholts. His thrifty father, who was so often looked upon as a failure in the shadow of Overholt, again helped his son when the Overholt relationship failed. By the end of the year, Tintsman had to sell his share to Henry Clay Frick, who then had a two-fifths share of Frick and Company. Tinstman continued to sell assets in an effort to save his mortgage. From that small coup, Frick proved himself a true financier and capitalist, while Tinstman's problems continued into 1874. Tinstman's railroad, the Mt. Pleasant and Broad Ford Railroad, had a ten-mile stretch that serviced the coke works of Frick. Frick worked with Tinstman to broker a deal for the railroad with the Baltimore & Ohio Railroad, which would gain direct access to the Connellsville coal region. It would give the B&O Railroad a big advantage over its competitor, the Pennsylvania Railroad. The deal did not require a large capital outlay by Baltimore & Ohio. They purchased the ten-mile railroad at cost. Frick, for his part, received a $50,000 commission (over $750,000 today), more money than Frick had ever had and over double what he had invested in the coke partnership.

Frick proved even more savvy, paying off his debts and landing coal lands at depressed prices. Frick was making a fortune in the panic that was toppling the rich of Wall Street. The price of coke dropped to 90 cents a ton, a level that only Frick could actually make a profit on. While Frick expanded, he kept a cash reserve to protect against any problems. Frick turned salesman in an effort to maintain volume at the coke works. He worked long hours at the works and went almost daily by train to Pittsburgh to increase sales. Frick had several inherent advantages, such as his ability to sell at 90 cents a ton and still make a profit. Connellsville coke was a better fuel than the anthracite coal of eastern Pennsylvania. He was able to convert mills and factories over to the better fuel in the down market. As Frick supplied volume at 90 cents a ton, his competition began to fail, further increasing sales. Furthermore, he was able to write his own "loans" by paying his workers in scrip. Frick opened his first company store (Union Supply), where scrip could be used. Frick also sold the goods at a profit and required his workers to buy at the company store. The scrip, however, started to circulate in western Pennsylvania like U.S. currency. Scrip from Frick and Company and the Pennsylvania Railroad was considered a stronger currency the U.S. dollars to many. Other than Judge Mellon and Andrew Carnegie in Pittsburgh, no capitalist in the country proved as successful in the Panic of 1873 as Henry Clay Frick.

Like Carnegie and Mellon, Clay (as he was then known) continued to expand in the depths of the recession. On the other hand, his main competitor, Morgan Mines, remained focused on making profits each day. Frick got a mortgage loan against company assets in 1874 from Mellon. Thomas Mellon was impressed and amazed at the dealings of Frick. Frick used $15,000 to purchase railroad cars to move coal and coke. Frick was able to get a revolving line of credit for another $25,000. Frick's expansion was balanced as he paid off personal notes that were likely to be called. He started to look to the future, buying coal lands, which were being sold at depressed prices. He studied coal seam direction and purchased troubled farms needing cash. Frick developed deeper mine technology, since the vast majority of the coal lay 60 feet or more below the surface. In 1874, he made his first unsuccessful effort to buy out his competitor, Morgan Mines. Clay had enough to money to offer $550,000 in the failed effort to obtain Morgan Mines. The recession, however, contained to deepen through 1874 to the point that it threatened completion of Carnegie's super mill at Braddock.

Unemployment nationally was running over 25 percent. Thomas Mellon called the Panic of 1873 the "most disastrous and extensive collapse since that of 1819." In New York City, over fifty soup kitchens were serving over twenty thousand. Carnegie remarked that he had to step over tramps to get to his New York office. The *New York Times* suggested that he get a dog with good teeth as protection against the tramps. By the end of it, over half of Pittsburgh's banks would fail, but Mellon remained a bastion of strength. Thomas Mellon did have to stop payments at times, but unlike other banks, Mellon never closed the doors. Oil had dropped from $3 a barrel to 50 cents a barrel. Agricultural products had dropped a similar percentage. The railroads that didn't fail were unprofitable. Many homeowners lost their homes. Judge Mellon noted, "Real estate was unsaleable at any price." Wages were falling, too, and immigration had been stopped. Cambria Iron Works had labor problems as well. By 1875, the recession was global, and it was at the time being called the "great depression." President Grant received many calls for help, but the federal government chose to remain on the sidelines.

The real blow to Frick came in late 1874, but not from the recession. In December of

1874, Frick's eighty-three-year-old grandmother died. Maria Overholt had 48 grandchildren and 28 great-grandchildren. Frick took the loss of his grandmother hard, and his own physical strength seemed to decline with the news. Biographer George Harvey noted that in Frick's typical work day he "got up at six, looked over the ovens and set things going, took the train to Pittsburgh at seven, reached his office at ten, legged it from factory to factory soliciting orders till three, reached home about six, and attended to details of mining till bedtime." This was a grueling schedule in the winter months, and by January 1875, it had taken its toll. On a business train trip, he suffered an attack of inflammatory rheumatism and was forced to return to his room at the coke works. He approached death as three doctors attended to him. Abraham Tinstman had him moved to the Overholt homestead, away from the smoke and dust of Broad Ford. He would be house-bound until March, unable to even bathe himself, but he did slowly recover. On March 9, Clay made it to the Broad Ford office to look over the books. Tinstman and Frick remained close through these tough times for both of them.

Tinstman's financial fortunes continued to decline. With all the problems, Tinstman and Frick remained close as cousins. They often played chess together in the evening. Tinstman was clearly receptive to selling Morgan Mines to Frick, but Tinstman was one of several partners. Frick tried in late March of 1875 to merge Morgan Mines and Frick Company, but again he was unable to close the deal. By late 1875, both Morgan and Tinstman needed capital to keep Morgan Mines going. Frick bought out the Tinstman and Rist shares in Frick & Company, so they could put capital into Morgan Mines. Tinstman was forced into personal bankruptcy and Morgan Mines failed in October of 1875. Morgan Mines closed tem-

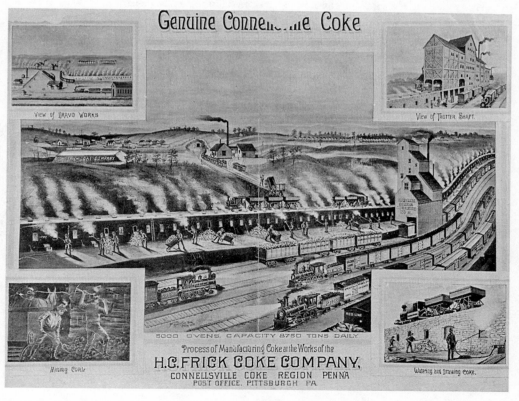

An 1893 advertisement of Connellsville coke for the World's Fair (courtesy Carnegie Library of Pittsburgh).

porarily as Frick assumed the deed for $60,000 and took on an additional $10,000. This was far less than the estimated value of $650,000 only a year earlier. Frick actually added a rider that allowed Tinstman to back it within two years. In the meantime, Frick slowly brought Morgan Mines back into operation, running only the best ovens and equipment. Frick proved brilliant at restoring Morgan Mines to profitability, combining operational skill with cost accounting. Frick also laid railroad track, built a steel bridge across the Youghiogheny River, and charged the railroad for access. In December of 1876, Frick was the volume and low-cost producer of Connellsville coke. Personally, he had little debt and a cash reserve while the other coke princes of the area were bankrupt. Still, the rise of the blast furnace throughout the country had kept demand high, and there were some thirty small coke operations in the area in 1876.

The Panic of 1873 would create a great troika of Pittsburgh titans: Andrew Carnegie, Thomas Mellon, and Henry Clay Frick. These men had been tried and tested in this earlier "great depression." Some how they managed to expand their businesses as others failed. Their companies represented strength in the downturn, and Mellon's banks stayed open, Carnegie continued building his mega steel mill, and Frick expanded his coking capacity. All three had kept their eyes on the future and the days grew darker. All three envisioned the rise of steel as the industrial backbone of the nation. All three would find their fortunes tied to the city of Pittsburgh, and they would soon find their source of strength was each other. Frick, however, would be the cornerstone of the fortunes of them all. Frick would live up to Thomas Mellon's assessment of 1876:

> That young man has great promise. He is very careful in making statements, always exact and wholly reliable. He is also able, energetic, industrious, resourceful, self-confident, somewhat impetuous and inclined to be daring on his own account, but so cautious in his dealings with others, disposed to take chances that I doubt if he would make a successful banker. If he continues along his own line as he has begun, he will go far unless he over-reaches. That is his only danger.[7]

It is very telling that such a young upstart could so impress the old industrial aristocrat Thomas Mellon.

5. Bessemer Converters, Strikes, and Carnegie

The Panic of 1873 in many ways built Frick and Company. The recession was deep, but many of the steel companies kept their eyes on the future. The Bessemer converter was making the volume and reasonably priced steel a reality. Steel was a marvelous material that was stronger than wrought iron and more flexible than cast iron. Tests in the early 1870s had proven that steel railroad rails wore better than those of wrought iron. Steel was replacing wrought iron in stream boilers, allowing high-pressure operation. Steel was being looked at for structural applications in bridges. The world's greatest armament company, Krupp Steel, was producing large steel cannon to replace cast iron. Steel's strength changed the industrial world. By 1875, Bessemer steel plants had been built in Chicago, Pittsburgh, and Harrisburg. The demand for steel meant demand for liquid pig iron to feed these Bessemer converters, and that meant bigger blast furnaces using coke. The use of coke, and in particular Connellsville coke, soared. Frick had been highly successful, but it was only Carnegie with his steel mills that could crown him the King of Coke.

Carnegie had been slow to see the future of steel, but once he discovered it, Carnegie made steel's future his. Actually, it was his brother Tom Carnegie that first saw the future in steel, and convinced Andrew to study it further. On a European trip in 1872, Carnegie stopped in Sheffield to see the inventor Henry Bessemer and his marvelous steel works. Peter Krass, Carnegie's biographer, described the moment:

> As Carnegie stood before the dazzling Bessemer converter, the white ingots glowed in his eyes and heat of the blow inflated his five-foot-three-inch frame until he was as big as President Ulysses S. Grant. He felt a surge of power, of enthusiasm, of confidence that steel would indeed replace iron, and he became determined to build a majestic mill.

That mill was his Edgar Thomson Works at Braddock, Pennsylvania. Named after Edgar Thomson of the Pennsylvania Railroad, the mill was to make steel rails. Carnegie and his partners endured the Panic of 1873 to see the mill roll its first rail on September 1, 1875. Edgar Thomson Works in turn created a huge demand for Connellsville coke.

Actually the man who probably most affected Carnegie and Frick was Henry Bessemer. The Bessemer converter allowed for mass production of steel. The first Bessemer plants at Pennsylvania Steel in Harrisburg, Cambria Iron in Johnstown, and Joliet Steel in Chicago used pig iron inefficiently. Carnegie's new Edgar Thomson Works was typical of the problem. Carnegie made pig iron at his Lucy furnace, casting it into 50-pound pigs, then loaded those pigs in rail cars to move to Edgar Thomson ten miles up the Monongahela River. Once at Edgar Thomson, the pig iron had to be melted to a liquid in an "air" furnace (using more coke as fuel) and then poured in a ladle that in turn poured the liquid pig cast into a Bessemer converter. The converter then blew air through the liquid iron, burning out the carbon with a shower of sparks and light. Carnegie started the project to build blast furnaces at Edgar Thomson with the idea of taking liquid pig directly to his Bessemer converters. Carnegie also continued his search for his own supply of coke to support his future furnaces. Bessemer steel represented a major breakthrough. The old puddling furnace could produce a ton of steel in eight hours at a cost of $300 per ton, while a Bessemer converter could produce 25 tons of steel in eight hours at a cost of sixty dollars a ton. Finally, steel could be used in major building projects, and the Age of Steel had begun. Steel production went from 2,300 tons in 1867 to 260,000 tons in 1875.

Western Pennsylvanian steel masters took to the Bessemer process because it was truly invented there, not in England. While most of Carnegie's future managers were learning their trade at Cambria Iron Works in Johnstown, William Kelly was developing a pneumatic steel-making process there. Kelly perfected the process in the 1860s and even convinced Cambria steel managers that steel would someday replace wrought iron in railroad applications. Carnegie, however, had licensed his rights from Henry Bessemer for his huge Edgar Thomson Works. Carnegie continued to make tons of steel as the patent battle heated up between Bessemer and Kelly. The Irish at Edgar Thomson Works, who controlled the melt shop, refused to call it a Bessemer converter, calling it a Kelly converter. Most of the managers at Edgar Thomson had formerly worked at Cambria Iron and were also aware of Kelly's invention. Many years later Kelly would win the patent battle, and near the end of both of their lives, Carnegie visited Kelly to thank him.

Eventually Frick's fortunes would be tied to Carnegie, but in 1876, Carnegie and Frick had competitors, depressed prices, and labor issues to contend with. In 1876, while significant in their industries, neither Carnegie nor Frick were dominant. They both, however, were low-cost producers in their industries, which had allowed them to prosper in lean times. While smaller, Frick was in the better position to grow. Carnegie was fighting to expand his Bessemer rail business; Connellsville coke was in demand across the nation. And while the price of pig iron declined in the latter half of the 1870s, the price of coke increased because of a shortage. Frick was getting coke orders from Joliet Steel in Chicago, Wheeling Iron in West

Bessemer convertor, 1879.

Virginia, Union Iron in Chicago, and many mills in the Youngstown and western Pennsylvania area. Frick needed more coke capacity as well as more coal, but before he expanded he was caught in a national wave of labor trouble.

Several biographers of Frick and Carnegie claim that in the late 1870s Frick had already gained the reputation of the "cruelest employer in the industry." Some of these charges are extremely hard to sort out. Frick in later years had bad publicity coming from his involvement in the Homestead Strike in 1892 and from Carnegie associates. Frick did little to create his own counterpublicity. What is clear in the 1870s is that Frick used immigrant labors, opposed unions, and ran his company store at a profit. All of these were common practices of the time, and were not unique to Frick. Still, Frick seemed only marginally interested in his workers; but in the 1870s, he basically lived in quarters not much better than theirs. In the 1870s, none of Frick's operations had major labor strikes such as were occurring in Ohio and Eastern Pennsylvania. With the depression, labor unrest in the western Pennsylvania coal fields had been relatively calm. Most of the strikes and union activity were in the anthracite coalfields of eastern Pennsylvania, where the immigrant Irish had formed the secret militant organization of the Molly Maguires. The Knights of Labor had also found success in eastern Pennsylvania, but in western Pennsylvania the Miners' National Association failed. Higher wages and a lower number of immigrants also contributed to the relative calm of the western fields. From the beginning Frick had opposed unions. Industrialists, including the most benevolent such as George Westinghouse and H.J. Heinz, generally opposed unions. Frick, however, was a leader in using immigrant labor; most of these were Slavs and Hungarians. While they offered cheap non-union labor, they did require housing. Frick found a very profitable business in supplying housing and food to his workers.

It was Carnegie, not Frick, who was making labor news in the 1870s. Carnegie had lost his late 1860s battle as the market demand forced him to end his lockout of the Sons of Vulcan at Union Mills. Still, Victorian managers and Pittsburgh's Pig Iron Aristocracy were determined to break the union. It was a matter of control, not property or human rights. Recession caused by the Panic of 1873 gave Carnegie another chance to break the union. This time he would have the state of the economy on his side. Carnegie and a number of owners moved for lower wages for the Sons of Vulcan and the Amalgamated Association of Iron and Steel Workers. The Amalgamated Association had formed to unite the puddlers (Sons of Vulcan) with the rollers, heaters, and nailers. In November of 1874, Carnegie and other owners locked the workers out. The owners extended the lockout as far as Cambria Iron Works in Johnstown, Pennsylvania. Ultimately, the lockout would put forty thousand men out of work, most of whom were not union members. The lockout highlighted the main weakness of the unions, which was their lack of amalgamation and solidarity. Puddlers, heaters, rollers and skilled laborers were pitted against each other in intercraft rivalry. The unskilled laborers had nothing to gain and generally were the most hurt. They were out of work and even if the wage increase was won, their wages remained the same.

The 1874–1875 lockout revealed a lot about Carnegie. Historian Paul Krause defined the importance of the lockout: "Overlooked by historians, the lockout of 1874–1875 was one of the most intense disputes of its day. It is the critical opening chapter to the history of Pittsburgh in the Gilded Age which closes with the Homestead lockout of 1892."[1] With reduced demand and prices, the owners' association could hope to break the union this time. The battle once again was over Carnegie's quest for a sliding wage scale based on product price. Carnegie had an additional advantage over the iron puddlers and rollers at Union Mills. Steel was replacing iron and the Bessemer process had spelled the death knell for puddlers. By mid–1875 Carnegie had lost the battle but not the war. Rising orders forced Carnegie to bring the men back under the old wages, breaking with the owners' association. Carnegie's use of hard times and technology would be his major weapon against unions. Carnegie's strategy would be to use the lockout in economic downturns; if the strike continued into an up economy, Carnegie would bail out to fill orders. Carnegie created the illusion of being more open to settle with unions, while he left others to fight it out. Carnegie always controlled the battleground and selected the time. Labor was coming under pressure to lower wages across the nation as the great recession continued. The lockout of 1874–1875 heralded something new as well. Pittsburgh Bolt Company and Black Diamond Steel brought 300 non-union black puddlers in from Richmond, Virginia. Black workers offered cheaper labor, and the union refused to accept them, further complicating the issue. These black workers became known as "black sheep." The end of slavery and the fall of the cotton industry had developed a large pool of cheap black labor. Ohio mine owners had used blacks to break the union in the Hocking Valley Strike of 1873–1874.

Interestingly, Carnegie's Edgar Thomson Works was union-free because of enlightened managers such as Bill Jones. Bill Jones was a dynamic plant manager who molded a managerial team that would become known as the "Boys of Braddock." Jones had been recruited from Cambria Iron Company as Edgar Thomson was being built. Jones had come up through the ranks and loved plant management versus the boardroom. Carnegie gave him a free hand, as Jones set world production records almost daily. Jones hated unions, but he loved his workers. They could count on Jones to take their grievances to Carnegie. He would give many a future president of United States Steel, such as a young Charles Schwab, their start at Edgar Thomson Works. He talked Carnegie into trying the eight-hour day versus the normal twelve hours of the steel industry. Carnegie allowed this work schedule only at Edgar Thomson, and only while Jones was there. Jones nurtured and even promoted the new immigrants that took the low-level laborer jobs at the mill. He kept Carnegie out of the operation, and Carnegie allowed him wide latitude.

Unfortunately, the Pennsylvania coal fields lacked the enlightened management of men like Bill Jones. In early summer of 1877, the rein of terror by the Molly Maguires in the coal fields of eastern Pennsylvania was nearing its peak. On June 21, 1877, ten Mollies were finally brought to justice and hanged. The Pinkerton Detective Agency became famous for bringing the Mollies to justice. The Mollies had been implicated in over fifty murders of bosses and workers. The Irish were forced to the lowest and most dangerous jobs while the English and Welsh controlled the mines. The Irish had migrated to America to escape British oppression, only to find it again in the mines of eastern Pennsylvania. The Mollies looked to improve their poor working and living conditions, but they advocated violence to achieve their goals. The hangings and the railroad strike of that summer would end public support for the Mollies, and they disappeared after ten years. Frick and the operators in Westmoreland and Fayette counties worried about the Mollies coming to their western coal fields. To avoid Irish labor, Frick tended to prefer immigrants from western Europe to operate the mines.

The turning point for many industrialists in their view of labor and unions came in the summer of 1877. The most momentous event of 1877 would have a personal impact on Henry Clay Frick and most capitalists. A deadly national railroad strike had started in late July when the east coast was caught in a major heat wave. The nation was still struggling with the effects of the Panic of 1873, with unemployment high throughout the nation. The stagnation of the economy had squeezed profits on the nation's railroad companies, and over 500 railroad-related companies had gone bankrupt. The Pennsylvania Railroad and Baltimore & Ohio Railroad had laid off thousands and asked the remaining brakemen and firemen to take a 10 percent pay cut while doubling up on the work. The wage cut did not affect anyone making less than a dollar a day, which was most of the workforce. The wage cut came with the news that the railroad companies were increasing dividends. The strike would start outside Baltimore at Camden Yards on July 16. The railroad strike moved quickly along the line to West Virginia and points west. Frick's rail connections were soon affected by the spreading strike. On July 19, the Pennsylvania Railroad workers joined the strike, taking control of the Pittsburgh station and the switches. On the morning of July 20, no trains were moving in Maryland, Pennsylvania, West Virginia, Ohio, and Illinois. Frick could no longer move coke as strikers closed the rails. Baltimore was now engulfed in a full-blown riot, resulting in the burning of the downtown area. In Baltimore, during the peak of the riots, gangs, socialists, and the unemployed joined the strikers. Dozens were dying by the day in Baltimore, and violence was moving across country on the railroad lines.

Frick at Connellsville used the sheriff and deputies to remove local strikers. On July 21, Pittsburgh erupted in riots, and the state militia arrived. Tracks were torn up and cars burned. The unemployed and street gangs joined in the riot. Shooting broke out on both sides. By July 21, 1877, 20 had been killed, including the sheriff, with hundreds wounded lying on the sidewalks. Pittsburgh's Catholic Bishop Tuigg walked the streets giving last rites to the wounded, as another nine would die in the streets. Men, women, and children joined in the pillage. Railroad cars were raided and the goods carried off by the mob, which now was much more than strikers. The Union Station was torched and freight cars of products were looted as regular citizens joined in. In all, 1,383 freight cars, 104 locomotives, and 66 passenger cars were destroyed at Pittsburgh. Damage came to over $5 million. Press pictures of the destruction looked like Civil War battles.

Chicago also had significant riots with property damage and at least eight dead. In Chicago, German socialists and the Workingman Party took control of the unrest. In many cities the unemployed joined the strike and looting. A mob of over 20,000 terrorized Chicago. The riots reached the west coast by July 24. The country had never known such violence except in war and would never see such civil unrest again until the civil rights riots in the 1960s. Americans had only read about such work-related violence in Europe in the 1870s, but the European immigrants of the 1840s could well remember the unrest and riots caused by socialists. Labor historian Joseph Rayback described the effect best: "The Railway Strike of 1877 thoroughly shocked a large portion of the public. Not since slaveholders had ceased to be haunted by dreams of a slave uprising had the propertied elements been so terrified."[2] And the violence had touched every major American city, including those of the far west such as San Francisco. It was the perfect storm as the recession, the heat wave, the unemployed, youth gangs, strikers, and socialists came to together on July 21, 22, and 23.

The Railroad Strike of 1877 had a profound effect on Pittsburgh's capitalists. The bloody Paris revolution of 1871, in which the Marxists took over the government and then were forcibly overthrown, was still fresh in the minds of capitalists. In Europe and in the American press, Marxism, socialism, and unionism were linked. The commercial press throughout the country started to use the terms communism, socialists, anarchists, and Marxism in relating the railroad riots. An editorial in the *Pittsburgh Leader* noted that "the workingman in Pittsburgh is really a communist, and there is no doubt that communist ideas have spread widely." There had been a Marxist convention in Pittsburgh in April of 1876, which many believed to be at the root of the problem. Industrialists such as George Westinghouse, H.J. Heinz, and Thomas Mellon were convinced that it was the work of immigrant socialists from countries like Germany. Unions became linked with violence and the political roots of socialism. The union movement in New York and Chicago had demonstrated strong ties with German socialists.

Even liberal industrialists such as Heinz and Westinghouse became deeply anti-union. The press and general public of Pittsburgh became anti-union as well. Socialists started talk of the right of ownership of the workers. For the 1877 American mind, the dispute between

Great railroad strike destruction in Pittsburgh, 1877 (courtesy Carnegie Library of Pittsburgh).

socialism and capitalism was a matter of property rights. Property rights were paramount in the American psyche and education. For decades, the *McGuffey Readers* in grade school stressed property rights as a constitutional right. The national press, which initially had supported the strikers, became fearful of unions and their possible links to the socialism of Europe. In the coal fields the strike created more tension between foreign immigrants and English-speaking workers. Some men such as Frick became determined to stop the spread of union-ism because he saw it as an attack on American capitalism and property rights. The riots of the summer of 1877 affected the soul of America as the race riots did in 1967. It is clear that a young Frick was deeply affected, and it colored his view of unions forever. Interestingly, the forgotten Railroad Strike of 1877 in Pittsburgh dwarfed in deaths and violence the 1892 Home-stead Strike that Frick would be blamed and remembered for.

By late summer of 1877, business returned to normal in Pittsburgh and Connellsville. In 1878, Frick formed a new partnership with the Ferguson brothers, who had capital and coke ovens in nearby Fayette County. Edmund and Walton Ferguson had come from New York and Connecticut in 1871 to invest in coke operations in Fayette County. The brothers also had other business investments in the east, and Edmund was an officer of the Merchants and Manufacturing National Bank in Pittsburgh, where he resided in 1878. This new part-nership brought in another 200 coke ovens and capital for coal expansion. Shortly after the formation of the partnership, H.C. Frick & Co. took over the Henderson & Co. Works in

Fayette County for $200,000, a deal that added another 100 ovens. The partnership was ideal for Frick. The Fergusons were wealthy investors and not businessmen. They had little understanding of the coke industry other than that it was a good investment. The price of coke moved up to around $1.20 a ton as more steel mills opened. Furthermore, Tinstman proved unable to buy back Morgan Mines and Frick took ownership. The company became H.C. Frick & Co. on March 9, 1878. Frick had achieved a cost and quality advantage but still lacked capacity to be a single supplier to these large blast furnaces. This forced Frick into the world of finance and investment.

Frick now was becoming more involved in finance and marketing, which required him to stay often in Pittsburgh. At Broad Ford, he had moved into a good boarding house known as Washabaugh House; but in Pittsburgh he took a room at the Monongahela House, one of America's finest hotels. In 1840, the Monongahela House had been built as a first-class hotel on a par with the best in the nation. It had five stories with 180 rooms and a world-class winding black walnut staircase. The ballroom could hold 1,500 and was considered the best west of the Alleghenies. Its guests would include eight presidents: John Q. Adams, Andrew Jackson, Zachary Taylor, William H. Harrison, Abraham Lincoln, Ulysses Grant, William McKinley, and Theodore Roosevelt. The guest list also included presidential hopefuls: Henry Clay, James Blaine, William Sherman, and Philip Sheridan. Out-of-country guests such as King Edward VII stayed at the Monongahela House. The bar served only hard Scotch-Irish whiskey, allowing those who drank beer to find a nearby German beer garden. Fresh oysters and sea fish were always on the menu, and horseradish was a natural condiment. The Pig Iron Aristocrats of Pittsburgh tended to be well educated and loved the theater and the arts, bringing such artists to the Monongahela House as Mark Twain, Ralph Emerson, Horace Greeley, Henry Beecher, and Thomas Benton. Nikola Tesla would be one of the great scientists who lived for over a year at the Monongahela House. Tesla, known for his expensive tastes, found the Monongahela House to be the only cosmopolitan entity in the Steel City. Frick spent a good deal of time decorating his room, which housed a Tiffany candelabra and clock. He also purchased several paintings from New York's Knoedler & Company, starting a lifelong relationship. Frick readily adapted to this type of living.

While business was booming, labor problems continued to rise at the coke works. Frick remained opposed to unions and any government involvement in the mines. The State of Pennsylvania investigated Frick's company store in 1878 and 1879. The final report was a mixed bag of facts, but the image of the overall operation of the stores was damaging. The stores operated at a profit of 16 percent, or about 8 percent of Frick's overall profits of $378,000 in 1879. This type of company store was common in the coal fields. Frick and his superintendent Lynch were actually proud of their operating efficiency. He did sell produce at a lower price than local grocery stores but was higher on such staples as flour. There was nothing illegal or even unethical about the operation, but the labor unrest of the time made it problematic in the eye of the public. Western mines were starting to get some scrutiny as labor problems spread from the east to the west in the 1870s.

These labor problems were, however, not in the Connellsville district but in the Monongahela Valley near Pittsburgh. The Monongahela mines were to be found in the streams (runs) that cut the hillsides to flow into the Monongahela River such as those at Braddock, Munhall, and Mifflin. They tended to be much smaller than those of the Connellsville area. The owners such as John Munhall, Abraham Hays, and A.H. Kenny were major landowners with large mansions on the hilltops. In stark contrast, the miners lived in shanties on the runs. In the recession following the Panic of 1873, the owners moved the price of a bushel of coal from 4 cents to 2 cents without raising wages. Miners tried to strike but the owners played cheap immigrant workers against the laborers and helpers. While mining was considered a craft,

the elements of mining could readily be learned by the unskilled labor. In addition, the owners acted as a group that pressured the whole district. The lost strikes brought forth a new
leader, D.R. Jones of Mifflin Township, who would cross Frick's path years later in the Homestead Strike of 1892. For Jones's part in the 1870s mining strikes, Judge Thomas Mellon had
conspiracy charges brought against him.

The biggest problem with the American union was the structure itself. The unions of the
nineteenth century were much different from the industrial trade unions of today. Unions
were crafts unions, which had evolved in Europe from the old crafts guilds. They were crafts-
specific unions of skilled workers such as miners, puddlers, glass blowers, iron rollers, iron
heaters, shoemakers, cigar makers, bricklayers, and colliers. The crafts guilds had been broken up in Europe, and early American immigrant craftsmen blended union strength with the
guild structure. Crafts unions acted in their own interest even when part of a large company,
controlling the production level. There were entrance barriers into the crafts union, which
favored families, clans, and nationalities. Once in the union, there was an apprentice program for the worker to progress to the master level. The master was in charge of his own
group of apprentices and helpers. Most of the time the company paid the master, who in turn
paid the helpers and apprentices. They were resistant to any management supervision or
direction. The crafts union usually set production limits, such as the puddlers, who worked
fours "heats" a day. The unions were sensitive to new technology, which allowed less skilled
workers to perform the work. They generally refused to allow entrance to new immigrants.
Many nationalities, such as the Germans in America, were anti-union because they felt they
had destroyed the guilds of Germany and were socialist, yet they wanted a strong guild system. It was a model that didn't fit the industrialization of the nation. Management saw other
problems with crafts unions, such as their control of the operation, production limits, and
independent operation. Still, their own independence and exclusiveness were the result of
many failed strikes.

D.R. Jones believed in amalgamation and all-inclusive approach. Jones was a brilliant
labor leader who is often overlooked in the history of labor. He was a member of the Knights
of Labor and rejected the violence of the eastern miners. Jones was one of the first to realize
the political element in successful unionization. The Knights of Labor were radicals of the
period; they had enemies among the capitalists and crafts unions. They believed in industry
and full shop representation of laborers and skilled workers. In a strike, all workers were to
stand together so that all workers would benefit. Workers would also include different crafts
that combined forces as well. The Knights also stood for the eight-hour day against the twelve-
hour day standard at the time. The Knights stood for the unpopular idea of including even
the immigrant workers, which the crafts unions hated. D.R. Jones preached solidarity, cooperation, and amalgamation. He pushed for alliances betweens the Knights of Labor and the
Miners' Association. When the economy picked up in 1879, Jones built an alliance of Monongahela miners, went out on strike and won. Jones became president of the Miners' Association but continued an informal alliance with the Knights. Jones remained involved in the
general labor movement, helping the steelworkers move towards an amalgamation. The miners in the Connellsville district, however, remained unamalgamated and divided.

D.R. Jones moved toward the Westmoreland County (but not Connellsville) mines in
1880. He rallied the Miners' Association to strike against Waverly Coal Company, which was
partially owned by Thomas Mellon. Jones called for a strike for higher wages, breaking the
contract, which required sixty days' notice. Mellon sued Jones for conspiracy, calling Jones a
"communist." The *National Labor Tribune*, published in Pittsburgh, took on Thomas Mellon. The *Tribune* called Mellon's actions "the direct outgrowth of a miserable selfishness which
regards a dollar as of greater moment than human flesh and blood," and found his approach

typical "of perverted minds that have come to consider the teachings of Jesus Christ a good theory for Sunday reading, but not intended for practice in the real affairs of life."[3] Jones was found guilty but got off with a $100 fine. Mellon sued the *National Labor Tribune* for libel. The Connellsville area, meantime, remained relatively free of major strikes. Frick had early on required "yellow dog" contracts, under which the worker pledged not to join a union.

Frick started to move away from the day-to-day operation of the mines in 1877 as prosperity returned. Thomas Lynch was promoted from a clerk for Frick to superintendent of mines. Lynch was a man made in Frick's own image and had learned the business from the ground up with Frick. He had worked in a country store prior and was proud of the company store at the mines. Lynch had extraordinary supervisory and organizational skills and could replace Frick as a daily manager. Like Frick, Lynch believed in hands-on supervision and the use of a company foreman, which the crafts union resented. Under the crafts system, the master craftsman miner had complete control. Frick's health was again suffering in late 1877, deteriorating to inflammatory rheumatism. This time his grandmother, who had so often nursed him back to health, was gone. Westmoreland County was no longer a pleasant rural community, but a smoggy industrial hamlet. Sometimes the smoke blacked out the sun to noon. Houses were covered with dust every morning. Farm pastures were becoming marked with sinkholes from the underground mines. It is little wonder that this time Frick chose to recuperate in the fashionable Pittsburgh suburb of Shadyside, home of his friend and partner Edmund Ferguson. While Pittsburgh's smog was the worst, the eastern suburbs like Shadyside remained free of the smog.

Frick was blessed with Lynch, who stepped in and ran the company as Frick lay ill. Frick recovered, and in 1879, at age thirty, achieved his goal of becoming a millionaire. Frick had worked hard to obtain his goal of making a million. He had lived in a shack, gone into the mines often, sacrificed much of the social life he loved, and breathed the smoke and dust of his coke ovens. Frick's aggressive building and investment during the recession had made him an extremely wealthy man. His poor health had necessitated that he learn the science of organization, which would be key to his future success. Illness had forced Clay to allow lieutenants such as Lynch to evolve into managers. Frick had learned the secret that Carnegie had found years earlier: that good managers could multiply his effort many times. The price of coke had recovered from its low of 90 cents a ton to around $2.00 a ton in 1879; and at times, Frick could sell a carload at the spot price of $3.00 to $4.00 a ton. Frick's cost-cutting had now put him in a position to make a profit of 80 cents to a dollar a ton. In 1879, Frick had nearly 800 ovens and 1,000 employees and controlled over a quarter of the Connellsville coke production. Frick was shipping over one hundred carloads of coke a day to over fifty customers. Frick still had not become a major supplier to Lucy Furnace of Carnegie. Carnegie was struggling to get high-quality coke, but he had internal coke supplies he was being forced to use. Tom Carnegie, the brother of Andrew, had been working with Frick to cut some smaller deals. Frick was supplying a large amount of coke for reheat and cupola furnace operations at Edgar Thomson Works. Andrew Carnegie's other partner, Henry Phipps, had shown that Frick had the higher quality and wanted a deal with Frick to supply Lucy Furnace.

6. The King of Coke

George Harvey tells the story of Frick's passage to millionaire status:

> On the evening of December 19th, his thirtieth birthday, Clay Frick dropped into the store on his way home from a prolonged game of chess following supper with his cousins, took a look at the books preliminary to the annual accounting, bought a fresh five-cent Havana cigar on credit, lighted it thoughtfully, strolled placidly around the corner to the Washabaugh House and went to bed. He had made his million.

There is no question that meeting this goal was a psychological achievement. The accomplishment and realization of it was probably not a one-evening event but months, even years, of realizing he was a wealthy man. Frick was on the verge of entering the most exciting decade of his life. He controlled some of the finest Connellsville coal, which was the best metallurgical coal in the world. By 1880, almost 60 percent of the United States coke production (3.3 million tons a year) was in Connellsville, and Frick could now see the path to taking control of the district. Frick the millionaire, however, was changing. The change in Frick's life had been showing since 1877; sickness had forced him to look at his life. He was living better and higher. He experienced that need to rest and contemplate that comes after achieving a major accomplishment. He was enjoying life more, playing more chess, painting a little, collecting a little, and reading a lot more. Sickness had forced him to make the transformation from operations manager and bookkeeper to business executive.

One change that had evolved, as Frick grew rich, was his social life. Clay had met Andrew Mellon, the son of his banker Thomas Mellon, in 1876. Frick was six years older than Andrew, but they had become good friends by 1877 as business drew Frick to Pittsburgh more often. Edmund Ferguson had introduced him to some of the best social events, and he often ran into Andrew Mellon. Mellon had many social ties, and the handsome duo became popular at the best parties in Pittsburgh. They seemed to have shared an interest in the fine arts and reading. Andrew was known to be shy and Frick was a bit too serious, but they seemed to have a symbiotic relationship. For several years these two young, rich bachelors were the princes of the social scene, learning to fully enjoy their wealth. Frick soon came to enjoy the cosmopolitan life of Pittsburgh over that of the coke ovens of Connellsville. Still, Frick was far from divorcing himself from business and industry, as he had been bitten by the wealth bug, and was wanting more. His hard-working manager, Thomas Lynch, had shown him that people and organization could allow him to increase his wealth while spending more. Certainly, men like Carnegie had shown the way.

Frick became involved in business clubs that combined social and business pursuits in this period, and these in many ways were the natural environments for Clay Frick. One of these was the Duquesne Club, which had a group predominantly of Pig Iron Aristocrats. Frick was a charter member of the Duquesne Club, along with Henry Oliver, Ralph Baggaley (who had originally bankrolled George Westinghouse), and James Laughlin. The Duquesne Club would combine Scotch-Irish Presbyterianism, Monongahela rye, and business. It would grow into a castle of pig-iron capitalism. At the Duquesne Club, the Pig Iron Aristocrats met daily in "room number 6." These old-line industrialists included Benjamin Jones, Henry Oliver, Henry Phipps, C.B. Herron, J.W. Chalfant, and C.H. Spang. Such meetings today would border on illegal. Frick as a new young capitalist had to slowly work his way into the inner circle. Frick's involvement was limited early on, but in 1881, Frick was a full member of this august club of capitalists. On a given day one might see Andrew Carnegie, H.J. Heinz, George Westinghouse, Henry Clay Frick, Benjamin Jones, Thomas Mellon, Henry Phipps, John Chalfant, E.M. Ferguson, and many others. It was often said that more pig iron was made in the bar of the Duquesne Club than in Pittsburgh's seven furnaces. Frick learned to relish this capitalistic club.

More revealing and problematic was his charter member in the South Fork Fishing and Hunting Club near Johnstown, Pennsylvania. Its dam would be pointed to in 1889 as the source of the Great Johnstown Flood of that year. The Queen Anne clubhouse was actually located at Cresson Springs forty miles from Pittsburgh. Cresson Springs had been for years a resort area for wealthy Pittsburghers. The South Fork Fishing and Hunting Club was initially a group of young Turks who were rising up in Pittsburgh's circle of capitalists. The club was built on a mountaintop lake, which had been artificially created in the 1870s by an earthen dam. This area of the Alleghenies was a short trip on the Pennsylvania Railroad from Pittsburgh, yet it offered a slice of true wilderness. While the initial forest had been lumbered out to fuel the charcoal iron furnaces of the 1700s and early 1800s, the area had returned to its former wilderness in the 1870s. Black bear and wildcats were still common in the area. Eagles, geese, and turkey were common. Huge flocks of passenger pigeons darkened the skies for hours at a time. The Mountain View Hotel had a clientele of the wealthy from Pittsburgh and Philadelphia, and cottages were rented by wealthy families in the summer. Tom and Andrew Carnegie had built a cottage in the area next to the Mountain View Hotel. The area offered an attractive real estate investment for young men like Frick. Frick had already started to make small personal investments in real estate in Pittsburgh's East End.

The club's creator was Benjamin Ruff, a businessman and coke broker, who purchased the mountain lake resort from Altoona's Congressman John Reilly for $2,000. Pointing out that Andrew Carnegie had a nearby vacation cottage, Ruff pulled in a young Frick in 1879 for a major share in the club. Initially, they were young and upcoming industrialists such as Frick and C.C. Hussey. Within a few years, the club had a galaxy of capitalists such as Andrew Carnegie, B.F. Jones (Jones & Laughlin Steel), Edgar Thomson (Pennsylvania Railroad), Henry Phipps (Carnegie Steel), Thomas Mellon, Andrew Mellon, William Thaw, Joseph Horne (Horne Department Store), and Philander Knox (future secretary of state and senator), to name but a few. The club built a dam to improve its mountaintop lake, and members built cottages near the clubhouse. The club became known as the "bosses club." David McCullough described the members thus:

> They were early-rising, healthy, hard-working, no-nonsense lot, Scotch-Irish most of them, Freemasons, tough, canny, and without question, extremely fortunate to have been in Pittsburgh at that particular moment in history. They were men who put on few airs. They believed in the sanctity of private property and the protective tariff.... They trooped off with their large families regularly Sunday mornings to one of the more fashionable of Pittsburgh's many Presbyterian churches. They saw themselves as God-fearing, steady, solid people, and, for all their new fortunes, most of them were. Quite a few had come from backgrounds as humble as Carnegie's.[1]

This new crowd of capitalists was a lot different from the old guard of the east, such as the Vanderbilts and Astors. The club would come to an end with the failure of their mountain dam and the famous Johnstown Flood of 1889.

Andrew Carnegie was starting to pay attention to the young millionaire Henry Clay Frick, who was building a club near his cottage, but not because of his resort. About this time, Carnegie was reported to have said: "We must attach this young man Frick to our concern. He has great ability and great energy. Moreover, he has the coke — and we need it."[2] Frick was increasing his shipments to Carnegie's Edgar Thomson Works but had only a minor part of Lucy Furnace's business. Frick was shipping over 750,000 tons a year, with about 120,000 tons going to Carnegie concerns. Frick was a major supplier to Carnegie's Pittsburgh competitor of Isabella Furnaces as well as competitors in Chicago. Meantime, Carnegie was struggling to use his own coke ovens with inferior coal. Carnegie wanted vertical integration; his partner Henry Phipps wanted higher quality coke for Lucy Furnace; and his brother Tom Carnegie wanted assured supply. By 1879 the economy and the demand for steel were on the increase, and Carnegie Brothers needed to address their coke supply. In addition, Carnegie was building some of the world's largest and productive furnaces at his Edgar Thomson Works in Braddock.

Carnegie had assembled a group of amazing managers at his Edgar Thomson Works, which had broken almost every record in the production and rolling of Bessemer steel, but initially Carnegie supplied Edgar Thomson with Lucy Furnace pig iron. Plant manager Bill Jones was a brilliant motivator of people, and he had two furnace geniuses in James Gayley and Julian Kennedy. They had been planning blast furnaces at Edgar Thomson Works for several years. Julian Kennedy had purchased the remains of an Escanaba, Michigan, charcoal furnace for $16,000 in 1879. Kennedy went on to build a huge blast furnace at Edgar Thomson Works. Within a few months after startup, the furnace was producing 4,722 tons of steel a month and consuming 2,700 tons of coke a month. Plans were already underway for a second, even larger furnace. Carnegie tried to form a group of steel companies to buy coke works to assure supply, but the effort fell through. Concerns about lack of a steady supply of coke were noted by Carnegie's partner David Stewart: "I do not like to depend on the chances of getting coke from manufacturers and we may have one of our furnaces out of blast or stop converting works. This would cost us more than a few dollars in coke property."[3] Carnegie then moved to purchase Morgan & Company, Frick's main competitor in Connellsville. Morgan & Company had developed from what was left after Frick took over Morgan Mines back in the 1870s. Still, Morgan & Company could only supply a small part of Carnegie's huge needs, but it was the highest quality Carnegie owned. Carnegie's partners were getting anxious to bring Frick in the supply chain, but things would have to wait.

At the time, Frick was mixing more enjoyment with business. Frick and Andrew Mellon had been planning a European trip since late 1879, and this was on Frick's mind. Frick had been dreaming and reading of a European art trip for years. He had collected a few prints and continued his own painting, but he dreamed now of becoming a true art collector. Frick had also invited Frank Cowen and another coke prince, A.A. Hutchinson. Hutchinson had been in the coke business since 1872 and had considerable coal and coke operations. In Westmoreland County alone, Hutchinson had 500 beehive coke ovens, compared to Frick's 1,000 ovens. All told, Hutchinson was a substantial competitor with a high-tech operation. His coke crusher and sizing were state of the art, allowing Hutchinson to supply a variety of markets. A.A. Hutchinson had the best and oldest Connellsville coal mines; his coal had been hailed at the Philadelphia 1876 Exposition as the world's best. His production in 1879 was around 360,000 tons a year in high quality Connellsville coke, plus additional capacity in Fayette County. In addition, Hutchinson had 1,500 acres of prime coal lands and access to the Pennsylvania and Baltimore & Ohio Railroads. Hutchinson and Frick together controlled about fifty percent of Connellsville coke production with the other fifty percent divided up among 40 or more smaller companies. Carnegie's partner Henry Phipps had approached Hutchinson about a possible deal, and Frick was well aware of Carnegie's interest. Hutchinson was actually a customer to Frick as well, buying coke to meet demands. Hutchinson Brothers Company was the key to control of Connellsville coke by either Frick or Carnegie. Frick and Tom Carnegie both realized the importance of Hutchinson in controlling the coke market.

Tom Carnegie had even been courting the Hutchinson Brothers to come into the Carnegie organization. But all would have to wait as the foursome left in June for New York to begin their trip. The trip was to focus on art museums in France and Italy, but there were other stops such as Ireland because Andrew Mellon wanted to see the land of his ancestors. The first stop in New York would be a very important one in Frick's plan. They hired a carriage to take them up Fifth Avenue to view the mansions of the old-guard capitalists. It appears Clay was in search of new goals to fuel his ambition. They stopped to view the new mansion of William H. Vanderbilt, the son of Commodore Vanderbilt, who was the principal owner of the New York Central Railroad. The mansion had an extensive art gallery connected to it that fascinated Frick. Many sources record the following speculation by Frick: "What do you suppose the upkeep of that place would be? Would you say three hundred thousand dollars a year — about a thousand a day?" There is no question that Frick drew new inspiration from his visit to the Vanderbilt mansion. Shortly after his return, Frick would purchase the four-volume set of *Art Treasures of America*, which detailed the Vanderbilt collection. Frick, unlike his traveling friends, was not second-generation wealth and was still full of ambition. The vision of the Vanderbilt Mansion and art collection would fuel his ambition for the next few decades.

The foursome arrived in Queenstown, Ireland, in July, on the part of the trip that was for Mellon. They visited the Irish cities of Dublin and Belfast. One memorable part of the trip was the kissing of the Blarney stone. The real surprise for Frick came in visiting the Irish castles with their extensive art collections. On the Fourth of July in Killarney, they hoisted an American flag over Ross Castle. From Scotland, the foursome went to London to focus on art museums. Martha Frick Symington Sanger notes that Frick found particular inspiration in visiting the five-generation art collection of Sir Richard Wallace in London. The Wallace collection was a European must visit for men like Frick. A few years later it would be one of the first stops for fellow Pittsburgher H.J. Heinz. Frick's daughter reported that the Wallace collection was "the high spot of the trip." Sanger suggests that Frick developed the idea to build an art collection that he could give to his countrymen. Certainly, the trip would lead Frick to such a collecting goal, which would also combine Frick's patriotism and his personal love of art. No doubt Andrew Mellon was also moved to a similar goal. Both men at their deaths would leave substantial collections for the public, with Mellon's becoming the core of the National Gallery of Art in Washington, D.C.

Frick took the opportunity to visit his namesake village of Frick in Switzerland. They moved on to the Louvre in France, stopping briefly to take some lessons in French. Frick was said to have found a romantic interest in a daughter of an American banker in Paris. The final leg of the trip was a dash across the continent, including Italy and Venice. Frick and Mellon did purchase some inexpensive paintings, but these in the end were minor works whose titles were not recorded. Frick was said to have purchased a popular beaver top hat but found it too trendy for industrial Pittsburgh. On their return to Pittsburgh in the fall, there would be even more socializing. Frick now was comfortable being removed from day-to-day business operations. Frick developed a strategic approach to business that Carnegie had discovered a few years earlier, which was not simply to distance himself from his operations, but to see them with a higher-level focus. In fact, Frick was to meet with Carnegie in New York on his honeymoon.

Returning to Pittsburgh in October, Frick took some time to visit his mother and family, who now lived in Wooster, Ohio. He turned to the reading and studying of art. He purchased his first painting, *Landscape with a River*, by Pittsburgh's most famous artist, George Hetzel (1826–1899). The painting was of the Allegheny Mountains near his South Fork Fishing and Hunting Club. Still at the Monongahela House, Frick and Mellon prepared for the

Pittsburgh social season. In addition, Frick got caught up with the latest industry news. Carnegie was becoming ever more eager to secure a supply of fuel. Carnegie controlled about 16,000 tons of coke a month, while Frick alone had 75,000 tons a month. Carnegie already had a second blast furnace on the drawing board for Edgar Thomson Works. Carnegie was also a high-cost producer of coke, and his coal was lower quality. Carnegie was convinced he had to find a new coke source. Carnegie estimated that Frick had the superior resources and transportation advantages over the competition. For his part, Frick was not totally committed to the steel industry. His coke was going to many different industries, as well as his coal. With Andrew Carnegie now living in New York, Tom Carnegie was the point man with Frick. Tom Carnegie hoped to get Frick to buy his unprofitable coke works and then supply Carnegie as a partner. Henry Phipps, on the other hand, wanted Carnegie to buy into Frick's company. Frick, however, was cautious about any proposals, wanting to reduce more debt in his coke company. Tom Carnegie was working on Frick's partners, the Ferguson brothers, just as hard.

Another concern would surface for many of the coke princes soon. The year 1881 was a busy one on several fronts besides business for Frick. His interest with Benjamin Ruff in the South Fork Fishing and Hunting Club was not going well. Initially, Ruff had spent $17,000 to shore up the mountain lake dam. The dam had broken on December 25, 1879, and work was postponed to the summer of 1880 while Frick was in Europe. Work had been completed, but again the dam developed problems from a winter thaw and rains damaged it in February of 1881. The history of the dam had been problematic since its construction beginning in the late 1830s. The resulting earthen dam and artificial lake, known as Lake Conemaugh, was the largest in the world. The dam held back a 40-foot-deep lake of 20 million tons of water on a mountaintop. It held back drainage into Conemaugh gorge leading to the city of Johnstown, which was a 450-foot drop in elevation. The rebuilding of the dam had aroused concern among the citizens of Johnstown, which was what the club wanted to avoid. While every effort was being made to keep things from the public, Johnstown and Pittsburgh reporters were fascinated, and in the case of Johnstown there was worry. Reporters highlighted the importation of 1,000 black bass by a special rail car in June of 1881. The fish were said to cost a dollar a bass after all expenses were accounted for. Reporters failed to uncover the exact membership, which added further mystery and speculation. Frick, in particular, was always secretive about his life. Carnegie was now interested in the project as a means to drawing Frick and his coke empire closer. While Frick was a major investor, he left the development of the resort to his partner Ruff. Until 1889, the South Fork Club offered Pittsburgh industrialists a beautiful summer getaway. Railroad connections to the business district made it ideal for the barons to stay close to their businesses. The eventual breaking of the dam in 1889 and the Johnstown Flood would, however, dog Frick for the last half of his life.

There was one powerful opponent of the Club: Daniel Morrell. Morrell was the owner of Cambria Iron Company in Johnstown and a fierce competitor of Carnegie. Carnegie had taken the best of Morrell's managers such as Bill Jones to run his Edgar Thomson Works. Daniel Morrell was the pillar of the community, and he didn't really care for this mountaintop fishing lake for Pittsburgh competitors. Morrell's bigger concern was the fear of Johnstown's residents about the water hanging over their heads. Morrell had his own inspection made of the dam and found it unsound. He wrote Ruff a number of times about improving the dam and reducing the possible danger. Morrell's own engineer and manager John Fulton had done the inspection. At the time Morrell was still unaware of the membership of the club but he suspected Andrew Carnegie was a member. After several letters, Morrell was unable to move Ruff to take action and decided to join the club just to keep an eye on things. Morrell never really exercised any membership rights or got socially involved. Ruff continued with his plans of cottages and a hunting preserve, convinced the dam issue was over. The dam was a minor concern, if a concern at all, to these captains of industry. Business was their focus, not conditions at their summer resort. Carnegie had secretly joined the Club in an effort to draw closer to Frick. By 1881, Carnegie was badly in need of a coke supply, as enemies such as Daniel Morrell, and in Pittsburgh Andrew Kloman, were building rail mills to challenge Carnegie.

Frick was in no hurry to deal with Carnegie because the old Pittsburgh Pig Iron Aristocracy was courting him to supply coke to their Pittsburgh blast furnaces. These old-guard pig iron producers had banded together to challenge the new steel man Carnegie, whom they particularly disliked. On October 21, 1879, an old Carnegie partner, Andrew Kloman, brought together the Pig Iron Aristocrats to form Pittsburgh Bessemer Steel Company. They planned a new Bessemer rail mill at the little burgh of Homestead, across the river from Carnegie's Edgar Thomson Works. It was a state-of-the-art mill. The mill began operation in August 1881, and someday it would be part of the Carnegie empire; but in 1881 its goal was to crush Carnegie. Kloman's syndicate included the Hussey family, James Park, and Reuben Miller. Kloman needed the expertise of the Amalgamated Union workers to supply the rail-making expertise. While the Pittsburgh Bessemer Steel Company took a swipe at Carnegie in the press, stating: "We recognize the higher type of Christian manhood," the company would prove to have even worse relationships with the unions.

Pittsburgh Bessemer's first manager was William Clark, who had led the Pig Iron Aristocrats against the Amalgamated Union and the puddlers in 1878. Clark was the lion of the strikebreakers and only Frick's handling of the Homestead Strike of 1892 would eclipse his legend. Clark was at the center of the "Pittsburgh Puddler Strike of 1878" that included James Park's Black Diamond Steel, Reuben Miller's Crescent Iron Works, the Hussey family iron works, and William Clark's Solar Iron Works. The puddlers had won a tough victory in 1874 under the Sons of Vulcan, but in 1878, Carnegie and Bessemer steel were challenging the puddlers. In 1878, the Amalgamated Union had made inroads into Pittsburgh's iron and puddled steel plants. Their organization efforts met the resistance of owners such as William Clark. Clark's strategy was to replace striking workers with "black sheep" scabs. Clark, even more than Frick, saw the union as an encroachment on workers' rights, to say nothing of owners' rights. Clark wanted to be able to set puddlers' working hours and production. Violence and hard feelings resulted, but the owners prevailed. Amalgamated's only hope would be to organize the Bessemer operations of Edgar Thomson Works and Pittsburgh Bessemer at Homestead.

The Amalgamated Association of Iron and Steel Workers infiltrated the Bessemer operation at Homestead but soon found conflict with William Clark, the new plant superintendent. Clark, a Welshman, ran into ethic problems quickly as the Irish were angered over the dominance of Welsh foremen. This struggle with the Amalgamated for managerial control would run deep at Homestead for decades. At Homestead, Clark first moved to fire all union sympathizers and demanded that new employees sign a "yellow dog" contract agreeing not to join a union. The problem reached a conflict when the blooming mill rollers asked for extra pay in hot weather, and Clark refused. The men secretly formed lodges of the Amalgamated, and as they gained strength, tension increased. Daily slowdowns and struggles were the norm at the Homestead plant. In March of 1882, the disagreement moved to a full-blown strike. The economy had again slipped into recession as 1882 started, and in response Clark asked for a wage cut, which immediately resulted in a strike. The battle ensued to the point that Clark brought in scabs to do the work. There was violence, and the county sheriff sent deputies to prevent further trouble. The mess forced the owners to fire Clark, but the damage was deep to management-union relationships. The strike was hailed as a great union victory and the reinforcement of the Labor Republic. The union difficulties had prevented the plant from solv-

Adelaide Childs, the new Mrs. Frick, in her wedding dress (courtesy Frick Collection).

ing its start-up problems, and the company was bleeding with financial losses. The scars from this beginning would haunt Homestead for decades, and it would be the taproot of the great Homestead Strike of 1892. Carnegie was able to purchase the struggling Pittsburgh Bessemer by driving Bessemer steel prices to new lows. In 1883, Carnegie took over but planned to gut the operation and turn it into an open-hearth shop. What he could not gut were the Amalgamated lodges in Homestead.

The years of 1881 and 1882 were more highlighted for Frick by social events than business. Frick also increased his reading about art, and he had found a compatriot in Andrew Mellon. They enjoyed reading and discussion trips to the Allegheny Mountains. They also made frequent visits to a small but growing art community in Pittsburgh. Frick, operating out of the fashionable Monongahela House, found he could combine social and business interests. Frick and Andrew Mellon were the most eligible bachelors on the social scene in 1881. In early June at one of these social events, Clay would meet his future wife Ada (Adelaide) H. Childs. Adelaide Childs was the daughter of Asa P. Childs, of an old New England family whose roots traced back to the Plymouth colony. Asa Childs had made a fortune in Pittsburgh making and selling shoes. The Childses had a mansion in Oakland at the present site of Magee Hospital. Asa had also been a leader in the Whig and Republican parties. Adelaide's brother Howard was a major supplier to Frick's company store at Connellsville. They would court for three months, with Andrew Mellon and Ada's older sister Martha chaperoning, and they became engaged in October. Adelaide was 22 and Frick was 32. The Childses were strong Presbyterians, but Frick had no trouble switching over (at least briefly) to the faith of Pittsburgh's greatest capitalists. Frick would be the first to donate to the new Presbyterian Church in Pittsburgh's East End, the First Presbyterian Church of Wilkinsburg, shortly after his wedding.

The wedding of Henry Clay Frick and Ada H. Childs was considered "one of the most notable of the season." It took place on December 15, 1881. Andrew Mellon was Clay's best man, and some of Pittsburgh's greatest capitalists were present. The *Pittsburgh Gazette* reported:

> The scene was one hard to describe. The spacious apartments were tastefully decorated with choice flowers and foliage plants, and soft strains of music from a hidden orchestra served to beguile the time to those waiting. Shortly after five o'clock, louder notes gave warning of the approach of the bridal party; and in a few moments the parlor was filled with elegantly dressed ladies and gentlemen. The officiating clergyman, the Rev. W.J. Holland, pastor of the Bellefield Presbyterian Church, and the Rev. Dr. W.H. Hornblower took their places, and the bride and groom attended by Misses Martha C. Childs, a sister of the bride, and Miss Overholt of West Overton and Messers Jacob Justice of Philadelphia and Howard Childs of this city entered the room. The bride was attired in a rich costume of broached cream colored satin, and wore the customary long bridal veil.... After this a sumptuous repast was served and the balance of the evening was devoted to dancing by the younger portions of the guests. Mr. and Mrs. Frick left on the Fast Line at eight o'clock for the East and will visit the principal cities before their return.[4]

On the six-week schedule was the meeting with Andrew Carnegie at New York's Windsor Hotel.

Tom Carnegie had never stopped his negotiating with Frick, including the day of the wedding, and laid the groundwork for a final deal. Tom Carnegie made arrangements for Frick and his new wife to meet Andrew Carnegie at his suite at the Windsor Hotel. The couple arrived in New York the next day. They spent a few days touring such sights as the Stock Exchange, the Metropolitan Museum of Art, and the Opera. They strolled across the new Brooklyn Bridge that had been built with steel from Carnegie's Edgar Thomson Works. On December 23 or 24, the couple met Carnegie and his mother for a luncheon. Carnegie was in

Frick and his new wife Adelaide (courtesy Carnegie Library of Pittsburgh).

the weakest bargaining position, but Frick wanted cash to pay off debt. The economy had taken a slight downturn and Frick wanted to expand. The initial deal arrived at was very favorable to Frick. It was a type of partnership, in which Carnegie purchased 4,500 shares of H.C. Frick Company for 11.25 percent ownership. Some of the purchase resulted from an exchange of Carnegie's coke operations using lower-quality coal such as that from Monastery Works in Latrobe. This increased Frick's coke ovens from 1,026 to 2,207. The deal required Frick to supply all of Carnegie's coke needs, including supplying the best Connellsville coke for Carnegie's furnaces. The distribution of shares on January 31, 1882, saw Frick holding 11,846, the Ferguson Brothers holding 23,654, and Carnegie holding 4,500 shares.

Henry Phipps was not pleased with the arrangement when he got news of it. Phipps argued that Carnegie should not agree to exclusive supply arrangements with Frick. It appears that Carnegie and Frick met again on January 6, 1882, to discuss some of the ancillary issues.[5] It was Carnegie who seemed to be hesitating after talking to Phipps. This type of buyer's remorse was common with Carnegie. Phipps also was concerned by the lack of control by Carnegie interests in the new company, which might allow Frick to change details. Carnegie may have been planning a full takeover of Frick in the long run. Tom Carnegie, on the other hand, wanted the deal badly, and he felt he could handle the Ferguson brothers down the road. Carnegie seemed at the time to be driven by his belief in backward vertical integration. At the time he was closing the deal with Frick, he was already looking at purchasing railroads and ore supply. Carnegie had jumped ahead of the deal to pressure the railroads for lower prices. On December 28, 1881, a day or two after his first meeting with Frick, Carnegie was already leaning on Robert Garrett, vice president of the Baltimore & Ohio Railroad, for reduced rates. Carnegie threatened to ship Frick coke on the Pennsylvania Railroad if the B&O did not lower rates.[6] Carnegie also realized that the Ferguson brothers were the major stockholders, although Phipps had told Carnegie that they followed Frick on any decision. Carnegie allowed for some flexibility in specifying an annual meeting of Tom Carnegie and Henry Clay Frick to review the agreement.

It had been accepted as corporate mythology that Andrew Carnegie's mother whispered to him at the time: "That's a verra good thing for Mr. Freek, but what do we get out of it?"[7] But Carnegie knew exactly what he was doing. Stock deals were Carnegie's turf, and he had a team of capitalists behind him. Tom Carnegie had been negotiating with Frick's partners, the Ferguson brothers, behind the scenes. In addition, over the next two years Carnegie's allies came in and purchased shares from the Fergusons. By August 1885, Carnegie's full plan would be played out with Carnegie holding 13,711 shares, leaving Frick with 8,665 shares, E.M. Ferguson with 8,665 shares, Walter Ferguson with 8,667 shares, Henry Phipps (Carnegie's partner) with 3,955 shares, and Tom Carnegie with 3,780 shares. Technically, the initial arrangement was a "partnership." At the time, Frick had no idea of Carnegie's long-run plans. In 1882, it looked as if Frick had gotten the best of the deal, and he trusted Carnegie as a new partner. When the Fricks continued their honeymoon into February of 1882, Frick was still the King of Coke because of the agreement. The couple went on to Boston, Philadelphia, and Washington, D.C. In Boston, they climbed Bunker Hill, and in D.C., they visited Congress and toured the Smithsonian. They attended the trial of Charles Guiteau, Republican President James Garfield's assassin. Frick had admired Garfield, who had supported an increase in protective tariffs as Chairman of the Ways and Means Committee. Politically, Frick was a strong Republican. Martha Frick Symington Sanger reported the couple visited President Chester Arthur.[8]

Frick would soon realize that he had been outfoxed by the steelmaster.

7. A Fox in the Henhouse

It didn't take Carnegie two years to make his move on corporate control of H.C. Frick Company. Carnegie was like the computer worm virus of today; once in, he would take control. He had demonstrated this with the Kloman Brothers, Keystone Bridge, and Union Iron Mills. Ownership of companies had always been a Carnegie principle, and his deal with Frick would be no different. The firm of H.C. Frick was reorganized and became H.C. Frick Coke Company, and while Frick's share remained the same, Carnegie could now move ahead with his plans to buy up more shares. The incorporation of H.C. Frick occurred in April of 1883 with capital of $2,000,000 and a little over 2,000 coke ovens in operation. Initially, Tom Carnegie, Andrew Carnegie, Henry Phipps, and the partnership of Carnegie Brothers owned less than 12 percent. Frick had just under 30 percent of the stock, with the Ferguson brothers in control of about 60 percent. The Ferguson brothers allowed Frick a free hand as president of the company. Frick expanded the company to meet the growing demand for his coke. The supply arrangement with Carnegie required expansion. Frick closed the deal with A.A. Hutchinson, the one he had been working on prior to the Carnegie deal. Carnegie hesitated on expending more cash, but he also realized it as a means to an end. The infusion of cash came from Carnegie and his associates at a cost as Carnegie gained more stock. Frick trusted the old master as he was mesmerized by corporate growth. Under Carnegie's guidance, and taking advantage of the early recession of the 1880s, H.C. Frick Coke Company became the largest coke company in the world, controlling 40 percent of the finest Connellsville coke. Frick had conquered an array of different markets. Frick was supplying coke to silver and gold smelters on the west coast as well as supplying home fuel to the east coast. What Frick didn't realize was the Carnegie brothers were courting the Fergusons to sell stock.

In February of 1882, Adelaide and Clay returned to the Monongahela House exhausted. Once again Frick was stricken with inflammatory rheumatism and was bedridden. It took several weeks for Clay to again recover. Once recovered, he began the search for a new house. Tom Carnegie suggested his neighborhood of Pittsburgh's East End, where the Mellons also lived. Frick, like the Carnegie and Ferguson brothers, had been making investments in real estate in the East End for a couple of years. The East End had a railroad station on the Pennsylvania Railroad, which connected this beautiful area to downtown Pittsburgh and the South Fork Club in the Alleghenies. The East End was considered the site of a future real estate boom and many investors were getting in. In 1882, some of the first horse-drawn streetcars became available in the East End, making it a suburban paradise. In April of that year, Frick purchased a two-story, 23-room, Italianate chateau-type house beside George Westinghouse's home, which was known as Solitude. A few years later H.J. Heinz would move in on the other side. Frick's new house had been built in 1876 and was located on a 5.5-acre lot at Penn and homewood Avenues. It had originally been owned by Carnegie partner John Vandevort. John was a close friend of both Tom Carnegie and Henry Phipps. The Vandevort family was part of Pittsburgh's original industrial elite. The original house was known as "Homewood" and had a stable and greenhouse. Frick hired Andrew Peebles, a prominent Pittsburgh architect, to expand and bring the house up to the standards of the wealthy. He named the homestead "Clayton." They had telephones installed, which were some of the earliest in Pittsburgh residences in the suburbs. The business activity in the East End required mail to be delivered as often as five times a day; so business could be transacted, telephone calls were limited to a few miles in the Pittsburgh area. The house was located on a special line of the Pennsylvania Railroad designed by George Westinghouse. The private station would allow for direct entry on the train to New York and points east. Adelaide was already pregnant, but the preparation of the house would take until late January 1883.

Frick was readily accepted into the social circles of this new suburb by Tom Carnegie and his friends. He would find much acceptance in the Carnegie partnership as well. Frick would quickly impress Carnegie's partner Henry Phipps and Carnegie's brother Tom. Like Frick, Phipps had a bookkeeping background. Phipps had started as a bookkeeper for the Kloman brothers but soon became an investor. Phipps took to technology and had become a blast furnace expert. He had become one of the first to promote Connellsville coke as a productivity booster. Lucy Furnace, under the supervision of Phipps, had become the world's most productive furnaces. Prior to Frick, Phipps was the partnership's only finance man. Phipps came to highly respect Frick's financial skills, and they would team up to build a Carnegie empire.

The year of 1882 was one of strikes in the steel and iron industry. These were centered on the problems that had started at Pittsburgh Bessemer Steel at Homestead. The problem was much deeper than a matter of the rich capitalists against the poor laborers. First, as we have seen, the poor immigrant laborer was excluded from union membership. These crafts unions were for skilled workers only. Second, the pressure to confront the union didn't only come from the boardroom or the owners. Lower and middle management had become frustrated by the pay scales of the skilled union workers. The steel foreman, for example, worked the same twelve-hour day as the steel puddler or blast furnace man but was paid considerably less. Usually, the foreman made half the wages of the highest-paid union worker. In the 1880s a blooming mill roller made about $6.00 a day, a blooming mill foreman about $2.50 a day, and an unskilled laborer about $1.00 a day. The blooming mill superintendent made about $6.00 a day. The average worker of the period made about $1.65 a day, so there was little public support at the time for these crafts unions. The internal control of the union by various nationalities, and rivalry among the crafts, created internal opposition. Still, companies often lost public support with their unilateral lockouts in recessions. The other part of the problem was a fear of the unions by the owners. Part of it was a control issue, but another part was European unionism, which was socialistic, political, and often violent. The newspapers were full of the violence and socialism of Europe, and the American Railroad Strike of 1877 had put fear into the general population.

The first Homestead Strike of 1882 against the Pittsburgh Bessemer Steel Company was both bitter and violent, and it would lead to the first national strike of the steel workers. The owners and the union across the country united for the 1882 struggle. The strike started in March, and by May there were 100,000 strikers, including 700 at Homestead. The three-month strike of 1882 at Homestead ended in a type of draw, but the strikers claimed victory. Carnegie, Frick, and most of Pittsburgh's capitalists were appalled that the Pig Iron Aristocrats had allowed the Amalgamated to take over the mill. It was the first solid agreement that the Amalgamated Iron and Steel Workers would represent the workforce. In June of 1882, union members from around the nation came to Pittsburgh to celebrate and meet. It was a call of unity by the Knights of Labor and the Amalgamated, plus other trade unions. On June 17, 1882, a "Grand Labor Parade" occurred, which many consider the first Labor Day. Thousands clogged the streets of Pittsburgh as banners proclaimed them to be "noble and holy," and "the source of all wealth." Capitalist H.J. Heinz was in the crowd that day and noted in his diary on seeing the banner "Labor and Brains against Capital": "What folly."[1] The parade highlighted local leaders such as D.R. Jones, who had led strikes against Thomas Mellon's coal mines. The Homesteaders of the Amalgamated were prominent in the parade, and Carnegie was not happy to see the Knights of Labor from Braddock. Another Braddock unionist, John McLuckie, was in the parade. He would play a future role in the Homestead Strike of 1892. Both D.R. Jones and John McLuckie were now residing in Homestead. The Grand Master Workman, Terrence Powderly of the Knights of Labor, was there as well.

The parade was a show of union solidarity and unity, at least on the surface. The Knights of Labor and the Amalgamated were in competition for the same workers. The main difference between the Knights and the Amalgamated was that the Knights were organized by industry and the Amalgamated by trades. The Knights favored representing both skilled and unskilled workers within an industry, and were more likely to accept immigrants. The Amalgamated favored representation of skilled workers, opposing the membership of the unskilled. Amalgamated represented the "tonnage" workers paid by the tons produced. The Knights were concerned with broad labor issues such as the eight-hour day and working conditions. The Amalgamated was focused on wages, crafts control, and pay scales. In 1882, the Amalgamated were in most of the steel mills with some competition from the Knights. The Amalgamated called their basic unit a lodge while the Knights called theirs a "forge." Unofficially, the Knights were strongest at Carnegie's Edgar Thomson Works, while the competing Pittsburgh Bessemer Company at Homestead was dominated by the Amalgamated. Some workers belonged to both unions.

The parade was a statement in many ways. An Irish police force assured perfect order, in contrast with the railroad riots of 1877 on the same streets. The Greenback Labor Party marched also as the political arm of labor. The parade and Homestead "victory" led the Amalgamated Association of Iron and Steel Workers to take a bold move to settle the wage issues that remained. In July, the Amalgamated called for a national strike. The strike would pit 35,000 members against 116 mills in seven states. Manufacturers united to battle the strike, which was focused on Pittsburgh. The growing differences between the Knights and the Amalgamated helped to weaken the effort. The Pittsburgh glass houses and mines joined in, taking the number of strikers to nearly 100,000. While local strikes continued for years, the main strike was crushed by November. D.R. Jones, as president of the Miners' Association, was forced to resign. In addition, the Greenback Labor Party was crushed in the November elections. Carnegie, with his progressive plant superintendent Bill Jones, had forged a relationship with the Knights at Edgar Thomson Works. The cozy relationship kept Carnegie's real nemesis, the Amalgamated, out of the plant.

Ironically, the great parade of 1882 to celebrate the rise of labor may well have led to its demise. The national strike of 1882 was a major setback for the Amalgamated and started a national decline. Between 1882 and 1885, the Amalgamated managed to win only one of eleven major strikes. The membership fell from 16,000 in 1882 to 5,700 in 1885. The main enemies of the Amalgamated craft unions were technology and mass production. The rise of Bessemer steel ended the day of the puddler, which had been the iconic representation of the industrial crafts. Pittsburgh factories were effectively de-unionized. Carnegie helped in a strange way to prolong the Amalgamated, which he wanted destroyed. Carnegie's Union Mills were involved in the national strike, but with an upturn in orders, Carnegie again broke ranks with the manufacturers and settled. The old-line Pig Iron Aristocrats were extremely angry at Carnegie for breaking the owner alliance. Carnegie again was ahead of the curve, building a favorable opinion with some union leaders, but he always had a strategy of provoking a strike in economic downturns. Carnegie was quoted as telling the *New York Times*: "The reason for signing is that they are crowded with orders which must be filled at all hazards."[2] At Edgar Thomson Works Bill Jones convinced Carnegie to move to the eight-hour day and to help workers purchase homes. The strategy declawed the already weak local Knights of Labor.

Playing on the setbacks, the Revolutionary Socialist Party met in Pittsburgh in October of 1882. The terrorist Johann Most brought these radical views to Pittsburgh in 1883. Johann Most called anarchists and radical socialists to Pittsburgh for a meeting known as the Black International. Most tried to bring the European-style street revolution to America. The socialists built a document known as the Pittsburgh Manifesto, which called for infiltration of the trade unions and the use of force against capitalists. Neither the union nor owners welcomed the socialist convention. The socialists were never popular in Pittsburgh, with its old German neighborhoods. The Amalgamated system of hierarchal pay systems was far from socialism and represented a type of union cells of capitalism. The Amalgamated even bordered on union aristocracy. The convention, to a large degree, helped spread the use of the term capitalism, which was a term drawn from Karl Marx's *Das Kapital*. The national tide appeared to be turning against the crafts union cause. Many of the labor leaders retreated to local politics, taking over towns such as Homestead. Homestead remained the industrial Alamo of the Amalgamated, but Pittsburgh Bessemer Steel was near bankruptcy by the end of 1882.

Carnegie had his hands full in 1882 as well. The downturn in the economy had started a price war between Edgar Thomson Works, Cambria Iron, and Chicago rail producers. The price war erupted as Cambria broke an agreement with Carnegie. Carnegie, however, had a major cost advantage with Frick coke, and Cambria lost out. With his new cost advantage, Carnegie went after the western rail markets of the Chicago mills. By the end of 1882, Carnegie united again with Cambria on price and took major orders from the Chicago market. Carnegie had been the master of such price arrangements, which under today's laws would be illegal. Frick, in the meantime, was working on some coke deals with the Chicago mill owners. Carnegie didn't like it, and Phipps and Tom Carnegie were concerned. Still, transportation gave Carnegie the advantage, so he allowed Frick to pursue these old Chicago customers. Furthermore, Carnegie was in a battle for the steel market, and Frick would wait.

Both Carnegie and Frick benefited for the first couple of years of the alliance. Carnegie was now the low-cost rail producer, and he took orders almost at will. The old Pig Iron Aristocrats' Pittsburgh Bessemer Steel was broken by early 1883, and even they had to turn to Carnegie. Carnegie bought Pittsburgh Bessemer out at book value. Carnegie offered the company's stock or $50,000 in cash, but only William Singer took Carnegie up on the offer, which eventually would be worth millions. Carnegie had plenty of rail capacity, so he planned to convert Homestead into the world's greatest structural and plate mill. Carnegie foresaw a buildup of the Navy and the protective tariffs of the Republicans as a future root of a steel plate boom. In April of 1883, Frick reported that the 14 months since the agreement, H.C. Frick Company had sold 950,000 tons of coke at an amazing profit of $378,000, for a net return of 23 percent. Frick had also scouted the local farms for more coal, purchasing more potential mines. The record showed he invested $44,000 in the same period for coal and coke improvements. The company still had a debt of $54,000.

Frick's personal life and marriage were at a high point as well. The couple had started decorating the house with furniture from many trips to New York. They purchased fine horses and carriages for the house as well. The couple found a common love of art and paintings. They spent time reading and collecting as they waited for the house to be finished. They purchased another painting called *Fruit* by George Hetzel. They purchased a similar painting by A. Bryan Wall, a member of Hetzel's group and a friend of Frick's father and family. The move caused another bout of inflammatory rheumatism. Frick took several days off work to help unpack boxes, which was very telling about the relationship and Frick's state of mind.

The workaholic of early years seemed to have been tamed by money and Adelaide. They had moved in at the end of January, and Adelaide gave birth to their son, Childs Frick, on March 12, 1883. Frick's friendship with Andrew Mellon deepened, and Andrew was often a dinner guest. On weekends the two might play cards and talk art into the night with Andrew staying over in the guest house. Adelaide strengthened her relationship with her sister Martha, who also had a room in the new house.

Frick and Andrew Mellon would meet for lunch at the Duquesne Club to discuss art and personal investments. Frick and Mellon were active in Pittsburgh real estate, banking and coal companies. The two loved to invest in small coal mines, looking for potential capital appreciation. Andrew Mellon joined Frick in buying the Overholt Distillery. Frick was brought in on several banking deals of Mellon, including Fidelity Title & Trust (a Mellon company) and Union Trust. In the early 1880s, both men put personal funds into small coal companies and railroads such as Fort Smith and Western Railroad. Many railroad executives would lunch with the two young friends. Like both their fathers before them, they enjoyed making deals in the coal industry outside of Frick's company. Frick would be one of the first investors in George Westinghouse's natural gas company. Mellon taught Frick banking and finance, while Frick taught Mellon art. Frick had a well-diversified personal investment strategy, while his future partner Andrew Carnegie had made the decision to put all his eggs in one basket. Frick's knowledge of banking, business, and finance was always far beyond that of Carnegie. Besides the Duquesne Club, both were members of the Union League Club. Frick, however, had close political, banking, and social ties that Carnegie lacked. Furthermore, Carnegie was based in New York and never made the Pittsburgh meetings.

Even with all his business, Frick would usually spend evenings with his family. Frick proved to be the ideal father, demonstrating an amazing love of children. Had the press and workers seen him, they would have been shocked. The picture of Frick carrying and burping his son would seem not to fit his demonic public image. His love of children and family would be a part of Frick that the public never saw. Martha Frick Symington Sanger reported a note from Adelaide's sister's diary: "I don't think his papa ever wrote any words that made him feel as rich and happy as those written in the Bible that day announcing the birth of Childs Frick."[3] Frick's love of children would be exhibited throughout his life but usually inside the family home and by anonymous donations to many children's charities. It is a part of what might appear as a paradox, but in reality it is part of the complexities of everyone's life. In any case, the birth of Frick's son brought great happiness into his life.

Now Frick was dreaming of becoming the major supplier of coke to the nation, but he needed more deep mines and coke ovens. Carnegie was not dreaming of the coke market, but of steel. Carnegie had his supply of coke assured and that was enough. He was not really interested in seeing Frick increase supply to his competitors. In an August 13, 1883, letter to Andrew Carnegie, Frick proposed a takeover of A.A. Hutchinson and Connellsville Gas and Coal Company.[4] Frick's plan showed his good business sense. The purchase would double their coke capacity and coal reverses. Frick reasoned such a takeover could be managed without an increase in office and management overhead. The acquisition of the 1,500 coke ovens would be far below the cost of building them. Frick had gained the support of Tom Carnegie; Andrew Carnegie passed, using a terse letter to say no, but Frick persisted. Frick offered Carnegie a bigger share of the stock arrangement in November, and Carnegie gave his approval. Frick moved quickly to purchase A.A. Hutchinson's Standard Mine in December of 1883, completing years of negotiating by Frick for this property. Standard Works, with its 500 coke ovens, was the largest coke maker in the Connellsville district. Frick also picked up an outstanding operations manager in superintendent and old friend Robert Ramsay. Frick, however, also became a major landlord of immigrant laborers in the deal. More problematic is that Carnegie moved just as quickly to take a 50 percent-plus share of H.C. Frick Company. Frick would soon learn Carnegie was a much different partner from what he was used to.

Before Carnegie took 50 percent control in mid–1884, Frick was able to purchase more operations and establish new supply relationships. Carnegie plants only accounted for 40 percent of Frick's 130,000-ton-a-month capacity. Frick put together an arrangement with Southwest Coal and Coke Company to supply his Chicago steel customers. Frick also entered a partnership with the Chicago steelmakers, creating the new company of Chicago and Connellsville Coke Company. Frick also used the new coke works to supply another Carnegie competitor, the Cambria Iron Company. Frick picked up another friend and strong manager in Morris Ramsay, the brother of William and Robert Ramsey. None of these relationships were of interest to Carnegie except when they affected the price of coke, competitive advantages with other steelmakers, or priority of supply. In reality, the Chicago steel men proved even more problematic than Carnegie. Both Carnegie and the Chicago steel makers were tolerant of lockouts and strikes in the steel industry, but pushed Frick to keep the coke supply open regardless of his labor issues. Frick was the only coke man among them; the rest were steel men. By 1884, Carnegie was convinced he needed to take stock control of H.C. Frick Company to assure there would be no supply disruptions.

Disagreements with Carnegie on coke pricing continued through 1884. Frick had formed a price-fixing syndicate (legal at the time) in 1884 known as the Coke Syndicate. The price of coke had dropped briefly to 90 cents a ton, sending shock waves through the Connellsville district. Frick brought together the leading coke manufacturers in the Connellsville district to hold a minimum of a $1.00 a ton. The Coke Syndicate would control 6,895 ovens, or two-thirds of the Connellsville district.[5] The plan worked well for Frick, who drove coke prices up, but Carnegie realized he had a problem. High coke prices increased the price of steel at Braddock's Edgar Thomson Works. Carnegie had to force Frick to consider his steel interests and that would require a new strategy.

The year 1884 was one of recession for industry. Carnegie had a simple strategy for recessions: cut prices, cut costs, and deal with the iron and steel unions. Carnegie pushed for lower coke prices against the wishes of Frick. Frick, for his part, wanted to take an interest in Carnegie's company, which Carnegie controlled tightly. Carnegie kept putting Frick off, saying he needed to focus all his energy on managing the coke operations. It is not fully clear why Carnegie opposed Frick's owning stock. Carnegie had started to use stock as an incentive for his steel managers. Frick could never really hope to become a major stockholder as long as the Carnegie brothers lived. Certainly, Carnegie saw that Frick would have a conflict of interest on a management level, but such a conflict could have made Frick more sensitive to the steel business side. Before Frick caught on, Carnegie realized that Frick was a skillful opponent who needed to be contained. Carnegie and his associates treated coke as a resource whose price had to be lowered. Frick offered more stock in H.C. Frick Company for more interest in the Carnegie partnership, but Carnegie was already on the brink of taking control. Frick was not blind to Carnegie's buying of stock and threatened to increase the capitalization of H.C. Frick Company, which would dilute Carnegie's share. While Frick's trust in Andrew Carnegie was declining, he still seemed to fully support Tom Carnegie. Tom Carnegie was a friend to Frick, but he was a brother to Andrew.

Frick and Carnegie realized that they were in a struggle for control of the coke company. Frick moved ahead with the increased capitalization, but Carnegie and his partners only increased their share by buying stock from the Ferguson brothers. Carnegie played to Frick's ambition by buying stock and allowing Frick to buy more coke and coal assets. The recession had crippled Frick's ability to get cash to buy assets. Frick wanted badly to expand H.C. Frick with the purchase of three coal operations: Southwest, Morewood Mines, and Dillinger Mines.

Carnegie refused to help, which sent a message to Frick that the friendly partnership was over. By early 1885, Carnegie would have his control by stock deals and buying by his associates. The Carnegie brothers had flanked Frick. Frick now was at the mercy of Carnegie's price demands and was required to obtain a full approval on investments. H.C. Frick Company was now an in-house supplier. Carnegie was the boss and would assert enough power to make sure Frick understood. Frick had formed a coke pricing syndicate similar to those of Carnegie in steel. Carnegie sent a representative once to demand a reduction in price against the Frick's syndicate. Frick had no choice but to obey, but it was a major blow to Frick's ego. Carnegie would later apologize, but it was also clear who was the boss.

Frick was not totally dependent on the commands of Carnegie. He owned many small mines in the Connellsville area as well as partnerships in Southwest Coal & Coke and Chicago & Connellsville Coke Company. Frick had many coke and coal interests, but he was a master of none. Still, Carnegie could not afford to allow Frick tactical freedom in the coke market and started to draw him with more financial interest in Carnegie Brothers in 1886. Frick started a personal quest to study and understand steelmaking. Frick might have been flanked, but he was far from out of the fight. Carnegie also needed Frick's knowledge in running H.C. Frick. Frick had also gained the respect of Carnegie's largest and oldest partner, Henry Phipps. More and more, Phipps turned to Frick for financial advice on his investments.

Carnegie now had a managerial genius working for him. Frick moved to increase the use of management foremen to supervise and set goals. Frick had been the earliest in the coal fields to put in underground management supervision. The move would create tension with the mining crafts system where the master miner functioned as an independent operator and subcontractor. As Frick opened new mines, he moved to supervised unskilled labor to replace the crafts system. The new model of trade mining divided workers into specialized jobs such as explosives man, loader, pick man, and daymen with a crew foreman. Frick was a leader in applying this hierarchal worker model. Technology helped Frick facilitate the change. Skilled miners had carefully hand-cut mines, but in the 1880s blast powder became available to blow out one to two tons on a face in one blast. By the late 1880s, cutting machines and compressed air drills became available as well. Miner jobs became unskilled, but these "inside" jobs were still paid based on tonnage mined. The "outside" general labor, repair, and maintenance jobs were paid a fixed hourly rate. A mine and coke works the size of Frick's Standard Mine would have one to two underground foremen with an additional twenty company men underground. There would be about 180 tonnage underground miners. On the surface, supporting the mine and coke works, were another pair of foremen and 20 company men with about 130 hourly paid coke workers. There would also be at least 10 clerks and about 20 skilled craftsmen such as carpenters and blacksmiths. Additional groups of carpenters were available to cover building and housing for the workforce, and these were usually employed by the company store. A store manager and clerk were used to run the company store. Frick used size to reduce overhead costs of his many Connellsville area operations. In Carnegie's view, Frick's cost-cutting had always put him in the category of a great manager.

Carnegie could be a tenacious bulldog between the scenes with his managers. Frick never gained the freedom of Bill Jones at Carnegie's Edgar Thomson. Carnegie had one of the best in Bill Jones of Edgar Thomson, but even Jones had to pay respects to the steel master. Jones's excellent and fair treatment of the workers at Edgar Thomson, but Carnegie's acquisition of Homestead across the river had brought the Amalgamated to Braddock's Edgar Thomson. The Amalgamated had built membership in many of the tonnage departments. In addition, the Knights of Labor had some footing at Edgar Thomson Works. The Knights had a larger following in the unskilled labor force with its growing population of Slavs, Hungarians, and Poles. Many of these Hungarians had been drawn away from the coal fields. The continuing recession had taken steel rail prices from $37.75 a ton in 1883 to $28.50 a ton in 1885. For Carnegie it was ideal time to deal with the union, particularly the Amalgamated. Even Bill Jones had little tolerance for the union. Jones had gotten the eight-hour day and pay increases for the men from Carnegie. Now Carnegie was outraged to find the Knights had not forced his competition to do the same. Carnegie had calculated that his labor costs at Edgar Thomson were higher than those of the Chicago steel mills. Jones felt the heat from Carnegie. The Amalgamated posed a bigger threat with potential wage increases on tons produced.

Using the economic downturn, Carnegie with Jones moved to finish off the growing Amalgamated at Edgar Thomson. In December of 1884, Carnegie shut the mill down for the installation of new equipment in the rolling mills. The plan called for the men to be discharged and then rehired, with the idea of eliminating union members. Once shut down, Carnegie and Jones hesitated on the rehiring until the Amalgamated forced increases at other mills or took a pay cut. This was a repeated strategy of Carnegie's. After a month, the men returned, agreeing to wage cuts of 20 percent to 33 percent. The Amalgamated was in effect crushed at Edgar Thomson but still was a force in the coal fields. Interestingly, by the end of 1885, Carnegie was going to report record profits and raised wages 10 percent. This up-and-down game was typical of the steel industry in the 1880s and 1890s. The problems at Edgar Thomson spread to H.C. Frick Company. Like Carnegie and Jones, Frick had an outstanding superintendent in Thomas Lynch. Like Jones, Lynch was close to the men; and while anti-union, he understood the problems of the men. Coal men claimed they were being cheated by the company weight scales and overcharged at the company stores. Both charges appeared to have a great deal of truth.

A mining industry study in 1884 showed how much the company stores were really a company abuse.[6] The state survey of coal companies showed that around 20 percent of a coal company's profits were attributed to the company store. Frick had truly invented a major side business with over fifteen general stores in 1884. Frick had major supply contracts with merchant king John Wanamaker. The study detailed the difference in prices. The comparison was striking:

Foodstuff	Company Store	Independent Store
Flour per barrel	$8.00	$7.00
Butter per pound	$.35	$.30
Bacon per pound	$.40	$.10
Ham per pound	$.13	$.11–.12
Cheese per pound	$.20	$.16–.18
Tea per pound	$.60–$1.00	$.25–.75
Coffee per pound	$.28–.37	$.25–.30

This type of pricing was taking a major portion of the workers' pay and contributing a major part to the company's overall profit. In addition, resentment built over the requirement to buy at the company store by paying the employee in company scrip. In 1882, a coal miner told an investigator: "If we do not deal in the company store we are not wanted at the mine, and are given a poor place to work. The company store system is a blot on the liberties of this county, and should be the concern of all whether in or out of the mine."[7] These abuses led to a short strike in 1885. The Slavs and Hungarians for the first time rose in solidarity to strike. Carnegie supported the strike initially. Frick took a strong stand, but as the coke ovens went cold and threatened to shut down Edgar Thomson, Carnegie wanted it settled. Again Frick reluctantly obeyed.

Carnegie failed to realize that this short 1885 strike augured a new era in unionization. The Knights of Labor were taking over and changing the Amalgamated in the coal fields. Technology and Frick's new management structure had broken the crafts nature of mining.

The aristocratic, skilled-oriented, and crafts-based structure of the Amalgamated union no longer reflected the reality of unskilled immigrant labor of the mines. The unskilled Slavs and Hungarians had to be brought into the union to stand against management. Even Frick didn't fully realize that technology was in reality beating the hated crafts union approach. The Amalgamated union itself failed to fully recognize the futility of a hierarchal crafts system.

With all the problems, Frick was extremely happy at the birth of his daughter Martha Howard Frick on August 9, 1885. For her first few years the family used her nickname "Rosebud." Family biographer Martha Frick Symington noted, however: "Martha's birth would mark the end of the last happy period in Frick's life and could never have been foretold."[8] Until this point, the many difficulties of business had been just part of a normal day's work. Frick went to work in Pittsburgh by carriage each day and made a weekly train trip to Connellsville. At Clayton he spent more time reading about art and playing with the children. Summers were spent more in the Allegheny Mountains. Frick, however, believed he could balance recreation and business. But unlike Carnegie, Frick dreamed of more strategic control of his investments and businesses. Frick had started to envision himself as a financial capitalist. He thoroughly enjoyed his Pittsburgh investment luncheons at the Duquesne Club. Carnegie did not share Frick's vision for himself; in fact, he feared allowing Frick's involvement in Carnegie's investments.

Things changed in the autumn of 1886. In October, Tom Carnegie died of pneumonia and hard drinking. This was a real blow to Andrew, who had allowed Tom to basically run the day-to-day operations of the company. It had been Tom who originally persuaded Andrew of the investment potential of Bessemer steel. Frick had also lost his best ally in the steel company. Andrew had lost his chief operating officer, and he was not willing to get more involved with tactical issues. Tom had remained living in Pittsburgh's fashionable East End, maintaining key local political ties for the Carnegie brothers. Carnegie had no real replacement for Tom. Henry Phipps had been a loyal friend and partner, but he lacked the executive skills needed. Now Carnegie had to turn to Frick as a possible replacement. In November, Carnegie allowed Frick to become a stockholder in Carnegie Steel. Frick purchased $100,000 of stock at $1.84 per share for about a 4 percent interest. Carnegie would slowly allow Frick to enter into the organization, realizing over the longer term that he needed help. For Frick, however, it would mean more involvement in the day-to-day operations, but he hoped that it would lead ultimately to more freedom. It would also mean more familiarity with the technical complexity that steelmaking required. Carnegie feared Frick's involvement after Tom's death and developed a legal document known as the "Iron Clad Agreement." This pact protected against an internal takeover from the partners. The agreement assured that on death of a partner, his shares would be purchased by the partnership. It also provided a means for securing the removal of a partner. Frick proved up to the task as he started a crash course on steelmaking through a reading campaign. Frick's knowledge would soon overtake his master.

In the meantime, Frick's business partners, friends, and neighbors were helping him break into not only Pittsburgh's social world, but its financial world. Frick's business partners, the Ferguson brothers, were wealthy and had connections in the banking world, as did Frick's best friend, Andrew Mellon. Frick had become a trustee of the Mozart Club, which promoted the appreciation of classical music. Mrs. Frick was also involved in the Mozart Club, which often sponsored struggling musicians. Frick became a director of the Pittsburgh National Bank of Commerce. In addition, Frick continued to expand his real estate investments in Pittsburgh's East End along with the Andrew Mellon. In the 1880s, Frick became a major landowner in the eastern suburbs. He invested with mayor and political boss Christopher Magee in utilities and streetcar companies to support real estate development in the East

End. Another important directorship for Henry Clay Frick was in the Philadelphia Gas Company of his neighbor George Westinghouse. The Philadelphia Gas Company was supplying natural gas to homes and industries in the Pittsburgh area. Natural gas was a new concept in the 1880s, and George Westinghouse had made it competitive with coal by developing a delivery system. Natural gas by 1887 would cut the use of heating coal in Pittsburgh by 30 percent. Such directorships were very important and were usually reserved for senior business leaders in the community.

Carnegie's profits turned up in the mid–1880s, and he continued with his plan to convert Homestead Works into a world-class plate manufacturer. This would require a conversion from the Bessemer converter to the open-hearth process of steelmaking. Bessemer steel had a high sulfur and phosphorus content, which made it too weak for naval armor plate as well as some specialty items such as big forgings. Carnegie had correctly predicted this as the next growth market as steel rail tonnage leveled off. Carnegie had been at the 1879 London meeting of the Iron and Steel Institute, where he had heard a talk on this new process and had purchased the rights to it. He asked Bill Jones to try what was then called the Thomas process in a Bessemer converter at Braddock, but the results were disappointing. On an 1885 trip to England, Carnegie saw the Thomas process working smoothly in a furnace invented by German Charles Siemens. On his return, Carnegie sent Charles Schwab, superintendent of Homestead, to Krupp Works in Germany. In 1886, Schwab led Homestead in a conversion to the open-hearth process, which produced a much cleaner and stronger steel needed for armor and structural steel applications. It, however, was a more expensive method to make steel than the Bessemer process.

Charles Schwab was one of Carnegie's superstars. Bill Jones discovered Schwab selling cigars at a Braddock drugstore. Captain Bill Jones hired Schwab to work at Edgar Thomson in the engineering department for a dollar a day. Schwab would become one of many young men known as the "Class of 1887" that Jones hired who would eventually become presidents and vice-presidents of Carnegie Steel and United States Steel. These "boys" would include Schwab's friends Alva Dinkey (future vice-president); William Dickson (future vice-president); and William Corey of Braddock (son of Mellon's old coal partner and future president). Bill Jones trained these "Boys of Braddock," and they admired Jones and honored his legend for decades. These friends would go on to manage as much as 40 percent of assets of industrial America in the early 1900s. Schwab worked hard at Edgar Thomson Works and took an interest in steel chemistry. Carnegie's partner Henry Phipps was an amateur chemist who gave the young Schwab a $1,000 for a home chemistry lab. Schwab moved fast to become Jones's assistant. He was sent as his representative to Carnegie's meetings in Pittsburgh. The gregarious Schwab was the opposite of the stern Frick. Schwab, however, lacked the corporate discipline of a Henry Clay Frick.

8. The Strike of 1887

The 1880s were some of the most turbulent years in American history. Between 1881 and 1886 there were 23,336 strikes.[1] Labor problems had hit the anthracite coal fields in the 1870s, and in the early 1880s, the problems moved to the Ohio coal fields. The bituminous fields of western Pennsylvania had at least avoided the violence. But the decade of the 1880s was one of labor problems all over the nation as well as the world. The coal fields in southwestern Pennsylvania consisted of company "patch" towns. The Knights of Labor had a large national following, but the Amalgamated Association of Iron and Steel and the Miners' Association were losing membership. Still, even the Knights had an unsuccessful strike record. The recession of the early 1880s had resulted in many lost strikes. Public opinion varied after the violence of the Railroad Strike of 1877, but local strikes over wages usually had public support. The unions were being forced to include immigrants into their organizations to win strikes. Capitalists were becoming more determined to resist, if not break the unions. Politicians had gotten involved in the 1880s, looking at six major points: child labor, women labor, working conditions, arbitration, the eight-hour day, and fair practices. Two factors were becoming a growing problem, immigrants and the socialists, both inside and outside the union. By 1886 a perfect storm was brewing over Frick's coal fields.

Part of that storm was the divide within the union movement itself. One part of the struggle was between crafts unions versus more general representation. The crafts union such as the Amalgamated represented only skilled labors, which accounted for less than 20 percent of most industries. The Knights of Labor called for all worker representation, which threatened the high wage structure and controlled membership of the crafts. The divide between the crafts and more general trade unions created a divide between nationalities. The Irish, German, and Welsh controlled the crafts, while the new immigrants such as the Slavs and Hungarians were discriminated against. As technology progressed, allowing machines and unskilled labor to replace skilled labor, crafts unions came under pressure for survival. Technology had broken skilled labor more in the mines, and the Amalgamated Miners changed to the Amalgamated Association of Miners and Mine Laborers to ward off membership drives of the Knights in the coal fields. An additional problem was the infiltration of the socialists into the union movement. The socialists had made inroads in the general trade unions, but they also played on the borders of the union movement, creating violence.

The labor problems were not so much rooted in the pay rate of the workers per se in the steel and coal industry, but in the sliding scales used. The skilled industrial workers were highly paid compared to the average workers. The unskilled workers tended to be paid the average national rate, but the work was by far more dangerous and the environment could be hot and toxic. The bigger problem was the policy of the capitalists to challenge workers for pay reductions in economic downturns, while in the good times of high profits, the capitalists did not offer increases. The idea of reducing wages in bad economic times was close to Carnegie's heart. The other problem was the short working life of these workers, which threatened families' economic well-being. Injuries were common, and often left a family without a breadwinner. Some historians like to picture it as a type of economic slavery, and while that is probably a bit extreme, the injury issue probably made the life of a plantation slave family more secure. The worker struggled for the opportunity that both Frick and Carnegie had known, yet Carnegie and Frick believed that, like themselves, a hard worker could rise from poverty. The rise of opulent lifestyles of the capitalists also created a problem. The distance of the capitalists from the workplace contributed to a type of blindness or ignorance as to the reality of the worker. Henry Clay Frick, living in Pittsburgh, lacked the closeness to the work of his grandfather Overholt.

Another problem of the decade was the well-publicized trips of Carnegie and Frick to Europe. While Pittsburghers like Frick and Carnegie were not as outrageous as the Robber Barons of New York, they still stood out in contrast to the miner or steelworker. The salaries of Carnegie's superintendents were large as well. Bill Jones of Edgar Thomson Works had demanded and received a salary equivalent to the president of the United States—$25,000 a year. Young Charles Schwab at Homestead Works received $10,000 a year, and Frick's right-hand man, Thomas Lynch, was making $5,000. While these men were respected and loved by the workers, their salaries were amazing, considering a skilled miner or steelworker made $500 to $700 a year, and an unskilled laborer made about $350 a year. The men were accepting of Jones and Schwab because they worked and lived in the steel towns. Jones was often right at the furnaces, and in fact, would die from a furnace explosion in 1889. The large superintendent company house still stood as a castle. Still, at least for the superintendent, the view of the mill or mine offered a daily reality. The mining towns, in particular, were dark and dirty. The miners lived a feudal type of life. There were economic chains which made them a type of serf to the company; some critics might say slave.

The decade of the 1880s was one of change in the coal fields of western Pennsylvania. First the crafts system of mining was breaking down from the use of technology, strikebreaking, and the use of immigrant labor. The technology of undercutting coal-mining machines and the use of explosives was taking the skill out of the miner's craft. A single miner could dig thirty tons of coal in a nine-hour day with the undercutting machine. Hand and pick mining could do ten tons (using three men) in a nine-hour day. The miner was reduced to a machine operator. The undercutting machine mined faster than coal could be loaded, requiring the hiring of cheap immigrant loaders. The influx of immigrants was a necessity because of the general unskilled labor shortage in the mill and steel districts. In addition, extremely low wages and political unrest in Europe made the move to America profitable for the individual. Laborers in America could earn a $1.00 a day, compared to 15 cents in Europe. This created a globalized labor competition similar to what we see today, except today capitalists take the factories to the cheap labor.

Eastern Europe became a major source of immigrant labor in the late 1880s. Slavs and Hungarians were brought in from Europe to fill laborer jobs and to break strikes. Agents usually offered a paid passage to America (although it was later deducted from their pay), and they received housing, upon which they paid rent. Some Slavs and Hungarians had worked their way into the tonnage jobs after several strikes, but the immigrants were asking for tonnage jobs. In addition, the nativists wanted the immigrants out of the coal fields. Nativist-hate strikes were not uncommon. As the industry grew, so did the number of immigrants taking jobs. Interestingly, the once-hated Irish immigrants of the 1820s were now the nativists opposing Hungarian and Slav immigration. The Irish-controlled Democratic Party took on the movement to pass immigration laws. This led to the involvement of politicians in the union issues.

The root problems in the mines were many and complex. Wages, of course, were a central issue, but there were many ancillary issues. Management control of the weight scales was considered an issue of fairness. Many miners questioned the accuracy and fairness of weights, which were the basis of payment. The strike in 1886 had resolved some problems such as the weight scales, but the anger was not pacified. Finally, the state of Pennsylvania passed a law against women going into the mines. The miners had been using their wives and children to dig coal. This family-type operation allowed the miners to dig more coal and thereby increase the income to the family. The same was true for the coke oven drawers, who were paid by the ton as well. There were more immigrants in the coke tonnage jobs. The owners tolerated this unusual arrangement because under the crafts system, the miner selected and paid his workers out of the price he received for coal dug. The whole system was in a state of flux and evolution. The use of mechanization and the breakdown of the crafts system created a void for needed supervision. The immigrant laborers were not of the apprentice system and required management supervision. Wages also needed to be adjusted for the increased productivity created by machines.

Frick was looking for wage cuts in 1886, but things were about to change. Frick imposed a large wage cut at the end of 1885 and the Coke Syndicate moved with Frick. In January 1886, women were prohibited from entering the mines, which ended the practice of wives working with the miner. This resulted in loss of family income. The Amalgamated Association of Miners and Mine Laborers, negotiating the tonnage paid to miners, wanted a five-cent-per-wagon increase on the seventy-five cents per wagon of coal paid. The Amalgamated also wanted about a 20 percent increase for the laborers making about a dollar a day. The complexities continued with the Knights of Labor, representing mainly the unskilled, asking only 10 percent. The demands started the Strike of 1886. The usually docile Slavs and Hungarians had a Spartacus-type leader in Steff Stanex, who endorsed a general strike on January 18 against Frick and all the owners in the Coke Syndicate. The tension between the Amalgamated and the Knights was patched over by the leadership of Steff Stanex. Now the skilled and unskilled united loosely, but progress stalled on all fronts. This was the first major show of worker solidarity.

Frick and the owners moved to evict miners from their homes, which took the tension to the breaking point. The Slavs and Hungarians turned to violence as a standoff froze any decision. The area exploded as idle miners fueled their anger with heavy drinking. Local sheriffs quickly lost control as armed battles started. At Frick's Morewood mine, shots were fired, and a number of workers were wounded and one killed. Many more were injured throughout the coal fields. By January 19, five immigrant miners and three American miners had been killed. Carnegie and his associates forced Frick to settle the strike quickly. The strike had shut down 75 percent of the nation's metallurgic coke supplies, and the Chicago steel men were on Frick to settle as well. Frustrated, Frick reinstated the wages and promised to review the other complaints. Frick now held less than a third of the stock in H.C. Frick Company, and Carnegie and his partners called the shots. The settlement had resolved very little and left many resentments. A grand jury refused to indict strikers who had been jailed for violence, and Frick had to pay court costs. With Frick forced to settle, the Coke Syndicate collapsed and the union won a 10 percent increase across the board. Coke prices went up seven to ten cents to the steelmakers, and direct labor costs increased seven cents a ton due to the wage increase.

One of these resentments arose from Andrew Carnegie's hatred of any bad press. America's most popular weekly magazine, *Harpers Weekly*, was giving negative coverage to Carnegie over his labor approaches. Carnegie, now living in New York and surrounded by writers and artists, started to see himself as a labor and capital philosopher. This was a strange twist for Carnegie, who had been playing hardball with the unions since the 1860s. He opened himself up to a great deal of criticism in 1886, when he published his essay "An Employer's View of the Labor Question." Carnegie argued the existence of a "worker republic." Carnegie declared: "Now the poorest laborer in America or in England or indeed throughout the civilized world, who can handle a pick or shovel, stands upon equal terms with the purchaser of labor."[2] The whole article was, at the very least, inconsistent with Carnegie's actions at Edgar Thomson Works. It was a slap in the face to Henry Clay Frick. One positive aspect was that Carnegie argued for national arbitration, which he would at least try. The article did, however, point out some differences between Carnegie and Frick. Carnegie viewed the labor-management dispute as a type of chess game, while Frick saw it as an actual war game. Neither Carnegie nor Frick could relate to the worker's view.

The most amazing statement in Carnegie's essay revealed his lack of understanding of the problem, which lay in his refusal to see that *he* was the problem he was describing. In the essay he stated:

> Salaried officers ... cannot possibly have any permanent interest in the welfare of the working-men.... It is the chairman, situated hundreds of miles away from his men, who only pays a flying visit to the works and perhaps finds time to walk through the mill or mine once or twice a year, that is chiefly responsible for the disputes which break out in intervals.[3]

Clearly, Carnegie in New York was the very person he was talking about. He must have rationalized that he had men like Bill Jones taking care of business, and even that would have made sense if Carnegie had let his managers on the scene make the call. Carnegie had the answer but he didn't realize it. Executives such as Andrew Carnegie, Henry Frick, Tom Carnegie, and Henry Phipps were no longer in touch with the workforce, as labor problems increased in the latter half of the 1880s.

Labor problems on the national level were also exploding. On May 1, 1886, the Knights of Labor staged a nationwide stoppage for one day in support of the eight-hour workday. The stoppage of 340,000 workers sent a strong message to the capitalists of the time. As violent as the coal fields had been, they received less press than labor problems in the cities. Nationally, Chicago had become the hot spot of labor problems. In Chicago, the Socialist Labor Party had formed an informal alliance with the Knights. The May 1 strike merged with problems at Chicago's McCormick Harvester Works a few days later. At the McCormick Works, socialists and anarchists mixed with the workingmen, triggering a riot. The police were called in to break it up. Shots were fired and four men were killed and many injured as the crowd panicked. The anarchists printed up flyers asking for revenge, and on the evening of May 4, over three thousand gathered in the Haymarket. This time, bombs exploded and more shots were fired, and eventually another ten were killed and hundreds injured.

Eight anarchists were found guilty and four were hanged. Many of the leaders were connected to earlier socialist conventions in Pittsburgh. In general, the Haymarket created a wave of xenophobia, filling American city newspapers with stories about local connections and links between unions and local anarchist cells. Even though Pittsburgh had only had small demonstrations that May, fear grew as Pittsburgh connections were uncovered. It would be considered the first "red scare." Capitalists and factory owners became sensitive to violence when union activities were organized. Pittsburgh still had the memories of the destruction of the 1877 Railroad Strike. The Haymarket was the peak of the great labor upheaval of the 1880s.

The Haymarket Riots polarized urban America. There was a type of anti-labor movement that associated violence with unionization. The countermovement was even more striking. In Chicago during the summer of 1886, the Central Labor Union, the Amalgamated, socialists, and the Knights of Labor formed the United Labor Party. In the fall elections the United Labor Party elected a state senator and six assemblymen. Labor parties won local and state elections in numerous states. In Carnegie's home city of New York, the Labor Party almost elected a mayor, and while losing, the labor candidate got more votes than the Republican candidate, Teddy Roosevelt. The elections pushed state legislatures to pass new labor laws. The capitalists reacted by forming more owner associations, and a public relations effort to link socialism to trade unionism. The success of labor would lead to fractionalization of the movement in 1887, and a lot was based on the exclusion or inclusion of socialists. It should be noted that in Pittsburgh and Connellsville, the socialists had a very small following, but the capitalists of Pittsburgh feared the socialists.

The Coal Strike of 1886 had never been fully settled, and in 1887 problems once again rose to the breaking point. Frick had reviewed the issues with Thomas Lynch and a friend and Catholic priest, Father Lambing. The assessment was that the Knights would settle for a 10 percent general increase, while the Amalgamated would require 20 percent. Frick and the syndicate made an offer of around 10 percent. Labor costs were critical to the owners. The coal and coke industry was extremely labor sensitive, with labor making up over two-thirds of the cost of production. Some estimates of labor costs were 85 percent.[4] Carnegie, the Chicago steel men, and the public wanted the issues in the coal fields resolved. The general strike was rapidly approaching the death rate of the Great Railroad Strike of 1877. Frick now was under public pressure to do something, and he knew that increasing profits would soon be reported. Carnegie was pushing for an end because the steel business was booming. Frick offered a wage scale increase and a labor increase of about 10 percent. No one wanted the violence to continue. Arbitration got everybody back to work and ended the major violence. Both sides, however, were on high alert and prepared for war. The owners brought in Pinkerton Guards and enlisted a Coal Police force. Strikers drilled and paraded their "troops." The Coal and Iron Police had been authorized by 1866 state legislation, which had resulted from early violence in the eastern Pennsylvania anthracite coal fields. Frick's operations under Thomas Lynch actually were more peaceful than most, but profit reports were about to change things.

In 1887, H.C. Frick Company (which Carnegie controlled) was about to report solid profits. The company now had 5,000 coke ovens or 45 percent of the region production. Frick was producing an amazing 6,000 tons per day. Henry Clay Frick remained the president of the Coke Syndicate of coke producers. The Carnegie brothers were demanding a scale reduction in the price of coke shipped to Carnegie mills, and Frick hoped to pass on the cost reduction to the miners. Carnegie had lowered rail prices in the 1885 downturn. Frick, however, saw the boom in the market and realized he would be lucky to hold the workers to a 10 percent increase. It was an example of the lack of coordination between Carnegie's various corporate divisions and his own total focus on the steel operations. In early 1887 the Carnegies agreed, under Frick's leadership, to ask again for a 10 percent increase, while the workers wanted 20 percent. The timing didn't follow the Carnegie model as the economy had taken an upturn. With Tom Carnegie dead, Henry Phipps headed up Carnegie's local empire. Both the Knights of Labor and the Amalgamated Association of Miners and Laborers rejected the wage scale offered but agreed to arbitration. The arbitration board allowed for three union representatives and three owner representatives and a seventh leader mutually agreed to. As the board deliberated, both sides prepared for a possible clash. The board ruled in favor of the owners for a 10 percent increase, and the national unions certified the result. The local lodges of the Amalgamated Association of Miners and Laborers refused to accept the decision, and the strike began on May 7, 1887. The Knights of Labor declared the strike illegal. The strike bordered on anarchy, with the workers split.

The strike turned violent quickly as machinery was destroyed and mines dynamited. The Hungarians and Slavs took to the town streets. Shots were fired. The involvement of the Hungarians changed the dynamics. Locals tended to be nativists and wanted the removal of the Hungarians. The local press supported the owners and demanded that the area be cleaned of Hungarians. Frick was preparing for the possibility of bringing in blacks for strikebreakers. The public generally supported Frick and the owners because of the hatred of the Huns (a generic term for Eastern Europeans). Even the union was split, led by nativists such as George W. Sarver. A *National Labor Tribune* editorial showed how deep and broad the hatred in answering the problem of the "Filthy Hun": "The general invitation to the oppressed of all lands to come to America ... certainly never contemplated the introduction of so miserly low carrion as these Huns, the worst probably of the civilized world's people. The republic cannot afford to have such ignorant animals within its borders."[5] The situation was chaotic and approached anarchy throughout western Pennsylvania. Still, the Hungarians had the numbers to continue to block production. Union leaders tried to maintain solidarity, but the Knights, by siding with the arbitration board, lost support. Skilled and unskilled workers forged a loose alliance, but Frick had gained public support and the upper hand. Frick also paid and stood behind his salaried employees during the strike. Frick was extremely generous and helpful to the foremen, who represented the newest and lowest level of management. Frick also was the first to promote Catholics (Thomas Lynch was a Catholic), Hungarians, and Slavs into this entry level of management.

The problems had developed quickly while Carnegie was preoccupied. The fifty-two-year-old Carnegie had been married in Pittsburgh on April 22, 1887, and had left for his honeymoon. Interestingly, just before the wedding Carnegie and his wife signed a prenuptial that stated Carnegie planned to give away his fortune. Carnegie was changing, but his new "calling" was more a justification of his accumulation of money. Frick, however, remained all his life simplistic, a businessman and a capitalist. Frick moved forward to hold out against the strike even with opposition in the Carnegie organization, some Chicago steel makers, and J. Schoonmaker of the Coke Syndicate. Victory for Frick was clearly near; furnaces going down at Edgar Thomson Works and Chicago, however, built pressure on Frick to end the strike.

Henry Phipps contacted Carnegie, who was in Scotland, and they decided to pull back their call for lower coke prices and further pressure Frick to end the strike. Carnegie had a huge increase in rail orders at Edgar Thomson in the summer, and he did not want to lose sales over a few pennies on the price of coke. Seven Carnegie mills had been shut down at a cost of $250,000 per hour. In addition, Phipps called on Frick to settle the strike at whatever the increase. For Frick, it was now a matter of pride. Carnegie once again had failed to support him. Furthermore, Frick was president of the owners' association, who wanted to hold out against the workers. The Syndicate charged H.C. Frick Company $90,000 for breaking with the association. Frick did have the support of Carnegie's competitor, Cambria Iron; but the Chicago steelmakers, like Carnegie, wanted coke to meet orders. More importantly for Frick's ego, he was reduced to a Carnegie puppet. Frick, the "King of Coke," had been struck down by the prince of steel. His leadership among the owners had been destroyed. Looking at it as an affront to his "manhood," Frick offered his resignation in three weeks pending Carnegie's acceptance. The strike standoff continued, but by the first week of June, Carnegie's Edgar Thomson furnaces were being banked, as well as those of the Chicago steelmakers. Carnegie sent an ultimatum to Frick to end the strike and restore wages. Frick obeyed but the headline read: "Coke Men Crushed. Carnegie Thunders from His Castle in the Scotland Highlands. His Bolt Wrecks the Syndicate. Millionaire Operators Mourn and Hungry Hungarians Dance with Glee. President Frick Overpowered. Resigns." It was a tough public rebuke of Frick and a rare personal defeat.

Once again Carnegie had saved his own reputation. For the Knights of Labor, their role in the coal fields had ended with the Amalgamated's holding out successfully. The Strike of 1887 and Carnegie's decision to force an end to the strike was a victory that miners could point to. It had also proved the importance of solidarity, which would become the hallmark of miners into this century. The Amalgamated Association of Miners and Mine Laborers set a path for American unions. The Amalgamated Miners in western Pennsylvania became the

Miners' National Progressive Union in 1888, representing the full workforce. This alliance would ultimately lead to the formation of the United Mine Workers of America in 1890.

Frick's resignation came as a blow to Carnegie, who badly needed men like Frick, so he could travel and write. Still, Carnegie, like his idol Napoleon, was a general who could not tolerate insubordination. Frick's reaction was quick and decisive; he not only resigned but offered to sell Carnegie all of his remaining shares in H.C. Frick Company. Carnegie ignored the stock offer but allowed Frick's resignation. Frick planned to vacation in Europe to get away from it all. On July 22, 1887, Frick, his wife Adelaide, son Childs, daughter Martha, mother-in-law Mrs. Childs, and Adelaide's sister, Martha Howard, sailed for London. They had been planning such a trip for art collecting for months and now was the perfect time to get away from the press. Frick arranged for Andrew Mellon to manage all his personal investments while in Europe. Frick would also write frequent letters to Andrew about the trip, art, and finances.

One of Frick's traveling partners, John Wanamaker (1838–1922), would become an important friend. Wanamaker, who had pioneered the idea of the department store with his "Grand Depot" in Philadelphia, had become a major supplier to Frick's string of twenty general stores in the coal fields. Wanamaker in 1887 was a major Republican fundraiser, and he would land a $20,000 donation from Frick for the Benjamin Harrison campaign. Wanamaker had also gained a reputation as a businessman known for his application of the Golden Rule and Christian principles. Yet Wanamaker was outspoken about his fear and hatred of unions. He had become a fierce opponent of the Knights of Labor; yet he pioneered such employee benefits as profit sharing, free medical care, pensions, and employee education. These were business practices Wanamaker shared with his good friend and Frick's neighbor H.J. Heinz. Wanamaker was a serious art collector much like Frick. This trip Wanamaker shared his love of art with Frick, and Frick would buy two of his earliest paintings, Tito Lessi's *The Reader* and Meyer von Bremen's *The Darlings*. Frick was struggling for most of this European trip with his problems with Carnegie.

Carnegie was also struggling with his relationship with Frick. Carnegie's mind about Frick's leadership changed dramatically when the July numbers showed that wages were 12.5 percent higher than his competition. Having higher costs than the competition was a cardinal sin for Carnegie. Carnegie had realized his mistake and realized the weaknesses of his partners Henry Phipps and John Walker. Phipps, who was Carnegie's senior partner, was loyal but not a great businessman. In particular, he lacked the ability to stand up to Carnegie when necessary, which men like Bill Jones and Henry Clay Frick could do. Carnegie was still missing his brother Tom, who had run the Pittsburgh operations so successfully. Frick had pointed out that Carnegie's failure to stand for the arbitration decision would erode the very progressive use of arbitration that Carnegie had called for as part of the "workers republic." The strike of 1887 would indeed convince steelmakers that arbitration did not offer a solution. Carnegie had made a major mistake in his pursuit to satisfy customers and the union. Carnegie badly needed managers that could tell him when he was wrong.

When Frick and his family arrived in London on August 2, he received a telegram from Carnegie inviting him to the castle in Scotland. Frick turned down the invitation and went on with his plans to visit France and Germany. In later September, Frick reconsidered and planned to visit Carnegie. As a result, the party split, with Frick, Adelaide, and Adelaide's sister heading for Scotland, leaving the children with a governess in Paris. The exact nature of the visit is unknown, but it went a long way to healing the rift. Carnegie had no real backup for Frick in coke production, so Carnegie needed Frick. During the visit to Scotland, it is believed that young Martha may have swallowed a pin. In any case, Martha started to exhibit a mix of symptoms. The European doctors were not sure what the problem was, but the family was anxious to get home and have their neighbor and doctor, James McClelland, look at her. Frick booked the earliest ship and on October 9 left for New York.

A few weeks after Frick's return, Frick was once again appointed president of H.C. Frick Company on November 10, 1887. Frick also received some additional compensation from Carnegie. First, H.C. Frick Company received the $90,000 lost to the Coke Syndicate. Frick received more stock in Carnegie's steel company and started to replace the retiring Henry Phipps. Frick was determined to prove himself as one of Carnegie's best steel lieutenants. Frick would never again, however, trust Carnegie fully. Interestingly, Bill Jones of Braddock noted: "I don't particularly like Frick, nor do I admire him, but at least, you always know where you stand ... with Carnegie, it is a different matter, he is a sidestepper."[6] Carnegie in 1887 was a writer, philosopher, labor historian, patron of the arts, millionaire, corporate mogul, and philanthropist. No one was sure which Carnegie might show up. Frick never envisioned himself as anything but a businessman and capitalist. Even in his art collecting, he was never an elitist but a passionate collector.

While Carnegie espoused the highest virtues of capitalism behind the scenes, he was a tough player. As 1887 closed, Carnegie's Edgar Thomson Works labor contract was due for renewal. Rail prices were down 20 percent, and Carnegie was again looking at wage reductions at the works. Carnegie viewed economic downturns as opportunities. Carnegie had been upset with the fact that Edgar Thomson's wages were 6 percent higher than the competing mills of Chicago. Some of the problem had been in the conversion of Edgar Thomson Works to an eight-hour day. Carnegie was again ready to overrule a trusted manager in Bill Jones of Edgar Thomson Works. Jones was no lover of the union, but he did believe in a fair deal for his workers. But while he could argue with Carnegie, Carnegie was still in charge. With prices down and winter starting, Carnegie had the high ground once again on the battlefield. On December 17, 1887, Carnegie announced plans for a shutdown to upgrade machinery.

It was an old ploy from Carnegie's playbook and illustrative of Carnegie labor tactics. The Knights of Labor, which was the only operative union, offered their proposal for the upcoming contract to Bill Jones on December 28. Jones did not respond immediately, having to discuss the details with Carnegie. Jones was told to ask for a 10 percent wage reduction. Next, Carnegie went to the press to present his case. His selection of the *New York Times* showed that he was addressing not the steelworkers of Braddock, but the his liberal and aristocratic friends. In a January 20, 1888, *New York Times* interview, Carnegie set the basic justification: "It is only fair to ask the men to submit to a 20 percent reduction in wages." Carnegie based this on a 20 percent decline in rail prices. Carnegie tried to seem benevolent by only requesting a 10 percent pay cut. The cut would apply to both skilled and unskilled labor. Finally, Carnegie announced that he would submit to arbitration. While arbitration was in vogue, both Carnegie and the union wanted to avoid it. Arbitration had not proved to be a useful way to resolve issues, as had been seen only a few months before in the 1887 coal strike. Still, Carnegie's many articles on labor and capital in 1886 had held arbitration up as a solution. Carnegie needed a way to avoid going to arbitration, or at least a public excuse to avoid it.

The Knights of Labor supplied that excuse. The Knights offered to go to arbitration for six months of the three-year contact. The union needed to get Carnegie off the high ground. Winter, lower rail prices, and low orders strengthened Carnegie's hand. The idea that the union would negotiate again in the summer would help. The men could live off their summer gardens, and chickens and hogs, which often roamed the streets of Braddock. Furthermore, heating coal was needed. The delay would also give time for the rail market to firm up. In this respect, this was a typical chess game for the union and Carnegie. Jones and Carnegie refused the arbitration deal, and Carnegie then toughened the deal by demanding a return to two twelve-hour shifts per day in place of three eight-hour shifts per day, which required more manpower. This would particularly hit the unskilled labor, which was paid by the day. Jones was in the middle. Carnegie argued the high costs of the eight-hour shift to Jones with the labor costs reports. On the other hand, Jones was also angry with the Knights of Labor, who had not pressured the Chicago mills to move to an eight-hour day, which would allow Carnegie to point to lower labor costs at the Chicago rail mills. The negotiations slowed and the rail market remained depressed. When Carnegie had a strong hand, he was a stonewall. Carnegie continued to make his case in the press, this time the local press directed at the union members and community.

In March, a union group went to New York to talk directly with Carnegie. As usual, he was a charming host and reaffirmed that he would not use scabs to replace the workers. Carnegie was happy to discuss his theory of a sliding wage scale based on steel prices, which he had put in writing since about 1886 in the nation's magazines. Carnegie suggested that the men at least give the sliding scale a trial. The sliding scale applied only to the tonnage (skilled) workers. This struggle between skilled workers paid by the tons produced versus unskilled workers paid by the hour was a problem for both the union and Carnegie. The Knights had always tried to maintain solidarity between the skilled and unskilled workers. The plant "closing" continued into April. Carnegie used the press to make his strongest case that Edgar Thomson Works was not meeting the competition of the Chicago mills, and Pittsburgh would suffer in the long run. Carnegie even won over the *National Labor Tribune* (paper of the Amalgamated Association), which stated Carnegie was "only submitting to market pressures."[7] In fact, the *National Labor Tribune* documented the difference as a total cost per position of $43.60 in Chicago and $46.35 in Braddock.[8] Both the Braddock Knights and Bill Jones had been undercut. Carnegie realized by mid–April that he had won the public relations battle, and Jones believed the men would return to work under Carnegie's offer, regardless of what the union said. Jones started to go through the motions of preparing the Works for a long shutdown. The people of Braddock were hungry and their morale was broken. Stores were closing down. Father Hickey, Catholic priest in Braddock, called for a referendum to return to work, but the union balked at such a vote.

Jones and Carnegie made the decision on April 19 in New York to open the mill to anyone that would agree to terms. The terms were tough, and were couched in an "individual" contract between the worker and company. In effect, it was a "yellow dog" contract requiring a worker not to join a union. Additional terms were a rate cut, new sliding scale, and the return to the twelve-hour day. Jones was confident that the majority of the workforce would be happy to return to work; if not, he was prepared to replace the needed workers. Jones was sure that the skilled workers would sign, but he was unsure of the Eastern European element, generically referred to as the "Hungarians." Jones hired a group of Pinkerton Guards to protect the mill against violence. Pinkertons were outsiders to the community, since local law enforcement often hesitated to fully enforce the law. The *Pittsburgh Press* headline on Monday, April 23, 1888, read "Braddock's Battlefield. Warlike Character Around the Edgar Thomson Works." Jones did send emissaries to Braddock's saloons to help calm things and talk directly to Hungarian leaders such as Joe Wolf. Bill Jones's willingness to talk directly to the men was his real strength. They might have opposed him, but they trusted him and even liked him. Jones was known to take money out of his own pocket to help a struggling worker. Jones had worked with the Knights over the years, although he felt let down by them over the eight-hour day. The Knights of Labor at Braddock were now divided along many lines.

The final result is that the men returned to work and the Knights were crushed at Edgar Thomson Works. For Carnegie, it was a complete victory. Even the immigrant unskilled workers broke with the union. Jones was happy to have the union out of his shop as well. The public had mixed feelings. Citizens after the Haymarket riots had little sympathy for unions, but bringing in Pinkertons seemed to be a step too far. Carnegie and Jones went a step further to eliminate the union by firing ringleaders. In addition, about a hundred workers were blacklisted in the Pittsburgh area. Still, the workers did not support the union's call for a boycott. This management victory was pulled off with minimum violence thanks to the skill of Bill Jones, the very personal skills so lacking in Henry Clay Frick. In the end, Edgar Thomson had reduced labor costs an amazing 18.8 percent with the reductions. Carnegie also got his trial sliding scale, which would tie production rates paid to the price of steel and the tons produced. It should be noted that tonnage workers, like those in the Amalgamated, liked the sliding scale (depending on rate) because it paid on production, not by the hour. The sliding scale was born out of the crafts approach to manufacturing. The more general approach to labor by the Knights of Labor favored an hourly wage scale per job, which is more common in today's labor management.

Carnegie, Frick, and the Pig Iron Aristocrats did have common goals and even alliances with the union on other issues. The congressional election of 1888 was as important as the presidential election for the steel industry. The Cleveland administration continued to push for lower steel tariffs, and Congress had been mired in a floor fight over tariffs. The tariff issue was split on political lines. The Democrats representing the farmers of the Midwest and non-industrial South wanted the low prices of free trade policies. The industrial North and the Republicans wanted American industry protected from cheap imports. The Democrats' success with unions had been due to the loyal support of the Irish, who controlled the leadership. The Irish loyalty to the Democrats had roots in the nativist and anti-immigrant groups (particularly anti–Irish) within the Republican Party. Interestingly, most non–Irish workers tended to vote Republican in the 1870s and 1880s. Republican Congressman McKinley of Ohio needed help in the House, and the Democrats had to be unseated. The Republicans targeted three free-traders: William Ralls Morrison of East St. Louis, Speaker of the House John Carlisle of Kentucky, and Frank Hurd of Toledo. Morrison had been a target of Republican gerrymandering for years, but all had been unsuccessful. The year 1888 was different in that Republicans had labor support, in particular the Knights of Labor. Strangely, the Knights might publicly support a candidate while its members secretly campaigned for another. Local Knights chapters often went against national endorsements to support high-tariff Republicans. The steel tariffs, however, were important to labor and capital. The Master Workman of the Knights, Terrence Powderly, is believed to have issued a directive to defeat Morrison.[9] The situation was similar with lodges of the Amalgamated Association Iron and Steel Workers. Pittsburgh iron and steel masters had a number of large funds for political action.

One Knight and Republican operative was John Jarrett. Jarrett had started as an immigrant puddler in Sharon, Pennsylvania. He had been a leader of the Knights and a Pittsburgh Lodge member. He had served as president of the Amalgamated Association of Iron and Steel Workers during the first Homestead Strike of 1882 with the Pittsburgh Bessemer Company. He had invested in the iron and steel industry over the years, although the sources of his investments and money are not clear. Jarrett had connections to Pittsburgh industrialists such as Frick and Carnegie. The owners' funds were hidden in organizations such as American Iron and Steel Association of the owners, and the Tinplate Association and Steel Sheet Association. Jarrett was sent to East Louis with a bag of money to oppose Morrison. Officially representing the Workingman's Tariff Club, which was a front for the owners' American Iron and Steel Association, Jarrett was also active in Carlisle's Kentucky district. In Toledo the Knights and the various glass worker unions united to target Hurd. Republican money poured into labor unions as well, such as the Window Glass Workers. The glass industry of northwest Ohio had been a huge benefactor of the McKinley tariffs. In the end, the Knights took down Morrison, Carlisle, and Hurd in stunning upsets, in particular the defeat of robber barons opponent and anti-capitalist Speaker Carlisle. Labor sent a strong message of its support for the McKinley tariffs, but it also created a type of all-out war between the Republicans and Democrats for the labor vote. This political war would spill over into the labor disputes of the time. The Democrats would remember well the Pittsburgh capitalists, like Frick and Carnegie, who financed their 1888 congressional election setbacks.

9. Providence

I went up on the embankment and looked across the bridge, which was filled full of debris, and on it were thousands of men, women, and children, who were screaming and yelling for help, as at this time the debris was on fire, and after each crash there was a moment of solemn silence, and those voices would again be heard crying in vain for help that came not.
— William Tice, Johnstown Flood survivor

Frick was not involved in the 1888 strike at Edgar Thomson, but he was a Carnegie partner and followed the actions closely. As Frick struggled to learn the steel business, his home life was changing as well. On September 3, 1888, the Fricks had a daughter, Helen Childs Frick,[1] while Martha continued to suffer from an unknown affliction. Dr. McClelland had prescribed a number of plant and animal potions to no avail. He performed a type of operation to remove the pin, but the results seemed to help little. Frick would always spend evenings with his children, and watching Martha suffer was very difficult for him.

On the business end, the years leading up to the Homestead Strike of 1892 were once again highly successful. Carnegie brought Frick into the company slowly, giving him the assignment to reduce transportation costs. Frick helped gain major reductions in moving ore from the Great Lakes to Carnegie's Pittsburgh mills.

The Carnegie empire of 1888 was the world's greatest manufacturing company. Edgar Thomson Works was the world's largest factory and steel mill and the largest supplier of railroad rails. Edgar Thomson alone made about 20 percent of the nation's rails. Carnegie mills also made about 18 percent of all the steel made in the United States, and Carnegie planned on further growth under Frick. H.C. Frick Company was the world's greatest coke maker. The massive Homestead Works used the open-hearth process to produce plate, forgings, and structural steel. Carnegie was making large inroads into the armor plate market. Carrie Furnaces across from Homestead produced the hot pig iron for the open hearths. Carnegie also had an integral transportation system linking supply and production.

Personally, Pittsburgh steelmakers had created unbelievable wealth in a time of no income or corporate taxes. Carnegie was worth about $20 million ($3.6 billion today). Henry Phipps' personal wealth was at $5 million (almost a billion today). Frick stood at $1 million in a list of over a hundred Pittsburghers worth a million or more. Most of the one hundred Pittsburgh millionaires lived in Pittsburgh's East End. In January of 1889, Frick and many of the East End millionaires converted their homes from natural gas to electricity with the help of George Westinghouse. Where New York and Wall Street millionaires invested in lavish parties, East End Pittsburghers invested lavishly in technology. Only a few years earlier, these millionaires had converted to natural gas from Westinghouse's Philadelphia Company (where Frick was on the board). President Grover Cleveland came to Pittsburgh to see the Philadelphia Company's distribution of natural gas. Cleveland hailed Pittsburgh's future of natural gas and electrical power. East End streetcars were the first to be converted to electrical power. Frick and Carnegie had also started to convert their factories to electricity.

Henry Phipps resigned in October 1888 as chairman of Carnegie Brothers. Carnegie's partner David Stewart formally replaced Phipps, but Stewart died on January 7, 1889, and

Frick was appointed president of Carnegie Brothers a week later. The deal included a prom-
ise to advance Frick's share in the company to 11 percent (the same share that Tom Carnegie
and Henry Phipps had held). Frick now was thrust into the public light, which was the most
uncomfortable part of the new job for him. Frick was, however, blessed with some of the best
business and operating managers ever assembled. These managers included Bill Jones at Edgar
Thomson, Charles Schwab at Homestead and Thomas Lynch at H.C. Frick Company, but they
also included some of the world's best lower and middle managers. Men like Julian Kennedy,
William Corey, James Gayley, and Alva Dinkey were the world's best furnace experts. This
collection of managers would become known as the "Boys of Braddock," and while loyal to
Carnegie and the organization, they were never fond of Frick. Some of this was the fact that
Frick had jumped ahead of Bill Jones of Edgar Thomson for the chairmanship.

Jones was ten years Frick's senior. Jones had just won over the union at Edgar Thomson
Works. While the adept strategy was that of Carnegie, Jones had a strong following among
the men. Jones had fought Carnegie on the twelve-hour day and got a trial for the eight-hour
day. Jones personally was part of the work force, often working alongside the laborer. Jones
had pioneered a true cooperative company store where prices were lower. He was a mechanical genius with many major patents. His "Jones Mixer" had revolutionized the steelmaking
process. He had been asked to speak at the iron and steel associations of Europe to explain
the efficiency of Edgar Thomson Works, which held every major world steelmaking record.
Engineers from the world over flocked to Braddock to see this marvelous steel mill. Nobody
in the Carnegie organization understood the steelmaking process better. Frick had little experience in steelmaking. Carnegie biographer Joseph Wall suggests that Carnegie had a different thing in mind. Wall notes:

> Frick would place the interests of his coke company over that of Carnegie's steel companies,
> Carnegie believed, as long as that remained Frick's only major interest. The best tactic, then, in
> redirecting Frick's loyalty would be to give him a larger share in the Carnegie association and, if
> possible, persuade him to accept a responsible position within the management of the company.[2]

While Bill Jones and his protégés such as Charles Schwab saw the promotion of Frick
over Jones as a injustice, Carnegie had made the right business call. Bill Jones was an outstanding plant manager, but he hated the boardroom. Jones would send his young protégé
Charles Schwab on the train to Carnegie's meetings. Bill Jones had no understanding of stock,
demanding to be paid in cash. Most of the other men who took Carnegie's stock would be
future millionaires. Jones could never have functioned as a corporate executive. Frick, on the
other hand, was comfortable in the boardroom and plant. He knew banking and investment,
serving on several corporate boards. Jones was the better manager with his people skills, but
Frick knew corporate games. Jones was a great motivator, but Frick was the better organizer.
Frick knew how to delegate. Jones, however, inspired loyalty in his subordinates, which Frick
never achieved. Frick lacked the personality of a Bill Jones or a Charles Schwab, and that
would cost him dearly. Frick was stately and sober, which would be critical to Carnegie, as
the company had become linked with the Republican effort to pass protectionist legislation.
Maybe Frick's strongest suit was his financial skills. Through friendships and business, Frick
had gained an expertise in finance and banking that no other Carnegie manager had. Frick
also had local political and business ties throughout Pittsburgh.

Frick would have his hands tied as Carnegie saw himself more as the prophet of labor
and capitalism. In early 1889, Carnegie started to write his essay, "Gospel of Wealth," which
would start a national debate. This was the type of publicity most steel masters and capitalists avoided. The first taste of this would come as Frick watched Carnegie dedicate his Braddock Carnegie Library in March of 1889. He included some of the ideas from the "Gospel of
Wealth," although toned down, in his speech. Carnegie biographer Peter Krass rated Carnegie's

speech with: "Here was Carnegie at his schizophrenic best: the hardened chieftain and sentimental benefactor, the man who could growl one minute and smile adoringly the next."[3] He tried to sell his sliding scale as opening a new era of harmony at Edgar Thomson Works. Carnegie used the opportunity to urge Homestead across the river to accept the Edgar Thomson Works' sliding scale. It was a warning shot to the Amalgamated Association, which Carnegie named, to turn around. Carnegie noted: "As a friend of labor, I advise them to accept the sliding scale and be done with labor disputes."[4] What Frick was hearing on that cold March day at Braddock's Leighton's rink would be the challenge and curse that would mark the rest of Frick's life. This type of public statement was contrary to the nature of both Frick and Jones, who would be there after Carnegie took the train back to New York. The sliding scale was not popular with the skilled tonnage workers, but Carnegie had forced it on the Braddock mill, and his next goal was Homestead. To Carnegie, the sliding scale offered a solution to keeping wages in line with market conditions. Carnegie had been pushing this sliding scale since his days with Union Iron Mills. The problem was that even if the market for steel remained high, the company seemed to want to adjust the contract scale down. In effect, the workers, based on history, assumed a lot of downside loss and limited upside gain.

At least Carnegie did believe the sliding scale, based on a three-year contract, would solve many problems. Carnegie defined the sliding scale approach in his 1886 *Forum* essay:

> What we must seek is a plan by which the men will receive high wages when the employers are receiving high prices for the product, and hence are making large profits; and per contra, when the employers are receiving low prices for products, and therefore small if any profits, the men will receive low wages. If this plan can be found, employers and employed will be in the same boat, rejoicing together in their prosperity, and calling into play their fortitude together in adversity. There will be no room for quarrels, and instead of a feeling of antagonism there will be a feeling of partnership between employers and employed.

It was a tough argument that the risk was the same for the employer and employee. Bad times had no affect on Carnegie's lifestyle, while the wage reductions to the workers caused major adjustments in the family budget. Work stoppages for workers meant a loss of income, not fewer dividends. The workers also had short earning lives due to injuries and age. Still, the Amalgamated union saw the possibility of some benefits, if favorable and flexible terms could be negotiated.

Unlike Frick, Carnegie's lifestyle was bigger than life. Frick's was one of work and family. George Harvey described Frick's day:

> None expected to work harder or longer than the Chairman himself, who rose methodically at six o'clock in the morning, walked two miles to his office to keep fit, was at his desk invariably at eight o'clock ready for business, conferred at lunch with one or more of his lieutenants, returned home when he had finished the day's work, joked with his seven-year-old son, played with his two little daughters, dined almost always alone with his wife quietly and quickly, studied business problems till early bed-time, and slept soundly till the whistle blew for the beginning of another identical day.[5]

Frick certainly worried much over Martha, who continued to suffer. On the weekends and Thursday nights, Frick might gather friends and neighbors such as Philander Knox, Andrew Mellon, Robert Pitcairn, James Reed, and George Westinghouse for a poker game. On Thursdays, Mrs. Frick held afternoon bridge and whist games for the neighborhood wives. Most nights were devoted to reading the newspapers, magazines, and books. Furthermore, Frick could spend hours viewing his paintings. It was a simple life compared to that of men like Carnegie.

Mrs. Frick also stayed out of the news. She managed the twenty-three-room and seven-servant home at Clayton. The staff included a cook, a maid, a butler, and a gardener. Clayton was beautiful but not overwhelming like most of the stone mansions in the neighbor-hood. Adelaide Frick was active in church and charities. A social paper described her in 1888: "The wife of Mr. H.C. Frick, the two or three times millionaire, is young and fair and charm-ing. Her home in the East End is one of the handsomest in the city and she is the fortunate owner of carriages, horses, diamonds and all the beautiful things that money can buy."[6] House cleaning was a major task in a Pittsburgh home, and Mrs. Frick managed it personally. Coal dust and metallic dust from the mills and factories left a coating each morning, which had to be swept from porches and walks. The dust required almost daily washing of light-colored fabrics. Dark-colored draperies and clothes were preferred. The sulfur in the air tarnished silverware quickly, requiring weekly cleaning. Studies had shown Pittsburgh to be number one in the world in soot fall (1,030 tons per square mile) followed by Glasgow (820 tons) and London (248 tons). The bad air was believed to complicate even minor ailments.

In the summer, Frick might "vacation" at Carnegie's "cottage" in the Alleghenies, at Cres-son, Pennsylvania, near the South Fork Hunting and Fishing Club and the Mountain View Hotel. Carnegie had built there because of the restorative powers of the air and water in the Alleghenies. Carnegie suggested that summers in the Alleghenies might help little Martha at least avoid the common Pittsburgh complications of thyroid and pneumonia. In reality, Carnegie's cottage was a beautiful two-story home, but it did lack central heating, cooking facilities, and servant's quarters. Carnegie would often rent a small cottage for his traveling staff of a coachman, a cook, a maid, and a nurse for his mother. Carnegie usually made his staff available to Frick when he vacationed there. Meals could be taken at the luxurious Moun-tain View Hotel. The hotel offered many family events and activities, and attracted the wealth-iest families of Pittsburgh and Philadelphia in the summer. The men could spend the evening at the nearby South Fork Club playing cards. Carnegie often had guests at his cottage. The nearby Cresson Springs were believed to have medicinal properties. The wealthy of Pitts-burgh had often fled to Cresson when typhoid epidemics hit Pittsburgh. Frick's neighbor Sal-lie Heinz (wife of H.J.) had died of typhoid across the street from Frick's Clayton. Of course, both Frick and Carnegie had suffered from serious cases of typhoid. Only a few years earlier another East End neighbor, Tom Carnegie, had died of typhoid. Typhoid, in combination with other ailments, was the number one killer of children in Pittsburgh, and Pittsburgh was number one in overall typhoid deaths. Since Carnegie's cottage was on the Pennsylvania Rail-road, Frick could commute to work.

In May of 1889, Frick faced a new problem with the famous Johnstown Flood following the failure of the dam at the South Fork Club. Frick had been an original member of the now large club for the wealthy, and he was a major shareholder. Frick remained an officer over the years, but his work schedule left him little time for recreation. The club had grown from 1880 into the summer club of America's wealthiest industrialists. Frick had made money on the growth of the club. Members now included most of Pittsburgh's East End. The club was not well known in Pittsburgh but had troubled Johnstown citizens for a decade. The artificially created mountaintop Lake Conemaugh was the world's largest and the center of local con-cern. Early in the 1880s, several dam problems had revealed that the dam had lots of engi-neering issues, but alleged negligence on the part of the club's officers was exaggerated.

This mountainous region around Pennsylvania is even today prone to flash flooding in which creeks might rise twenty feet in a matter of hours. Western Pennsylvania had just expe-rienced a winter of record snowfall in 1888–1889, and the rains continued throughout the spring of 1889. The spring floods of the Monongahela River and Allegheny River in Pittsburgh had been some of the worst on record. Downtown Pittsburgh had suffered some of the worst floods in recent history. The dam at South Fork had suffered problems every year, and this year the record snow and rain would put an additional strain on the dam. The rains of May

30 and 31 had caused the streams to overflow, resulting in some localized flash flooding. Friday morning, May 31, things were peaking, with the river at Johnstown rising a foot an hour, filled with trees and debris. That morning, lake rain gauges recorded five inches in a couple of hours, and the lake was rising an inch every ten minutes. The water input was a once-in-a-century event that would test even the best engineering of the area. The citizens of Johnstown had worried for ten years about the dam and such an event. That morning the rains and winds accelerated.

Johnstown was a main switching yard for the Pennsylvania Railroad and had towers in the hills to monitor traffic. The track up the line had been washed out, and east and west-bound trains were being held. A little after noon the tower telegraphed the yardmaster: "South Fork Dam is Liable to Break: Notify the People of Johnstown to Prepare for the Worst."[7] Amazingly, no one at the telegraph office took it seriously. The downpour was the hardest many had ever seen. Creeks and runs that were usually only a few inches deep were now up to four feet deep. Few of the actual club members were there because of the poor weather. Around three o'clock in the afternoon, the dam burst, and Niagara was unleashed on the Conemaugh Valley. The valley passage from South Fork to Johnstown is a narrowing gorge of about twelve miles, which created a wave 75 feet high! The wave reached Johnstown 57 minutes after the dam collapsed and would take ten minutes to fully pass through Johnstown with its devastating force of 20 million tons of water. Trains, houses, and the iron furnaces of Cambria Iron were torn away. The disaster would result in more than 2,200 deaths with many missing, putting it on a par with the 2001 attack on the Twin Towers. The Johnstown Flood remains number 3 on the list of U.S. natural disasters (the Galveston Hurricane of 1900 is number 1, Hurricane Katrina in 2005 is number 6, and the San Francisco earthquake of 1906 is number 7). It remains America's worst flood. The statistics were grim: 98 children lost both parents, almost 400 children under the age of ten dead, and 99 families completely wiped out. Many of the bodies were never found. After the killer wave, oil tanks caught fire, and the town burned for another day. The stories of death were unbelievable, including stories of a whirlpool of screaming men, women, and children. The property damage would reach $17 million.

The word of the catastrophe reached Pittsburgh within a few hours, even with telegraph lines down. Much of the response of Frick and the South Fork Club has been tainted by the labor issues of the period, but the initial national newspaper coverage had blamed the South Fork Club. The scale of the disaster meant it got national coverage. Reporters rushed to Johnstown to find unbelievable stories of horror. Surviving townspeople pointed to the South Fork dam and its mysterious capitalist members — a perfect story. Interestingly, like Hurricane Katrina, the initial headline in the *New York World* was "10,000 Dead." A few days later the later the *New York Sun* headline — "CAUSE OF THE CALAMITY — The Pittsburgh Fishing Club Chiefly Responsible." The *New York Times'* headline of June 9, 1889, was "An Engineering Crime — The Dam of Inferior Construction — According to Experts." As the reporters searched for the club's highly secret membership, the name Henry Clay Frick stood out. Frick's name had been on the incorporation papers, while most members were never noted in print records. There were a total of 61 members who paid a membership fee of $800 in 1889. It is believed that the members took a secrecy pact after the flood. Carnegie's membership remained secret for another year.

It took years for a full disclosure of members' names. The Johnstown Flood National Memorial lists the following members: Edward Allen (founder of Pacific and Atlantic Telegraph), D. Bidwell (owner of a mining explosives company), James Brown (treasurer of Hussey Company and future U.S. congressman), Henry Brunot (Pittsburgh lawyer), John Caldwell (Westinghouse partner), Andrew Carnegie, C.A. Carpenter (freight agent), John Chalfant

(Pig Iron Aristocrat, steelmaker, and banker), George Christy (Pittsburgh lawyer), Thomas Clark (Pittsburgh lawyer), Charles Clarke (Pittsburgh investor and Frick neighbor), Louis Clarke (son, inventor, and car manufacturer), A.C. Crawford (lawyer), William Dunn (building supply executive), Cyrus Elder (lawyer for Cambria Iron), Daniel Euwer (lumber baron), John Ewing (real estate baron), Aaron French (manufacturer of railroad springs), Henry Clay Frick, Walter Fundeburg (dentist), A.G. Harmes (machinery manufacturer), John Harper (banker), Howard Hartley (manufacturer of industrial products), Henry Holdship (industrial investor), Durbin Horne (owner of Horne Department Store), George Huff (industrial investor and future U.S. congressman), Christopher Hussey (owner of Hussey Metal Company), Lewis Irwin (lawyer), Philander Knox (lawyer, future Secretary of State and U.S. senator), Frank Laughlin (manufacturer), John Lawrence (paint manufacturer), John Leishman (Carnegie partner), Jesse Lippincott (baking powder manufacturer), Sylvester Marvin (founder of National Biscuit Company-Nabisco), Walter McClintock (merchant), James McCord (hatter), James McGregor (lawyer), W.A. McIntosh (president of Cleveland Gas Coal Company), H.S. McKee (banker), Andrew Mellon, Reuben Miller (steel executive), Maxwell Moorhead (iron manufacturer), Daniel Morrell (president of Cambria Iron Company), William Mullens, Edwin Myers, Frank Oliver (merchant), H. Patton (glass manufacturer), Duncan Phillips (glass manufacturer), Henry Phipps (Carnegie partner), Robert Pitcairn (superintendent of Pennsylvania Railroad), D.W. Ranking (doctor), James Reed (law partner with Knox and future federal judge), Marvin Scaife (Pig Iron Aristocrat), James Schoonmaker (coke producer), James Schwartz (president of Pennsylvania Lead Company), Frank Semple (banker), Christian Shea (Horne Department Store executive), Moses Suydam (industrial manufacturer), F. Sweet, Benjamin Thaw (Pig Iron Aristocrat and coke and iron manufacturer), Colonel Elias Unger (hotel owner and president of club), Americus Vespecius (banker),

Houses destroyed in the Johnstown Flood (courtesy Carnegie Library of Pittsburgh).

Calvin Wells (president of Pittsburgh Forge and Iron Company), James White (manganese ore producer), John Wilcox (civil engineer), James Willock (banker), Joseph Woodwell (hardware baron), William Woodwell (hardware baron), and H.C. Yeager (dry goods).

The condemnation of the press tainted what would otherwise be considered a swift, efficient, and committed response by Henry Clay Frick, although historians still question his motives. The night the dam broke, the East End members of the club met at the home of Charles Clarke, and a Pittsburgh Relief Committee was proposed. An executive committee was founded that included Henry Clay Frick, Henry Phipps, Robert Pitcairn, and James B. Scott (superintendent of Lucy Furnaces). The committee dispatched an army of volunteers, which included Bill Jones and 300 Braddock steel workers. With Frick's approval, Jones shut down Edgar Thomson at a cost of $15,000 a day. Frick worked his financial magic as well. The money flowed from many sources to the Pittsburgh Relief Committee. H.C. Frick Company donated $5,000, and Carnegie Company donated $10,000 (about $185,000 today). The Pennsylvania Railroad gave $5,000, and T. Mellon & Sons gave $2,000. The South Fork Fishing and Hunting Club gave $3,000 and emergency goods. Robert Pitcairn held a meeting at the Pittsburgh's Old City Hall and collected $48,000 in less than an hour. Citizen collections from cities were impressive—Pittsburgh, $560,000; Philadelphia, $600,000; New York, $516,000; and Boston, $150,000. Capitalists added tens of thousands, such as Benjamin Thaw, $3,000; John Astor, $2,500; Jay Gould, $1,000; George Westinghouse, $1,000; and Joseph Pulitzer, $2,000. The New York Stock Exchange gave $20,000; Macy & Company, $1,000; and Tiffany, $1,000. Foreign aid came as well, with Germany giving $30,000, and the London Stock Exchange $1,000. Buffalo Bill Cody held a benefit show at the Paris World's Fair, which Carnegie was attending at the time. Schoolchildren added thousands in pennies and nickels. It was the first major relief effort by the American Red Cross. All told, $3.7 million (about

Johnstown's main street after the flood (courtesy Carnegie Library of Pittsburgh).

$68 million today) in cash was donated. Non-cash donations were just as impressive, with 20,000 hams from Cincinnati and sixteen carloads of flour from Minneapolis. In general, food and supplies clogged the rails and roads, and the army was needed to distribute the supplies. Unfortunately, the heroic work of the executive committee was lost in the search for somebody to blame. To a large degree, Frick's reserved and cold personality worked against him publicly.

The Johnstown Flood filled the papers for months, and Frick remained the major link to the South Fork Fishing and Hunting Club. A number of suits were filed, but none proved successful. The Carnegie and Club lawyer Philander Knox always argued that there was no negligence, only an act of God. Historians continue to research the question of involvement, but the only issue appears the silence of the club members. The issue may best be summarized by flood historian David McCullough:

For to prove that any living member of the club had been personally negligent would have been extremely difficult. And in all fairness, it is quite likely, as the *Boston Post* suggested, that the clubmen themselves knew no more about the structural character of the dam than did anyone in Johnstown.[8]

While an original investor and listed officer, Frick never appeared to be very active in the club, but the catastrophe would be linked to his name.

10. Labor Disputes and
Personal Setbacks

In 1889, Frick was chairman of Carnegie Brothers, which had control of Edgar Thomson Works. William Abbott was Chairman of Carnegie, Phipps and Company, which controlled Homestead. William Abbott (1852–1930) had started as a clerk for Carnegie in 1873 at Edgar Thomson. Abbott had worked his way up to superintendent of Union Mills, and on to chairman of Carnegie, Phipps and Company. The Johnstown Flood had barely slowed Carnegie in the summer of 1889 as he toured Europe and plotted from his Scottish castle. He had one goal that stood out—break the Homestead Amalgamated union—but just as important was the implementation of his sliding wage scale. Carnegie had set the tone in his March 30, 1889, dedication speech at Braddock; but in May, he asked William Abbott to prepare a request for the union. Pressure was building at Edgar Thomson Works from Bill Jones to bring other Carnegie plants in line with Edgar Thomson. The contract was up at Homestead in July, so the work had to be done quickly. The proposal given to the union amounted to wage cuts as high as 30 percent for some workers. The unskilled laborers were not represented by the Amalgamated, and no wage cut for them was proposed.

For the time, Frick could only watch developments at Homestead. Carnegie, the steel Napoleon, assigned Frick to another front—that of crushing the emerging competition of Allegheny Bessemer Company across the river from Braddock at Duquesne, Pennsylvania. Carnegie and Abbott would take on the challenge of the Amalgamated union at Homestead. Carnegie made the proposal to the union at Homestead himself. The proposal at Homestead was quickly rejected and a strike began on July 1, 1889. The Amalgamated had won a great battle at Homestead in 1883, and it was confident that Carnegie could be broken, too. The union called the strike, but the unskilled non-union workers were not supportive; still, the plant was effectively shut down by a lockout. The union represented only about 800 of the 2,500 employees. Carnegie then offered individual contracts for the workers, which had worked at Edgar Thomson Works. Employees were dismissed who would not sign the new contract. Abbott made arrangements to bring in scabs and Pinkerton Guards. Allegedly Abbott made the call himself, but that seems inconsistent with Carnegie's interest in the proposal. In any case, tensions rose as trainloads of Italians and blacks arrived to replace the workers. Pinkertons were kept nearby in case of violence. The unskilled workers had to support the union to protect their jobs. On July 10, the scabs moved toward the mill, but more than two thousand Homestead employees blocked their entrance. As the day progressed, women and children joined the guard. The county sheriff tried to move the workers but then threw down his revolver and badge, unwilling to cause a riot. The cheering crowd had carried the day. Carnegie had underestimated the strength of the Homestead union. The union at Homestead, unlike the one at Braddock, had a long history of resistance.

Realizing the situation was bordering on serious violence, works manager Charles Schwab and union officer Hugh O'Donnell started negotiations. Meanwhile Abbott was openly advertising in the paper for scabs. As negotiations progressed, the Homesteaders set up barriers to prevent scabs or the Pinkertons, who were now across the river in Pittsburgh, from coming to retake the mill. The Amalgamated was also getting support at Edgar Thomson Works for a sympathy strike. On July 14, a young Slovak father and laborer was patrolling the bridge between Rankin and Homestead for scabs or Pinkertons. John Elko was accompanied by his wife and five-month-old daughter. A train approached and Elko tried to board it to check for scabs. He fell and his leg was cut off. He died shortly after. The *Pittsburgh Post* reported he died for "the cause." Hundreds of Homesteaders stood with the Slovaks and Hungarians at Elko's funeral. Elko's death at least temporarily united the workers. Charles Schwab realized the tide had turned, but the union wanted to settle too. The agreement gave the Amalgamated the right to negotiate for the men, and Carnegie got his sliding scale and wage reduction. The contract would be good until July 1, 1892. Carnegie, however, was extremely disappointed that Abbott allowed the Amalgamated to survive. Carnegie would ultimately blame Abbott's management skills for the failure, and it would mark the fall of Abbott in Carnegie's eyes. Carnegie had a bad habit of wanting a scapegoat for any setback. Carnegie cabled Frick from Germany: "It's too bad but we must expect three years or so of trouble now."[1]

Frick's efforts in the coke business were more successful in the summer of 1889. He successfully bought out his three biggest competitors. Frick had launched a brilliant strategy in 1889 that rivaled his boss and mentor's strategies. Acting as chairman of Carnegie Brothers, Frick moved to drive down coke costs to the steel mills. Frick took the price of coke to 80 cents a ton to take away competitors' customers. The consequences would be a reduction in steel costs and pressure on other coke producers. In addition, Frick gave his coke operators and miners a 5 percent wage increase, putting wage pressure on his competitors. The wage increase created strikes at Frick's competitors. First to fall was Ned Leisenring's Connellsville Coke & Iron Company. The Leisenring family's local history went back to the early days of Overholt. They had bought prime coals and had developed deep mining technology. By August, Connellsville Coke & Iron sold out to Frick for $3 million. Frick got 1,500 coke ovens and 9,000 acres of coal. Shortly after, Frick's old rival and nemesis Colonel Schoonmaker sold his 1,500 ovens and 5,000 acres of coal to Frick. Finally, J.W. Moore, one of the oldest coke producers, sold all 509 ovens and 2,000 acres of coal. Now Frick was the king of Connellsville coke with 7,000 ovens controlling 70 percent of the Connellsville coke production. Frick had proved his financial prowess, having built only two ovens in his career, but controlling 7,000 coke ovens through takeovers. Carnegie was duly impressed at Frick's competitive strategy to crush the competition.

September of 1889 brought a new challenge for Frick and Carnegie. On Friday, September 26, blast furnace "C" at Edgar Thomson bridged. Bill Jones, as was his nature, went to the scene of the problem. The captured gases caused an explosion, which fatally injured three men, including Jones, and injured another dozen. Two men died on Saturday, but Jones struggled at Homestead's Homeopathic Hospital for days. Carnegie even rushed his personal physician to him. Jones's death was a blow to the whole Carnegie organization. The funeral shut down the works and an estimated ten thousand people lined the streets of Braddock for the funeral of this popular manager. Frick, Phipps, and Carnegie's lawyer were part of the group that paid Jones's widow $35,000 ($675,000 today) for the patent rights for the Jones Mixer. The Jones Mixer had given a major advantage in the continuous flow of iron from the blast furnaces to converters. Many historians feel Frick was less than tactful, claiming the price paid was too low. The deal seemed reasonable at the time and was a necessary business transaction. Without the Jones Mixer, Edgar Thomson Works would not be the most productive in the world and the world's lowest-cost producer.

Biographer Peter Krass reported that Carnegie was so distraught over the death of Jones that he offered to sell his interests to an English concern.[2] Certainly, Jones's death was a blow to Carnegie, but nothing suggests Carnegie was seriously ready to quit. The hole in the Carnegie organization, however, was serious. Charles Schwab petitioned Carnegie for Jones's Edgar Thomson job. Jones had been Schwab's mentor and hero, and Edgar Thomson was the jewel in the Carnegie crown. Carnegie hesitated because, with Schwab at Homestead, he had his best "people person" in his most difficult mill. Schwab was persistent about the job. The decision to move Schwab to Edgar Thomson appears to have been finally made by Carnegie, although Schwab would now report to Frick. With Tom Carnegie and Bill Jones gone, Carnegie lacked managerial leadership. Abbott also appeared too weak without Schwab to settle things at Homestead. Carnegie also would begin to discuss matters of both his organizations with Frick. Carnegie was losing faith in Abbott. The larger problem would be the selection of John Potter to replace Schwab as superintendent of Homestead. Carnegie felt obligated to promote longtime employee John Potter.

John Potter was an introvert, more like Frick than Jones, but he had superior engineering skills. Potter had started at age fourteen in Carnegie's Union Mills as a greaser boy. He became an expert in metallurgy and steel rolling, which brought him to Homestead. Schwab had named him chief mechanical engineer. While Potter was known to lack people skills, Carnegie felt his bigger problem at Homestead was technical. Carnegie was negotiating with the government for a major naval armor contract. It would require the rolling of new one percent nickel steel, which required stronger rolling equipment and special heating practices. The success of one percent nickel armor was creating demand from all over the world, including a deal with Russia that Carnegie was working on. At the time America's only naval armor maker was Bethlehem Steel, and the American navy was expanding its fleet of armored battleships. Some of the first armor rolled by Potter went into the famous battleship *Maine*. Carnegie was even dreaming of entering the large cannon business by challenging Krupp in Germany and Midvale Steel in the United States. Carnegie was in the process of retooling Homestead to make armor, and Potter seemed like the necessary pick to achieve his goals. Frick probably had no say, since Homestead was under Carnegie, Phipps, and Company under Abbott.

Carnegie tied up Frick at the time with a major strategy play, and it would be a test for Frick in the steel business. Carnegie had focused Frick on rail competition of Edgar Thomson Works. A new company with superior technology, Allegheny Bessemer, was challenging the rail business of Edgar Thomson. Allegheny Bessemer had evolved from the failed Duquesne Steel, five miles up the Monongahela from Homestead. It had some old-line Pig Iron Aristocrats such as William Clark of Solar Iron Works and the Park Brothers of Black Diamond Steel. Clark and the Park Brothers were actually part of Frick's Duquesne Club network. The plant had been built by rolling master C. Ansler of Macintosh & Hemphill Company. The plant was fully integrated with blast furnaces, Bessemer converters, and rolling mills. The design was that which Sir Henry Bessemer had dreamed about in the 1850s—a direct rolling from ingot to finished size without three to four reheating steps. This method would cut processing costs significantly over those of Carnegie Edgar Thomson Works. In March of 1889, the works had started rolling but lacked the completion of the blast furnaces and was forced to heat cold pig iron in cupolas to supply hot metal to the converters. Carnegie realized that the direct rolling coupled with blast furnaces would be tough to beat, and Frick got the assignment to drive them out of business or purchase them before they could reach full efficiency.

In the summer of 1889, as Homestead was battling the Amalgamated Union, so was Allegheny Bessemer Company up river. Allegheny Bessemer had hoped to run non-union, but Homestead unionists had got into the works at the very beginning, when the company was known as Duquesne Steel in 1887. The battle of Carnegie Brothers & Company against Allegheny Bessemer was an example of cutthroat competition. It would initiate Frick into the steel business, and it would be Frick's financial prowess that supplied the final blow. Carnegie first started a campaign to put concern into the minds of railroad purchasers about the direct rolling process. Edgar Thomson Works even went to an extra heating of billets, suggesting it was needed to assure quality. Carnegie salesmen kept the pressure on the creditability of the Allegheny Bessemer direct rolling process. The Carnegie people, of course, had no real concerns about the process. In the meantime a combination of normal startup problems and union problems plagued Allegheny Bessemer. Allegheny fought hard by reducing prices and taking large orders away from Edgar Thomson Works. Frick used his tonnage leverage to drive prices down and put stress on Allegheny, which had a high-cost contract with the union.

Frick countered, cut, and pressured Allegheny Bessemer at every turn. He took the battle to the smallest of orders, as he had in the coke business. He and Carnegie worked with competitor Illinois Steel to cut prices and take orders from the new company. Allegheny Bessemer was highly productive, being able to produce almost 17,000 tons of rails in a month. However, the production costs were extremely high. Allegheny Bessemer's investors were now weakened, as the company needed cash inflows to keep moving and lacked profits as stoppages increased cost. Frick circled around the plant like a buzzard, offering key investors a chance to sell. They at first refused, but then came to terms for $1,000,000 in November 1890. Frick's old ties with Pittsburgh's Pig Iron Aristocrats gave him an inside track in making a very favorable deal in bonds at a price that represented a huge bargain. The owners had invested three times that much in the works. Historian Joseph Wall called it "a legend among steel manufacturing everywhere as the greatest bargain in the history of steel manufacturing."[3] Frick was off on the same strategy of buying physical assets cheap versus building. Carnegie was even more impressed with Frick's financial prowess.

Frick's managerial brilliance started to be noticed as well when he conceived of the Union Railway, which would connect Carnegie operations in the Monongahela Valley. Frick had made his first big money with the railroads, and he had gained valuable expertise in railroad operations and costs. Carnegie had been paying high freight rates to the railroads to move material and product between plants. Even within the plants, the Pennsylvania Railroad and B&O railroad owned the tracks and charged for internal moves. Carnegie had expanded his Pittsburgh plants with almost total disregard for the transportation costs, but after raw material costs, transportation costs were the largest cost factor for the Carnegie plants. Carnegie's bullying of the railroads to reduce rates had been unsuccessful. By the end of the 1890s, the Union Railway, with only a hundred miles of track, carried more freight than the nation's larger railroads. The building of Carnegie's own company railroad proved highly cost-effective, and building costs were repaid in months. Frick reduced the railroad switching costs on iron ore by an amazing 25 cents a ton. Frick reduced coke railroad rates from Connellsville by threatening to extend the Union Railroad. With a company railway, Frick looked to connect the blast furnace hot metal of Carrie Furnaces to the open hearths of Homestead directly. Seeing Frick's success, Carnegie wanted a railroad to pick up iron ore from the Lake Erie docks. The Union Railway was the beginning of integrating Carnegie Steel into a modern corporation. It was the business genius of Frick, not Carnegie, that laid the foundation for United States Steel. George Harvey called 1890 the happiest year of Frick's life because of his initial success in the steel business.

The success would prove that Frick could apply his financial and managerial skills learned in the coke industry to steel. Railroad companies started to look to Frick to join their boards. In a short time, Henry Clay Frick had crushed competition and contributed to a major reduction in costs. Carnegie had worked closely with Frick on the Allegheny Bessemer project and had been impressed with Frick's Union Railway Company. Carnegie was in Scotland most of the time but Frick executed orders perfectly and made quick tactical decisions when necessary. Carnegie was starting to talk to Frick more on matters at both of his partnership companies. Abbott's ability as chairman of Carnegie, Phipps, and Company looked extremely weak compared to that of Frick. Frick was pressuring Carnegie to put the two Carnegie companies together under Frick. Frick even talked to Abbott about the combination and Abbott agreed, realizing he had lost Carnegie's trust. Still Carnegie hesitated to promote Frick. Carnegie had some financial concerns as well as questions about Frick's ability to deal with the union. Men like Jones and Schwab had buffered Carnegie from real violence in his conquests of the sliding scale. Carnegie wanted that buffer between him and the union. Frick would prove himself to Carnegie in the winter of 1890-1891.

The real loser of the Allegheny Bessemer purchase had been the Amalgamated Union. Now the Amalgamated hoped to cause trouble at Edgar Thomson, which was non-union. The three-year sliding scale that Carnegie had negotiated at Edgar Thomson was about to expire on December 31, 1890. It would be an opportunity for Frick to prove himself in steel negotiations. The opportunity grew as Carnegie was distracted by a sickness of his wife in New York. Frick needed some freedom from Carnegie, who was always ready to overmanage and second-guess. Frick's first strategy was to downplay the growing problem at Edgar Thomson to Carnegie. The unskilled workers at Edgar Thomson were the bigger problem this time. Over the protests of Bill Jones, they had been moved to a twelve-hour day by Carnegie in 1888. Frick was not requesting a reduction for the skilled tonnage workers; even though the market had turned down. Other companies were asking for reductions, so the majority of non-union skilled workers seemed willing to continue under the sliding scale. Frick wanted to let the works remain non-union for a continuation of the sliding scale, in effect, holding wages in a downturn. The issue at Edgar Thomson focused mainly in the blast furnace department by workers who felt they were underpaid in comparison to wages at the rolling mills. In addition, the twelve-hour day in the hot and dangerous furnace department was particularly problematic. Frick would show tolerance in dealing with the non-union workers of Edgar Thomson.

The year-end trouble at Edgar Thomson offers a contrast and is instructive. Carnegie instructed Frick: "Advance in wages or cost at present time of course impossible.... Would have Schwab say to men at a time when we are trying every means to get orders even at a loss ... when Eastern mills have reduced wages we are asked to increase cost. It is not in our power to do so ... public sentiment will be with us."[4] Frick didn't believe there would be much trouble. Frick was well aware that the sliding scale agreement of 1888 had resulted in major cost reductions. Edgar Thomson plant manager Charles Schwab had even asked Frick and Carnegie to increase the wages in the blast furnace department, which had seen a 32 percent increase in productivity. The sliding scale had proven it could not only adjust wages in down times but also increase productivity, as the men tried to increase wages by more production. The issue, however, appeared to be mainly with the unskilled labors. The bigger influx of Eastern Europeans in the lower jobs was Hungarians, who tended to be young and single. Many came to earn money and then return to Europe. Frick had often recruited these workers as a form of temporary labor. The problem with the Slavs was that more were staying on and bringing over family. They were now looking to establish themselves and were stakeholders in the mill and community. The Knights of Labor had made some inroads with the Hungarian and Slav laborers and were threatening an uprising.

Frick made all the right decisions in this Edgar Thomson uprising. In particular, he kept Carnegie out of the tactical details. The protests were focused in the unskilled furnace jobs at the blast furnace department. Frick had a skillful popular manager in Charles Schwab to help out. Schwab lived up the hill from the Carnegie Library in the superintendent's home, but he was close enough to measure the pulse of the workforce. The problem elevated New

Year's Eve as heavy drinking continued up to the midnight deadline. Schwab was in his "mansion" but receiving information from many friends in the workforce. Schwab was also in constant communication with Frick at his home at Clayton by telegraph. When the raw materials handlers walked off the job at midnight, Schwab made the short carriage ride down the hill to the blast furnaces. Schwab had a group of friendly workers in place to keep the blast furnaces running. By three o'clock in the morning, Schwab telegrammed Frick that he had the situation under control. Schwab was able to get Wolfe's Tavern to close down, which dispersed the crowd. Schwab suggested that Pinkertons be brought in, but Frick refused. Instead Frick sent company lawyer Philander Knox to Pittsburgh to get the sheriff. Frick realized that no strong stand was needed. The sheriff took the train to Braddock and swore in deputies from among Schwab's best men. They needed to keep the blast furnaces running or major costs would be incurred.

Frick's response demonstrated the type of restraint he would be accused of lacking in the future Homestead Strike of 1892. Frick realized the problems of bringing in outsiders, and he preferred the sheriff's deputizing of loyal company men. Frick instructed Schwab: "If, in this manner, I can get our men to stand right by us, I would much prefer this to getting Pinkerton detectives."[5] Things calmed down at Braddock as Schwab and the sheriff worked things out. Frick showed restraint and blast furnace superintendent James Gayley was skillful in keeping the operation up and running. Frick's success seemed to result in part from Carnegie's being distracted by his wife's sickness. Without Carnegie second-guessing and interfering, Frick and Schwab showed good managerial skills in their approach. The sheriff showed similar restraint and managerial skills in meeting with the workers. Another plus in this Edgar Thomson uprising was the absence of a union, outside socialists, and reporters. Frick also had no interest in doing anything that might give rise to unionism. Carnegie was pleased that the sliding scale and twelve-hour day remained in place. The results for the workers were mixed. They avoided a general industry decrease in wages but had little say with any other grievances because they lacked a union.

Frick showed another side also in this uprising. Frick showed a kindness to one of men who had helped Schwab. Frick wrote:

> I understood you to say today that Michael Quinn, who died recently from injuries received at the hands of some Hungarians, while he was on duty at the works, was a widower, and left three children, a boy 12 years old and two girls younger. Such being the case we feel that we should make some provision for the children, and you are hereby authorized, when there is a satisfactory guardian appointed for them, to say that we will pay him, for their use, $3,000 [$55,000 today].[6]

While many have dismissed such kindness as an aberration, it is totally consistent with Frick's demonstrated soft spot for children. He was continuing to see his own daughter Martha suffer, who by this time had lost her hair. Frick was tormented daily seeing his young child waste away. Frick had also demonstrated a history of loyalty to foremen and front line managers who suffered during strikes.

The next crisis was a strike of 10,000 against H.C. Frick Company in February 1891. This represented a difficult problem in that Frick realized Carnegie would not stand for steel production to be reduced. Frick had anticipated this and had stockpiled months of coke to keep the mills running. He had learned that Carnegie had a low tolerance for shutting down furnaces at Edgar Thomson. Carnegie had gained the coordination that he needed by having Frick head Carnegie Brothers & Company overall interests. H.C. Frick Company in 1891 had 9,000 beehive ovens and 35,000 acres of coal. Though H.C. Frick Company dominated, the strike was a regional one against all the Connellsville operators. H.C. Frick Company was huge, dominant, and very profitable. Contrary to many reports, the company had the most peaceful relationships with the miners. Carnegie was hopeful that he could impose his sliding scale on the miners and coke workers. The workers were asking for an increase, but for Carnegie and Frick, this was a much bigger issue. They both saw this as a struggle for control with the union.

Union activity in the coal fields had been on the rise. The United Mine Workers of America had been formed on January 25, 1890, but there were other unions in play. The various unions, however, had built solidarity to protect against efforts to break them such as had been used previously. The issues in the mines were more extensive than in the steel mills. Safety and social issues needed to be addressed. On January 27, 1891, H.C. Frick Company had suffered a major cave-in at their Mammoth Mines and 109 miners were killed. The accident pointed out the danger of mining but did not reflect poorly on H.C. Frick Company. Thomas Lynch had made the company the model for safety in the industry. Both Lynch and Frick had always applied rigid work rules to address safety. Frick, Carnegie, and Lynch reacted quickly to the accident with a relief fund for the workers. A $25,000 relief fund was set up, administered by a relief committee consisting of two Catholic priests, a Methodist pastor, and the union.

The accident didn't slow the movement towards a strike. The owners still had the upper hand, but many union leaders sensed things were changing. The facts, however, suggested it was a poor time. The coke market was depressed and operations were at less than 70 percent capacity, and the Carnegie mills had stockpiled coke. There was a split between Carnegie and Frick on methodology. Carnegie wanted Frick to hold out without negotiations as long as possible, putting pressure on the miners and their families. Frick and his general superintendent Thomas Lynch felt they could force the issue in mid–March, as did the other independent owners. The United Mine Workers Association was asking for a ten percent pay raise, extra money for narrow work, extra for working a wet place, a limit on house rent, and an eight-hour day. Both sides appeared entrenched. Frick was working with the sheriff closely and had deputized a coal police force. The union had formed their own quasi-military unit. Riots broke out in late February, and increased as Frick's major competitor, W.J. Rainey, brought in Pinkertons.

What came next was one of the area's bloodiest strikes, forgotten to history and overshadowed by Homestead. The Morewood Massacre was bloodier than the Great Homestead Strike, but it is overlooked for several reasons. First, the rural nature of the mines caused few outside newspapers to follow events. The other reason was the hatred of the Eastern European immigrants, whom locals considered a plague.

In any case, Frick moved to bring the men back in mid–March on an individual contract basis. This was a typical owner strategy of lockout followed by individual contracts. He offered a sliding scale and a nine-hour day. The hope was the men would return, abandoning the union. The majority of the workers, particularly the Hungarians, stood in solidarity. Slowly, by the end of March, Frick had about 30 percent of the operations going. The presence of men working put pressure on the strikers. Frick and the other owners started to bring in blacks from the South, as well as Italians; these two groups were considered on a lower social level than the Hungarians. The strikers used violence where possible, since it was the only bargaining tool they had. Frick had strong political ties with bosses such as Senator Matthew Quay, and he persuaded the Democratic governor to send troops. The governor had hesitated because the Democrats were using these opportunities to build labor support in elections, but Frick's Republican bosses were able to call in favors. Using the National Guard gave perfect cover for the owners to get tough.

The prime operation of Morewood Mines became the focus of a final stand in the first two days of April. Morewood had 162 coke ovens ready for operation and was the center of the Hungarian community. It was said that the Hungarian's mental map was better known as Pennsylvania, and it had been the first large colony of Hungarians in the United States. A march of 1,000 miners led by a band was repelled on March 30, but a great deal of damage was done to the works. The National Guard was authorized to use force. Early morning on April 2, another group of 400 to 700 miners approached again. This time shots were fired, which ultimately resulted in nine dead miners and many wounded. The shooting resulted in arrests on both sides. More militia was called in, and Frick hired Pinkertons to guard company properties. Violence continued as the strike slowly moved to an end in May. On May 21 the United Mine Workers called for a formal end of the strike. It is not clear whether either side gained much. Carnegie got his sliding scale and pay cut, but the union, though beaten, was not crushed. Another setback for the unions put more pressure on the building crisis at the Homestead Steel Works. Carnegie seemed pleased with the results and publicly supported Frick. During the struggle, Carnegie and Frick often talked about the mistakes that Abbott had made at Homestead. Frick had proven himself up to any task, and Carnegie was looking forward to the Homestead contract in 1892.

Carnegie and Frick believed that the area Hungarians were involved in a type of conspiracy, as did most in western Pennsylvania. They had overestimated the bond between Hungarians, but the struggle with the capitalists had managed to unite them. The Hungarians did have a communications network that gave them an advantage over company spies. The Hungarians were demonstrating a type of solidarity that hadn't been seen since the 1850s and the Irish Molly Maguires of the eastern coal fields. The often-unrepresented Hungarians in the steel mills were being driven to support the strikes of the skilled workers on principle, but in the coal fields they were part of the bargaining. The United Mine Workers had reluctantly added the Hungarians, becoming an industrial union instead of a crafts union. The support and blood of the Hungarians were paving the path for a type of social acceptance by fellow workers. They would teach the United Mine Workers the need for internal solidarity. Within a few years blacks and Italians followed the Hungarians into the union. Frick's policies of strike breakers and house evictions made him a national enemy of the Hungarians. It is ironic that Frick had been the first of the industrialists to bring Hungarians into the mines and factories of western Pennsylvania. Frick had also been the first to promote Hungarians into management positions, and Frick had even fought against nativist laws.

Frick's house eviction policy was clearly over the top and created hard feelings, but Frick saw it as a property rights issue. The worker was only renting at a cost of $6.50 a month on $1.12 a day. Add coal for heating at $1.50 a month, and a worker was using 24 percent of his wages for housing. The eviction policy was almost impossible for more reasonable managers to justify. The practice, however, probably did more to promote worker solidarity than the union. Still, with all Frick's hardheaded policies, the workers preferred Frick's mine operations. Italians and blacks often paid the Frick bosses to get on the crew. Part of the reason was Frick's superior organization. Workers were paid on time, and jobs were standardized by pay, neither of which was common with the other owners. In smaller operations, pay rate might be determined on the basis of personal connections. The union as the standard often cited the "Frick scale." While Frick stores overcharged, workers were allowed some credit in bad times.

The Morewood Massacre and the upcoming Great Homestead would be nothing compared to the death of Frick's daughter Martha in July of 1891. Martha Frick Symington Sanger best tells the story of Martha's final months, and it presents a much different Frick from the one people know from history books. It shows a very human side of a loving father, and a man whose heart was easily broken by his daughter's suffering. This is a side of Frick that must be considered for any balanced view of the man. It also shows that capitalists are as human as their laborers and are not easily defined as heartless monsters. This side of Frick can be paradoxical and confusing to those wanting to characterize him as pure evil. It creates many questions but it also explains his soft spot for children and children's charities. The fact that Frick could be a harsh taskmaster while being a loving father is not unusual. It points to Frick's ability to see business as a separate part of life where harsher rules applied. Such mental separation is not unusual for managers in heavy industry. In any case, Martha's illness tore Frick apart for years.

Martha continued to worsen during 1891, with homeopathic doctor and neighbor Dr. McClelland visiting her daily, but there was little that could be done. In the spring Frick had taken the kids to New York to shop. Frick bought Martha a tricycle and Helen a doll, but Martha would soon become unable to ride the tricycle. Frick tied to cheer up the children, but Martha's slow decline was heartbreaking for the whole family. As her condition worsened, Martha had the full-time assistance of Annie Blumenschine Stephany. On a short walk to Philander Knox's home with Martha, Frick noticed the girl's limp, which had abated, had returned. For Frick, early summer of 1891 was the most difficult, as Martha could be seen to weaken daily. Martha Sanger described the struggle:

> As June warmth began to turn into July heat, the final stages of Martha's long, slow death from peritonitis and septicemia began. Bacteria had claimed Martha's abdominal cavity and bloodstream. Her vital organs, starved for nutrients and oxygen, were now on the verge of collapsing, one after another like dominos.[7]

Adelaide, Frick, and Annie established a nightly routine of sleeping in Martha's room. Frick stayed in the room to around three o'clock every morning. During the day Frick commuted to the Pittsburgh office from the temporary home at Lilac Street and returned early to play with the children.

In late June, Dr. McClelland and Carnegie recommended Martha be taken to Cresson Springs and the Mountain House Hotel. Cresson Springs had always been hailed for its restorative air and water. The Carnegie cottage was prepared for Frick as well as four rooms at the hotel. A full staff of servants, nurses, doctors, and helpers were brought in. They remained there through July, with Frick commuting by the Pennsylvania Railroad to the Pittsburgh office. Frick would bring Martha a gift every time he returned to the cottage. Frick took the fragile Martha outside to enjoy the fresh air and play with her dog, Brownie. In later July, Carnegie sent his personal doctor, Jasper Garmany from New York's Bellevue Hospital, but there seemed that little could be done. The struggle would end on July 28, 1891, with the family around and Frick holding his daughter's hand as she passed. Robert Pitcairn sent his private railroad car to return the family to the East End. The family was devastated and accepted an invitation from E.M. Ferguson to stay at his vacation home on the Connecticut coast. Carnegie had even suggested a European holiday at his castle, but Frick needed to return to work.

The impact on Frick could be seen throughout his entire life. Martha was buried in Homewood Cemetery about a tenth of a mile from Clayton, and Frick had the trees cleared so his could see the grave from Clayton's second floor. Frick had to spend more time with young Helen, who may have been the most affected. Frick would commission sculptors and painters to recreate Martha in art. Frick hired Roman sculptor Orazio Andreoni to create a beautiful life-size marble bust of Martha, which still can be seen at Clayton. He had her picture engraved on his personal checks and wore a pansy (her favorite flower) in his lapel. He carried her picture in his wallet. A few years later, Frick donated the painting *Christ and the Disciples at Emmaus* to the Carnegie Institute in "memory of Martha Howard Frick." Martha Frick Symington Sanger demonstrates how the memory of Martha influenced Frick's collecting. Sanger is not alone in seeing this theme, which was noted in a *Pittsburgh Post* article of 1898 describing the painting of *Emmaus* at the Carnegie Institute: "Somehow we feel could she [Martha] who is daily kept in memory be given place in a painting, not otherwise could she appear than does this beautiful, sweet, singularly pure and charming face."[8] Annually, Frick's most difficult day would be Martha's birthday, August 5, when he would always be saddened by her memory. Frick seemed to find some happiness that in his Christian view he would again see Martha. In 1896, he donated one of the first X-ray machines (a machine that might have saved Martha) to Pittsburgh Mercy Hospital. Years later, as Frick lay dying, the only picture in the room of the great collector was Romney's *Lady Hamilton*, which was said to remind him of Martha. The impact on Adelaide was deeper, and she made Martha's room a living tribute to her. Adelaide suffered from a low-grade type of depression for the rest of her life. Frick suffered similarly but could find some relief in his work.

11. The Run-Up to Homestead

Frick had proven himself as chairman of Carnegie Brothers through the tough years of 1889 through 1890. He had quickly learned the steel business and started to apply his system of corporate infrastructure. Frick had proven himself a Carnegie man, but at a career and personal cost. Frick had often gone too far in his struggle for control with unions and by 1891 had become a hated man among the Eastern European immigrants because of his tough union policies.

The Amalgamated union at Homestead had also overplayed their hand. Facing technology and a new management system, the Amalgamated dug in, holding to the crafts union approach. The Amalgamated pushed for unnecessary staffing along the lines of the old guild structure, choosing to take a stand against the trend. The miners had realized that the guild structure no longer fit the modern workplace, and the guild jobs no longer fit the actual mill jobs of steelmaking. Carnegie and Frick had fought the miners to a draw, but they showed flexibility in moving from a crafts union to an industrial union. The miners blended skilled and unskilled to build solidarity. The Amalgamated Association of Iron and Steel Workers (AAISW) was a union divided on many levels as to how to proceed. Until 1890 it refused to admit unskilled labor, which might be up to 90 percent of the employees in the mills. Even after 1890, the rule allowed admission at the discretion of the locals, but only Homestead had taken advantage of the rule. At the 1891 Amalgamated union meeting in Pittsburgh, a union leader noted: "I should not be surprised to see the Amalgamated Association reorganize under vastly different rules and regulations. The trouble has always been that the association has extended protection to the few at the expense of the so-called unskilled laborer."[1]

Personally, Frick had thrived through the tough years. He had expanded his own personal investments in Pittsburgh real estate and utilities. Unfortunately, his daughter Martha continued to decline in strength. Frick had also launched a renovation of Clayton, using Pittsburgh's best-known architect Fredrick Osterling and decorator A.J. Kimbal. Osterling had designed a number of East End homes including H.J. Heinz's "Greenlawn." The Frick project began in the winter of 1891, and the Fricks moved to a temporary home in Shadyside. Frick's library and office were to be expanded, but so were the children's rooms. A solarium and portico were added. The innovations cost $131,300. The house had some of the first machine-made carpets, plus curved glass windows, as well as some machine-lathed wood decorations. One of the more interesting improvements was the use of aluminum foil as a wall covering. Aluminum foil at the time was novel and as expensive as gold. The Mellons were investing millions in the production of aluminum, but this special foil came from France. The music room had velvet on the walls, and the dining room was paneled with mahogany with a dado of painted leather. Later a bowling alley was added to the cottage house, turning it into a playhouse for Childs and Helen. Frick also was becoming involved in a number of investment projects that brought him into contact with Pittsburgh's Republican machine of Christopher Magee. Carnegie had pulled Frick into the world of national politics. Frick had been asked early in his career to run for Congress as a Republican in Westmoreland County, but he had declined, wanting a career in business. His business career, however, would lead him to become adept at politics. Frick would become the Republican kingmaker and remain so until his death.

In the winter of 1890, Carnegie had turned to Frick to pull some strings with Pittsburgh's city boss Christopher Magee. Frick had made investments in Magee's streetcar company and had some small real estate dealings with Magee, but he would find that Magee was not impressed with the power of Carnegie. Carnegie wanted to buy some additional land for his retooling of the Homestead works, in particular to add a more powerful armor rolling mill. The land needed was city property where a poorhouse was located. Political bosses controlled the state and city in 1890. Christopher Magee controlled city council, and his partner William Flinn in the state house assured state support. On a national level, Matthew Quay supplied the ties to national politics for Pittsburgh and Pennsylvania through his statewide machine. Although Frick had opposed Quay on many local issues, he supported Quay's strong stand on protectionism in Congress. Frick was able to use Quay to pressure the Democratic governor.

No company, no matter how powerful, could do anything in Pittsburgh without Magee's approval. Bribery and back-room deals were a way of business in the 1800s. Frick enlisted his neighbor, company lawyer, and friend to help Frick get the land for Carnegie. They seemed not to have greased Magee well enough, and when bids on the land were offered, Magee set up a dummy bidder to win. Carnegie and Frick needed to bribe Magee further. They were successful, but Frick learned a valuable lesson about Pittsburgh politics. Magee was the king, and even coke kings and steel barons had to pay tribute. Frick never really cared for Magee, nor did his best friend Andrew Mellon and the Mellon family, but they were forced to deal with Magee until the early 1900s. Frick, the Mellons, Carnegie, Westinghouse, and Heinz were all manufacturers and Republicans but cared little for the Pittsburgh Republican machine. Frick had little respect for local bosses, and the Mellon family had always been critics of Magee's type of boss politics. Since Frick was a local Republican, many over the years have linked him to Magee. The relationship with Magee was a matter of convenience. Magee was ever the pure politician whose end goal was not friendship as much as maximum return for himself. It was national politics that interested the Pittsburgh capitalists more.

The Tariff Bill of 1890 was the career signature of William McKinley. McKinley at the time was chairman of the powerful Ways and Means Committee. The Fifty-first Congress of 1888 formed with what was believed to be a mandate for tariff reform. The Republicans controlled the White House and both branches of the legislature in 1888. Frick and Carnegie had actively supported the campaign of President Harrison. Providence seemed to favor McKinley's tariff, and McKinley's power was peaking. The tariff issue, now preeminent, was what McKinley had studied for all his life. The new president, Benjamin Harrison, was for high tariffs. Although not a personal friend of McKinley, he drew on old friends such as former President Rutherford B. Hayes. McKinley had deep ties to the Pittsburgh capitalists. Westinghouse had worked with young Congressman McKinley in the 1880s to get railroad safety laws passed. As a young lawyer, McKinley had defended Carnegie lawyer and Frick neighbor (and future attorney general) Philander Knox on a college drinking charge. McKinley showed true brilliance in his compromises and teamwork, not only in the House, but also with the Senate and White House. The tariff bill of 1890 included many innovations that helped American farmers. The bill completed the evolutionary steps of American tariffs from revenue generation to protection of industry development. No bill before had been directed at policy to build industries such as tin plate and sugar. The steel industry was marked for major protection as well. Frick sent McKinley $5,000 for Carnegie Brothers & Company in 1889 to support his effort. Frick and McKinley developed a relationship, and Carnegie often used Frick as the go-between. Frick also became an informal consultant for McKinley on steel and iron tariffs.

McKinley's Bill of 1890 was the best researched ever and used science and statistics to apply the tariff rates. First, McKinley argued that the revenue tariff approach was the real problem and that tariffs needed to be protective. His statistics were convincing: "Before 1820 nearly all our imports were dutiable; scarcely any were free; while in 1824 the proportion of free imports was less than 6 percent; in 1830, about 7 percent.... The percent of free imports from 1873 to 1883 was about 30 percent, and under the tariff revision of 1883 it averaged 33 percent."[2] American industry boomed under the high tariffs. For his 1890 bill it would be 50 percent. The difference was that it focused on the nation's needs, not on revenue production, which for years had been the only major source of government income. The McKinley plan was a result of years of study, and none knew more about tariffs than McKinley, but he would have to make political compromises to get it passed. McKinley pored nightly over the tariff schedules and surveyed his colleagues on industry needs. Pittsburgh capitalists such as George Westinghouse and Henry Clay Frick consulted with McKinley often. Carnegie had written a number of articles in support of the tariff. Frick saw political action as part of his job in heading up Carnegie Steel. Frick developed the model of the modern CEO and the necessity of being involved in politics.

McKinley argued that protective tariffs had not restricted exports, and again the numbers supported him: "We sell to Europe $449,000,000 worth of products and buy $208,000,000 worth. We sell to North America to the value of $9,645,000 and buy $5,182,000. We sell to South America $13,810,000 and buy $9,088,000." McKinley was not alone in his evaluation. In 1882, Bismarck had hailed the protective tariffs of America: "Because it is my deliberate judgment that the prosperity of America is mainly due to its system of protective laws." The McKinley tariffs were focused on building America, not restricting trade. They were applied in a manner that did not produce trade wars. Still, McKinley was clear that his tariffs were nationalistic: "The free-trader wants the world to enjoy with our citizens equal benefits of trade in the United States. The Republican protectionist would give the first chances to our people, and would so levy duties upon the products of other nations as to discriminate in favor of our own." The Tariff Bill of 1890 passed over the outcries of the Democrats, who launched a national campaign to throw the Republicans out of power. McKinley had the strong support of John Dalzell and George Huff, who were Pittsburgh congressmen and friends of Frick. Frick, in particular, had supplied funds to the overall victory of the Tariff Bill of 1890. McKinley would actually lose his House seat as part of the Democratic campaign. The national battle about tariffs would continue through 1896, and it would become an issue at Homestead in 1892.

The unions, which had tried to stay neutral, sided with the Democrats in public. Union leaders supported the Democrats because of the Republican links to the owners. Union leaders were often ignored when they supported Democrats, since the workers preferred the Republican "Full Dinner Pail" approach to protecting American industry. The Republicans argued that tariffs had created large profits for the manufacturers, and they should pass on those profits in the form of increased worker wages. Homestead, which had been a Republican stronghold, was moving towards the Democrats over union issues. In addition, the Democrats argued the tariffs had increased the prices of basic needs while doing nothing to help wages. Homestead offered the perfect political wedge for the Democrats. Frick had been an active fundraiser for President Benjamin Harrison, and that worried the union because Frick might be able to get troops involved. Harrison had shown a propensity to supply troops to prevent violence in labor disputes. If Harrison were to use troops, that could also be used to turn the workers against the Republican Party. The Knights of Labor and the Amalgamated unions had supported the Democrats in hope of keeping the troops out of strikes. Unions were starting to realize the importance of political ties to counter those of the capitalists. The gathering storm at Homestead was becoming a microcosm of the political struggles of the two parties. In Homestead, the individual Amalgamated lodges had used their political power to vote in many local government jobs for union members.

The Amalgamated lodges had decided that never again would Carnegie send the county sheriff and his deputized army into Homestead. Sheriff's deputies, troops, and company police forces had been successful in allowing the companies to run mines and mills with scabs, rendering the strikes useless. Union leaders started to see an unfair advantage in the alliance of the capitalists and local government. One of these leaders was John McLuckie, who had fought with the unions in Braddock in the 1880s. McLuckie was an assistant roller at Homestead and had been a member of the Knights of Labor and the Amalgamated. McLuckie and the Amalgamated realized that Carnegie and Frick controlled Pittsburgh through the Republican machine of Christopher Magee. McLuckie and others ran for local offices in 1888, and McLuckie was elected a burgess.

Another part of the preparation for the battle at Homestead was a strengthening of the bond between skilled Amalgamated workers and unskilled workers. The lodges had supplied the money to win local elections, but ties with the unskilled workers had allowed the steelworkers to control the local government. These political ties had brought skilled and unskilled laborers closer than ever. The earlier nativists who had controlled government were particularly hard on the Eastern European immigrants. Shortages in labor had allowed a few Slavs and Hungarians to move into the lowest apprentice positions of the lodges. Blacks and Italians were still under an absolute ban from membership. It was far from perfect, but the unskilled workers' best hope was in support of the upcoming strike. They even formed the first unskilled lodge of the Amalgamated Association of Iron and Steel Workers. It was more of a symbolic concession on the part of the Amalgamated. Some of the unskilled were members of the Knights of Labor, which had some support for the Amalgamated. Homestead union leaders realized they needed the support of the unskilled workers, even though there were very little immediate gains for the unskilled worker. Generally, the unskilled worker was in the middle with nothing to gain from a strike.

Another factor in the prelude to the Homestead Strike of 1892 was the rapid advance of technology. Technology was making it easier to make steel and had greatly increased the rate at which steel was produced. It also had eliminated large numbers of skilled workers. Maybe more problematic was that the union structure of crafts no longer reflected the structure of the work place. The year 1892 marked the death of the skilled puddler. Puddlers had been the top of the iron and steel craftsmen. As an engineering tool, puddle iron had become too expensive to compete with mass-produced steel. High technology Bessemer converters throughout America had ended the need for puddlers. Early in the year Pittsburgh's Jones and Laughlin Steel closed over thirty-five puddling furnaces, dismissing all their high-paid puddlers. In April 1892, Carnegie closed all of his Thirty-Third Street Mill puddling furnaces, putting over two hundred puddlers out of work. Many believe that Carnegie was making a point of the advance of technology and the ultimate end of the crafts approach. The Amalgamated union, which represented the puddlers and steelworkers, became divided. The union could not mount sympathy strikes to support the puddlers. Amalgamated unions had little solidarity even among the various crafts. At the 1891 convention of the Amalgamated, some cried out in the wilderness that the "puddler of today will be the steelworker of the future." The shift in technology had left the union's majority craftsmen unemployed, which had fatally wounded the national union. It was not the puddlers alone who were suffering from technology. Roll and heating technology had replaced 108 out of 132 workers in a rolling mill at Edgar Thomson in 1885, but rollers are still needed even today.[3]

The fact was that in 1891 the Amalgamated Association of Iron and Steel Workers (AAISW) had 26,046 members, most of whom were ironworkers, dominated by puddlers. The steelworkers were rapidly distancing themselves from the puddlers. Worse yet, other crafts lodges, such as the rollers, which were still needed in steelmaking, were distancing themselves from the puddlers. The steelworkers put their hopes of stopping the slide of the union by taking a stand at Homestead, but the workers of Homestead were divided between two unions, different skills, and nationalities. The decline and division resulted in the defection of AAISW secretary William Martin to go to work for Carnegie as a labor analyst. As a union officer, Martin had negotiated what many owners believed to be a reasonable Homestead contract in 1882, but many workers believed Martin and others had sold out. Frick had made the suggestion to Carnegie to hire Martin. At the time Martin was editor of the *National Labor Tribune*, and no one was in a better position to know the wages and inner workings of the union.

William Martin would give Frick and Carnegie insights into the very heart of the union. Frick would use Martin as a personal advisor to bring him up to speed on the complexities of the Amalgamated Association of Iron and Steel Workers. William Martin was given the assignment from Carnegie to design the sliding scale for the upcoming Homestead negotiations. Frick hoped that Martin could help avoid the frontal assault building between the company and the workers at Homestead, but Martin's analysis and report would inflame Carnegie. Martin found that Homestead rollers were paid 50 percent higher than ten other competing mils.[4] Martin also found unskilled laborers at Homestead, and even more damaging was the finding that union work rules required more workers than needed. Carnegie cabled Frick in June: "It is not only the wages paid, but the number of men required by Amalgamated rules, which makes our labor rates so much higher."[5] Carnegie was now determined that the union had to go.

Martin's report confirmed both Carnegie's and Frick's different views of the union problem. Carnegie and his "Boys of Braddock" had a simple yet powerful philosophy. They believed in driving wages down below the competition and pushing for new production records. For them, the union problem was all about wages and the competition. Frick came to the same anti-union position, but for him it was about union work rules and management control. Frick saw union work rules as supporting a nonexistent crafts structure, which required over-manning of the mill. Frick had even increased wages in the mines to ward off unionization. The crafts approach also gave production level control to the union, which caused major problems for Frick and Carnegie. A ten percent increase in jobs was much more costly than a ten percent increase in wages. The eventual breaking of the union at Homestead proved Frick's point with a 25 percent reduction in the manning requirements. Frick was much more focused on the structure of the workplace, while Carnegie liked the simple straightforward attack on wages.

In April 13, 1891, Samuel Gompers of the American Federated Union visited Pittsburgh to promote the eight-hour day among the various unions of western Pennsylvania. Gompers would become known as the father of labor unions, but in 1891 he had his hands full. Gompers was a very progressive leader but had come from a crafts union of cigar makers. Gompers differed much with the Knights of Labor, but he believed in the eight-hour day. Where he disagreed strongly with the trend was the involvement of the unions in politics and the rise of the socialists in the unions. The Pittsburgh unions had few connections with the socialists, but they were forging ties with the Democratic Party. Gompers warned against this. Gompers was well aware of the tension building at Homestead and in the mines of western Pennsylvania and hoped that politics and the socialists could be kept to the sidelines. The socialists, in particular, had turned public opinion against the unions.

Things were changing for Carnegie and Frick as well in 1891 and 1892. Going into 1892, Carnegie had two companies—Carnegie Brothers & Company, with Frick at the head, and Carnegie, Phipps & Company, headed by Abbott. Frick's flagship at Carnegie Brothers was

Edgar Thomson Works, which mainly produced rails. Abbott's flagship plant was Homestead, which produced structural steel and steel plate. While the companies had the same owner-ship, the administration of the two was separate. Carnegie had learned to count on Frick's advice, but William Abbott had lost favor. By the end of 1891, with Frick's help, Carnegie had completed months of study about bringing the two companies together. Carnegie wanted to get Frick in charge for the upcoming negotiations at Homestead. In January of 1892, the deal was cut to bring the assets of Carnegie Brothers and Carnegie, Phipps & Company together as the Carnegie Steel Company. H.C. Frick Company was kept as a separate company with Thomas Lynch as general manager. Frick would become CEO of all and Abbott would be removed from active management. Charles Schwab would be general superintendent of Edgar Thomson; John Potter, general superintendent of Homestead; and Thomas Morrison (a Carnegie relative), general superintendent of Duquesne. The partners had evolved over the years as Carnegie rewarded his key managers with shares. The shares and partners of Carnegie Steel were as follows:

Andrew Carnegie	$13,833,333	
Henry Phipps	$2,750,000	[oldest partner and boyhood friend]
Henry Clay Frick	$2,750,000	
George Lauder	$1,000,000	[a cousin of Carnegie]
Henry Singer	$500,000	[joined when Carnegie bought American Bessemer]
Henry Curry	$500,000	[Manager of Lucy Furnace, joined as partner 1886]
Henry Borntraeger	$500,000	[started as clerk 1878, mgr. 33 Street Mill, joined in 1886 as partner]
John Leishman	$500,000	[joined in 1886; became U.S. ambassador]
William Abbott	$250,000	[started as employee in 1871, partner in 1886]
Otis Childs	$250,000	[Frick's brother-in-law]
John Vandervort	$200,000	[one of the original six and friend of Tom Carnegie]
Charles Strobel	$166,666	[Carnegie bridge designer from Carnegie's Keystone Bridge — started as employee in 1872]
F.T. Lovejoy	$166,666	[Carnegie Company secretary]
Patrick Dillon	$166,666	
William Blackburn	$125,000	[started as sales clerk; became regional sales agent]
William Palmer	$83,333	[sales manager]
Lawrence Phipps	$83,333	[Henry Phipps's nephew]
Alexander Peacock	$83,333	[Carnegie sales vice-president]
J.O. Hoffman	$83,333	[Carnegie sales agent]
John Fleming	$83,333	[Carnegie sales agent]
James Simpson	$62,500	
Henry Bope	$27,777	[started as sales clerk and worked up to agent]
F.T. Lovejoy	$918,0555	[joined in 1881; trustee]

Carnegie Steel consisted of Edgar Thomson Works at Braddock, the Homestead Works, the Duquesne Works, Carrie Furnaces at Rankin, Lucy Furnaces in Pittsburgh, the Keystone Bridge Company, Union Mills and Beaver Falls Mills. There were ancillary companies, which included the Pittsburgh & Lake Erie Railroad, Carnegie Natural Gas Company, Youghiogheny Coke Company, and American Manganese Company. In addition, Carnegie Steel Company also had large iron ore holdings in the Lake Superior region and some small ore mines in central Pennsylvania. Total employment was over 13,000, and capitalization was $25,000,000. While H.C. Frick Company was a separate company it was controlled by the partners. All of the partners were bound by the "iron-clad agreement" that required a partner, if asked by the other partners, to sell back the shares at book value. The "iron-clad" agreement gave the partnership rights of purchase in the case of a death as well.

12. An Industrial Waterloo

The fight between centralized capital and organized labor may as well be pushed to the finish here at Homestead, and unless I am badly mistaken, it will be fought out there.
— A Homestead steelworker, July 6, 1892

The gathering of forces at Homestead would lead to an end of many icons in America. Men like Frick and Carnegie would no longer be admired or get favorable press. It would the beginning of the end of the Amalgamated Association of Iron and Steel Workers. Both the Carnegie Empire and the Amalgamated approached July 1892 at the peak of their power. Homestead had been recognized by both Carnegie and the union as the location of Armageddon. The battle had been prophesied by the *Pittsburgh Post* months prior.[1] It was to be Waterloo for more than just Frick and the Amalgamated; many others would end their reputations, careers, and living there. President Benjamin Harrison, who sent in federal troops, would lose the November election largely because of Homestead. The Amalgamated Association of Iron and Steel Workers, one of the world's largest unions, disappeared within five years after Homestead. Steelworker and mayor of Homestead, John McLuckie, was blacklisted and banished to Mexico. The various union men brought to trial were acquitted, but hundreds were blacklisted and never again worked in the industry. Plant superintendent John Potter would some years later commit suicide in Los Angeles. Carnegie and Frick would eventually part as friends over Homestead. The heroic age of American industrialization ended there.

Homestead would also represent beginnings. It was not the birthplace of the steelworkers' union, but it may have been the birthplace of lower-level industrial management and the foreman position. Homestead did start the process of breaking the racism of the union towards Eastern Europeans as the immigrants joined the battle in a show of solidarity. The union movement would take a new direction that would focus on inclusiveness and solidarity, but it was a slow transformation. Homestead would take until the late 1930s for the dream of a union at Homestead to be realized. It would bring politicians to understand the issues of labor. Both political parties would look to improve and get the votes of mill workers, but Homestead would break the Republican Party's control of the workingman's vote. The Democratic Party began its strong connection with unionization. Unions came to understand the power of the press in the union movement. Homestead would open the eyes of America to the problems of industrialization. To a large degree, it even opened the eyes of Carnegie and Frick. However, these were not the results envisioned only a few days before the strike.

In 1892, Homestead had become Carnegie's most technological advanced mill, and the palace of America's Industrial Revolution. Its plate, structural beam, and armor plate mills were the largest in the world. The complex covered more than 100 acres and employed 4,000 at capacity. It was the biggest factory in the world and was the world's largest integrated mill. Its huge 50-ton open-hearth furnaces were supplied by Carrie blast furnaces across the river. Unfortunately, Carrie Furnaces initially supplied cold pig iron to be melted in cupolas at Homestead. The mill had some of the world's first electric cranes and electric lighting. It utilized natural gas in its reheating and annealing furnaces. Homestead had special handling equipment on a scale that existed nowhere else in the world. Its 12-ton forging press had made the world's largest forgings of nearly 100 tons. The works had its own railroad with nineteen locomotives. It had its own large blacksmith shop and a major machine shop to make its own parts and tools. The works had just signed the largest armor contract in the world. Homestead's nickel armor would change naval warfare. The growth of the mill had created a thriving community of 12,000.

The workforce was changing, as was the makeup of the town. One estimate is that at the time of the 1892 strike, only 1,200 workers were native born, and 800 of the workers could not speak English. The original residents of the area were Scotch-Irish, followed by German Lutherans. Homestead and associated Mifflin Township had been a farming community in the early 1870s. Its first development was the building of the "poor farm" where Pittsburgh's poor were sent to do farm work. The first commercial works was the Bryce Highee Glass Company in 1879, and in a few years employment had reached 500. Coal mining was also done in the valleys created by streams running into the Monongahela River. By 1880, there were over 1,000 miners in Mifflin Township operating the rich coal seams. The town of Homestead had boomed to 3,000 in 1882 and was the home of glass and mining craftsmen. The Republican Party dominated the town, with deep roots going back to the election of Abraham Lincoln. It was the opening of the Pittsburgh Bessemer Steel Company in 1882 that started a second boom. Still, this town, often referred to as "a workers republic," was an enclave of craftsmen and middle-class skilled workers. Homestead was the logical home for the growth of the largest crafts union, and that tradition continued after Carnegie bought Pittsburgh Bessemer in 1882.

The buildup to the 1892 Homestead Strike started at the 1891 convention of the Amalgamated Association of Iron and Steel Workers. The convention had 261 delegates representing 24,068 members. It was America's largest union representing the skilled crafts workers of the iron and steel industry. The union, however, was fighting the inherent changes of industrialization. The Amalgamated was opposing disturbing trends, which eroded the crafts system infrastructure. The union was holding to its apprenticeship system of seniority, control over the amount of production that could be scheduled, and banning overtime until all crafts workers were employed. The union remained opposed to the entry of any Eastern Europeans such as Slovaks and Hungarians. The union opposed any type of foreman having a say in the operation of the crew. The battle was, for the most part, against the advance of technology, which was reducing the skill level needed. The union had a major problem in inter-crafts rivalry, which had cost them to lose many strikes. The owners used this rivalry to their advantage. The highly paid steel rollers cared little for the problems of the declining puddlers lodge, which was being eliminated by Bessemer steel technology. To some extent, greed is a basic human fault, and it crosses class lines. The individual crafts wanted the highest pay and showed little concern, let alone solidarity, for the struggling lodges. The unskilled majority was not allowed membership in the union. In any case, the Amalgamated believed it needed to make a stand against the encroachment of the owners, and the high-tech mill at Homestead was the obvious place.

Homestead represented a stand for management as well. Carnegie had purchased the failed Homestead Bessemer steel mill and gutted it, putting in the latest technology. Carnegie's 119-inch rolling mill had eliminated hundreds of skilled workers and made high production rates possible. Carnegie had brought in thousands of Eastern European unskilled workers, and was expanding their role in the operations. Frick was implementing a foreman supervision system. The lockout of 1889 had been considered a draw as back orders forced Carnegie to settle early. The 1889 lockout at Homestead had reduced wages and gained a great deal of ground, but Carnegie believed they could get more. Carnegie realized the size of the union was misleading, and their weaknesses could be exploited. Furthermore, the economy was now in a downturn, which gave Carnegie the upper hand that he had played so well in the past.

For most, the facts of Homestead are surprising, since Homestead is now mythology. The union workers at Homestead numbered 800 out of about 3,800 total employees. The union tonnage men accounted for about 325, and these were the only employees addressed in the contract.[2] These 325 workers were all German, Welsh, English, and Irish. The union represented only the highly skilled workers organized into lodges by the trades of puddlers, boilers, heaters, rollers, hookers, catchers, and roughers. The Amalgamated Association of Iron and Steel Workers represented this small group. The wage argument was initially with those 325 workers. Even more surprising might be that the average American worker at the time made $8.50 a week, while a union steelworker at Homestead averaged $35.00 a week. The brutal twelve-hour day was not a matter of contention since the long hours represented income. In fact, most of the high-tonnage workers liked the pay of the twelve-hour day. Even the immigrants who were paid by the hour liked the income but struggled with the long shift. The lodges had made only small concessions to the Slavs and Hungarians, allowing them to enter at the lowest level and grandfathering them at that level.

In all, seven workers were killed at Homestead, as well as three Pinkerton Guards. This was slight compared to the number of dead and wounded of the Railroad Strike of 1877, whose riots left the city of Pittsburgh looking like a bombed-out German city of World War II. But Homestead represented ideology and the collision of cultural change in America. It was the last stand of the great crafts union and the end of America's idolization of industrial titans. It was the realization of the industrialization of America, and the passing of Thomas Jefferson's agrarian America. Homestead was an American event, somewhat predetermined by the union, the management, and the press. To a degree, it had the buildup of an early Super Bowl and was one of the first national events shaped by the press coverage. Homestead later became something of folklore and mythology. Many Pittsburghers still claim to have had family killed in the great strike. Most believe it to have represented Frick's effort to crush the low-paid immigrant steel workers, a struggle of the very poor against the wealthy, the root of the successful American union movement. The fact is the battle was not over the wages of the immigrant workers, but of the highest paid of America's industrial workers. The laborers could not join the skilled union, and their wages were of no concern to the union lodges. Still, it was a struggle between labor and management. Homestead is remembered more than the struggles of the same time involving the Knights of Labor, who stood for all labor and workers, an eight-hour day, and good working conditions.

Another part of the problem at Homestead was Carnegie's sliding pay scale. Carnegie had believed the sliding scale would be the resolution of labor problems, but its application at Homestead and Braddock had surprisingly increased costs. The Amalgamated was actually quite happy with the scale through 1892. The 1889 contract had been signed when a steel billet sold at $26.50 a ton of steel. The contact increased wages when the price went above $26.50 a ton and decreased it when prices fell below $26.50 a ton. The contract called for a $25.00 a ton minimum below which rates would not be reduced. The contract called for the rate to be adjusted every three months based on the preceding three months. The contract would be in effect for three years. This was the sliding scale Carnegie and Abbott had fought for. When the contract was signed in July of 1889, as noted, the price was $26.50 a ton; and by the end of 1889, it reached $36.00. In 1890, it declined all year to finish at $25.75 a ton; and then in 1891, it fell to $23.00 a ton. The men were being paid at the $25.00 rate, the contract minimum. As negotiations started, Frick offered a $23.00 minimum, while the Amalgamated would only go to a $24.00 minimum. In addition, to the scale just discussed, management wanted a reduction in the rate or percentage for various parts of the scale. The union refused to go to the $23.00 base minimum, "notwithstanding the fact that the improved machinery would enable their members, even at $23.00, to earn more than is paid in other Amalgamated mills."[3] Management was also asking for the contract to hold only for a year instead of three, so they could adjust quickly to billet market prices. This was the heart of the wage issue; the union itself was probably the bigger issue on Carnegie's and Frick's minds. Frick, in particular, wanted the union out, so that union work rules could be eliminated. Union work rules mandated crew sizes and production rates.

Much has been made of the fact that the scale changes suggested by Carnegie and Frick would have only amounted to two cents per ton increase, or a total of $20,000 on a million tons.[4] On profits in the millions, it seems a small amount, the assumption being the increase of 325 skilled workers' wages. Based on this analysis it would seem trivial, but Carnegie and Frick were capitalists and cost cutters. It was not unusual for Carnegie to replace new equipment for even newer based on two cents per ton savings. His managers were trained to go after the smallest of savings. More importantly, Carnegie was a fierce competitor, and the report by former union officer William Martin showed Homestead paying skilled workers 50 percent more than ten other competing mills, as well as his own mills at Braddock and Duquesne. Frick was also looking at white-collar waste and cutting clerks of senior partners such as Francis Lovejoy. It is often impossible to understand business and make judgments based on one time frame. Carnegie and Frick were always consistent in viewing costs long-term and competitively. It is never remembered that these cuts led to competitive advantage that created tens of thousands, if not hundreds of thousands of jobs, over the next decades. It is unfortunate that the seeming coldness of capitalism is the very engine of job creation many times. Yet no system to date has found a way to create full employment at high wages. In fairness, there have been capitalists, such as Westinghouse and Heinz, who executed the system of capitalism with more heart and a touch more warmth than Frick and Carnegie.

The dollar amounts earned by Homestead workers ranged from about $12.00 a day (skilled) to $1.40 day (laborer) in the operating departments. The highest tonnage union man earned $3,280 a year and the lowest $378 a year. The top skilled worker at Homestead made $50.00 per week ($2,500 per year); the average American worker made $8.50 a week ($425 a year).[5] An average laborer at Homestead made from 75 cents to $1.40 a day, or around $380 a year. A foreman made about $6.00 to $8.00 a day, or $1,900 a year. The average days of work for the year was 270 days. The average day was twelve hours. Poverty level for a family was considered $300. Entry into the middle class probably required an annual salary of $800. Walt Whitman put the middle class test at $1,000 per year. The new white-collar jobs of the 1890s put many into the middle class. The press framed the Homestead Strike as labor against capital, but in reality only the highest workers would benefit, and these were some of America's highest-paid workers. There was a clear aristocracy in the union jobs. Rollers in the slab and billet mills made around $9.00 a day ($2,400 a year), a melter in the open hearth made $3.10 to $4.14 a day ($850 a year to $1,200 a year). First helpers in the open hearth made $2.80 a day. The lowest man on the crew made $1.40 a day or $380 a year. The proposed contract at Homestead said nothing of the laborer making less than a dollar a day. In terms of a percentage cut the new proposal from Carnegie meant a cut of from 40 percent to 20 percent.

Some occupation salaries for the 1890s were:

Skilled craftsmen	$800 per year
Department store buyer	$1200
Department sales person	$400
Bookkeeper	$2,000
Insurance agent	$1,200

Railroad clerk	$800
Warehouse clerk	$1,100
Editor	$2,500
Schoolteacher	$500
Woman worker H.J. Heinz	$200
Frick's head butler at Clayton	$960
Frick's gardener at Clayton	$720
Frick's chef at Clayton	$720
Production worker at Westinghouse Electric (male)	$485
Average Homestead skilled	$1,900
Average Homestead unskilled	$340
Average American worker	$425

Based on an 1890 survey of steelworkers at Homestead, the following statistics stand out. Of the 3,800 employees at the Homestead Mill, rollers, who represented less than 0.5 percent of the workforce, earned $7.00 to $7.50 a day; 109 skilled laborers (2.9 percent) earned between $4.00 to $7.00 a day (these included furnace operators); and 800 skilled workers (21 percent) earned $2.50 to $4.00 a day (these included first and second helpers in the hierarchy/apprentice system and craftsmen outside the Amalgamated such as carpenters and blacksmiths). The balance was represented by an unskilled group of 32 percent earning $1.68 to $2.50 a day, often hired by the tonnage crews, with the remaining 43 percent earning less than $1.40 and as little as 60 cents per day and working twelve hours. The company to a degree even reinforced the hierarchy and aristocracy of the union by supplying more than forty special houses for the master craftsmen at Homestead.

At the time of the strike (1892), four men (rollers) received an average of $7.50 a day ($2,025 a year), and the next 23 highest paid men received $5.40 to $7.04 per day ($1,460 to $1,900 a year). For comparison, a roller in Eastern Europe was making 39 cents a day (about

Pittsburgh and Homestead in 1892 (*Harper's Weekly*).

$100 a year). Of the total of 3,800 men, 113 earned an average of $4.00 to $7.50 a day ($1,080 to $2,025 a year), 1,177 earned an average of $1.68 to $2.50 a day ($434 to $675 a year), and 1,625 earned $1.40 or less a day ($378 or less a year).[6] Frick testified before Congress that the wages of the 900 or more skilled workers were a bit higher: four men received from $10.00 to $12.65 a day, twelve received $8.00 to $10.00 a day, thirty received from $6.00 to $8.00 a day, eighty-two earned from $4.00 to $6.00 a day, 443 made from $2.00 to $4.00 a day, and 335 made $2.00 a day ($540 a year) or less. Frick probably included ancillary skilled workers such as blacksmiths, carpenters, engineers, machinists, and bricklayers in his numbers. Frick had gotten his numbers from William Martin, who had compared all skilled workers.[7] Frick's estimate of the unskilled workers also appears very high. Regardless of which estimate is used, some conclusions about wages can be drawn. The skilled workers involved in the wage reductions made five times the average American worker. The unskilled majority made less than the average American worker ($340 versus $450 a year), only slightly above the poverty level.

A family budget from the same Homestead study of the time is enlightening. The family budget is a true testimony to the creativity and industry of these immigrant families. The average Homestead steel family took in $663.58 annually, of which at least $85.00 or more was from other members in the family. One of the bigger issues for the worker was economic slowdowns, which could mean a significant drop in days worked from the average 270 days. Injuries could also cause lost pay (there was no insurance or benefits). Forty was considered old in the mill, which took years off the lives of many men. Young boys might pick up some day work, as well as the women, to help support the family. Women did sewing and cleaning. Daughters were often employed in the H.J. Heinz and Westinghouse plants, which were major employers of young women. The pay there might be as high as $1.50 a day in 1892. Immigrant families functioned as one economic unit with all employed in various ways. Many of the Slavs and Hungarians sub-rented their two-room apartments, often putting six to a room. The budget consisted of 45.1 percent for food, 19.5 percent for clothing, 15.3 percent for rent, 6.6 percent for tobacco and alcohol, 11.6 percent for things such as books, entertainment, and newspapers. This left a surplus of 15 percent for the family income, which could be applied to savings.[8] Often steelworkers who worked at Homestead lived in nearby burghs, which were connected by an extensive streetcar system. The rail fare was estimated at $3.50 month, or as high as 6 percent of the income of a non–Homestead family.

The immigrant workers took advantage of the capitalistic opportunity to save and invest on their sometimes-meager wages. The workers faced extremely difficult contingencies such as loss of work due to injury, sickness, disability, and economic slowdowns. Saving was almost a necessity. The savings, in addition, were used to buy houses or bring family from Europe. Thrifty German skilled workers were able to save 10 to 15 percent of their wages in good times, but an economic downturn or injury could eliminate those savings in a short period. In tough times, community supported struggling families. Nationality groups formed fraternal lodges, as did churches, to pool money for injury and disability insurance. Monthly dues were about 70 cents to $1.30 a month, and there was usually an initiation fee of $1.00 to $8.00. The death benefit was from $600 to $1,000. Accident benefits ranged from $100 to $400. Sickness benefits were weekly payments of $5.00 to $7.00 a week up to 20 weeks. Total disability payments were $400 to $8,000. Workers religiously maintained their lodge dues even in the most difficult of times. The lodges and churches also supplied social activities for the workers and their families. Churches also helped in education and citizenship courses. Many immigrants stayed only a few years, saving for a return to Europe with extra cash. These returnees were usually young and single. One benefit, which these immigrants truly respected, was public education for the children. Pittsburgh's public school system was extensive and one of the earliest. The Homestead schools were extremely poor, but highly appreciated. Public education was lacking in Europe, so it offered hope for a better future.

Some typical food prices were: corned beef at $.06 a pound, coffee at $.14 a pound, flour at $.02 a pound, and butter at $.22 per pound. Bread was around $.05 a loaf and potatoes were $.39 a bushel. A pound of ham was about 11 cents and a pound of crackers was 4 cents. Ketchup in a prepackaged bottle ranged from 50 cents to $1.00 a bottle. Ketchup from the grocer's barrel was around 30 cents a gallon or 40 cents for a pint bottle, which was a considerable amount based on wages of $1.00 to $1.50 a day. Ketchup, however, was popular because it added spice to an extremely bland diet. Horseradish was popular for the same reason, and a young H.J. Heinz in the Pittsburgh area had made a fortune selling horseradish for 10 cents a jar. Pickles cost four to eight cents a dozen and were an important part of the diet. Hogs and chickens were raised and often roamed the streets. Gardens were critical, and cabbage for sauerkraut was a major crop. Sauerkraut could be stored through the winter. Cucumbers for pickles and horseradish were also popular garden items.

Landlords often abused the industrial slum workers, overcharging for rent in many cases. A two-room apartment might run $7.00 to $11.00 per month without toilets, baths, or heat. Fuel costs were about 80 cents a week (coal heating). The two rooms would house a family of six with a possible sub-renter or two. Other costs were $1.00 for a man's shirt, 5 cents for a linen handkerchief, $2.50 for a wool blanket, and $3.00 for gallon of whiskey. A starter house would cost from around $2,000 to $3,000. Running water, if present, cost $15.00 a month. At the time of the strike, the company had loaned 69 men about $48,000 at 6 percent for home purchases, or about $695 per worker. Savings rate at the time was around 6 percent.

The worst months for the workers' budgets were January through July. The winter months, of course, had the strain of heating bills. Stored garden products such as sauerkraut and pickles were thin through May, June, and July, and generally new garden products didn't start until mid–July. Seasonal work for women at the nearby Heinz plant didn't start until September. The steel business was somewhat affected by seasonal trends, with a pickup of orders starting for delivery in June, making the winter months a time of short work weeks. Generally, management liked to do lockouts from January to May. The union tried to have contracts up in the summer, when they were in the best resource position. The Homestead crisis was coming at the beginning of July, which probably was the closest time to a balance of power between labor and management. Significantly, Carnegie and Frick were asking that the new contract specify January for renegotiation.

Frick's problem with the union was deeper than Carnegie's. Carnegie focused mainly on the labor costs, but to Frick, work rules and operating control were the bigger issues. This control was the issue with men like Bill Jones, George Westinghouse, and H.J. Heinz as well. Carnegie's secretary James Bridge clearly described the problem at Homestead:

> Every department and sub-department had its workmens' "committee" with a "chairman" and a full corps of officers, who, fearing that their authority might decay through misuse, were ever on the alert to exercise it.... If a man with a desirable job died or left the works, his position could not be filled without the consent and approval of an Amalgamated committee. Usually this committee had a man in waiting for it; and the firm dared not give it to anymore else. The method of apportioning work, of regulating the turns, of altering the machinery, in short, every detail of working the great plant, was subject to the interference of some busybody representing the Amalgamated Association.[9]

The Amalgamated held on tightly to its role as the employment department for the mill in the crafts. The local fraternal lodges often supplied day laborers. The issue of control frustrated Frick and management down to the foreman.

In fact, the union work rules and control represented a major roadblock to Frick's foreman infrastructure. The structure of the Amalgamated had a union lodge of skilled workers representing each operating department. The union lodge was the basic unit, and it had its own organization and work rules. The union crafts lodge represented a unique operating department and part of the process. For example, the open-hearth furnaces, 119-inch rolling mill, and the 32-inch slabbing mill had their own lodges. In total, Homestead had seven lodges. Each lodge elected a president and officers. Each crafts lodge was represented on an advisory committee, which had a weak union president over the individual lodges. Hugh O'Donnell was the president of the advisory committee, but he had less power than the lodge presidents. The lodges were far from democratic, and nationalities often controlled various lodges; for example, the Irish worked in the furnace department and the Welsh and Germans in the rolling departments. Job seekers at the mill "applied" to the crafts lodge, not the company. The union lodges also had many social functions. The lodges would often underwrite funerals or supply financial help in tough times. The lodge could peg production if it chose to. The men could refuse to work if the heat was too high. No man could be dismissed without the lodge's agreeing to it. Like the subcontracting craftsmen in the coal mines, the steel lodge had almost complete power over the company foremen. In many cases, the real costs in the mill operations were not in labor wages but in work rules. Frick understood this better than Carnegie. The same is still often true today.

The personal buildup to Homestead was stressful for the whole Frick family. Adelaide was living in a type of nervous depression after the death of Martha. Adelaide and the children stayed in New York until March of 1892. Frick called daily as he continued work in Pittsburgh during the week. Threats to Frick's life from a Braddock steelworker had reached the newspapers, and Frick requested that newspapers be kept from his wife. Rumors of anarchist plots against Frick abounded, and local authorities were requested to watch Clayton closely for problems. Frick took no bodyguards, as friends had suggested, but continued his daily commute and routine. The staff was told to never let Adelaide walk outside alone. The death of his sister and the house restrictions affected Childs as well. Childs loved to study nature in the ravine (present-day Frick Park) in the back of Clayton. On weekends, Frick would also take the children for walks in this area. The steep ravine had become a nature preserve in this

The Homestead Works in 1892 (courtesy Carnegie Library of Pittsburgh).

industrial city. Childs's grades dropped off, which disturbed Frick. Frick had often pushed his son hard, hoping he would have the academic experiences that he had missed. Frick was also a demanding perfectionist, which Childs seemed to resist. Helen, on the other hand, learned how to please her father. A tutor, Clyde Augustus Duniway, was hired to help Childs, and Frick monitored his progress closely. Eventually, Childs would combine his love of nature and improved academics in a career in paleontology. Childs and his tutor were sent to a Boston boarding school in 1892 in an effort to improve his studies.

13. Homestead — The Battle

Homestead in many ways has grown in myth and legend since 1892. In 2006 the History Channel put the Homestead Strike in its *Ten Days That Unexpectedly Changed America*. The battle of Homestead was far from unexpected. The Amalgamated had discussed the need to make a stand at Homestead a year prior to its convention. The battle for Homestead had been in the planning stages with Carnegie for three years. The plan was to adjust the sliding scale, but just as important was to eliminate the Amalgamated union at Homestead. The strategy had been used many times before by Carnegie. It consisted of asking for a pay reduction, then closing the mill, waiting several weeks, and then offering the workers individual contracts to return. Carnegie realized that union negotiations were mostly psychological warfare. Carnegie had been discussing strategy and tactics a year before Henry Clay Frick took over as Carnegie Steel president with direct responsibility for Homestead Works. In fact, in December 1891, Carnegie asked Frick to have his brother-in-law Otis Childs, who was a manager at Homestead, start a rumor that business might be moved to the non-union Duquesne Works. Both Carnegie and Frick were closely reviewing the labor cost data of William Martin by January 1892 when Carnegie Steel was formed. Martin had been developing the data for over a year. Likewise, the Amalgamated were comparing their own data. Both sides moved slowly and with restraint, realizing public opinion was important to both sides. In fact, public opinion was Carnegie's Achilles' heel. Carnegie had strong ties at the *Pittsburgh Dispatch* and prompted positive articles early in 1892, detailing the disadvantage of Homestead in the overall industry. Frick also had "spies" in the works to pick up information and distribute rumors. It was the first industrialist strike where both sides actually used the press and public opinion.

The battle centered on about 300 skilled workers and their wages, ignoring over 2,000 unskilled workers. These skilled workers made about $2,500 a year (compared to $450 for the average American worker) based on the tons of steel processed. The company demands were: (1) reduce the minimum sliding wage scale in the rolling mill to $22 per ton; (2) reduce the tonnage rate paid in the open-hearth furnace departments; and (3) change the contract date to December 31 from June 30. The justification for the tonnage rates was the installation of new equipment, which boosted production. The date change was to put the company in a more favorable position for contract negotiations. The unwritten goal was to eliminate the Amalgamated because of its control and work rules. Carnegie wrote to Frick to note this strategy: "As I understand matters at Homestead, it is not only wages paid, but the number of men required by Amalgamated rules which makes our labor rates so much higher than those in the East.... The chances are, you will prepare for a struggle in which case, the notice (i.e. that the works are henceforth to be non-union) should go up promptly on the morning of the 25th [June]."[1] By the "East," Carnegie meant Bethlehem Steel and Midvale Steel, which were bidding against him on large naval armor contracts. Carnegie had lost large portions of available naval contracts to Bethlehem. Frick was just as interested in getting his foreman system to replace the master craftsmen as the managers of the operation. Still, Frick and Carnegie seemed to waffle on the idea of breaking the union as the contract expiration date approached. Frick seemed more willing to deal, apparently sensing that breaking the union might be unachievable.

Carnegie headed for Scotland in late June to dedicate a library there. Carnegie seemed sure of victory, but Frick was not. Carnegie sent a number of encouraging letters from New York prior to leaving.[2] Frick met with the union, against Carnegie's directions, the day Carnegie left for Scotland. The group consisted of the national president of the Amalgamated, William Weihe, and Homestead's central committee head Hugh O'Donnell and his committee. O'Donnell was a roller making about $2,000 a year. Frick was with his superintendent William Potter and partners H.C. Childs and F. Lovejoy. Frick did move his demand of a $22 a ton minimum to $23 a ton, but the union held that it had to be $24 a ton, and there was no movement on the other two points. Rails at the time were selling for $22.50 a ton. Potter seemed even more willing than Frick to negotiate. Then Carnegie seemed to waver in a telegram when he landed in Scotland. It is clear that there was doubt in everyone's mind about where the situation was going. Frick was becoming aware that the unskilled might stand with the skilled workers, which would make things difficult. Frick and Potter also seriously lacked the people skills needed for successful negotiations. On June 25, Frick closed off negotiations and started plans for a lockout. Meantime, reporters from all over world were flooding into Pittsburgh. One paper estimated there were at least 135 journalists from all over the globe.[3] Homestead was a story waiting to happen.

Frick posted notices that the negotiations had failed, and he was proceeding to close the works. Frick, the union, and the public expected violence based on Homestead's history alone. Frick started building an 18-foot wooden fence with barbed wire and allegedly with rifle slots. Sewers from the mill were provided with gratings. Arc light searchlights were also installed on twelve-foot towers. It was rumored (falsely) that the barbed wire was electrified, using Westinghouse's new alternating current. Alternating current was widely feared at the time. Frick had little confidence in the county sheriff, who had cut and run in the 1889 Homestead strike. Neither could Frick count on the Democratic governor; in fact, the governor initially refused to send troops, seeing the problems at Homestead as a political opportunity for more Democratic votes. In addition, worker politicians controlled Homestead and would not protect property against the workers. The mayor was a skilled union worker, John McLuckie, who was making about $1,700 a year, and had a personal stake in the strike. In early June, Frick had contracted with Pinkerton for an army of three hundred guards. The hiring of Pinkerton or private guards, while unpopular, was not unusual; however, the number needed for America's largest industrial plant *was* unusual. Pinkerton was short on trained guards because of prolonged strikes in the mines of Utah and Colorado. Pinkerton had been advertising in Western cities for armed guards at five dollars a day plus food and lodging. They mustered raw recruits in Chicago, a mix of college students, drifters, and laid-off workers. The union similarly prepared their forces, which included the unskilled workers. They patrolled the river, railroad tracks, and bridges, assuming scabs would be sent in. Scouts on horses were set up and down the river to warn the town of any approaching company men.

Things had reached the breaking point in Homestead as the saloons filled up, and effigies of Carnegie, Frick, Potter, and others were hung on telegraph poles. Frick, from his offices in Pittsburgh, called in Sheriff McCleary, politician boss Magee, and company lawyer Philander Knox on June 28, a group Frick would stay in contact with throughout the strike. The sheriff committed to work with Frick and the Pinkertons. Frick laid out his plan to have the Pinkertons enter the works via the Monongahela River and turn it into a fort. Meanwhile, the workers were meeting at the opera house. They had managed to gain the support of the unskilled workers, which surprised Frick and Carnegie, but it was a weak alliance. The unskilled were caught in the middle and could only hope for a quick settlement. Frick started the final phases of closing the mill, with the rolling mill coming down last. By July 1 both sides had laid their plans as an uneasy calm descended on Homestead. Frick, with spies in the mill and town, was the better informed. By July 4, the workers had gotten word of men being hired by Pinkerton in Chicago. On July 5 the workers pushed down the fence and surged into the mill. Local authorities were overwhelmed. The die was now cast, and the union went to full alert, posting workers up and down the Monongahela River.

The hired Pinkertons were moving by the Pittsburgh and Fort Wayne Railroad from Ashtabula, Ohio, where Potter had met them. They would muster at Bellevue on the Ohio, a few miles from Homestead. The sheriff met them with his deputy Joseph Gray, who would travel with them and deputize them if necessary. Deputizing these outsiders would put the responsibility on the county and make things legal. Frick was able to bring the necessary political pressure on the sheriff through boss Christopher Magee. Carnegie was cabled as to the movements. On July 5, the sheriff performed what was considered a tactical feint to confuse the workers. He went to Homestead with twelve deputies to discuss the law and the need to protect the works from damage. The sheriff returned across the river to Pittsburgh, knowing the Pinkerton landing was planned for two o'clock in the morning of July 6. The hope was to slip into the works under the cover of darkness. The Pinkertons moved by two river barges from Bellevue to the Homestead plant. The barges had been purchased and converted to covered troop carriers in Allegheny City (Pittsburgh's north side). These were floating forts described as "Noah's Ark." They were equipped with dining halls and kitchens, each had a hired steward and twenty waiters. Winchester rifles were in closed boxes to be opened only by command.

As the barges moved toward the plant, fog helped cover their approach. Pittsburgh was experiencing a July heat wave and a temperature inversion, making it hot and humid. The Smithfield Bridge on the Monongahela River was lined with watchmen, as were the riverbanks. A horseman was sent to awake Homestead. At 2:30 A.M. the Homestead Electric Works sounded a whistle alarm. Residents and workers, like the minutemen of old, got out of bed and picked up old family guns. Hugh O'Donnell, a former newspaperman, made sure reporters were on hand. As the barges approached the mill landing at 4 A.M. they faced the guns, men, women,

The scene of the Homestead Strike as illustrated in the July 1893 *Harper's Weekly* (courtesy Carnegie Library of Pittsburgh).

and children. Old Civil War cannon, mounted as monuments, were worn from their mountings and loaded for action. The Pinkertons started to land, armed with new Winchester rifles. The union leader Hugh O'Donnell and the Pinkerton leader Captain Heinde came within speaking distance and exchanged peaceful intents. There was some pushing, and then shots were fired. Three steelworkers were killed on the spot and dozens wounded. An old twenty-pounder cannon was fired from the Braddock side of the river, missing the barges and hitting and killing a steelworker. The Pinkertons had wounded as well, and the Pinkertons retreated to their floating forts. Telegraph sent the word to the hotels of Pittsburgh, and an army of reporters flew into action. The word was now moving out to the world. Pittsburghers and Valley residents started to assemble on the Swissvale hills across river to view the battle.

Frick had received the message of the Pinkertons on the move and now took a carriage to the Pittsburgh office. Chris Magee and the sheriff were at their offices. As the shooting started the sheriff telegraphed the governor to send troops, which he refused. Governor Robert Patterson was a Democrat, and the Homestead uprising played into his party's political advantage by breaking the Republican support by the workers. Inaccurate cannon fire and gunshots continued as the Pinkertons huddled in their floating forts. Hugh O'Donnell, realizing he was losing control, had the saloons in Homestead closed as anger was mounting in the streets. Another effort to land at 8 A.M. failed. The huddled Pinkertons had some protection, but the barges, in the days before air conditioning, were becoming sweaty iron furnaces. These men were not professionals, so they doubted whether this strange action was worth their lives. Most had never envisioned such duty. In Pittsburgh, Frick, the sheriff and Magee tried to use the courts to put pressure on the governor to send troops. Homesteaders added to the barrage by tossing dynamite. Telegraph wire reports to Washington brought calls to repeal the tariffs that had helped Carnegie Steel. Meanwhile, the Homesteaders poured oil into the Monongahela and started a few surface fires. By 7 P.M. the Pinkertons had had it and raised a white flag. The body count was thirteen dead and 36 wounded.

The Amalgamated advisory committee accepted the surrender but lost control of the crowd. The mob of men, women, and children were half-crazed by this point. The Pinkertons in their blue uniforms became the prisoners of the crowd, and were beaten and stoned. The Pinkertons were forced to run the gauntlet of angry workers and townspeople. The advisory committee eventually got the Pinkertons to a safe place in the railroad yard. The sheriff arrived by special train at 11 P.M. to remove the beaten Pinkertons. Homestead continued to celebrate as the train moved out of town. Frick returned to Clayton protected by personal bodyguards. Frick made arrangements to have his son Childs go to Fisher's Island. On July 8, Adelaide gave birth to a very sick Henry Clay Frick, Jr., at Clayton. Helen would remain at Clayton to be with her mother. Frick had major concerns for his family as the press turned extremely negative.

The sheriff struggled to find deputies, and the advisory committee in Homestead struggled to regain control of the town. Lookouts were still posted as the town took the next couple of days to bury the dead. The struggle degraded to a political one, with Carnegie's unionized mills in Beaver and Pittsburgh offering support. Union men in Chicago talked about sending men and guns. The United States Congress debated daily. The governor finally sent troops after political bosses Magee and Flinn pulled every string possible; still, the troops were not greeted in Homestead. Rails were torn up to slow the trains, but the troops were in place by July 12. Once the town was under military control, Congress sent a special committee to hold hearings. With Homestead peaceful and under martial law, the advantage passed to Carnegie Company. O'Donnell called unsuccessfully for a national boycott of Carnegie steel product, and Samuel Gompers came to help support the unsuccessful boycott. O'Donnell continued to work the press and Congress, which now was his best hope. O'Donnell appealed by letter on July 16 to Republican vice-presidential candidate Whitelaw Reid to allow the union to save some face by reopening the negotiations.[4] A strong-willed Frick, however, refused, sensing he had a victory. On July 17, Hugh O'Donnell went to New York to try to win over the Republicans, who were counting on the labor vote for high tariffs in the fall election. While O'Donnell was in New York with the Republicans, McLuckie was in Homestead adding to the Democratic rhetoric against the Republicans. Frick started to advertise for scabs on July 14, according to the long-range plan. On July 21, Frick tried the old strategy of opening the mill and allowing men to return on an individual contract. The move failed, making the lockout a true strike.

Things changed again as the socialists entered the crisis. On July 23, a clean-cut Alexander Berkman in a suit entered Frick's office at the *Chronicle-Telegraph* Building on Pittsburgh's Fifth Avenue. The socialist and anarchist movements in the United States had been following the action at Homestead. The most radical left fringe were the anarchists, who even rejected the minor organizational bent of Karl Marx. The anarchists had always looked for opportunities to get involved in labor strife. They were best known for the Haymarket riots. For them, the capitalists were the root of all evil of the world. In their fervor, the anarchists approached the religious homicide bombers of today. They believed the greatest political accomplishment was to die creating a scene for the cause. Dying was the highest form of propaganda for them. Homestead was now the ideal location for creating such propaganda. Their philosophical leader was the orator Emma Goldman, and her lover was Alexander Berkman. Years later, Emma Goldman would be called "the most dangerous woman in the United States" by J. Edgar Hoover.[5]

Berkman had arrived alone in Pittsburgh around July 16 with little money and a gun, and wearing the suit Emma Goldman had suggested. He responded to a newspaper ad that Frick had placed for scabs and set up an interview at Frick's office. The first visit was more to check on the routine and the guards. Frick was without bodyguards and was following his routine of taking lunch at the Duquesne Club and then returning to the office. At the Duquesne Club, he usually lunched with his friend Andrew Mellon and Mellon's younger brother, Robert. Frick had his own little club within a club at the Duquesne Club, which included his Thursday night poker friends.[6] This group included George Westinghouse, Philander Knox, Andrew Mellon, Henry Oliver, Robert Pitcairn, Henry R. Rea and E. Ferguson. This little club was said to have had its own rules and initiation. Frick's group lunched in a special room, modeling themselves after the Pittsburgh Pig Iron Aristocrats, who met daily in "room number 6." These old-line industrialists included Benjamin Jones, Henry Oliver, Henry Phipps, C.B. Herron, J.W. Chalfant, and C.H. Spang. Henry Oliver had helped found the aristocratic club of the pig iron manufacturers — the Duquesne Club. Frick's group represented the new aristocrats, and it was one of Frick's pleasures to lunch with the group. Frick often lunched late and returned to the office by himself without guards.

Berkman's first visit allowed him to learn about Frick's well-known routine. Berkman stayed in an anarchist cell in Allegheny City across from Pittsburgh. Berkman's second visit was on July 23, and a nervous Berkman was forced to wait until a telegraph boy delivered a message to the office. Frick was in the office with his partner and second in command John Leishman. Berkman rushed in and fired a shot, hitting Frick in the shoulder. Frick fell and Berkman fired again, hitting him in the neck. He took aim for the third shot, but Leishman intervened, forcing the shot to go wild and hit the ceiling. Leishman wrestled Berkman to the ground. Frick jumped in, and Berkman took out a sharpened file dagger and struck Frick in the leg and knee. The office boy got a sheriff's deputy who took aim, but Frick called him off, only wanting to see his attacker's face. In the struggle with the deputy, Berkman was found to have an explosive pill in his mouth, but it failed to go off.

The burning of the Pinkerton boat (courtesy Carnegie Library of Pittsburgh [and Frick Collection]).

Doctors were called for immediately and performed an operation to remove the bullets. Frick refused anesthesia and the bullets were removed. Then, amazingly, he seemed revived. He wrote short telegrams to his wife, Carnegie, and the press. He even talked of returning to the office on Monday. The doctors stayed with him for some time. Finally an ambulance was called to take Frick to his home. Now a crowd had gathered at the office building and hospital. Frick returned home bloodied and weak, but the first thing he asked about as he saw his wife was the health of his newborn son. The doctors tried to calm Adelaide and Annie, a nurse who had arrived for Frick. Adelaide's bed was moved from her room to Frick's, so they could be together. It was six days before the first anniversary of the death of Martha. Twenty years later Frick admitted to a reporter that when Berkman first aimed at him he saw Martha at his side.[7] Frick would always contend that it was the spiritual light of Martha that blinded Berkman, who had reported that sunlight from the window caused him to miss the headshot.

Berkman's entrance into the crisis changed things. The union wanted no part of Berkman's act. While the press continued to vilify Frick, they also hailed his courage and nerve. Frick still refused to have guards at Clayton and the office. He continued his routine of taking the trolley from Clayton to his office. A New York reporter stated: "Those who hate him most admire the nerve and stamina of this man of steel whom nothing seems to be able to move."[8] Still, union papers continued to demonize him. A poem in the *National Labor Tribune* included the chorus: "Of all slave drivers, for spite and kick,/No one so cruel as Tyrant Frick." Public opinion did turn a bit in favor of Frick. The religion of the workers was Catholicism, and the local priests and press saw more evil in anarchists than capitalists. The *Pittsburgh Catholic* noted: "The attempt on Frick's life is an eye opener. We are no better, no safer, no securer, than the people residing in France, or Germany, or Russia. Our lax laws have given the Anarchists a foothold here."[9] An editorial in the *Catholic World* in 1893 noted: "The distribution of wealth is frightful in its very inequalities. Still I do believe that the social system is radically and hopelessly wrong. I do believe that the American workmen can right their wrongs by the machinery at their disposal and without violating any law human or divine."[10] After that, capitalists, religious workers, and particularly Catholic priests were on the European socialists' hit list. The public across the nation was concerned about the existence of anarchist cells in major cities and the rising tide of socialism. Still, the public had little stomach for the use of Pinkertons and troops in labor disputes. Homestead for the next few years would be debated in major newspapers across the nation. The final vision of the Homestead Strike became something much different from the reality.

Personally, the crisis was far from over for Frick. Adelaide slipped into depression and needed to be at Frick's side. Meantime, baby Henry Clay Frick, Jr., struggled for life. Frick had extra telephone lines installed to Clayton to better manage Carnegie Steel. He took daily reports from the plant superintendents. Frick had newspapers from all parts of the country coming in. He also stayed in close contact with Carnegie by telegraph. Frick seemed determined to recover from his wounds in order to keep Carnegie from returning and taking over. The baby had a fulltime nurse, Adelaide's sister, and daily visits from doctors. Still, little could be done, and on August 3, the child died. Adelaide was devastated, and Frick felt more pain than that inflicted by Berkman. Frick made the funeral arrangements, but both he and Adelaide remained in their room during the actual service in the house. The baby was buried beside his sister in Homewood Cemetery.

The drama at Homestead continued as Frick and Potter brought in scabs and tried to restart the mill. Scabs were housed in the mill, and the military assured protection. Wages were around $1.50 an hour plus meals and housing. Food and supplies were brought to the mill via the river. Frick brought in blacks from Richmond, Virginia, which heightened racial tensions in middle of the crisis. Strikers did their best to threaten deliveries and new workers. Most of the initial work was maintenance, although Frick was determined to run the mill. Frick went to the office by trolley on August 5. He remained more than ever determined to win this battle, holding out against weak-kneed Republicans wanting an end to the conflict. The unskilled immigrant laborers, needing money and with nothing to gain from the strike, started to break ranks. Carnegie was also going back and forth with public opinion. Frick was well aware that he couldn't count on Carnegie. On August 31, Frick visited and made a full inspection of all Homestead departments. Frick pushed forward and was able to start rolling steel in September, but it was more symbolic than full production. With direct involvement in the hiring of the men, Frick also continued to pursue every legal avenue to charge the leaders of the strike. By the end of September, Frick had the mill running at 45 percent capacity, an amazing feat.

The White House was watching the problems at Homestead closely. Benjamin Harrison was struggling and needed the labor vote, and the Democrats were linking Homestead to the Republicans. Harrison privately was opposed to the use of armed Pinkertons. Harrison sent his friend John Milholland to talk to Frick about ending the strike. Frick's reply was that he would not end the strike even "if President Harrison himself should personally request him to do so."[11] Frick had gone too far to consider a change of tactics. Democrats felt they could carry western Pennsylvania for the first time since the formation of the Republican Party in the 1850s. Torchlight parades in Homestead had floats portraying "protectionism" as black sheep, as politicians injected their own brand of racism into the crisis.

Things were changing in October. The unskilled laborers realized that their jobs were being lost for good, and they had nothing to gain in continuing the strike. The sheriff was having no problem recruiting deputies at $2.50 a day, and the military left on October 13. Desperate strikers dynamited a Homestead Hotel where scabs were being housed, but Frick pressed on. Slowly, the scabs were learning to deal with the job and the strikers. An October 15 survey of the mill by the union concluded there were 2,000 employees working at the mill and 200 were former employees. It was becoming clear the strike was lost, but the union did gather thousands for political rallies for the Democratic Party. Samuel Gompers visited again in an effort to shore up morale. The unionists tried to harass the scabs some more, but the sheriff responded with more deputies, and Frick offered rewards to name offenders. Money was flowing into the union from around the nation, but the most affected by the strike, the unskilled laborers, got very little of it. Frick visited the mill almost daily to build morale. On October 28, he replaced the unpopular Potter with Charles Schwab. Schwab had the respect of both scab and unionist. Schwab started to personally recruit old hands. Schwab moved inside the mill and started the rebuilding. The works was badly in need of repair, he reported to Frick. The strikers were losing, but their only hope was that political pressure from the upcoming election would break Carnegie or Frick.

The Homestead Strike had badly damaged the campaign of President Harrison to hold the White House. John Wanamaker, postmaster general and Philadelphia department store king, tried to pressure Carnegie and Frick into ending the strike to save the election. Frick and Carnegie had been major contributors to the Harrison campaign. Wanamaker was a friend and a supplier to Frick's Union Supply mine stores. Furthermore, Wanamaker had done a number of political favors for Frick, such as the naming of a Fayette County friend, Robert Paterson, to postmaster.[12] Carnegie and Frick resisted the plea, but Carnegie dispatched Frick to Republican headquarters to help save the election. Pittsburgh boss Christopher Magee and Pennsylvania Senator Matthew Quay accompanied Frick in late October. At the time Magee and Quay were Pennsylvania's most powerful bosses. John Wanamaker and Quay came by special Pullman car to Pittsburgh's East End station for the trip to New York.[13] They had tried unsuccessfully to avoid reporters. The *New York Times* headline read: "Frick Here with Boodle — Pennsylvania Millionaires to Buy Presidency."[14] The Allegheny Plateau, which included Pittsburgh, Youngstown, Wheeling, and Buffalo, had supplied a Republican plurality of 10,000 votes in every election since that of Abe Lincoln. The strike now threatened a loss of all of industrial Pennsylvania, New York, and maybe even Ohio. Frick probably was aware that the election was lost but felt obligated to the party to try to help financially.

Election Day, November 8, proved to be the last victory for the Homestead union as the Democrats carried the election. The Republicans managed to hold Allegheny County as the violence had cost the union public support locally. Homestead went Democrat for the first time. Frick started to bring in more blacks and Italians, a signal to the Slavs and Hungarians that they were going to be permanently replaced. The unskilled Slavs and Hungarians had no choice but to return to work. The union broke on November 18 as mechanics voted to return, but there were few jobs. The rumors of job shortages caused a panic of returning applicants. Frick and Schwab were now in a position to eliminate unionists. The mill showed 2,715 employed on November 18. A rush of 2,200 men applied to be reinstated, of which only 406 were hired. Most of the 406 were unskilled labor. The union was completely crushed. The last act of the union was to call for funds to help the unemployed. A Homestead relief fund was set up by the *Pittsburgh Press*. Money did come in, which allowed for an orderly absorption of the unemployed into the area workforce. Most of the union leaders left for different cities.

Schwab, who was only thirty at the time, helped make the mill transition a successful one. Schwab's biographer described his first four months:

> Schwab did not step outside of the plant; he lived in one of five executive houses on the grounds. Drawing upon an uncommon ability, Schwab was able to work for seventy-two hours at a stretch, taking on short snatches of sleep. He decided that in his first weeks he should go everywhere to greet and to speak to everyone on both the day and night shifts and to compile an inventory of physical and human assets on which he could base the reconstruction of Homestead.[15]

Schwab worked with Frick to help skilled workers who were behind on their rent payments. Schwab proved every bit the equal of his mentor Bill Jones. For his part, Frick also got to the mill often. The strike was over by the end of November, but Schwab needed time to repair and called for a brief closing.

The debate over the nature and fault for the strike would continue for years. Altogether three Pinkertons and seven workers were killed and over a hundred wounded. Stories, myths, and legends developed almost immediately. One of the Pinkertons told the following story the next day in the paper:

> When we saw that preparations were being made to burn the barges, I loaded my revolver and made up my mind to blow my brains out should the boat be set afire. I am just as positive that not less than a dozen of our men committed suicide during the day, as I am that I am standing here. I saw four jump into the water and sink and I have been told that several others made away with themselves in the same way.[16] Checks of the Pinkerton roster showed no suicides. All of this made great copy in a presidential election year. Popular national weekly magazines such as *Harpers Weekly* made it their cover story. Even European papers loved to cover the labor violence in the New World, which greatly angered Carnegie. Frick held a rare interview on July 7 that was carried around the world the next day. Frick summarized it: "It is whether the Carnegie Company or the Amalgamated Association should have absolute control of our plant and business at Homestead. We have decided, after numerous fruitless conferences with the Amalgamated officials ... to operate the plant ourselves."[17]

The costs of the strike were substantial. The 148-day strike cost the men about $1 million ($18.5 million today) in wages. The union and other union relief funds doled out in $170,000 in assistance to the workers. The loss of wages in sympathetic strikes at Beaver Falls and Union Mills was $950,000. The state of Pennsylvania estimated the cost of law enforcement at $440,000. The total was probably over $4 million ($74 million today). The company's profit loss was estimated at $750,000 ($13.8 million).[18] Harvey reported that the combined company cost of lost profits and expenditures was $2 million ($36 million today).[19] Still, the profits of Carnegie Steel only dropped $300,000 in 1892 from $4,300,000 in 1891 to $4,000,000 in 1892. More amazing was that Carnegie's greatest competitor, Illinois Steel, reported a loss of $1,000,000 for 1892. Even considering that expenditures for the strike continued into 1893, the company still reported profits of $3,000,000 that year.

The greatest loser of the Homestead Strike was the union. The Amalgamated union was smashed and the Carnegie mills would not be unionized again until the late 1930s. The membership of the Amalgamated dropped from 24,000 to 14,000 after the strike. The Amalgamated lost power and eventually became a finishing mill organization — the National Amalgamated Association of Iron, Steel, and Tin Workers. Hugh O'Donnell ended up being blacklisted by the company and union. The union opposed his secret efforts with the Republican Party. O'Donnell had always been a supporter of the Republican tariffs, which he believed key to American industry. Hugh O'Donnell left Homestead to manage a music company. Other leaders like Thomas Crawford and Jack Clifford similarly tried their hands at other businesses. After the union, the biggest losers were the unskilled laborers who lost their jobs, numbering well over a thousand. These unskilled laborers entered into a growing recession with no job skills. They had supported the union but had nothing to gain from a union victory. Most of these workers moved on to cities like Cleveland and Detroit to find work.

The biggest winner of the Homestead Strike was the Democratic Party. The Homestead Strike was used as a political hammer to pay back the Democratic defeats funded by Pittsburgh steelmakers. Frick and Carnegie had helped to defeat the Democratic Speaker of the House, John Carlisle, and others in 1888. The political side of Homestead is one reason it gained national notoriety. Herbert Casson summarized this in 1907:

Democratic editors were shrieking that "Slavery had its Legree, Protectionism its Frick." Free trade propagandists stood behind the strikers and cheered them on to the bitterest resistance. Every incident was exaggerated. It was not the loss of life, which attracted attention, but rather the dramatic and political nature of the struggle. Twice the damage has been done in other strikes of which the public has heard comparatively little.[20]

One might write Casson off as sympathetic to the steel managers, if it were not for the fact that the congressional inquiry into the strike was filled with questions about protectionism. Clearly, the fight over protectionism was at least a factor in the amount of publicity. For years, Homestead would be pointed to as proof that profits from tariffs did not help the worker. It was a wedge Democrats could use to break worker loyalty to the Republican Party. It was a populist cry, but the facts showed that tariff-generated profits were poured into plant expansion, consistent work, and jobs, although, the union would argue, not high-paying jobs.

The Democratic Party used Homestead as the poster child to oppose tariffs and break worker support for the Republican Party. The Homestead Strike opened a division in the Republican Party between the more progressive wing and the old guard. Frick, a staunch and loyal Republican, was thrust into the internal party politics. The Harrison administration lobbied Frick to recognize the union for the good of the party. Neither Frick nor Carnegie would bend to the political pressure. For Frick it was a difficult stand since he realized it would mean a Democratic victory. Frick realized this would defeat his strong belief in tariffs, property rights, and American exceptionalism. Carnegie, on the other hand, felt Grover Cleveland differed little in reality from the Republican candidate. Cleveland won by over 100,000 votes and carried the Electoral College 277 to 145. There were Democratic majorities the House (218 to 127) and the Senate (44 to 38). Amazingly, the Republicans carried western Pennsylvania, but most other industrialized areas went Democratic. With Democrats controlling the White House and Congress, capitalists prepared for a tariff reduction, but on other issues Cleveland was pro-business.

In retrospect, neither Carnegie nor Frick had a high regard for Harrison. Carnegie even seemed to prefer Grover Cleveland, who was a good friend of J.P. Morgan. Frick had believed Harrison to be weak in his support of tariffs and protectionism, and Frick was not alone in the Republican Party on Harrison's lukewarm support of tariffs. William McKinley, chairman of the House Ways and Means Committee, who had written the 1890 Tariff Bill, was defeated in Ohio. The defeat of McKinley was viewed by Frick as a major setback for American industry. The Democrats had made the case that the tariffs had created manufacturing, but the capitalists had put the profits in their own pockets. The Democratic celebration would be shorted-lived as the Panic of 1893 started to reach the factories of America. The Democrats made some efforts to reduce tariffs, but the economic downturn became a bigger priority. Probably the only valuable legislation came out of the Pennsylvania legislature. Known as the Anti-Pinkerton Law, it prevented the deputizing of nonresidents.

John McLuckie was typical of many of the Amalgamated leaders who were blacklisted by Carnegie Steel. Frick had pursued legal actions against McLuckie, but Carnegie seems to have ordered his blacklisting. McLuckie left Pittsburgh and remained active in political efforts such as the Populist Party, which got over a million votes in the 1892 elections. The Populist Party called for income taxes on the capitalists, and government ownership of railroads and communication companies. McLuckie remained an outspoken critic of Carnegie and Frick. Later revelations suggest that he worked with Emma Goldman to get Berkman out of jail.[21] McLuckie was last noted working in a copper mine in Mexico. There is also some evidence that Carnegie supplied him money in 1898.

As for Berkman, he was found guilty and sentenced. During the trial, much was made of a possible conspiracy. Part of this was because Berkman was a follower of the most violent branch of anarchism and socialism, led by John Most. Most became known in Pittsburgh in 1882 when he wrote a violent strategy known as the "Pittsburgh Manifesto." Pittsburgh's old German population had a deep hatred of socialists. Two north-side anarchists, Carl Nold and Henry Bauer, were arrested but were let go after the trial showed no evidence of a conspiracy. Goldman years later claimed that the original plan was to use a bomb, but Berkman lacked the expertise. Berkman served fourteen years in the Western Penitentiary, and after his release continued in the anarchist movement. Berkman spent most of his time in jail, being arrested again in 1917. He was deported to Russia in 1919 with Emma Goldman. Frick had died a few weeks prior, and Berkman noted, "Well anyhow he left the country before I did."

Many of the union leaders were arrested for treason and murder. Interestingly, most of the Amalgamated leaders, such as McLuckie and O'Donnell, were acquitted of all charges. Hugh Dempsey, a Master Workman of the Knights of Labor, was convicted. During the fall, the scab laborers had become sick and many died from a mysterious illness. Dempsey was arrested when some helpers testified that they were paid to add a yellow powder to the meals. Analysis of the yellow powder showed it to contain arsenic and antimony.

Frick would forever be labeled the anti–Christ of the labor movement. Many old friends started to distance themselves from him. Though he was only forty-four, Frick's beard had started to gray. While Carnegie never blamed him in public, Carnegie did so with friends in an effort to improve his own image. Carnegie's style, unlike Frick's, was always behind the scenes. Frick actually fared a little better than Carnegie in the final analysis. Insiders realized that Carnegie was pulling the strings and was in full control. Carnegie, scrutinizing every move Frick made, was perceived as hiding in Scotland. A Joseph Pulitzer *St. Louis Post-Dispatch* article, which was republished throughout America, concluded: "Say what you will of Frick, he is a brave man. Say what you will of Carnegie, he is a coward. And gods and men hate cowards."[22] Carnegie's public image was forever tainted. His philanthropy was now considered giving money to ease his conscience. Homestead would haunt him, but Frick always saw

Clayton at the time of the Homestead Strike (courtesy Carnegie Library of Pittsburgh).

it as a capitalistic struggle for property rights and the right to manage one's company. Towns throughout the world hesitated to accept libraries from Carnegie. Even Pittsburgh City Council tried to reject a Carnegie offer for a Southside Library.

Frick did have a few capitalists such as Rockefeller and J.P. Morgan come to his aid, but the press was overwhelmingly negative. Rockefeller, who cared little for Carnegie, sent a congratulatory telegram.[23] A pastor who knew both men from Uniontown defended both Carnegie and Frick in a national weekly, *The Independent*. Reverend Thomas Boyle boldly stated:

> No one regretted the shedding of blood more than Mr. Frick and if any financial sacrifice would have called back to life these dead, he would have willingly done it. His silence was then caused by lack of feeling or indifference, but it was feared that an expression of sympathy from him would be interpreted so as to intensify the spirit of lawlessness that had taken possession of his employees. It is easy to look backward and say that another policy would have brought different results, and yet if his plans had been fully carried out then his wishes would have been realized, and no injury should be done to any body. Mr. Frick is neither heartless, stubborn, nor overbearing. He is a man of great will power and when clearly convinced he is right, he is disposed to go forward and take the consequences.[24]

Interestingly, Frick got a fair amount of support from churches, which feared lawlessness and violence more than capitalism.

The year 1892 ended with more tragedy in Frick's life. His boyhood friend and Morewood superintendent Morris Ramsey died of stomach cancer. Ramsey's struggles had started in July, and Frick had sent him and his family for a vacation in Scotland. As Ramsey's decline continued, Frick hired the best doctors to work on him. Ramsey was brought to Allegheny City Hospital in December of 1892. He died on December 29. Ramsey, like Thomas Lynch, had been key to Frick's coke empire. With the death of Morris, Thomas Lynch was general manager of H.C. Frick Company and Morris's brother William Ramsay was general superintendent. Frick was a pallbearer and gave much financial help to Morris's family and widow. His biographers often overlook these acts of financial help to Frick's loyal managers. Frick ended the year surrounded by death and depression.

John Potter was made the Homestead scapegoat, to a large degree by Carnegie, and to some degree by Frick. All realized that his "promotion" to "chief engineer" was a demotion. As early as July 17, Carnegie had suggested in a letter to partner George Lauder, "Potter should be sent abroad and Schwab sent back to Homestead."[25] "Sending someone abroad" was an organizational phase for eliminating managers. Frick held off replacing Potter until the strike was won, not wanting to show any weakness. Nothing could be more demoralizing to these overachievers of the Carnegie Empire than a demotion. Potter had been one of the Carnegie "boys" and remained well liked by his peers. Potter eventually left Carnegie Steel to enter mining in South America. He never fully recovered from his loss of power in the Carnegie organization, of which he was so proud. He was invited to the twenty-first annual meeting of the Carnegie Veterans Association in 1925. On the day of the meeting he committed suicide in Los Angeles. Frick would never be invited to the meetings of the Carnegie veterans.

The new managers of Homestead, including Frick, all took pay cuts. The new group of managers under Frick and Schwab at Homestead would become known as the "Boys of Braddock" and would supply three future presidents of United States Steel, one president of Bethlehem Steel, and one president of Midvale Steel (#3), in addition to over ten vice-presidents of these companies. Schwab had some loyal family members and friends brought in, including Alva Dinkey (his brother-in-law from Braddock), Joe Schwab (his brother), William Dickson, and William Corey (both friends from Braddock).[26]

14. The Aftermath

The struggle of Homestead would soon be replaced by economic depression and unemployment. Panics were feared by both capitalists and laborers. The Panic of 1893 had started, like most, as a financial crisis in the financial firms. The root cause remains debatable to this day. Part of the problem was a reduction of European investment in America. In 1890, the famous British investment firm Baring Brothers went bankrupt. Baring Brothers was a major stockholder in American firms. This financial failure caused investment to dry up in America in 1892. But another view is that J.P. Morgan created the panic because he benefited by building his railroad trust and electric trust. Most of the failed railroads would come under Morgan's control. There was also a drain on treasury gold, which Morgan attributed to the Sherman Silver Bill. Another theory was the generosity of the Republican pensions for veterans drained the treasury. In fairness, however, the tariff revenues from the McKinley Tariff Bill more than covered the pensions.

In any case, the first signs of a panic came ten days before President Cleveland took office, with the failure of the Philadelphia and Reading Railroad. Before the Panic of 1893 ended, a quarter of America's railroads would fail, and steel prices would crash. In 1893 alone, 15,000 businesses failed, along with 158 banks. Of America's 253 blast furnaces, 116 shut down in 1893. As the panic deepened, the public increased its demand to get gold for their silver certificates, which drained the treasury to the crisis point. President Cleveland, Democrats, Republicans, the Senate, and the House all lacked a complete answer to the panic.

Homestead in many ways changed American politics in industrial towns. Prior to the Homestead Strike, most labor towns voted Republican, supporting the protectionism of the Republican Party. The Democratic Party had carried the farmers with their anti-tariff policies, which were intended to keep prices down. Homestead became a rallying point for the Democrats as an example that the profits from the tariffs were not being passed on to the worker. The union lost at Homestead, but that fall the Democrats took back the White House with Grover Cleveland. The labor vote turned Democratic. The use of troops by President Harrison particularly hurt the Republicans. When congressional hearings were held on the Homestead Strike, the Democrats used the opportunity to show that tariffs had not helped labor. The Democrats would have tightened their hold on labor had not the Panic of 1893 spread to Main Street.

The defeat of Ohio Congressman William McKinley, the architect of the 1890 Tariff and chairman of the House Ways and Means Committee in the 1892 election, had been a bigger setback to Pittsburgh capitalists than the election of Grover Cleveland. Cleveland, a close friend of J.P. Morgan, was considered a safe Democrat to have in the presidency. Carnegie, unlike Frick, was not necessarily a loyal Republican. William McKinley was planning to run for the Ohio governorship in 1894, and many Republicans such as Frick saw him as the future of the Republican Party. Never a wealthy man, McKinley had been forced into bankruptcy in the 1893 downturn. Needing to support his family, he wanted to go back into the law. McKinley's friend Mark Hanna looked for help to pay McKinley's debts to free him to campaign.[1] Henry Clay Frick headed up a group of Pittsburgh capitalists such as George Westinghouse and Philander Knox to help. McKinley accepted the money as a loan and did pay all parties back.[2] Frick and Knox had foreseen the rise of McKinley to the presidency in 1896.

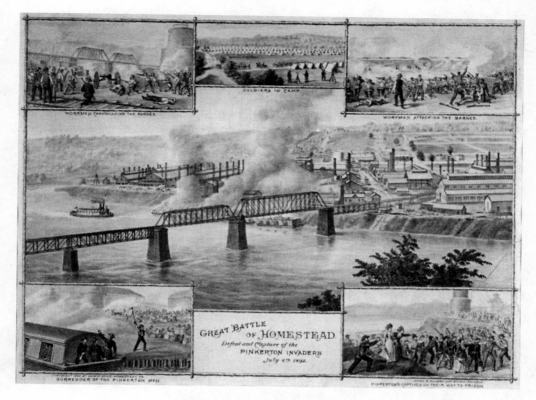

Postcard of the Homestead Strike (1894).

It usually takes months for the force of a Wall Street meltdown to hit the factories. As Homesteaders were returning to work, the full force of the panic hit. By December 1892, Homestead Works barely had orders to run at 40 percent of capacity. Unemployment was running over 50 percent in the steel valleys of Pittsburgh, and those who were employed were working a two- to three-day week. The *Pittsburgh Press* reported:

> In Homestead there are today 1,800 men, most of them with families for whom no employment can be found. For many of them the Christmas prospect is an empty cupboard and a cheerless hearth.... The wolf is at the door; innocent children, hard-working mothers, fathers who in the majority of cases simply obeyed higher authorities—all suffering in a land of plenty.[3]

These panics, not strikes, were what the average steelworkers feared most. Steelworkers in Braddock and Homestead took to the hills to dig coal to heat their homes. Those who got a few days' work shared food with family and friends. It was a common practice for workers to include a homeless visitor for Sunday dinner. Hunting small game become popular in the heavily wooded ravines of the area. Frick and Carnegie even discussed some form of company relief for the steelworkers. Homestead Works was able to come on line in early 1893 and was extremely competitive with the wage reductions. With armor and structural steel orders, Homestead became a rarity in the 1893 depression by running near full capacity. It was Edgar Thomson Works that was struggling with most of the nation.

The Panic of 1893 hit full force in the winter of 1892–93. Jacob Sechler Coxey of Massillon, Ohio, formed the idea of a massive march on Washington to highlight the rising unemployment. Coxey owned a sand quarry that mined high-quality silica sand for the steel and glass industry, which was closed by the panic. Coxey had also run for Congress as a Populist candidate. The depression had idled his operation for months. Coxey had some unique ideas that would augur those applied in the 1930s. Coxey hoped to form a Christian nation based on charity. He called also for an eight-hour day and a minimum wage of $1.50 as well as a national bond issue to support the unemployed. Coxey suggested a massive influx of money and public works for the unemployed, but it was the idea of a national march that struck fear into the hearts of Congress. The idea of an army of tramps, socialists, and anarchists marching through the country struck a nerve. The politicians remembered the railroad worker revolt of 1877 and the more recent riots in Chicago and Homestead. Many believed the country was ripe for a socialist revolution like those seen in Europe. The concerns were further stirred by the press, which descended on Massillon, Ohio. The Chicago press was one of the first to arrive. While editorials denounced the march, the headlines promoted fear to move Congress. Money and support started to pour in from labor unions, Populists, and probably a few Republicans. In the midst of the Coxey outcry, Governor McKinley was dealing with an outbreak of worker violence in Ohio. The strikers were attacking trains carrying coal into Ohio from West Virginia. Rails were being torn up, trains shot at, and bridges burned. Governor McKinley summoned John McBride, the president of the United Mine Workers, to his office. McBride had noted he had "fourteen cannon pointed on one mine." His cajoling failed, and McKinley ordered a massive call-up of the National Guard. The show of overwhelming force ended the violence. One train alone carried twelve men and two Gatling guns.

Coxey's gathering army remained peaceful as Coxey used torchlight parades and speeches to muster his troops. Finally, Coxey gathered several thousand to start the march, with thousands more to converge with his main column along the way. The initial body reportedly reached 20,000 at its peak in Ohio. The Ohio column was to meet the columns from New York and Philadelphia in Pittsburgh. Pittsburgh was to be the mustering point. The march started on Easter Sunday with a plan to reach Washington on May Day. Coxey and his "officers" rode horses at the front of the column, along with a band. Hugh O'Donnell, one of the Homestead leaders, led the way. Reporters were astonished as they rushed reports to their papers. Headlines seem to rally more from all parts of the country. New armies from Philadelphia, Pittsburgh, and Maryland mustered as well. Coxey's Ohio army followed roughly today's Route 30 to Pittsburgh. Towns offered food as the marchers passed through. As the army reached Pittsburgh on April 3, it swelled to 300,000 in the city.[4] At times it appeared to be a party as workers released frustrations. It was labor's spring break.

Pittsburgh was the forge of the nation and the fortress of American labor, and many hoped it would nurture the seed of a social revolution. The winter of 1892–93 had been the toughest ever for this industrial center. Hobo towns lined the great railroads leading into the city and the streets were filled with beggars. Immigrants in tent cities struggled to stay warm and eat. The rich suburbs lived in constant fear of looting or attack. The city had emptied its coffers to supply relief. Andrew Carnegie kicked in an equal amount of about $125,000, and other capitalists, including Frick, chipped in another $100,000. The money was used for city work projects such as Coxey had been calling for. The army's appearance lifted the hopes of the city. Bands and crowds gathered as if Coxey's division were a liberating army. Pittsburgh, however, would be the climax of the national march: the swell in the ranks fell quickly as the army left Pittsburgh.

In Maryland, roads were mud from a rainy spring and the army bogged down. Food became scarce and towns less supportive, and workers turned to the practice of foraging for food. The local authorities restricted foraging as the army dwindled with each mile. It entered Washington with under a thousand hungry marchers. President Grover Cleveland had braced for any trouble, and Coxey was arrested for walking on the grass (trespassing on Capitol lawn). Mounted police had an easy time intimidating the weary army. Some fighting broke out, but the police suppressed the army quickly. Populists in Congress read Coxey's petitions, and in the Senate, a bill was unsuccessfully introduced. The New Deal in the thirties would finally see many of Coxey's ideas implemented, and Coxey's march would be a model for the civil rights movement. Another army, known as the "Industrial Army," was formed in California and got some press as Jack London joined the march. In Montana, a group of 650 miners started a march, but the spring of marches had come to an end. The unrest, however, was far from over.

Homestead remained a hot spot of unrest, although muted by the economic downturn. Homestead Works saw few benefits from the aftermath of the strike. Schwab proved a better manager, but he was every bit as opposed to unions. The tense relations remained at Homestead. The union effort continued on an underground basis. A special type of spy organization was created as a "Bureau of Information" under J.R. Mack as manager. The Bureau placed a number of spies throughout the workforce. Interestingly, underground unionists were able to identify many of them around Christmas 1894, as the company had turkeys delivered to their homes. The practice of giving turkeys was ended but the bureau remained in place until the 1920s. When William Corey replaced Schwab as plant superintendent in 1898, Corey actually strengthened the function of the bureau. Corey was able to head off a major unionization drive in 1899, thanks to his spies.

While spies roamed the mill, Carnegie looked to pacify the townspeople in more public ways, planning a new huge library for Homestead. Frick's actions during the Panic and depression were less ostentatious but better addressed the problems. Mr. and Mrs. Frick became financially involved with the social outreach project of Kingsley House, which opened in December 1893. Mrs. Frick became personally involved as well. Kingsley House was the ideal type of Frick charity. It was the idea of Frick's pastor, George Hodges at Calvary Episcopal Church, and Father Sheedy of St. Mary's Church in Pittsburgh's poorest area. Kingsley House was a type of YMCA and YWCA, both of which Hodges was active in with George Westinghouse. The purpose of the house was to address the "ethnic, social, and economic conditions" of children. Kingsley House provided clubs for youth as well as a variety of classes. Classes stressed skills for future employment, such as typewriting, needlework, and manual arts. The house had a kindergarten for poor children and a nursery for working mothers. Kingsley House inspired neighbor H.J. Heinz to open a similar operation, the Sarah Heinz House, on the north side of Pittsburgh. Originally Kingsley House was located at 1707 Penn Avenue, but moved closer to the city on the suggestion of Mrs. Frick. Frick donated $50,000 (almost $1 million today) to purchase a new house and expand it. Kingsley House was a working effort for Adelaide and the Frick children. Adelaide often took young Helen to help distribute clothes and food. The Christmas party for orphaned girls was a tradition that Helen carried on for decades. Frick was particularly enthusiastic about funding these Christmas parties. He served on the Pittsburgh Free Dispensary Board, which was like a local emergency room for children and young mothers. Throughout his life Frick made quiet donations of expensive equipment to area hospitals. Another charity was the Salvation Army, which Frick gave to quietly his whole life. Discretion would be the hallmark of Frick's type of giving, as opposed to Carnegie's press releases of his giving.

Clubs were formed at Kingsley around interests and activities. Club members received general training in parliamentary practice, basic business practices, and banking skills. Clubs often ran social events to collect income for trips or to pay membership dues. These young boys learned business principles first-hand in the management of their own clubs. The House acted as a city social network, tying into organizations such as the YMCA, YWCA, and Sarah Heinz House. This network was critical in helping immigrants through offering citizen training and courses in English. The Kingsley House Association opened the clubs to a ten-day camping experience at its country camp, Lillian Home, at Valencia, Pennsylvania. This camping experience was free to the youth. Kingsley House also coordinated lectures with the Carnegie Museum. More cutting edge was the Kingsley House work with the neighborhood "little mothers." Magee Hospital had a maternity dispensary at the Kingsley House. The City Health Department offered free help and training for these young mothers. There was also coordination with the Juvenile Courts. Overall, no charity better expressed the type of charity Frick preferred. One minor embarrassment for Frick occurred in the fall of 1893, when Carnegie purchased a one-ton Orchestrion for him in Europe. The Orchestrion was a huge nine-foot-high mechanical "collection" of an organ, drums, and cymbals driven by metal recordings. The huge musical piece, which weighed two tons, took special handling at the railroad and a team of ten horses to pull the delivery wagon.

Frick's personal life changed also with Homestead. The family dinner remained important, but silence continued for a while. Frick, who rarely showed humor at work, liked a bit of playful teasing of the wife and children at home. The subtle joking and teasing at the table slowed, and with Childs at boarding school, Helen sat beside her father at the long, mahogany dining table. Frick did demonstrate some humor during the Homestead crisis with his purchase of the painting titled *The Mine Mule*. The mule wore a sign saying "Non-Union Helper." It certainly was a painting that required little expert interpretation. The Orchestrion played Frick's favorites, such as "Ave Maria" and "The Last Rose of Summer" during dinner. Things had also changed with the earlier death of Martha. While many demands were made of Childs, it was only natural that Helen became overprotected. For Helen, a major change was the loss of her governess to marriage. A young Swiss governess, Mademoiselle Ogiz, replaced Annie. After dinner, the family went to the second floor sitting room, which had a gas fireplace.

The Orchestrion continued to play as Frick would relax reading the paper. He might read weekly papers such as the *New World*. He might also play solitaire. Frick might then look over a few business papers for the next day. He never read novels but enjoyed biblical selections such as the Psalms and the Sermon on the Mount, Shakespeare, the *Sayings of Marcus Aurelius*, and the *Autobiography of Benjamin Franklin*. In difficult times Psalm 55 was a favorite of his. Frick always retired very early except when he had his friends over for cards. This was certainly a much different picture from Carnegie's dinner routine of having a Scottish piper lead in a group of richly dressed guests in his castle for an evening of expensive dining. It was much different from his New York counterparts and their nightly parties as well.

The Panic of 1893 continued, the greatest American depression to that point. Frick had ordered repairs and preparation of the Homestead mill in the fall of 1892, but when the mill was ready, the orders were gone. The United Mine Workers and the Knights of Labor called for a national strike in April 1894, and over 200,000 miners were involved nationwide. The Knights of Labor, who called for an eight-hour day, led the strike. This two-month strike was bloody far beyond the deadly violence; however, in the two-month period at least eleven miners died in the Connellsville region. The strikers were a roaming army of "Huns." The Hungarians, Poles, and Slavs united in the new union, which provoked the owners with violence. Scabs were often beaten to death and mines dynamited. The universal and national nature of the strike resulted in diffused reporting. Violence and deaths occurred in Alabama, Illinois, West Virginia, and Ohio. Governor William McKinley ordered out troops and mounted machine guns on rail cars. The strike lasted about eight weeks, as the workers broke along ethnic lines But again the rural nature of the operations suppressed press reporting. While H.C. Frick Company was struck, it was spared the worst, with the blacks and Poles returning first.

The Connellsville district slowed with the steel industry. The economy helped end the strike. The coke companies in the Connellsville area brought in over 2,000 blacks and Ital-

Helen Frick's dolls enjoy a ride in the neighborhood (courtesy Frick Collection).

ians, paying agents $3 per head. The owners created an army of a thousand deputies at $5 a person. The economy, scabs, union division, and hired army ended the strike in Connellsville by June 1894. The Knights, representing the unskilled, were involved in much of the fighting. Most of this was over the elimination of Hungarians and Slavs in the union. In this case, H.C. Frick Company was considered worker friendly, and the Hungarians did not target Frick mines. While Frick often used Hungarians, blacks, and Italians for strikebreakers, he would allow them to stay on in the workforce if they proved themselves. The strike had been triggered partly because mining companies were unable to meet payroll, but the H.C. Frick Company didn't have that problem. In addition, Frick workers were making, on average, better wages, since the Frick pay scale was the highest in the Connellsville district. Frick's competitor, W.J. Rainey, paid lower wages, discriminated against Eastern Europeans, and had a poorer safety record. Frick took pride in the better operation of his coke works. One tragedy for Frick during the strike was the beating to death of his chief engineer, Joseph Paddock. Frick would continue to help the family of Paddock for many years.

The unsuccessful strike led to the resurgence of the United Mine Workers. The United Mine Workers had become the dominant union for the mining districts with 20,000 members in 1890. The 1890s was a decade of depression and lost union membership, but the greater foundations of the UMWA were forged in the Panic of 1893. In the universal strike, the UMWA, affiliated with Samuel Gompers's American Federated Labor, replaced the Knights of Labor and smaller groups. The new union elected John B. Rae with a salary of $1,000 a year. The disaster of the national strike highlighted the lack of unity among the miners. To win these labor battles, the membership needed to change and promote new leadership. The AMWA embraced all races and religions in its membership and adopted the motto "United We Stand, Divided We Fall." Wages did improve with the upturn of the economy in 1895. The H.C. Frick Company led the way in 1895 with a 15 percent wage increase as the economy improved. With all the condemnation of Frick and Carnegie Steel, many lost sight of the improvements at the H.C. Frick Company under Thomas Lynch.

Hidden in history after the Homestead Strike would be one of Frick's greatest business moves. In fact, it was a deal that Carnegie saw no profitability in. It was the expansion into iron ore mining. Amazingly, it is Carnegie who gets credit for the massive application of vertical integration, yet he forcefully opposed Frick's moving Carnegie Steel into ore mining. In retrospect, Frick appears to have been the true architect of vertical integration. In 1890, Frick had worked on the favorable supply arrangements of limestone, a minor but necessary ingredient of steelmaking. Carnegie was content to stay out of raw materials unless supply problems threatened steel pricing or production. While Carnegie veterans looked back and attributed Carnegie with the concept, insiders of the period such as J.P. Morgan, John Rockefeller, and Henry Oliver attributed it correctly to Henry Clay Frick. The Panic of 1893 had brought the great mining complexes of the Mesabi Range to a halt. The mining companies needed cash and partners to continue. The use of Lake Superior ores in the blast furnaces of Pittsburgh had gone back to the 1850s. These early Lake Superior ores were "hard" ores that were mined in large chunks. The newly discovered Mesabi ores were "soft" and sandy, and furnace operators didn't want to experiment with them.

The Mesabi ore boom began in 1888, when the Minnesota range was determined to be over 100 miles long and 10 miles wide. Basically it covered the whole state north of Duluth to the Canadian line and west to the prairies. Mesabi is an Indian name for "Grandmother of All." The possible cost savings of 85 cents a ton was causing experimentation in the Chicago mills. Blending of up to 20 percent, Mesabi ores seemed to work without problems. The original owners, the Merritt brothers, were looking for partners in 1892. They initially approached Frick and Carnegie but got no response. They did find Carnegie's old friend Henry Oliver[5] to be interested. Oliver had even tried to interest political bosses C. Magee, William Flinn, and Matthew Quay, by taking them to see the range after the 1892 Republican convention. John D. Rockefeller became interested as the Panic of 1893 depressed the mine prices. Rockefeller and Oliver got involved in 1893.

Carnegie thought little of Oliver as a businessman and warned Frick to beware. On August 29, 1892, Carnegie wrote Frick: "Oliver's ore bargain is just like him — nothing in it. If there is any department of business which offers no inducement, it is ore."[6] A few years later in a letter to the Carnegie Steel Company Board, Carnegie wrote: "You will find that this ore venture, like all other ventures in ore, will result in much trouble and less profit than almost any branch of our business. If any of our brilliant and talented young partners have more time or attention than is required for their present duties, they will find sources of much greater profit right at home. I hope you will make a note of this prophecy."[7] These are hardly the words of the inventor of vertical integration.

Frick, however, did not lose interest. The cost savings in using Mesabi ore was worth many Homestead wage victories. Frick continued to study ores closely. In 1894, Henry Oliver's financial troubles deepened and Frick made a deal to take half interest in the Mesabi mines. As chairman, Frick was able to get some support from the partners. The deal was deemed a "gift" by Carnegie Steel Company, giving Oliver a $500,000 loan. Frick had pulled off a major future savings for the company, but it would take years for Carnegie to admit he was wrong. For Frick's part, it took strong leadership to continue to get the furnace operators to include more and more of the cheaper Mesabi ore.

Frick had now proved himself a steelmaker. Mesabi ore production went from 29,245 tons in 1892 to 1,913,234 tons in 1894.

15. The Foundation of
a Great Corporation

Homestead had returned to full business in 1893, and within a year was the flagship of a highly profitable Carnegie Steel. In 1894, as the depression continued and steel prices fell, Frick's cost cutting allowed Carnegie Steel to remain profitable and keep employment high. As many as 34 iron and steel related businesses went bankrupt in the Panic of 1893. One of them was a Carnegie competitor, Pennsylvania Steel, and his biggest surviving competitor was losing money. Carnegie Steel controlled a quarter of the nation's steel production. Homestead was productive and profitable, but there were many scars. In addition, the Democratic Party was taking a hard look at all of Carnegie's operations. The success of the company in large part was due to the armor production at Homestead. After the strike, armor production was progressing under plant superintendent Schwab and armor department manager William Corey[1] (both would be future presidents of United States Steel). William Corey was the only Carnegie man to have less personality than Frick. While Schwab referred to workers by their nicknames, such as Joe or Tommy, Corey thought of them by their employee numbers.

In September of 1893, all was about to change. That month, a Pittsburgh attorney came to see Secretary of the Navy Hilary Herbert about armor problems at Homestead. The attorney represented four armor department employees that wanted to sell information about irregularities in the production of Homestead armor. They had tried to sell the information to Frick, but Frick had rejected them.[2] Frick saw the offer as blackmail, but he did notify Schwab and Corey of the visit.

Frick also got a warning from his partner, Francis Lovejoy, of possible irregularities in the armor department. Frick would have nothing to do with producing inferior armor for American ships, having had a lifetime record of being more than fair in production for American forces. Frick wrote to Schwab in a September 16 note:

> Would say that I cannot too forcibly impress on you the importance of not permitting the heads of your departments there, or any employee under them, to do anything that would even look like slighting work that we turn out for the Government, and I trust you will give the matter your close personal attention and see that all matters and things in connection with armor are done strictly in accordance with specifications in our contracts with the Government.[3]

Schwab assured Frick that their inspection was valid.

The informant employees took their case directly to the government but again wanted money in return for information. The employees wanted 40 percent of the penalties and fines, but the Secretary of Navy persuaded them to settle for 25 percent. The information prompted Secretary Herbert to appoint a board of inquiry to research the complaints. The board, which never contacted the management of Carnegie, proposed a fine of 15 percent of the value of all steel produced for a total of $210,734. The four informants would receive $13,170 each (about $243,000 today). Carnegie wrote President Cleveland directly asking for a second board to be formed. Cleveland let the ruling stand but reduced the fine to 10 percent.

Letters from Carnegie to Secretary of the Navy William Whitney in 1887 suggest that Carnegie had little respect for the required tests:

> Your "specifications" are serious point, as our experience with Government officials of Army and Navy — is they are martinets only and insist upon technical points to absurd degree. Practical men know that "tests" are necessarily approximated, no two can result alike — that we can give you plates equal to any made in the world is true but we believe "inspectors" aboard know that variations exist and allow for them. I do hope we shall have to deal with a practical experienced inspector should contract.[4]

Clearly, Carnegie's lack of concern for Navy "specifications" would have been reflected throughout his organization of loyal lieutenants. Frick's organizational approach put less emphasis on loyalty. Frick wanted the real picture of the operations.

Frick suspected failures within the organization. He was well aware of the propensity of the Schwab and the boys to push tonnage. Specifications only represented roadblocks to achieving tonnage goals. For Frick, it also offered an opportunity to take a close look at the Homestead organization that had basically been that of Carnegie. Frick had a technical assistant in Millard Hunsiker. Hunsiker was a technical armor expert who had been hired by Henry Phipps to help Carnegie Brothers enter the market. Hunsiker understood the chemistry and processing of armor, and at the time reported to Frick. Carnegie cared little for Hunsiker's technical descriptions and had even asked his ideas be shortened in the "minutes" going to him. Frick could now use him as an organizational troubleshooter. Frick loved the use of a troubleshooter to look at problems, cost cutting, and organization. Hunsiker found a number of operating and testing deviations that required the firing of employees, including the plate mill's Leo Bullion. Schwab appeared to hesitate with Bullion, and Frick wrote Schwab: "It seems to be very difficult to get anything into your head, or to have you follow out instructions as given to you. I told you that I wanted Mr. Bullion's services dispensed with.... I shall expect prompt action on your part in this matter, on receipt of this."[5] It sent a clear message to the young Schwab (who was not yet a partner) as to who was in charge. Furthermore, Frick made it clear that the organization had to lose its "we know better attitude." Specifications were to be part of doing business in the future.

Other problems Frick found in the armor scandal was that Abbott had originally agreed to a delivery penalty for late delivery. Frick realized that this caused sales as well as organizational problems. Delivery pressures were part of the problem that caused managers to ship questionable product. Frick mandated no delivery clauses in future contracts. Frick addressed the overall delivery problems by organizing production meetings to review delivery requirements weekly. This would evolve into a new department, the Operating Department. A young William Dickson, from an old Braddock coal-mining family, would run the department. The Operating Department was the first industrial "Production Planning" function, which would be critical in future large corporations. Frick's organizational changes resulted in many improvements as a result of the scandal.

Politics quickly got involved in the armor scandal as the Democrats had a chance to show that while Carnegie Steel had been protected by tariffs, the company had produced more quality armor for the country's navy. At the time, the Wilson Tariff Bill was being debated to reduce tariffs of the McKinley Republican bill of 1890. With the Democrats controlling Congress and the presidency, the opportunity was too good to pass up. The House of Representatives formed a special investigatory committee. The hearings went on for weeks with the usual attributes of a political circus. The public and Congress lacked the knowledge to understand the sound and technical arguments made by Schwab and Frick. The hearings remain a matter of debate, with over a thousand pages of testimony over five weeks. The result was a foregone conclusion. The facts suggest a mix of poor behavior from the congressmen, navy inspectors (who were at the plant), Carnegie Steel testers, and Carnegie Steel management. The retesting, reworking, and questioning of the specification requirements of defective material is not uncommon to manufacturers but makes sensational reading if crafted by newspapermen. The Democrats achieved the scandal they had hoped for. Interestingly, Frick appeared to be cleared of most of the fraud in the press. The scandal shifted directly onto the shoulders of Charles Schwab, who had made some serious errors in his testimony. Schwab, known for his direct speaking, did not fare well in the one-sided questioning of politicians. Frick was much better suited to this type of testimony.

From an operating standpoint, there were problems probably related to the style of Charles Schwab and his Braddock Boys. Schwab and his boys were tonnage men, always driving productivity with numerical goals. The armor physical testing was new and one of the first quality control techniques in the industry. It had little creditability among the "old" steel makers. Their now-deceased mentor Bill Jones had been an outspoken critic of steel testing other than fitness for use, and Carnegie had adopted the same approach to testing. Even chemistry was in its infancy. Schwab's strength was his ability to motivate using numerical productivity goals, but it was also a weakness in the production of strict quality requirements. From the interviews, notes, and congressional record, Frick appears the cleanest, but the hearings also showed a weakness in his new corporate structure as to which department heads had absolute day-to-day control. Frick clearly laid the blame on Schwab, but Carnegie saw it all as a matter of worker revenge. The scandal would be a learning experience for all. Carnegie Steel and operating managers got a hard lesson in the importance of quality control in the future applications of steel. Frick started to require more organization reporting, but not in the paternal style of Carnegie. Frick focused on department reports to the works manager and a daily/weekly report to him.

Charles Schwab, the first president of United States Steel and leader of the "Boys of Braddock," in his thirties.

In the end, the press and the Democrats got their pound of flesh and the results of company misbehavior came to light. The Democrats got Carnegie to actually support the lower tariff bill, and the Wilson-Gorman Bill was signed in August of 1894. New shipments of armor showed superior results in ballistic testing. Homestead would continue to produce armor for the government, losing more business to its tough competitor than to the scandal. The press had a field day. Carnegie, Frick, and Schwab all wrote the scandal off as the final chapter of the Homestead Strike. The amazing performance of Homestead armor in the great naval battles of the Spanish-American War did much to move the scandal to the background. Carnegie's image was further reduced in the public eyes, but Frick had already been condemned to Hell by the public and lost little in the public's eyes. Unfortunately for Schwab, the public got to know him as a member of Carnegie Steel's ruling troika, and his image was hurt the most.

The armor scandal and the continuing bad publicity of the Homestead Strike had caused a rift in the Carnegie empire. Carnegie's lack of presence was taking its toll on the organization; even old partners such as Phipps, Lovejoy, and Leishman started to look to Frick for advice. For years, Frick had put up with Carnegie's second-guessing and meddling in hopes that the old man would retire, but Carnegie seemed to find endless joy on "running" the company while on perpetual vacations. In 1893 and 1894, Carnegie started to use Carnegie Steel as his personal bank to finance philanthropy, which Frick resented. Carnegie and Frick had many differences over the management of H.C. Frick Company, iron ore mines, organization, and the partnership. Some refer to the second showdown between the two as the "power struggle of 1894." In 1894, Frick asked Carnegie to double his salary and reduce the interest of a $1.7 million loan. Carnegie doubled his salary but would do nothing about the loan. For his part, Frick had been talking to Henry Phipps about buying his shares and breaking Carnegie's ironclad agreement. Frick played the role of a loyal executive; he never criticized Carnegie in public or with lower executives. It was the type of business executive behavior to which Carnegie never could adhere.

Carnegie and Frick also continued to disagree on a variety of little things. For Carnegie it was a matter of control. Frick had made gains among the partners and formed a structure in the Carnegie organization. Frick had believed that Schwab and Corey were probably the root of the armor scandal and should have been removed. Carnegie, however, enjoyed having young loyal lieutenants in the organization. It is clear that Frick would have liked to see Schwab gone. Frick had worked miracles to reorganize as much as he did with Carnegie watching every move. Carnegie was getting fearful of the organization's having too much of Frick's influence. He started to write Frick about needing a vacation. Frick had started to return to his workaholic tendencies. It was a tough period for Frick. He carried the burden of the strike and scandals and had to deal with Carnegie's overseeing. Frick, however, whether he realized it or not, was at the height of his power. Old partners like Phipps believed Frick was the man behind the company's great success.

Carnegie finally convinced Frick to bring his family to Cluny Castle for a visit in the spring of 1895. Before the visit, however, they would again clash over H.C. Frick Company. It may have been a brushback pitch by Carnegie for Frick's organizational moves in Carnegie Steel. Carnegie vetoed Frick's effort to establish a pricing pool with William Rainey in the coke business. Rainey had always been one of Frick's toughest competitors, and Frick had a great dislike for Rainey. Carnegie wanted Frick to merge with Rainey instead. While Frick was not in control of stock of H.C. Frick Coke, it was his baby. He had paid $80,000 for an exhibition of H.C. Frick Coke Company at the Chicago World's Fair. The coke company had over 11,000 employees. Nothing bothered Frick more than when

William Corey, second president of United States Steel.

Carnegie got involved with coke. Clearly, Carnegie was sending his own message about who was in charge. Frick made his visit to Cluny a short one. Things continued to decline between the two men. Whenever Frick pushed his way on something, Carnegie pushed back. Carnegie's meddling continued, and it wasted Frick's time by making him maintain his authority in the organization. Carnegie continued to foster Schwab as his little Napoleon.

The end of 1894 once again took the relationship to the breaking point. In November of 1894, Carnegie would commit the unforgivable sin. Carnegie met directly with William J. Rainey without telling Frick. Carnegie was still interested in merging Rainey and H.C. Frick Company. Carnegie had even discussed the renaming of the company as the Frick-Rainey Company. It is hard to understand what Carnegie was thinking, knowing Frick as he did. The reaction was predictable when Frick found out. Frick sent his resignation on December 18. Carnegie realized he had gone too far, but he also wanted to justify Frick's resignation to his partners. Carnegie notified senior partner Henry Phipps, now semi-retired in southern England.

Phipps was extremely upset with the resignation, fearing the worst for the partnership. Phipps had learned to trust and respect the management skills of Frick, believing him more important than Carnegie. Phipps cabled Carnegie on December 22, 1894: "Mr. Frick is first and there's no second, nor fit successor, with him gone, a perfect Pandora box of cares and trouble would be upon our shoulders."[6] Phipps had clearly been enjoying retirement under Frick's very profitable reign. Carnegie started to realize that Frick was serious this time. Carnegie even went so far as to offer to get out of the partnership and go into philanthropy. The terms of the offer were never well defined, but Carnegie had a large share in the company, which would require debt bonds to be issued to partners. Frick refused the offer, which confused Carnegie, who had believed Frick would not turn it down. Strangely, Carnegie continued to negotiate with Rainey, which had had much to do with Frick's anger. Carnegie went on to write Phipps, suggesting Frick was not well and possibly having a breakdown. Carnegie's behavior suggests he really believed Frick's reaction was irrational. Frick believed Carnegie had been just as erratic. Carnegie had started the year supporting the Democratic initiative to reduce tariffs, against which Frick and the Republicans stood. Carnegie had met secretly with Frick's most hated opponent about a merger, and Carnegie had even accidentally sent a letter meant for Phipps to Frick instead, complaining about Frick's possibly being ill. Carnegie had figured this to be a fit of anger on Frick's part that would go away, but Carnegie was wrong. Phipps tried to act as a mediator and broker.

Phipps seemed to have been instrumental in hammering out some form of resolution, the meaning of which historians are still debating. This probably is because the agreement was met to allow face saving by all. What we do know is John Leishman became president of Carnegie Steel and Frick became chairman of the board. The facts say a lot. Leishman was an easygoing Frick protégé; Carnegie would have wanted Charles Schwab, who would, in fact, take over in a few years. Carnegie realized that as chairman of the board, Frick could sit at the Board of Managers meeting. The Board of Managers was made up of partners, most of whom Carnegie believed to be loyal to Frick. Carnegie's living in Pittsburgh hardly worried Frick. Carnegie instructed Francis Lovejoy, who was the company secretary, to record individual votes on projects. Later he wanted voting reasons included in the minutes. Furthermore, Carnegie had Philander Knox update the "Iron Clad" Agreement to assure that any revolution could be put down.

The "Iron Clad Agreement" had gone back to the original partners of Tom Carnegie and Henry Phipps. The agreement was meant to protect the partnership in case of a death; in fact, it had been put together in 1887 when Carnegie was seriously ill. Over the years, it had evolved into a much different tool. Carnegie used it to control the partnership and avoid the loss of control that might come from becoming a corporation selling stock on the open market. The agreement called for the partnership, upon the death of a partner, to pay the estate at book value. Book value was generally a small percentage of the actual value of the share. Still, in later years book value was significant enough to cause problems for the partnership in the case of a larger-share partner. The death of Carnegie might well have bankrupted the partnership. The clauses allowed three quarters of the members to force a partner to sell his shares at book value, with the exception, of course, of Carnegie himself, who could not be forced to sell. William Abbott and John Walker had voluntarily asked to be removed. Only John Leishman would be forced to sell under the agreement, and Carnegie had targeted Leishman early on.

Frick could count on Leishman, and Carnegie immediately started a punishing campaign to discredit Leishman's ability. Letters from Carnegie in 1896 were brutal to Leishman. On finding that Leishman had lost money in iron speculation, Carnegie paid the debt but wrote: "You have much to do before you regain the confidence of your partners as safe man to be the executive head of the company. I cannot read the trade papers without being stabbed to the heart."[7] Carnegie would never be happy with the appointment of Leishman, but it appeared to be part of the deal. Frick would not have accepted a strong Carnegie loyalist in the position of president. This setup was ideal for Frick's purposes. Frick was relieved of day-to-day responsibilities while holding the real power. Partners such as Phipps could rest assured that Frick could step in on strategic matters. Frick did sell half his interest back to the company, but now he could pursue art and family once again.

Carnegie actually seemed to help Frick return to his old interest in art. Carnegie had been telling Frick for over a year he needed to work less and become involved in community and philanthropy. Carnegie planned to open the Carnegie Art Gallery in 1895, and he already had a "loan" exhibition under way. In addition, in 1896 Carnegie had planned an international exhibition to be held in Pittsburgh. He wisely put Frick on the Board of Directors for the Art Institute and made him treasurer of the Art Acquisition Fund. It was more effective than Carnegie's frontal attacks in getting Frick out of day-to-day management. Still, even in art, the two men had their differences. Frick loved the classical and old masters, while Carnegie favored the young artists of the current times. Frick's collecting during 1895 and 1896 did see a significant increase. Frick also commissioned a number of portraits by Theobald Chartran as gifts, including ones of Thomas Mellon, Henry Phipps, Mrs. Thomas Mellon, Andrew Carnegie, and President McKinley. Theobald Chartran was the most popular portrait artist in Europe and America. Chartran's portrait of Carnegie remained a favorite of Carnegie's and remains in the president's office of the Carnegie Institute to this day. Chartran also did a portrait of Frick and became a close friend of the whole family. Chartran would also do a posthumous portrait of Martha and a portrait of Helen.

Frick's work on the Carnegie "loan" exhibition greatly expanded his collecting hobby. Frick dealt with all of the world's greatest art agents in setting up the loan program. In preparing the "loan" exhibition, Frick worked with some major art dealers, such as Roland Knoedler of New York, Charles Carstairs of Philadelphia, Thomas Agnew of London, Arthur Tooth, and Henry Duveen of London. Early on, Frick had done most of his collecting with Knoedler's gallery in New York. It was through Knoedler that Frick came to know one of his favorite painters, Theobald Chartran. Frick got to know Duveen better through the loan exhibition. Frick seemed to personally like Joseph Duveen, who dealt with J.P. Morgan. In fact, Duveen's major clients included Andrew Mellon, William Randolph Hearst, Samuel Kress, John D. Rockefeller, and Henry E. Huntington. J.P. Morgan had mainly dealt with the founder of the firm, Henry Duveen. Morgan had extended the Duveen firm a line of credit to make purchases. Joseph Duveen was an ex-furniture salesman with a great sense of value. Duveen, who would become known as "Dealer King," was the subject of playwright S.N. Berhrman because of his idiosyncrasy and his Dickensian characteristics. Duveen became well known for his helping Andrew Mellon in building the core of what would become the National Gallery. While a knowledgeable collector, Frick liked value in his purchases. Duveen clearly was more suited for Frick than for Morgan, who often collected without any sense of cost or quality. Duveen's strategy was to search out bargains and offer them to Frick, often buying with his own credit. Duveen also shared with Frick an interest in photographing masterpieces around the world. Duveen often promoted the collecting rivalry between Frick and railroad magnate Henry E. Huntington.

Duveen and his London and New York Galleries were also experts in display. The Duveen Gallery used a concealed spotlight in the ceiling to highlight the paintings. Frick had the lighting system installed at Clayton (later improved upon at his New York mansion). Harvey reported the following:

> Often late at night, at the end of a trying day, when perfect stillness reigned, he would slip noiselessly, almost furtively, into the darkened gallery, turn on the lights and sit for an hour or more, first on the divan then on another, absorbing solace and happiness through the mirrors of his heart before seeking mental and physical relaxation of dreamless sleep.[8]

Martha Frick Symington Sanger attributed a deep relationship of Frick with his paintings.[9] Sanger further reported that Frick found solace in the art that reminded him of his daughter Martha. There was certainly a type of meditation that Frick found late at night with his paintings. Frick had a personal involvement with his art collection that men like J.P. Morgan lacked. Morgan collected art as he collected money, while Frick studied art. Frick was often criticized that he used art as a decoration, but he made art part of living. Frick's method of purchasing included keeping a painting for approval in his home to assure it was pleasant to live with.

The family life at Clayton appears to have improved. Childs, who had been at school in Boston, was allowed to return home and attend Shadyside Academy. Initially, Childs attended Sterrett School, but poor grades and security concerns moved Frick to send him to a Boston boarding school. The Shadyside Academy had been founded by most of the Pittsburgh greats, including Henry Clay Frick, Robert Pitcairn, Henry Laughlin, Mr. Dalzell, E. Ferguson, A.H. Childs, George Westinghouse, and many of Carnegie's lieutenants. Frick was a founder and charter member. Childs loved being back home, and while his grades did not improve, his passion for science did. Frick purchased a small shotgun for Childs, and Childs took up taxidermy. He loved to trap and keep animals at Clayton. The extensive woods (today's Frick Park) were a rich nature preserve. His parents purchased additional pets such as a baby alligator. Childs was a fun-loving kid who pursued his own interests over those of school. He collected the famous seashell fossils common in the Pittsburgh-area Ames limestone deposits. It was these same limestone fossils that had interested a young Andrew Carnegie in natural science. Childs formed a group of cadets who paraded and marched. Childs also was an early lover of football and played with a neighborhood team in 1895. The return of Childs lifted his mother's spirits more than those of Frick, who continued to push Childs on his poor schoolwork. As was the case with most Victorian fathers, Frick tended to be demanding on his son. Childs did take up his father's habit of teasing, and often Childs was quite mean to his sister.

Helen, on the other hand, appeared to thrive under the demanding Frick. She was an outstanding student and loved being around her father. Helen's governess, Marika Ogiz, turned out to be the ideal pick for Helen. In a fourth-floor room at Clayton, Ogiz schooled Helen. Helen's grades and her notebooks were given to Frick weekly, and he often returned them to Ogiz with notes. Frick always found time to monitor the education of his children, which was a priority in his life. Helen and her father had time to take walks in the neighborhood and visit Joseph Woodwell's home art studio. Helen took an interest in painting and music, following the interests of her father. In 1897, Frick built a beautiful two-story playhouse/cottage for Helen and Childs. The first floor had a bowling alley and a photography laboratory for Childs. There was a room of child-size furniture for Helen to play house. The upstairs was for dancing lessons and other activities.

One area after the reorganization that Carnegie and Frick found they agreed upon was an increase for the workforce. Both realized they had a public relations nightmare on their hands with the opening of the Art Gallery and the Art International. The company was having a very profitable year; in fact, profits were up 25 percent. They were also launching a plan to build four new blast furnaces. The memories of Homestead, however, were still fresh in the minds of Pittsburghers. For Frick, conquering the Amalgamated didn't mean it was now all right to oppress the remaining workers. Both Carnegie and Frick believed, like Alexander the Great, that conquered men and organizations needed to be incorporated into the empire. Instead of increasing the sliding scale or the rate, Carnegie suggested a 10 percent bonus.[10] A bonus represented an increase for good times without building the increase permanently into the wage structure. Frick was very agreeable to the use of a bonus versus an increase to the base wage. Frick released the bonus in June of 1895.

The Rockefeller and Mesabi ore deal of 1896 had been a point a contention between Frick and Carnegie. Still, in his new position Frick pursued his strategic initiative into iron ore, working with Henry Oliver. Frick had been pushing the use of Mesabi ore for years, but he faced tough resistance by Carnegie, Schwab, and the Carnegie furnaces men. Frick forced trials at the mills; and by 1895, James Gayley, the furnace expert, changed his mind, believing Mesabi ore could be mixed in for up to 50 percent of the load. In the meantime, Rockefeller had quietly taken over the Mesabi Range with the exception of Oliver and Frick's interests. Rockefeller went on to built railroads in the ore fields but faced a roadblock with Lake Superior shipping firms. Rockefeller enlisted Samuel Mather to build a new generation of super ore carriers. In 1896, Rockefeller and Mathers had the largest ore fleet in the world. These 475-foot-long steamships were a new class of ships known as super whalebacks. While other shipping firms charged $4.20 a ton of ore, Rockefeller was able to ship it at 80 cents a ton. Rockefeller improved his docks to load 1,700 tons an hour and could ship over 2,000,000 tons of ore in a season. Rockefeller had a significant advantage in acquiring the main component of steel. Rumors started that Rockefeller was considering building a super steel mill at the port of Cleveland or South Chicago. Carnegie tried unsuccessfully to purchase and use lower grade ore in Pennsylvania and West Virginia. While Frick seemed interested in backward integration, Carnegie was more motivated by the potential entry of Rockefeller into the steel business.[11]

Frick had been working with Henry Oliver for years and had some Mesabi Range ore under his control. Now Carnegie realized how wrong he had been. Carnegie had for decades been building barriers of entry into the steel business, and now Rockefeller was about to enter through the back door. Carnegie also realized that he would need Frick's expertise to form an alliance with Rockefeller. Rockefeller had great respect for Frick but little for Carnegie. The deal would be extremely complex. The final deal required Carnegie Steel to purchase all of Rockefeller's ore production of 600,000 tons of ore, and in return all ore would be shipped on Rockefeller's carriers, including the ore from the Oliver mines. The arrangement was a leasing deal that required Carnegie Steel to pay a royalty of 25 cents a ton (the going rate was 65 cents a ton). The lease would be good for fifty years. Rockefeller added the restriction that he wanted payments made in gold, fearing that the United States was about to get off the gold standard. Frick and Carnegie did go back and forth on the details, but both agreed in December of 1896. Frick started, immediately after the deal with Rockefeller, to look into a new ore find known as the Gogebic Range. Frick continued to work with Henry Oliver, who was outside the Carnegie loop. Frick tried to interest Rockefeller in a further deal, but he refused. Eventually, Frick and the Board agreed to purchase ore mines in the Gogebic Range, which would in the future put the corporation in charge of its own ore supply. Also, Carnegie Steel gained a huge advantage over the competition in the price of ore shipped to the mill. The less noted advantage was the overall efficiency and management of the supply chain.

The success of Frick's backward integration helped form a platform for the future United States Steel Corporation. In 1892, when Frick and Oliver combined, the Mesabi Range produced only 4,245 tons of ore; and in 1896, it produced 9,669,000 tons. Finally, when United States Steel was formed in 1900, Mesabi ore production reached 19,059,3993 tons. Frick continued to work with the 80 percent ownership in Oliver Iron Mining Company to purchase and lease more ore lands in 1897. By 1900, Oliver Mining was producing 4,534,372 tons a year compared to 1,347,268 tons from the Rockefeller lease under Lake Superior Consolidated Iron Mines. More importantly, Carnegie Steel had control over its iron ore needs with a favorable transportation rate. Frick's vertical integration had got the eye of J.P. Morgan, who believed large, integrated companies were the key to the future.

16. Big Steel

The new arrangement of Frick as chairman of the board seemed to have changed things little. Both Frick and Carnegie were dreaming even bigger dreams of super mills and integrated railroad systems. The nature of the steel industry would go through its biggest changes. In 1896, the American iron and steel industry overtook that of Britain to become the world's largest, and Carnegie Steel was the largest American steel company. The Carnegie empire was itself changing. John Leishman's main function was to manage day-to-day details. Carnegie continued to override all company decisions; Carnegie did not respect Leishman's opinion. Carnegie, who tried to stack the board with partners favoring him, also brought in a new group of young partners from management. These included Charles Schwab and many of the "Boys of Braddock," such as Joe Schwab (Charles's brother), A.C. Dinkey (Schwab's brother-in-law), William Corey, and James Gayley. On another front, the 1896 election of Republican William McKinley changed everything. For Carnegie, it was a case study of being careful of what you pray for. McKinley's favorable business polices created a new economic boom, but it also created an era of trusts. Bankers like J.P. Morgan had become interested in the steel industry due to the huge profits of Carnegie Steel. In 1898, Illinois Steel became part of a Morgan trust known as Federal Steel. This new integrated company had advantages on a par with Carnegie Steel.

Frick was starting to leave his mark on the management of Carnegie Steel. Frick instituted routine weekly luncheon meetings on Tuesdays of all key managers. Frick then assigned special committees from these managers to look at special projects. The size of Carnegie Brothers now required a corporate approach versus the one-man management of Carnegie. Frick's corporate style and increased involvement were becoming a threat to Carnegie's authority. Furthermore, Frick read and studied hard, and that, combined with his business network, made him more knowledgeable than Carnegie on the state of the industry. The managers and partners were starting to look to Frick for decisions and leadership. Frick's integration of iron ore into the corporation had enhanced the profits. Frick was proving every bit the man Carnegie had named him. Carnegie had started to worry that the company was getting too big for him to manage, but he hated to give up authority.

Bringing in iron ore as part of Carnegie Steel's vertical integration inspired Carnegie in another way. Carnegie had always given Frick much credit for the successes of his intercompany railroad known as the Union Railroad. Now Carnegie looked to build a Lake Erie-to-Pittsburgh railroad to move iron ore. For years, Carnegie had been locked in a battle with the Pennsylvania Railroad, and this new plan was a way to strike back. The idea, however, was again from the creative genius of Frick. Frick had been studying location and production costs in the newly evolving steel industry. Typical of Frick's managerial style, he had hired a specialist, George McCague, to study the issue and make a report. The report was a mixed bag, demonstrating some transportation disadvantages while concluding that the rates had been fair to Carnegie Steel. The United States government had dredged the village port of Conneaut on Lake Erie near the Pennsylvania state line so ore ships could dock. Carnegie believed this port could be connected to his Pittsburgh mills.

On reading McCague's report, Frick saw hope in a long-term rate arrangement with the

Pennsylvania Railroad. Additionally, Frick did not want a battle with his best steel rail customer. Frick and Carnegie had even considered getting the government to build a canal if the Republicans took back the White House. This time Carnegie wanted his own railroad to end a feud with the Pennsylvania Railroad. Carnegie moved ahead with the purchase of a run-down railroad known as the Pittsburgh, Shenango, and Lake Erie Railroad. This old line ran from Conneaut to Butler, a few miles north of Pittsburgh. With additional cash from Carnegie, Frick, and Phipps, Carnegie Steel purchased the near-bankrupt railroad and renamed it the Pittsburgh, Bessemer, and Lake Erie Railroad. The matter of rebuilding and extending the line was turned over to Frick in the following note: "Her case is respectfully submitted to the attention of Dr. Henry Clay Frick, Surgeon, and Physician (amputations may be necessary.)"[1] Frick did just that by rebuilding the roadbed and laying new steel rails. James Reed of the Union Railway was made president of the Pittsburgh, Bessemer, and Lake Erie Railroad. The new railroad could handle the largest locomotives and largest steel freight cars. The huge locomotives were capable of pulling 25 freight cars of ore, which was the heaviest freight train in the world. Frick upgraded Conneaut harbor into the world's best material handling operation. The Pittsburgh, Bessemer, and Lake Erie railroad at Conneaut Harbor could have achieved the lowest rate per ton in the nation and the highest average length of revenue haul in proportion to its track mileage. A sixteen-thousand-ton lake ore ship could be unloaded in fourteen hours into freight cars. The freight cars moved to Bessemer, Pennsylvania, to be redistributed to the Union Railroad for delivery to Mon Valley mills. It was an amazing tribute to the management skills of Henry Clay Frick. Many joked that the railroad made Pittsburgh a "lake port."

Frick's amazing railroad sent a hard message to the Pennsylvania Railroad. Carnegie Steel purchased the entire Conneaut dock area and built a new dock unloading system. Still, the Pittsburgh, Bessemer, and Lake Erie could only carry 1,500,000 tons annually, which was about half of Carnegie Steel's needs. Frick's unloading technology was just as amazing. Studies years later showed that it took 770 men shoveling daily to unload boats. Automated shoveling could reduce that to 55 men.[2] Frick's success was not overlooked, and new rates were negotiated with the Pennsylvania Railroad for the balance. In fact, the new contract got rate reduction on all, as Carnegie had commissioned Frick to look at building a coke railroad to Connellsville. Frick had already been considering a deal for the Monongahela Southern Railroad owned by the Mellon family, and Frick had some personal investment in it as well. The agreement reduced rates on iron ore from $1.15 a ton to 63 cents a ton, on coke from 55 cents a ton to 35 cents a ton, and on limestone from 85 cents a ton to 55 cents a ton. The agreement called for Carnegie Steel not to build any other railroads. The railroad saved Pittsburgh as the center of the nation's steelmaking, which was under challenge from Chicago, Cleveland, and Carnegie's dream of a super mill at Conneaut. It was now Frick who again saved the jobs of so many Pittsburghers.

Even Carnegie's dream of a super mill at Conneaut was a result of one of many Frick business analyses. Frick used both project troubleshooters and committees to analyze issues within the large organization of Carnegie Steel. It was a technique that Rockefeller learned from Frick to apply to Standard Oil. In this case, Jay Morse, formerly from Illinois Steel and now with ore shippers Pickands-Mather, approached Frick about building two blast furnaces at Conneaut. Jay Morse had stock in Federal Steel and a loose alliance as a pig iron producer for Federal. Frick formed a committee under his best furnace expert, James Gayley, to study the question. The analysis suggested that a fully integrated mill at Conneaut was a possibility. Carnegie became a believer in Conneaut as a site for a super mill to produce tubes. Frick, however, had studied a much different location as a possible super mill site. Frick had used Schwab and others to study the possibility of a mill on the seaboard at Sparrows Point, Maryland. Sparrows Point could use iron ore from Cuba and ship to the American south and international ports. Sparrows Point was also close to the Pennsylvania coal fields and had excellent rail connections. Frick believed in the analysis of Sparrows Point, but Carnegie refused to consider it. Years later Charles Schwab at Bethlehem Steel would build the nation's largest steelmaking complex at Sparrows Point.

Another Frick committee had led Frick to purchase land along a ship canal at Indiana Harbor for a possible super mill. Frick continued his overall analysis of the steel industry and had overtaken Carnegie in his understanding of the aggregate industry and competition. Frick correctly predicted the rise of Chicago as a major steel center. John Gates of Illinois Steel in 1895 was looking to expand aggressively. Frick was convinced that Chicago had a major raw material advantage, which could result in a major cost advantage. Deep-water ports allowed Great Lakes iron ore to flow directly to the blast furnaces. Illinois also had an emerging coal mining business, which would prove competitive. When Carnegie again balked, Frick purchased the lakefront land for $105,000, which years later made Frick a handsome profit. In 1916, Youngtown Sheet and Tube would build on the exact location, and United States Steel's super mill of Gary Works would be located a few miles away. Frick's analysis once again proved perfect. Unfortunately, Carnegie was slow to realize the full scope of Frick's genius.

The presidential campaign of 1896 was one thing that brought Carnegie and Frick together, at least in donations. Frick had been disgusted with the Grover Cleveland administration's reduction of tariffs. Carnegie tried to appease his liberal friends by supporting the reduction; but Carnegie's support came from realizing that the Democratic Congress would pass it regardless of his stand. Frick, on the other hand, had remained a strict Republican and supporter of the tariffs in the face of liberal condemnation. For Frick, Republicanism was his life's philosophy; for Carnegie, Republicanism was part of a business strategy. The presidential campaign of 1896 was between William Jennings Bryant of Nebraska and William McKinley of Ohio. Frick had always been a strong supporter of protectionist tariffs. McKinley's manager, Mark Hanna, approached Frick for help. Hanna obtained $250,000 donations from Frick, Carnegie, Rockefeller, and J.P. Morgan. Of the four, only Frick was an enthusiastic supporter. Carnegie, Rockefeller, and Morgan were concerned about McKinley's weak support of the gold standard. For Frick, however, the issue was tariffs. Frick was the most active in his support, following up with calls to others for financial support. Frick truly had his heart in this election, believing it was critical to the very future of the nation. Even Frick's son Childs named a pet rabbit after presidential candidate McKinley. Even before McKinley started the campaign, he was pulled into personal bankruptcy, but Frick helped pay off his debt and allowed McKinley to purchase a new suit for the swearing-in ceremony.

The campaign was a tough one, with McKinley running his famous "front-porch" campaign. Frick paid train fare for Braddock and Homestead steelworkers and their families to make the trip to Canton, Ohio, on the Pennsylvania Railroad, a two-and-half-hour trip. The families were also supplied a picnic-style lunch at the McKinley home. Actually, McKinley found substantial support because his protectionist policies meant steel jobs. Steelworkers poured into Canton, not by the thousands but tens of thousands. Carnegie's rail mill at Braddock sent thousands alone. Carnegie and the Pennsylvania Railroad offered special trains for workers and families. Braddock's Edgar Thomson was one of the largest factories, producing most of the steel rails for the booming railroad expansion. The mill had started in 1875 and owed its very existence to the Republican tariffs. Over 90 percent of rails were imported at the time Edgar Thomson started up in 1875. Thanks to tariffs, it survived and thrived, overtaking the domestic rail market by 1882. In 1889, British steelmakers hailed Edgar Thomson Works as the most productive mill in the world. By the end of the 1890s, Edgar Thomson Works made more steel rails than the rest of the world combined. When the crews visited McKinley, they presented him with a gold-plated piece of steel rail, which he cherished.

Support was not only coming from the mill at Braddock; a huge delegation from the troubled Homestead Works came by thirty-three special train cars in September. McKinley avoided any reference to the 1893 labor lockout, which had generated Democratic criticism, as McKinley had no direct ties to that strike. Even though Carnegie paid for the Homesteader visit, McKinley was very popular with the steelworkers. Steel tariffs had been the source of their income, and they were thankful to the politician who had made a career out of the tariff issue. Charles Schwab headed the delegation. A large parade was organized to march the Homesteaders from the train station to McKinley's home. The mile-long path from the railroad station was lined with food and souvenir stands. The Homestead speech exemplified the model of the front-porch campaign. McKinley used what would later be called the "rhetoric of silence." McKinley avoided the local issue, and keyed in on a national and future path. Mrs. McKinley served the workers lemonade during the speech. After the speech, the workers were escorted to a tent for lunch.

The McKinley presidency would offer an expansion of American jobs through steel tariffs. Frick was a firm believer in nationalistic capitalism using tariffs versus free-trade capitalism. McKinley carried the election and the Republicans took the house back, but the Congress was hesitating to take on increased tariffs. Senate leader Nelson Aldrich consulted secretly with Frick on how to proceed with the tariff bill.[3] Frick went on to suggest a specific review of specific metal products. Frick argued not for arbitrary higher tariffs but focused tariffs to promote American business. McKinley won the election 51 percent to 47 percent over Bryant. In 1897, McKinley and Aldrich pushed through a bill based on Frick's suggestions, which ushered in one of America's greatest industrial booms. Frick got another favor from McKinley. After the election Frick wrote McKinley suggesting his partner, neighbor, and fellow poker player Philander Knox for Attorney General. McKinley did select Knox. Frick would commission a portrait of McKinley as a present for his election, and another after his 1900 re-election. While the two were not close friends, McKinley was one of a few politicians who had the respect of Frick. Frick thought McKinley a bit weak but saw his own philosophy of capitalism in that of McKinley. Both McKinley and Frick were strong supporters of protecting all American industries. McKinley and Frick also shared a strong belief in the principles of Freemasonry and the importance of the YMCA and YWCA in developing America's youth. Frick never fully understood McKinley, who had the same love of capitalism but had none of the benefits of wealth.

The year 1897 brought changes for Carnegie Steel leadership as well. Leishman seems to have been a concession of Carnegie to Frick, and Carnegie had no intentions for Leishman to function long-term as president of Carnegie Steel. Carnegie constantly belittled Leishman to the point that he wanted out. In February of 1897, Frick gave in to Carnegie, and Charles Schwab replaced Leishman as president of Carnegie Steel. Leishman retired and thus received $800,000 from his shares. Frick obtained for him a job in the American embassy in Switzerland. Schwab, who had been made a partner two years ago, received an interest of one to three percent. Alexander Peacock, Frick's neighbor and sales agent, became the vice-president of Carnegie Steel. Schwab was clearly a Carnegie man, but he also had respect for Frick's business decisions. Schwab was well aware that he needed friends among the partners to deal with Carnegie's tantrums and fits of anger.

McKinley's industrial boom would in a strange way mark the end of the Carnegie empire. J.P. Morgan had built an "electrical trust" in the 1880s. A "trust" used a holding company and interlocking boards to control an industry. Rockefeller had done it in oil. Carnegie had a great dislike for corporations and trusts, seeing them as speculative stock arrangements.

Carnegie preferred to conquer the competition. While he had entered pricing pools over the years, Carnegie was quick to pull out if it was beneficial to him. Carnegie truly believed in social Darwinism in business. J.P. Morgan, by contrast, saw competition as wasteful, and saw trusts as a way to stabilize competition and maximize efficiency. The trust movement in steel started in the finishing mills such as the wire producers. In 1898, John "Bet-a-Million" Gates joined 14 wire mills into the American Steel and Wire Company. Similar efforts joined together tin plate mills into the Tin Plate Trust. As finishing mills combined, the need for bigger steel-making combinations was needed. Even the huge Carnegie Steel produced only 23 percent of the needed steel demand.

Morgan got involved in 1897 in the building of a steel trust. On September 9, 1898, Morgan created a $200 million competitor to Carnegie Steel. Morgan's Federal Steel was formed around Illinois Steel and Minnesota Mining, but was fully integrated, including coke ovens, ore mines, and finishing companies such as Lorain Steel. Elbert Gary was elected president of Illinois Steel. Frick started a corporate analysis of the threat of Federal Steel. The results were sobering. The new combination gave Illinois Steel Division an ore advantage similar to that which Carnegie Steel had gained with the Rockefeller deal. Illinois Steel could not only get Mesabi ore through Minnesota Mining, but it also had the advantage of being on a lake port, giving it a transportation advantage. Frick was not surprised; in fact, he was well aware of the move by Morgan to bring about a true steel trust. The idea that Morgan was drawn into the steel industry by a dinner talk of Charles Schwab is mostly mythology. Soon after the Federal Steel deal, Morgan was working on bringing all the country's tube mills together as National Steel. In effect, Morgan was taking control of Carnegie's customer base. He realized that price wars between Federal and Carnegie Steel would be wasteful. Morgan was aware of the need to bring Federal and Carnegie Steel together, but the issue was how and at what price. Carnegie was opposed to such alliances, but Frick was much more open to the building of a trust that would include the sale of Carnegie Steel. From mid–1898 to 1899, Frick was involved in a number of possibilities of the sale of Carnegie Steel. He had the strong support of Henry Phipps, who wanted the cash for his retirement. One of these options even included a purchase of the company by Rockefeller.[4]

Frick also started to size up this new Chicago steel master, Judge Elbert Gary (1846–1927). Gary's steel background was limited. He had entered the steel business as a legal consul to John "Bet-a-Million" Gates (1855–1911) in the amalgamation and formation of Consolidated Steel and Wire of Illinois in 1892. In 1895, he became a director and helped in the formation of American Steel and Wire. Later Gary worked with Gates to create Federal Steel. Gary was one of the early proponents of a large steel trust and had even tried to convince Morgan to help form such a trust in 1898. Gates was a gambler whom neither Gary nor Morgan had confidence in, but he had gotten the ear of Frick. He was talking to Frick as early as 1898 about steel mergers and trusts. Gates would play a role in the formation of Republic Iron and Steel in 1899. The era of McKinley (1896 to 1901) was one of mergers, trusts, alliances, and integration across the steel industry.

With Federal Steel, Carnegie realized he had an integrated competitor and began to talk about "reorganization." A growing number of partners were talking about buying Carnegie and the possibility of joining Federal Steel. The motivation seemed to be Carnegie's partnership and its "Iron Clad Agreement." Many of the older and younger partners wanted to be able to sell shares. The younger ones were "paper" millionaires and the older ones wanted more money for retirement. Dod Lauder, Lovejoy, Peacock, and even Schwab now joined Frick and Phipps. The group wanted at least a stock plan, which would allow members to sell freely at market prices. Frick clearly assumed the leadership for this movement. Frick even became willing to bring H.C. Frick Company fully into Carnegie Steel, which would make sale of all assets easier. Frick and Schwab even pursued business deals with the new Federal Steel. They worked on a price pool with Federal Steel on rails, but Carnegie vetoed it.[5] For his part, Carnegie started to pose other options.

Carnegie became interested in horizontal integration into finished steel products. Carnegie suggested a move into the manufacture of pressed steel railroad cars. Frick at first objected but later was agreeable if favorable terms could be found. The real objection came from Alexander Peacock, who favored supplying steel to their large customer, the Pressed Steel Car Company, rather than entering the business. In the end Carnegie and the Board never came to full agreement. Carnegie also looked into gun forgings for cannon. Frick started to see these projects as taking up too much time from the business of running Carnegie Steel. Schwab and Carnegie, however, felt horizontal integration was an option to battle the trusts, which were forming in the finished steel industries, such as tubes, wire, tin plate, and sheet products.

Carnegie also looked at some old practices that had served him well, such as pooling agreements on price. In October of 1898, Carnegie invited the president of the new Federal Steel, Elbert Gary, to lunch over duck at his New York apartment. Frick was also invited. It was the first time that Carnegie and Frick would see Gary. The three came to an agreement to equally divide the steel rail market.[6] Such "pools" were legal at the time. The arrangement stayed in place until the formation of United States Steel.

Carnegie had one hold over the partners in the Iron Clad Agreement. The agreement called for any partner to be bought out at book value. The underestimated book value of Carnegie Steel was $50 million in 1899. This was clearly low considering earnings were estimated at $21 million. The true value was around $250 million. For Frick's 6 percent share, this meant $15 million versus book value of $3 million. For Phipps, it was $27 million versus $6 million, and for Lauder, it was $10 million versus $2 million. These differences were a powerful inducement for the partners to sell. Frick was 51 and many of the partners were older, wanting the benefit of years of reinvestment. Schwab was only 38, but he had a taste for high living. Frick and Philips (unknown at the time to the others) had also been offered bonuses of up to $5 million to facilitate a sale. Even Carnegie, at 54, was busy with a young child and moving into his new Skibo Castle in Scotland. Dod Lauder, Carnegie's cousin, was probably the only partner besides Carnegie who strongly opposed a sale. Carnegie was ambivalent, however, torn between so many interests. What transpired next is what would become a common Wall Street experience in corporate America. It had all the intrigue of modern takeover battles, and the color of a Victorian background.

In the summer of 1898, Carnegie moved into his new Scottish home of Skibo Castle. The time seemed perfect to approach Carnegie about selling and retiring. Both Frick and Phipps were also vacationing in Europe at the time. Carnegie offered for Frick's family to stay at Skibo, but Frick excused himself, suggesting it would be too damp for his ill wife. The trip was to be one of relaxation and art collecting. Andrew Mellon accompanied the Fricks on the White Star (of *Titanic* fame) liner *Germanic*. It was on the crossing that Frick would introduce his best friend Andrew Mellon to his future wife. Once in Europe, Frick did make a short visit to meet Carnegie and Phipps at Skibo. The discussion centered on the new threat of Federal Steel and the future of Carnegie Steel. At least the potential of selling to J.P. Morgan or John Rockefeller was discussed, but Carnegie remained defiant about retiring.

In January 1899, an amazing meeting took place at Carnegie's New York home. The meeting was led by four partners—Henry Clay Frick, Henry Philips, Dod Lauder, and Charles Schwab. These partners had been negotiating and dealing together and on their own for a possible sale or merger of Carnegie Steel. Carnegie was open to the idea, as he got more involved in politics, social issues, and philanthropy. The others wanted the ability to take more cash out in stock. Carnegie had sent mixed signals for years, and now the discussion was brought into the open. The time seemed perfect as profits for 1899 were expected to double to $21 million. Federal Steel, with Morgan's money, was becoming too strong to take down. The National Steel tube-making trust was looking at moving into steelmaking versus buying off Carnegie Steel. Partners came to the meeting with their own agendas. At the time, Frick was dealing behind Carnegie's back with William Moore, who had put together trusts in steel tubes and steel plate. Frick hoped to achieve Carnegie's approval to sell or at least combine H.C. Frick Company in Carnegie Steel to make a future sale easier. Carnegie still wanted to fight, but he could count and realized that most partners wanted to sell. The result was that Frick was given the go-ahead to negotiate a sale at a price of at least $250 million. The deal for combining H.C. Frick was tabled as a concession to Carnegie. Dod Lauder, however, was suspicious of Frick and Phipps. Lauder probably realized there was more going on than Frick was telling.

Frick wasted little time in initiating his own campaign to sell or merge Carnegie Steel. Frick's first plan was to combine with Morgan and Gary's Federal Steel. Frick met with Judge Gary in the early spring of 1899 to compare properties and the possibility of a merger.[7] One hang-up resulted from the need for the combination to include H.C. Frick Company. A good supply of high-quality Connellsville coke was one item Federal Steel lacked. While negotiations failed because Frick would not assure support from the Carnegie organization, it was the beginning of an exchange that would ultimately lead to the formation of United States Steel.

Carnegie had reluctantly agreed to move ahead with the sale, but he was determined to oppose the uprising of Frick. Dod Lauder was sent to talk to individual partners to oppose any move to sell H.C. Frick Company to Carnegie Steel, but he had little success. Frick and Phipps continued to negotiate with William Moore on a buyout. Both kept the buyer a secret, knowing Carnegie would have a problem with Moore, whom he disliked. They also knew they only had to deal with Carnegie in the final details; if not, they would have to deal with Carnegie's interference. Frick finally negotiated with William Moore a very favorable deal, particularly for Frick. Carnegie Steel would be purchased for $250 million and H.C. Frick Company for $70 million. Carnegie did not know the buyer but probably figured Rockefeller or Mellon was involved, although some believe that Carnegie had to know that it was Moore. Carnegie asked for $2 million as a retainer for the partnership in return for his power of attorney. As always, Frick proved his mastery of financial deals in dealing with Carnegie's requirement. Frick and Phipps were to give the partnership the $2 million by negotiating with Moore and the other Carnegie partners; they needed only $170,000 out of their own pockets. They realized the importance of speed once Carnegie was aware of the buyer's identity. Carnegie was hesitant, and the more time he had to think about it, the likelier it became that he would back out. On May 4, 1899, they cabled Carnegie in Scotland that $170,000 had been deposited and the deal was imminent. Carnegie handwrote his farewell to the business world in preparation of the sale.[8]

With all parties now assured of the deal, Providence stepped in and changed America's industrial history. Moore was having trouble raising the money, and the death of one of the partners, Roswell Flower, caused a major problem. Moore intended to sell stock to the public to raise the cash, and word of the deal got out. Frick was extremely upset, as was Carnegie (whether he knew before or not).[9] Frick and Phipps tried to save the deal by upping the price and asking for more time to complete the deal. They realized they needed to close the deal or face the revenge of Carnegie, the senior partner, especially since Carnegie was now aware that Frick and Phipps stood to get a commission, and Carnegie would be in a position to turn the other partners against them. In June, both Phipps and Frick left for Skibo Castle to talk it over with Carnegie. Moore was to raise $50 million to help convince Carnegie the deal could be closed. It was doubtful to all whether Moore could raise the money. The meeting at Skibo failed to convince Carnegie, who was still determined to pocket the $170,000 retainer. While Phipps stayed on in Scotland at his own castle, Frick returned to Pittsburgh, realizing his days at Carnegie Steel were numbered, but he proceeded with a new type of reorganization plan to fit Carnegie.

The final break was near, and three months later the last dispute erupted. Frick remained chairman of the board for both Carnegie Steel and H.C. Frick Company. Carnegie remained the majority stockholder of both companies. Frick was in the weaker position but had developed an alliance with many partners in both companies. Now Frick's alliance at Carnegie Steel had been weakened. It was probably clear to both men that there would be one last and final battle. In fact, Carnegie was probably looking for the right field of battle to put an end to Frick. It is interesting that both men saw Napoleon as their personal hero. The battle would come over the price of coke charged by H.C. Frick Company to Carnegie. Carnegie biographer Joseph Wall described the situation:

> If desire for monetary gain had been the motivating force that drove men like Carnegie and Frick, as the "robber baron" proponents argue, then this dispute would never have arisen, for neither man had much to gain whichever way the issue was settled, and everything to lose if the issue should end in an open break. For every ton of coke sold by the Henry C. Frick Coke Company, Carnegie and his steel company took the major share of the profits. For every ton of steel sold by Carnegie Steel, Frick's interest in that company became more valuable. Both companies were so interrelated that the success of the one could not help but profit the other.[10]

While Wall saw the battle as trivial and unnecessary, for Carnegie and Frick, it seemed a battle like Waterloo ordained by Providence. Frick had violated one of Napoleon's adages: that when you battle with a king you must kill him. Probably all partners including Carnegie and Frick knew the split in management could no longer continue.

In 1899, H.C. Frick Company had dominance in metallurgical coke greater than that of Carnegie Steel in steel. H.C. Frick had about 16,000 beehive ovens of the total 20,000 in the Connellsville district. Carnegie knew that the best way to punish Frick was to attack "his" coke company. Twice before Carnegie had pushed Frick to the limit by moving on coke issues. One of the weak points and corporate inefficiencies had always been the relationship between H.C. Frick Coke Company and Carnegie Steel. Frick was chairman of the board of both companies. Frick allowed the weak point because he looked at H.C. Frick Coke Company as his company, although Carnegie was the major shareholder. This arrangement had been awkward from the start. While Carnegie originally wanted H.C. Frick to be a separate entity to filter cash through, its separate status became a concession to Frick. It went against Frick's very belief in corporate integration, but it was a matter of pride. While Carnegie owned the coke company, Frick controlled it. The president of H.C. Frick Coke Company, Thomas Lynch, was a strong Frick man, as were most of the Board.

The final showdown would come as it had begun: over coke pricing. In the winter of 1898, Frick and Carnegie had come to a "verbal" agreement to set the price of coke to Carnegie Steel at $1.35 a ton. The price did not affect the aggregate balance sheets of the two companies, but it affected their reported profits individually; thus it was a matter of pride between the companies and partners. The price meant nothing to the individual wealth of Frick and Carnegie. In the future United States Steel Corporation, the price would merely be a transfer cost assigned by the accounting department. It was a loose arrangement with H.C. Frick Coke billing Carnegie Steel monthly. Connellsville coke was the nation's metallurgical standard for steelmaking. The pricing to Carnegie Steel was more than fair, since H.C. Frick Coke Company was charging the competition, such as Federal Steel, at least 90 cents more per ton.

H.C. Frick Company started to charge $1.75 to Carnegie Steel while charging $2.60 to Federal Steel. By late fall the price of coke had reached as high as $3.25 a ton.

The negotiations to sell Carnegie Steel meant Carnegie overlooked the higher-than-agreed-upon price, as Schwab simply paid the invoices. In the fall of 1899, Carnegie was back in Pittsburgh looking over the books and attending board meetings. In reviewing the October minutes of the H.C. Frick Company, Carnegie saw the pricing and wrote on the minutes "Declaration of War." Carnegie lined his supporters up to confront Frick at the November board meeting of Carnegie Steel. Carnegie was absent, allowing Schwab and Lauder to carry the message. Frick made comments about Carnegie and the stage was set. In reading the minutes, Carnegie took it as a major insult. Carnegie went on to write his partner and cousin Dod Lauder: "Frick goes out of the Chairmanship of Board next election or before.... He's too old–too infirm in health and mind."[11] Carnegie had started his campaign among the partners to get the necessary vote. Carnegie knew he could count on Schwab and Lauder, but most of the partners did not want to be forced into a decisive vote. Schwab had tried for a year to hold things together, but Carnegie was determined to oust Frick. Schwab wrote Frick telling him the situation and suggested Frick resign. Frick didn't hesitate and sent his resignation to the Board.

Frick's resignation from the Board of Carnegie Steel was only the beginning of one of America's first great corporate battles. Frick still had some assets: He had a six percent interest in Carnegie Steel and board control of H.C. Frick Company. Carnegie's first order of business was to replace enough Board members in H.C. Frick Coke to take the control that he had in stock. The bylaws allowed for a new vote based on ownership. Frick was able to name two—Thomas Lynch and himself. Carnegie named five—Dod Lauder, Daniel Clemson, A. Moreland, James Gayley, and Thomas Morrison. Lauder and Morrison were Carnegie relatives. In January 1900, Carnegie took control of H.C. Frick Coke, and Frick and the position of chairman were eliminated. The meeting of the new Board now voted 5–2 to sell coke at $1.35 a ton to Carnegie Steel; and at this, Frick lost his temper and walked out.

Carnegie was well aware that he must kill a king. To that end, Carnegie started to plan to force Frick out of the partnership. Carnegie came to Frick's office on January 8, the day after the Carnegie Steel Board meeting. It would be the last face-to-face meeting for the two partners. Carnegie wanted Frick to back out of the partnership peacefully. The book value for Frick's 6 percent in Carnegie Steel was about $1.5 million, while the market value was around $15 million. Carnegie planned to enforce the Iron Clad Agreement at book value. The result was an explosion of Frick's temper. Frick yelled, "For years I have been convinced there is not an honest bone in your body. Now I know you are a god damned thief."[12] Carnegie left and called a special meeting of the Board of Carnegie Steel to remove Frick. Carnegie moved, and over two days got 32 partners out of 36 partners to sign off on the ouster of Frick. The four who did not sign off were Frick, H. Curry (who was ill), Phipps, and Francis Lovejoy. For his part, Frick was off to see his lawyer. Ironically, Frick would contest the very agreement he had used against others. Frick was out of the direct management, but he would contest the sale of his share of the partnership at book value.

Frick and Carnegie seemed to get the same advice: Hire the best, John Johnson of Philadelphia. Frick closed the deal with Johnson by phone while Carnegie was on the train to Philadelphia. Frick got Johnson to work on the brief, while Carnegie took a Florida vacation, assuming the Iron Clad Agreement to be just that. The numbers clearly suggested Frick's share was worth more than the book value. Frick soon realized that he could turn this setback into an opportunity. If the Iron Clad Agreement were found illegal, it would force reorganization and the ultimate sale of the company. Carnegie was slow to realize the danger. Phipps joined the fight in the hope that reorganization could be forced legally. Most partners wanted this feud ended. The problem was that the court proceedings were public and the press followed it like a big Hollywood divorce today. The Allegheny County Court of Common Pleas became the rallying point for the national press. The dollar amounts mesmerized the public. The timing coincided with attacks on "Big Business" from the press as trusts mushroomed in the late 1890s. For the Democrats in the upcoming election, it offered a way to break "Dinner Pail Republicanism," which had forged a weak alliance with labor and capitalists.

Frick had some very favorable documents in his possession. Carnegie's own internal analysis during the potential sale to Moore showed the value to be $500 million. Phipps found an additional document where Carnegie noted the value to be well beyond book value. In board meeting minutes of August 1898, a letter from Carnegie estimated the value of Carnegie Steel at a prophetic $300 million.[13] The court battle and records worried even the Republican Party, with McKinley facing reelection in 1900. In early 1900 rumors were everywhere, and it was clear that there would be no winners in a court case. Frick had the stronger case, but Carnegie could bring millions of dollars and armies of lawyers to the fight. The bigger fear for the Republican Party was that costs would become public knowledge. In particular, steel rails were selling at $23.50 a ton but costs were only $12.00 a ton.[14] The Democratic Party could use this against the tariffs on steel, which had been imposed by the Republicans. It was more of a political issue or image problem since tariffs had in reality created thousands of jobs, producing steady income for steelworkers, and Carnegie re-invested most of the profits in building more mills.

George Westinghouse, a neighbor and outside friend of both, tried to mediate a settlement to no avail. Westinghouse was one of President McKinley's biggest supporters as well. Lovejoy and Schwab suggested a face-to-face meeting but Carnegie refused. Schwab, Lovejoy, and Phipps forced a meeting with Carnegie, and without Frick, to settle this outside of the public eye instead of in an ugly court battle. The meeting took place on neutral ground — a playground in Atlantic City, New Jersey. The issue was settled with Carnegie Steel to become a corporation at a value of $250 million and merged with H.C. Frick Coke at $70 million. That would mean Carnegie's value was $176 million, Phipps's was $35 million and Frick's share was $31.6 million. Frick's $15.5 million in stock and $16 million in 5 percent bonds was considerably better than book value of $1.5 million. Frick and Phipps would then have shares to sell or keep. Frick, however, was to be banned from active management. For his role in helping Frick, Lovejoy was ostracized by Carnegie and died financially and mentally broken. Phipps sold most of his shares to fully enjoy his retirement. Interestingly, Frick held onto most of his shares, probably realizing a takeover would drive prices up. Frick resigned from the board of the Carnegie Library and Art Institute, being replaced by Charles Schwab.

Carnegie and Frick would never meet again. Years later, Carnegie tried to patch things up, and Frick sent a note: "Meet you in hell."

17. United States Steel

Among those who have done most to make it a success without any effort to claim credit is Henry Clay Frick.

— Joseph G. Butler, Jr., 1923

The amazing formation of United States Steel created a company that produced more than all the steel made in Great Britain and Germany, and nearly a quarter of the world's production with a capacity of 7,000,000 tons annually. It represented about two-thirds of the total United States production. It was the first billion-dollar corporation in history, and the first time the phrase "billion dollar" entered the average American's lexicon. The company's $1.4 billion capitalization was four times the federal budget of $350 million in 1900 and a full 7 percent of GNP. It had over 160,000 employees and was the world's largest employer. The company was the largest coke producer in the world, with almost 19,000 coke ovens and 75,000 acres of coal land. It would control 80 percent of the Lake Superior ores. The company also had 115 steamships to deliver the iron ore to its 80 blast furnaces. There were 250 open hearths and 33 Bessemer furnaces. It included 15 nail mills, 14 tin plate mills, 22 wire mills, and 3 pipe mills. In all, there were 149 steel plants with 9,400,000 tons of raw steel capacity and 7,700,000 tons of finished steel capacity. The corporation consisted of 213 manufacturing plants, forty-one mines, and over a thousand miles of railroad track. It had as much land as the states of Massachusetts, Vermont, and Rhode Island. United States Steel controlled around 70 percent of the American steel industry and 30 percent of the world's industry. The story of the formation of United States Steel has a strong bias from the Carnegie spin machine. Schwab usually is seen as the prime mover, with the critical work of Frick overlooked. Another colorful story is that John "Bet-a-Million" Gates dreamed it up while shooting pool at the Waldorf Astoria Hotel. Gates's involvement seems unlikely since J.P. Morgan had a low opinion of Gates and had refused him a seat on Federal Steel's board.[1] A more likely scenario is that the dream evolved in the mind of J.P. Morgan with the help of men like Henry Clay Frick.

The new company formed on April 1, 1900, was called Carnegie Company. Charles Schwab became president of the company. Carnegie Company was the largest in America, three times as big as the next largest corporation, Standard Oil. Frick publicly took credit for Carnegie Steel's success. Carnegie seemed determined to prove himself with a strategy to crush Federal Steel. Carnegie planned to move aggressively into finished steel products, taking on the steel trusts of men like J.P. Morgan. The following memo to Schwab illustrates Carnegie's charge:

> Crisis has arrived, only one policy open; start at once hoop, rod, wire, nail mills, no half way about last two. Extend coal and coke roads, announce these, also tubes. Prevent others building.... Never been time when more prompt action essential, indeed absolutely necessary to maintain property.... Have no fear as to result, victory certain. Spread freely for finishing mills, railroads, boat lines.[2]

Part of this was the announcement to build a super tube mill at Conneaut. Charles Schwab estimated that this super mill would have a $10 a ton advantage over J.P. Morgan's Federal Steel.

Frick was hardly out of business except for his equity position in the new company; he had private interests, he had his share with Andrew Mellon in the investment firm of Union Trust, and he served on the board of many companies. A few weeks after the Carnegie ouster, Union Steel was formed with Frick, Andrew Mellon, Richard Mellon, and William Donner of Cambria Iron Works and National Tin Plate. Union Steel was a wire-making operation geared to the production of nails and barbed wire. A new mill was built on the Monongahela River at a town named Donora after Donner and Andrew Mellon's wife, Nora Mellon. Frick, the Mellon brothers, and Donner all had equal shares in Union Steel. Long-term plans were to make Union Steel a fully integrated mill, and in a couple of years, Union Steel approached being a mini version of Carnegie Steel. Union Steel added blast furnaces and open-hearth furnaces. Frick worked to vertically integrate the company with Connellsville coke operations and ore mines. Frick was even adding sheet, tin plate, and rail plants. The Union Steel deal seemed to also be a direct attack on Gates's wire trust. Gates had started to work with Carnegie behind Frick's back and had told Carnegie he was interested in taking over H.C. Frick. A few months later, Frick invested with Andrew Mellon, who had invested in the New York Ship-building Company. New York Shipbuilding became a major builder of cargo and tanker ships. The Union Trust, in which Frick and Mellon were involved, was a holding company, bank, and underwriter. It had massive investments in local coal and transportation companies. Frick was still Pittsburgh's greatest capitalist, and his financial relationship with the Mellons was growing.

The formation of United States Steel came from two people who disliked each other. Carnegie saw Morgan as a speculator and, more recently, an unwanted force in the steel indus-try. Carnegie also deplored Morgan's womanizing. Morgan saw Carnegie as all that was wrong with American industry. Morgan noted that Carnegie had "demoralized steel by undermin-ing coordination, order, and ultimately stability."[3] Both Carnegie and Morgan had been on a track to the sale of Carnegie Steel for two years. If would be left to the charming Charles Schwab to bring these two together. The project, which Morgan called "on a scale that only Jupiter" could create, required two other great capitalists.[4] Morgan needed the iron ore fields of Minnesota and Michigan to assure the independence of the steel trust, and that required John D. Rockefeller. Morgan and Rockefeller had even less love between them. To bring these two titans together required the financial genius of Henry Clay Frick. Morgan, Gary, Carnegie, and Frick had been studying the possible consolidation of the industry for years. Carnegie represented the main hurdle, since he seemed to waver daily as to the question of his retire-ment.

The formation of United States Steel was not an event but a process of evolutionary steps. The first part of the process was getting Carnegie to be open to selling. The breaking of the Iron Clad Agreement, the forming of a stock corporation, the combination of H.C. Frick Coke into the Carnegie Company, and the failure of Frick and Phipps to facilitate a merger or sale, all contributed to Carnegie's indecisiveness. Carnegie loved the power of running his steel empire while on a seemly lifelong vacation. After the partnership breakup, Carnegie looked to a new power drive to smash the growing competition. This type of power drive is what Carnegie loved; however, the old partners had come to see the dollar potential of a sale. Frick held onto his 6 percent stock hoping to cash in on a future sale. For the previous two years, the prime movers such as J.P. Morgan, John Rockefeller, Henry Clay Frick, John Gates, and Henry Phipps had been talking and manipulating. It would take J.P. Morgan's money, and it may well have been Morgan that really spun the web to bring all the players together. On April 1, 1899, Frick met with Judge Gary, president of Morgan's Federal Steel, to bring six or so companies together.[5] Gary favored it, but Morgan and the Federal Steel Board did not. Money was the issue. It is clear that Morgan didn't need convincing about the need to buy

Carnegie out. It is also clear that as the story took turns and twists, Morgan had a bigger vision than the others. Morgan wanted the type of market control he had in the railroad and electrical industries. Morgan's business campaign was the systematic takeover of complete markets. Carnegie had made overtures to Morgan in the summer of 1900.[6] Charles Schwab did meet with Judge Gary to propose buying out Carnegie. In turn, Judge Gary enthusiastically proposed it to Morgan. At the time, Morgan believed he could not raise the money, or at least that is what many believe.

J.P. Morgan would be the central player to convince Carnegie that the time had come for him to retire, as would Carnegie be pivotal in convincing Morgan he could raise the money needed. Carnegie's aggressive moves to build a super tube mill at Conneaut and a wire mill at Pittsburgh were a direct threat to Morgan's trusts of Federal Steel and National Tube. The threat to build a tube mill, in particular, seemed a direct shot at Morgan's steel trust. Morgan hated this type of wasteful intra-industry competition. Morgan was said to see "competition as destructive, inefficient, and instinctively favored large-scale combinations as the cure."[7] Carnegie's threats and plans suggest that he was trying to push Morgan into a deal. Both Morgan and Carnegie were locked in a battle, which would result in one winner or a merger. Psychologically, Carnegie was more suited for the one-winner option, while Morgan would have preferred the merger. The battle of competition would have been a clash of titans that Carnegie — with a new son, a new castle, and other interests — seemed unsuited for at this time in his life; so probably both men were coming to the same ultimate conclusion of merger. In addition, the ancillary players such as Judge Gary, Henry Clay Frick, Charles Schwab, John Rockefeller, and John Gates saw more gain personally in a merger. Morgan had two concerns; first, whether he could get enough money together; and second, whether the government would allow such a monopoly.

A week before the famous dinner meeting of Schwab and Morgan, another important meeting took place. This meeting was a dinner given by Vice-President Teddy Roosevelt in honor of J.P. Morgan. Morgan must have at least discussed the potential of a steel trust with the McKinley administration. The more publicized dinner came on December 12, 1900, at New York's University Club. The dinner included some of America's greatest bankers and industrialists, including Morgan, William Vanderbilt, Chauncey Depew, Jacob Schiff, George Baker of First National Bank, and H.H. Rogers of Standard Oil. Andrew Carnegie was there only briefly before leaving for another appointment. Schwab, the guest speaker, was to talk on the future of the steel industry. Schwab emphasized the power of Carnegie Company's steel-making capacity and its future interest in moving into steel finishing. According to corporate mythology, the talk was the turning point for J.P. Morgan. The idea that Morgan had an epiphany seems to be more fantasy than reality. Morgan had studied the possibility of a steel trust. It may be more likely that Morgan planned all along to win over the young Schwab to mediate between him and Carnegie. Some even believe that Carnegie engineered the dinner.[8] The history of the rest of the night has several versions. Most of the sources are Senate antitrust testimony 12 years later. One version has Morgan and Schwab talking till early morning. Schwab biographer Hesson suggested Schwab talked for 45 minutes and then Morgan held a side meeting with him for 30 minutes.[9]

A few weeks later, on January 8, 1901, Schwab announced (at Carnegie's request) plans to build the world's largest tube and pipe mill at Conneaut. Carnegie seems to have again wavered on wanting to sell.[10] Joseph Wall suggests Carnegie was even dreaming of his own final victory in steel with his Conneaut mill.[11] Morgan's National Tube stock took a beating on the news. A few weeks later, John Gates confirmed with Morgan that Schwab would be the key in getting Carnegie to sell. Gates is sometimes given credit for conceiving of the steel trust while shooting pool at the Waldorf Astoria. Interestingly, Morgan used John Gates, a poker buddy of Schwab, to deliver the message. Morgan may well have been the best poker player of the three. Morgan knew that only Schwab could gain Carnegie's final approval. Morgan's pick of Gates shows Morgan had other things in mind. Schwab could have easily been drawn to a Morgan meeting. Morgan wanted a secret meeting without Carnegie's knowledge. Schwab took a chance and agreed, and it was this meeting that went into the early morning. Schwab was now walking a dangerous tightrope. Schwab, however, was a gambler and he realized that if he pulled off a deal for Morgan, he would have a secure place in the new corporation. Gates was probably thinking the same thing. Morgan wanted Schwab to get a price from Carnegie on what was needed. The presence of Gates at the meeting suggests Morgan had a bigger vision than just bringing in Carnegie Company. Gates owned American Steel and Wire, a major customer of both Federal Steel and Carnegie Company. Schwab left with the assignment to get Carnegie's price. Schwab realized that Carnegie seemed to change daily on whether to sell or not.

Schwab approached Carnegie at his New York home. Schwab went over the whole story with Mrs. Carnegie and then went off to meet Carnegie at his cottage for a cold game of golf. Schwab told Carnegie of the meetings and asked what price he needed. Carnegie asked for a night to think it over. Schwab returned the next morning and Carnegie wrote it on a piece of paper. He wanted $480 million, to be paid in $160 million in gold-backed 5 percent bonds, $240 million in stock in the new company, and $80 million in cash. Morgan accepted the price with the details to be worked out. Morgan and Carnegie did meet for fifteen minutes a few days later. Carnegie would not be a stockholder, and his stock exchange value would be paid in gold-backed bonds and some preferred stock. For Morgan, there was much to do before the final formation of United States Steel in March. He wanted Gates's American Steel and Wire and he needed Rockefeller's ore mines. Carnegie Steel was only leasing the Rockefeller ore lands.

First, Morgan settled with Gates. Judge Gary was working on Gates with little success. Morgan simply threatened to build his own wire mill, and Gates sold. More importantly, Morgan needed ore or Rockefeller could control him. Without Rockefeller's iron ore, United States Steel would not control its own destiny. Rockefeller was no Gates; indeed, Rockefeller was every bit Morgan's equal. Morgan's direct approach with Rockefeller failed, and Morgan enlisted Frick to negotiate the deal. Morgan had a liking for Frick, and they both shared an interest in art. Rockefeller had always admired and trusted Frick. Without Frick, a key part of the future steel trust would have been missing. Frick also quickly became Morgan's key advisor on additions to the new trust. Frick tried to get Jones and Laughlin Steel to join but failed. Frick got Rockefeller to agree to sell for $80 million in stock of the new company. Morgan had now pieced together a true steel empire, but Frick was the architect. Acting as banker, Morgan took a profit of $12.5 million in fees and $50 million in subscription fees. Altogether it took $150 million to float the deal. Frick's stock value in the exchange would be $61 million. Schwab's share was $25 million. Some problems still existed for the April 1, 1901, formation. Amazingly, Carnegie was still hesitant and actually suggested to Schwab he wanted out, but Schwab reassured him. Probably only J.P. Morgan and Henry Clay Frick fully understood the illusion of United States Steel. The steel behemoth had real assets of only $682 million against $303 million of bonds, $510 million in preferred stock, and $508 million in common stock. No wonder after the deal Frick began to sell his common shares, particularly after the initial upward stock movement. Morgan and Gary were still looking to add more operations, working on the principle set forth in the presidential campaign that staying under 50 percent of market would not trigger antitrust suits.[12] This 50 percent number was about where United States Steel stayed for years.

Judge Gary was to be chairman of the board with a salary of $100,000, and Charles

Schwab was to be president of the new corporation with a $100,000 salary and a 1 percent profit-sharing bonus. Because of Schwab's endless spending, it was rumored he made a million-dollar salary. Rockefeller was a major shareholder and the Board of United States Steel reflected this with the presence of John Rockefeller, John Rockefeller, Jr., and Henry Rogers. Charles Schwab balked on hearing that Frick would be a board member, but Morgan promised that Frick would not attend meetings. Other board directors included Elbert Gary, Charles Schwab, Robert Bacon (Morgan's partner), Marshall Field, James Reed (Carnegie Steel lawyer), William Moore (National Steel), Edmund Converse (National Tube), Francis Peabody, Charles Steele, Norman Ream, Peter Widener, William Edenborn (American Steel and Wire), Daniel Reid (American Tin Plate), Alford Clifford (American Steel and Wire), Clement Griscom, William Dodge, Nathaniel Thayer, Percival Roberts (American Bridge), George Baker (First National Bank), and Abram Hewitt. Frick's $61 million in stock became $88 million in a few days as prices of the new company stock rose from $38 per share to $55 per share. Carnegie's old (but many young) 35 partners became instant multimillionaires. The structure of United States Steel was based on the model of Frick and Rockefeller, who believed in committee structure versus a powerful autocrat. The committee structure continued with an executive committee consisting of Elbert Gary (chairman), Daniel Reid, William Edenborn, E. Converse, Percival Roberts, and Charles Steele. The executive committee was the real power in the new corporation. President Schwab needed to clear major decisions through the executive committee. There was also a finance committee consisting of Robert Bacon (chairman), H. Rogers, Norman Ream, Elbert Gary, and P. Weldener. Clearly, Elbert Gary had all the real management in the structure. The committees further assigned special subcommittees, usually consisting of three members to look at specific projects and purchases. This was the same style Frick had used at Carnegie Brothers. The three managing committees were top-heavy with Morgan and Gary men; in fact, only Schwab was a true Carnegie man. The Carnegie men filled the key operating positions, but they lacked the power to spend the capital needed to upgrade their operations.

The corporation was made up from the constituent companies of Carnegie Steel, Illinois Steel, National Tube, American Sheet & Tin Plate, American Steel & Wire, American Bridge, H.C. Frick Coke, Lorain Steel, Lake Superior Iron Mines, Union Railroad, and United States Steel Products. Each of these companies had its own president and managing board. The constituent companies initially varied in polices and practices. Union agreements varied between companies, but United States Steel started the process of bringing some unity. While the management of the corporation was difficult for the "Braddock Boys," the managing of their new-found wealth was more so. To improve operating efficiencies and share improvements, Frick's style of a technical committee system was set up. For example, the Open Hearth Committee had 23 members that met in New York every three months. The Blast Furnace Committee met every month in New York. In addition, consultants such as Carnegie's old furnace wizard and Frick's neighbor Julian Kennedy were hired to make industry-wide comparisons. The blast furnace committee compared the costs and operating costs of over 80 of the company's blast furnaces. Of course, Schwab added his approach of internal competition to the committee proceedings. In its first year of operation, the committee saved United States Steel over $4 million.[13] The new one-billion-dollar company was too large for the average man to envision. The joke around the mills was, "God made the world in 4004 B.C. and it was reorganized in 1901 by J.P. Morgan."[14] After the formation, over forty Carnegie partners became millionaires as the money was freed from the "Iron Clad Agreement." Seven of them took their families to Europe, including Carnegie, Phipps, Frick, Morrison, Lauder, Oliver, and Singer.

These instant Pittsburgh millionaires created a real estate boom and brought international attention to Pittsburgh. Most of them built beautiful mansions in Pittsburgh suburbs such as Shadyside, Sewickley, and East Liberty. Oliver, Phipps, and Frick invested millions into Pittsburgh real estate. Some, like Alexander Peacock, became Father Christmas, giving millions to help friends pay their debts and have a better life. Some lost their millions, like Francis Lovejoy, who invested unsuccessfully in gold mining. Some built personal libraries and art collections. Products of all types were engraved; one partner had 50-cent cigars made in Cuba with his name and coat of arms. They took up exotic hobbies such as automobiles, motorcycles, exotic flowers, and special mushroom farms. Pittsburgh boomed as real estate agents, art agents, and countless other salesmen descended on the city.

Carnegie and Frick knew now to handle money, but these young partners had worked for Carnegie on the "work now, pay later" system. Carnegie had become the richest man in the world, and had a special vault built in Hoboken, New Jersey, for his $300 million in bonds. Carnegie went on with his public philanthropy. Frick went on being a capitalist with anonymous giving. Schwab, however, went on a public spending spree, including mansions, parties, trips, mistresses, and gambling. Schwab's $3 million New York mansion was said to make Carnegie's look like a cottage. It was four stories with a 116-foot lookout tower, 90 bedrooms, an Olympic-size pool, a bowling alley, a wine cellar, a gymnasium, a network of phones connecting all the bedrooms, and a coal-powered electric plant. He installed a $100,000 pipe organ and added a two-story art gallery. The full-block mansion, known as "Riverside," was the most lavish ever built in New York. Men like Carnegie, Frick, and Morgan could accept huge mansions, but it was Schwab's partying that worried them all. His gambling at Monte Carlo was making bigger headlines than Carnegie's giving. Schwab's socializing without his wife and his poker games with John Gates at the Waldorf-Astoria also caught the public's eye. Judge Gary had deep Methodist roots and was opposed to any form of gambling. Gary wanted Schwab out. Schwab's affair resulting in the birth of a daughter had also become public knowledge. Carnegie was embarrassed by Schwab's behavior and wrote Morgan about it. Probably Schwab's greatest sin was that it affected his ability and drive to manage the new corporation.

Another problem for Schwab was his desire to be number one. United States Steel Corporation had been designed on the Frick/Rockefeller committee system. As president, Schwab reported to the executive committee headed by Judge Gary. The bylaws restricted Schwab's ability to act independently. In addition, while Frick was in the background because his Union Steel competed with United States Steel, Rockefeller, Rogers, and Frick were a force to be reckoned with on the board. The merger had created some inside organizational divisions and corporate clashes of culture. There were the Carnegie "Boys of Braddock" and Gary's old Federal Steel gang. Then there was the new power structure of the Rockefeller/Frick column. As he often did in mergers, Morgan was waiting and watching, although, he was no a big believer in the "Boys'" ability to run a diversified corporation. Schwab took on major directors such as Marshall Fields and Percival Roberts, creating strong enemies.

Early on, Schwab tried to challenge the complex committee system. Morgan and Gary saw United States Steel as a financial corporation run by committees. This was the system of Frick and Rockefeller. These were the only two men in the country who had experience running mega-corporations. Frick had successfully started the transition of Carnegie Steel to the committee system in the late 1890s. The old companies in United States Steel, such as Carnegie Steel, remained subsidiaries with their own presidents and company boards. These subsidiaries came under the control of United States Steel's executive committee, where Schwab wanted the subsidiaries to run their own affairs. Gary maintained that the executive committee could review and adjust policy. Schwab circulated his proposed plan for company operations. Gary and the executive committee soundly beat Schwab's plan with Morgan's full support. It was a clear rebuff of Schwab, and he realized his limited power in this new organization. Schwab would not be a little Carnegie, but a corporate executive as Frick had been in the old Carnegie organization.

The first challenge to the United States Steel executive committee system came from the Amalgamated Union in the spring of 1901. The formation of United States Steel was a mixed bag of union and nonunion plants. Although it was weak, the Amalgamated Association of Iron, Steel, and Tin Workers was the only union left in the steel industry. While the Amalgamated Union had been beaten back at the steel mills at Homestead and Braddock, the Amalgamated was still very strong in the finishing mills in the tin plate operations. The Amalgamated wanted to deal with the corporation as a whole in hopes of spreading unionization. Schwab wanted the individual division presidents to have the authority. Gary took the position that they would deal with the union by division, but like everything else, the executive committee would have oversight. The Amalgamated challenged the corporation over wages and union rights with a strike. The strike was far from successful, with the big plants continuing to work. The strike was particularly ineffective at South Works (Chicago), Homestead, and Edgar Thomson. The unionized tin mills and hoop mills were the core of the strike. The corporation brought in strikebreakers and the strike collapsed along with the Amalgamated. The Amalgamated leaders appealed directly to Morgan without success. A similar appeal to Samuel Gompers to make the strike a national union issue failed as well. With plenty of finishing capacity, the corporation chose not to open most of the unionized tin mills. This final collapse of the Amalgamated was again rooted in its inability to gain the support of the unskilled laborers.[15] Frick, of course, had little to do with this crushing blow to the union by Gary and Schwab. United States Steel also launched a quiet campaign of closing union mills in the corporation. The process was called by the union the "starvation and petition method."

Schwab's earlier dealings with the company, his investments, and his personal life continued to be problematic. Eight weeks into his presidency, Schwab tried his hand at being a financier in the mold of Frick. Schwab negotiated a deal to buy Bethlehem Steel, which was a manufacturer of armor, gun forgings, and heavy plate. He intended it as a personal investment, and planned to merge it with U.S. Shipbuilding Company. Morgan, however, saw this as a major conflict of interest and purchased Bethlehem Steel from him. Schwab then purchased Bethlehem back from Morgan and sold it to the shipbuilding trust of U.S. Shipbuilding. Morgan made a profit of $2.5 million, while Schwab gained control of Bethlehem Steel's Board and became a bondholder. Schwab was a great mill manager, but he lacked the financial expertise of a Frick. The deal never really worked well financially for Schwab, and it caused more government scrutiny of United States Steel and bad publicity for Morgan. In the end, it would offer an escape route for Schwab.

With the formation of United States Steel, Frick took a summer trip to Europe in 1901. He returned to New York on September 12 to very disturbing news. President McKinley had been shot a week earlier at the Buffalo World's Fair and was dying. The assassin, Leon Czolgosz, was a socialist and anarchist. Leon Czolgosz had a link to Frick's past. Czolgosz's girlfriend, Emma Goldman, had been the earlier girlfriend of Frick's own would-be assassin, Alexander Berkmann. Emma Goldman had also been taken into custody. Frick, who was visually shaken, made a statement to the reporters: "I hope that the president will live. His death would be a serious blow to the great commercial interests of this country, which have grown along such healthful lines during his term at the head of our government. The country cannot afford to lose him."[16] McKinley would die on September 14. Frick had supported McKinley since his early days in Congress. Frick never fully understood McKinley, but they shared a belief in American capitalism and exceptionalism. The McKinley assassination shook the nation as badly as John F. Kennedy's assassination would in later years. Frick and the Pennsylvania Railroad Board of Directors supplied a special funeral train for McKinley's body, cabinet, and family. The body of McKinley moved from Buffalo to the Capitol and then to his home of Canton, Ohio. The train with Attorney General Philander Knox and McKinley's body passed by the mills of Braddock and Homestead. Work was stopped for ten minutes as steelworkers lined the tracks holding their dinner pails high as a tribute to the "Napoleon of Protectionism."

The funeral train passed in view of the Monongahela House, where presidents from Lincoln to McKinley had stayed, as had Frick in his early days. Pittsburgh was an important port of call in this industrial era, and McKinley had visited here often, twice as president. McKinley was a close personal friend of Frick's neighbor, George Westinghouse. At Pittsburgh's Second Avenue, the train passed the exact location where the railroad air brake had been tested successfully, saving the life of a peddler. McKinley had later passed legislation that made air brakes mandatory on American trains. Also in the crowd at the Pittsburgh station was M.M. Garland, who was president of the Amalgamated Association of Iron, Steel, and Tin Workers at the end of the Homestead Strike. Garland had become a McKinley supporter and was working with him for peace with labor. Garland, like Samuel Gompers, had come to realize that prosperity meant both union membership and corporate profits. Union membership quadrupled during the McKinley administration as industry rapidly expanded.

Frick would attend the massive funeral for McKinley in Canton, Ohio. He would be among tens of thousands to do so, and United States Steel called for a holiday to allow steelworkers to travel by rail to Canton. McKinley was an extremely popular president. His full cabinet, most of Congress, all of the Supreme Court, and countless politicians descended on the small city of Canton. In addition to America's aristocracy, hundreds of steelworkers and miners came to Canton. Frick would always remember this gentle middle-class president who was the political lion of capitalism. Frick could not fully understand McKinley's passionate defense of capitalism, since McKinley, unlike Frick, had gotten very few rewards from it. With McKinley gone and Teddy Roosevelt as president, Frick realized that capitalism would have a new competitor in progressivism. Roosevelt was generally disliked by the capitalists; even J.P. Morgan, who had been happy with Grover Cleveland, had little good to say about Roosevelt. Roosevelt would live up to their fears in the first year by breaking up Morgan's railroad trust and forcing a labor settlement in the eastern anthracite coal fields by threatening to nationalize them.

After the formation of United States Steel, Frick expanded into many commercial interests as well, such as banking and real estate. In 1900, Frick was

Philander Chase Knox (courtesy Carnegie Library of Pittsburgh).

one of the largest real estate owners in Pittsburgh and one of the wealthiest in the East End. In 1899, Frick purchased the old St. Peter's Episcopal Church at the corner of Grant and Diamond streets in the city of Pittsburgh for $180,000. In late 1900, he launched the building of the future Frick Building. It would stand next to the Carnegie Building of 1893, which was known as the city's first skyscraper. Frick planned a 24-story skyscraper 265 feet tall to cast a shadow on Carnegie's 15-story building. The building was a steel frame with carved stone of classical Doric design. Each office had two 47-inch-by-62-inch mirror windows. The interior had rich Italian marble, Honduras mahogany, and bronze metalwork and doors. The primary tenant was to be Frick's Union Savings Bank. Another tenant was Equitable Life, of whose board Frick was a member. Frick maintained his own personal office there as well. The top floor was reserved for the Union Club, and the basement had the Union Restaurant, paneled in Flemish Renaissance oak. The Union Club and Union Restaurant had two refrigerating plants to produce ice. Also in the basement was the largest nickel steel plate vault in the world, which weighed 17 tons. The whole building had a central vacuum system for cleaning. The next year Frick planned a major hotel, which would be known as the William Penn Hotel. The William Penn was to be the second largest hotel in the United States at the time. He would also continue to invest in land around the Oakland section. By 1904, Frick was the largest owner of real estate in the city of Pittsburgh.

Frick's financial ties continued to grow with the Mellons in the early 1900s. Frick's investments outside of H.C. Frick Company were extensive. Frick and Andrew Mellon had continued their informal investment lunches at the Duquesne Club, and Frick became part of the Mellon enterprises. They formed a unique investment firm in the 1890s, which had tentacles in industry and mining throughout western Pennsylvania. Over the years, Frick and Mellon invested in a series of small coal mines on the Monongahela and Youghiogheny Rivers. Mellon formed the Monongahela River Consolidated Coal and Coke Company through Union Trust. This company put together a string of Frick and Mellon mine investments over the years. In 1899, Monongahela Coal was an amalgamation of 96 mines. In addition, Union Trust supplied the financing for the nation's largest coal mining company, Pittsburgh Coal Company. Mellon, Frick, Henry Rea, and Henry Oliver served on the boards of these companies, which merged in 1916.

Frick had been a major stockholder in Union Trust and Citizens National Bank with the Mellons. In addition, Frick formed Union Savings out of Union Trust. Union Savings was on the cutting edge of banking at the time, allowing deposits by mail. Union Savings was also known for its high rate on deposits. The Union Savings idea was to attract deposits from Europe. Union Savings became an important source of cash for the venture capital investments of Union Trust. Frick again had proven his amazing knowledge and skill in financial institutions. On July 2, 1902, Mellon National Bank was formed from T. Mellon & Sons, Pittsburgh National, City Deposit Bank and Frick's Citizens National Bank, making it the second biggest in Pittsburgh after Farmer's Deposit National Bank. Frick and Henry Phipps would serve on Mellon National Bank's board. Mellon biographer David Cannadine noted that Frick was "virtually an adopted member of the Mellon family, so far as banking and financial influence were concerned."[17] At the same time, Union Trust was reorganized, giving the Mellons 2,413 shares and Frick 1,503 shares.[18] Mellon National Bank and Union Trust had interlocking directorships and stock arrangements, which made Mellon National Bank a wholly owned subsidiary of Union Trust. The Mellon-Frick combination was a powerful engine behind the majority of Pittsburgh's many industries. It was estimated that Andrew Mellon, Richard Mellon, and H.C. Frick controlled a third of all the bank money in Pittsburgh in 1902. Frick was rapidly approaching the financial circle of a Carnegie. Union Trust was really a type of venture capital firm, which created many huge companies such as ALCOA in the alu-

Adelaide and Helen Frick in 1901 (courtesy Frick Collection).

minum industry, Gulf Oil, Pittsburgh Coal, Standard Steel Car Company, and Philadelphia Company. It is clearly overlooked that Henry Clay Frick, more than anyone else, built the city of Pittsburgh. Frick had deep roots in Pittsburgh banking, transportation, real estate, coal, steel, and manufacturing. More so than Carnegie, Frick was the builder of industrial Pittsburgh, and history shows he was the real force behind United States Steel Corporation.

Frick's contribution to United States Steel Corporation (USS) and the steel industry continued for years after the formation of United States Steel. Through Frick's leadership, Union Steel had developed a significant hold on the United States' steel wire business. In 1902, a stock exchange merged Union Steel's finishing operations at Donora, Pennsylvania, on the Monongahela with Sharon Steel in Lawrence County, Pennsylvania. Sharon Steel brought in primary steel production and could now challenge United States Steel, where Frick sat on the board. The merged company had an estimated capital value of $50 million. Union Steel was a fully integrated operation, which many saw as a miniature of United States Steel. Union Steel had ore mines, coal mines, gas wells, lime mines, ore ships, three blast furnaces, twenty-four open heaths, two blooming mills, a bar mill, rod mill, wire mill, and nail wire mill. Thanks to Frick, Union Steel had bought prime coal operations at Connellsville and ore mines at the Mesabi Range. Frick's railroad board memberships assured future rail connections from Lake Erie to the mills. The new company lasted less than two months, as United States Steel decided to buy it at $75 million. Both Frick and Mellon made as much as $20 million each from their small investment. The takeover would be reviewed years later, and Congress found the whole deal created overinflated profits for Frick and Mellon. Frick and the Mellons also moved into the steel freight and passenger railroad car business, again in direct competition with United States Steel. Frick and the Mellons made a $3 million investment with executives of the old Pressed Steel Car Company. Standard Steel Car started production in Butler, Pennsylvania, and soon was outselling United States Steel. In its first annual report December 31, 1902, the company had assets of $1,546,544,234 and an income of $15,657,083 with total employees of 168,000.[19]

Frick was involved in a number of other steel companies through his directorship on the Pennsylvania Railroad. Frick's close ties with the Pennsylvania Railroad and the Baltimore & Ohio gave him advantages over all steel masters. William H. Donner and Frick acquired interests in Pennsylvania Steel and Cambria Steel through their ties with the railroads. Cambria was to be managed by Donner. Besides his directorships with the Mellon investments, Frick was a director of a large array of corporate boards around the nation. These included National City Bank of New York, the Mercantile Trust Company, Franklin National Bank of Philadelphia, Commercial Trust of Philadelphia, and Equitable Trust Company of New York. He also served on the boards of Equitable Life Assurance Society, National Union Fire Insurance, and Union Insurance Company. He also served on the industrial boards of United States Steel, Diamond Light and Power Company, Union Steel, Standard Steel Car Company, Philadelphia Company, Reading Railroad, Baltimore and Ohio Railroad, Norfolk and Western, and Pittsburgh Coal. By 1906, Frick was one of the largest railroad investors and was added to the boards of Pennsylvania Railroad, the Chicago and Northwestern, the Atchison, Topeka, and Santa Fe, and the Union Pacific. The railroads remained United States Steel's major customer and supplier, and Frick was active in steel sales, pricing, and railroad charges to United States Steel. Frick and Mellon were also involved in the New York Shipbuilding Company. This was an amazing amount of involvement in the nation's business. It seemed everyone wanted the skillful Frick. He had become central to the nation's business and government, second only to J.P. Morgan. Frick was the world's greatest capitalist, often representing the best and worst of capitalism. There is no doubt that if Berkman's bullet had hit the mark, America's business, Pittsburgh, and the nation would be different today. Frick was a man whom presidents and corporate leaders now called on for help and advice. Frick was the world's expert on the steel industry.

By 1903, the excitement over the formation of United States Steel was gone. The company was struggling internally and externally. Schwab and his "Boys" and the old Federal Steel gang were fighting it out for control. These corporate loyalties between old competitors ran deep, especially among the Carnegie managers, who had been raised on the red meat of beating the "Chicago Mills." Morgan was growing tired of Schwab and his socializing; in addition, Morgan's partner William Perkins believed Schwab needed to go. The stock, once high-flying at $55 per share, had hit $10 a share in 1903. Frick was unloading his common stock. Even Carnegie, whose core fortune was in United States Steel bonds, was worrying about United States Steel's ability to pay on the bonds. Gary was not able to bring the company into one unit, especially with Schwab as president. Frick was starting to show up at board meetings when Schwab was gone. The company was short on cash, as expenses related to the merger grew and business turned down in 1902. Morgan realized United States Steel had serious problems and made the decision to bring in Frick. Of course, the Rockefeller's major holding put pressure on Morgan to bring in someone acceptable to the Rockefeller group, and that man was Frick. Frick was no Carnegie man, but he differed with Judge Gary on policy; still, he was the most accomplished steel executive in the corporation. Gary was an executive, as was Morgan's man George Perkins, but "neither knew steel as a metal. To them it was a stock — a purely financial entity."[20] While Frick did not attend the finance committee, he was assigned to endless special committees to review mergers, ore lands, coal lands, and technology. Minutes of meetings were sent to Frick, and Gary consistently asked for Frick's advice on major decisions. Clearly, Morgan valued Frick as the main consultant on industry questions. Frick also was the man who could go between the two factions inside the company.

Hotel Schenley (courtesy Carnegie Library of Pittsburgh).

Morgan was aware of the overfunding of United States Steel, and that it would have to be addressed as the economy slowed near the end of 1902. Judge Gary had had it with Schwab and was threatening to resign.

Morgan needed to do something or the ship was going down. A meeting set the stage for Frick in late 1902 on Morgan's yacht the *Corsair*. Frick was the only man with actual large corporation management experience that Morgan trusted (he disliked Rockefeller). The content of the discussion remains unknown, but clearly Morgan wanted to know what could be done to turn things around. He also wanted to discuss Union Steel, which was owned by Frick, and was competing with United States Steel in wire. Furthermore, Frick was active in the strategic decisions of Union Steel. It was leaked that Frick suggested a dividend cut on common stock, but Morgan felt that would cause the stock to collapse. Morgan has been hailed by many as saving the company by continuing a dividend in 1903, but it would be Frick who proved right in the longer run. In 1904 and 1905, United States Steel would have to suspend the common stock to infuse the capital needed to improve the operations. The Union Steel deal could be settled and that would free Frick to take a more active role on the executive board and the financial board. The deal was real for Frick. United States Steel would buy Union Steel, which was capitalized at $10 million, for $30 million. Frick was then freed to spend his time with United States Steel. In later news reports, this meeting of Frick and Morgan was believed to have been key to turning United States Steel around and maybe even saving the corporation.[21]

The other issue at the *Corsair* meeting was what to do with Schwab. Morgan wanted him out because of the bad publicity. The government and press were looking at the evils of Big Business, and Schwab's bigger-than-life socializing was a problem. For Frick's part, he had never seen Schwab as an executive. Schwab's strength was at the plant operations level. Morgan believed he needed one of the "Boys of Braddock" to replace Schwab, or it might further widen the split between Carnegie men and Gary men. The Braddock gang still had James Gayley, Ava Dinkey, William Corey, and William Dickson in high operating positions. At the time Gayley was Schwab's vice-president and Dickson was his assistant and second vice-president, Corey was president of the Carnegie Steel Division, and Dinkey was manager of Homestead. Frick, who never was a Carnegie man, saw Corey as the least of four evils. Frick also had old ties to the Corey family. Corey's quiet personality seemed best from Morgan's view as well. As the 1903 recession progressed, United States Steel stock hit a bottom of 8¾ per share, and the plan was fully implemented. Frick purchased 50,000 shares of common and 5,000 shares of preferred to show his support of the corporation.

This final showdown was a clash of many rather large egos. In early 1903, Schwab was aware of the side meetings discussing his fate. George Perkins, one of Morgan's assistants, had been the first to call for the elimination of Schwab; but Schwab had also done battle with his boss and chairman of the board Judge Gary. In addition, after the *Corsair* meeting, Frick started to attend board meetings, which was a clear signal that things had changed. It had been Schwab who had demanded Frick not attend board meetings. The June 1903 board meeting had Frick and Schwab meeting for the first time. Schwab had been acting strangely, avoiding work; in his own words, Schwab was suffering from "nervousness."[22] Schwab actually had no one on the board to consult except Frick. They appeared to have worked out a face-saving approach to Schwab's resignation. Schwab would retire ostensibly for health reasons, but the press never bought it. Frick held to the story; he was never the type of man to destroy even an enemy in the press. It was a courtesy never offered Frick by the Carnegie men. At the July board meeting, another phase of the plan was initiated with the election of William Corey to director. On August 4, Schwab gave his resignation to the board. Schwab had also prepared a soft landing by taking over as president of Bethlehem Steel (the nation's second largest steel company).

The final part of the reorganization of United States Steel to rebuild the powerful executive subcommittee was known as the Finance Committee. This committee consisted of Frick, Rockefeller representatives, and Morgan men. The committee membership included Henry Clay Frick, Elbert Gary, Robert Bacon, Percival Roberts, Jr., and George Baker. Robert Bacon retired and was replaced by George Perkins. The executive committee was disbanded, and the Finance Committee had central control of the corporation, which made Frick the real power broker in the corporation. As chairman of the board, Gary would have supreme powers, but almost all major decisions were discussed with Frick. Historians noted a major change as Frick took an active role on the Finance Committee. It would be Frick who developed a true corporate strategy. The Finance Committee issued the following directive in 1905: "The subject matter of formulating a comprehensive plan for the future development of all properties in which the United States Steel Corporation is interested, considered as a unit, was referred to a special committee to be appointed by the chairman of the Board for consideration and report."[23] Frick led that critical committee to break down the regionalism in the corporation. It must also be remembered that no company so large had ever been managed by central control. Frick certainly deserves the title of the father of corporate management.

Frick had maintained an aggressive personal investment strategy during the period of 1900 to 1905. He and his old friend Andrew Mellon continued their investments in Pittsburgh real estate. They also moved into the new field of real estate development. One of the more interesting was his investment in the St. Clair Improvement Company, which was a real estate development company in Clairton, Pennsylvania. Clairton, 14 miles up the Monongahela River from Pittsburgh, became the site of two small steel companies, which came under ownership of Crucible Steel in 1901 and were known as Clairton Steel. The St. Clair Improvement Company was a partnership of A.G. Mitchell (neighbor and Pennsylvania Railroad executive), Karl Overholt (nephew), F.W. McElroy (Frick business associate), and Henry Clay Frick. Frick owned 1,990 shares out of the 2,000. Real estate development around the steel mills had become a very profitable business. Frick had partnered earlier with Frank Nicola on developing neighborhoods for steel and mine workers. Karl Overholt, who also functioned as Frick's Pittsburgh office manager, did a lot of day-to-day managing of St. Clair. The company started building a middle-class community. The community, supported by Frick and Mitchell, had the Pennsylvania Railroad build a beautiful modern station at Clairton. It was advertised as "the ideal home of the man of moderate means ... for everybody who wants a home away from the smoke and dirt of Pittsburgh."[24] Clairton Steel was to be a major integrated mill employing

Henry Clay Frick, age 45 (courtesy Carnegie Library of Pittsburgh).

over 2,000 employees. Frick targeted the skilled workers and those unskilled who would work their way up. This model city was Frick's version of Pullman City in Chicago and George Westinghouse's Wilmerding. Frick arranged for the construction of community schools, churches, and banks.

The St. Clair Improvement Company community lacked the personal touch of Westinghouse's Wilmerding as well as the positive publicity. Earlier on in the mining business, Frick had realized the profits in developing boomtown communities. Union Supply continued to produce 25 percent of the profits of H.C. Frick Coke. Clearly, supplying and housing workers could be highly profitable. The St. Clair Improvement Company lacked the altruism of Westinghouse's Wilmerding, but it did not overcharge house owners as did Pullman City. It was just another profitable business venture. The company built and paved roads, built sewers, developed a natural gas pipeline, and built a water system. The company built the first-class Clairton Hotel, as well as the lower-level Tattnall Hotel that was targeted at single immigrant workers. Frick was removed from day-to-day management but still got involved. He purchased land and gave a park to the community. The company was so successful he formed Union Improvement Company with the Mellon brothers. Union Improvement Company developed the community of Donora around the Frick-Mellon Union Steel plant. In Donora, the Union Improvement Company built the Donora Hotel.

Frick's interests soon went beyond the community and to the new Clairton Steel mill. The mill was state of the art, having blast furnaces that could handle 100 percent Mesabi ore, something Frick had worked on while with Carnegie. Crucible Steel had been a tool steel and specialty operation in New York, but Clairton Steel was fully integrated and capable of direct competition with United States Steel. The plant had open hearths with finishing operations for tin plate, sheet, bars, and rails. Frick was even more impressed by its use of electricity to power cranes and material handling systems. Frick had pushed the United States Steel Finance Committee to purchase the mill in 1902. In 1903, the deal to purchase Clairton fell through.[25] Clairton Steel, however, was forced into receivership over cash flow problems. Frick and United States Steel quickly purchased the mill below cost. In 1905, again at Frick's suggestion, he had United States Steel purchase more land at Clairton, which in 1919 would become the state-of-the-art Clairton Coke Works. It was becoming clear that the structure of the massive United States Steel Corporation was the handiwork of Henry Clay Frick.

18. The World's Richest Neighborhood

In 1900, Frick's East End neighborhood was the world's richest. It was the rich suburb of what had become America's fifth largest city. In a short walk, one might run into Andrew Carnegie, George Westinghouse, H.J. Heinz, or one of the Mellon family. Mail was delivered seven times a day to keep America's greatest capitalists in touch with their factories, banks, and markets. The residents of Pittsburgh's East End controlled as much as 40 percent of America's assets. Two major corporations, Standard Oil and ALCOA, were formed in East End homes. It was the first neighborhood to adopt the telephone, with direct lines from the homes to Pittsburgh's biggest banks. The neighborhood had its own private station of the Pennsylvania Railroad. This wealthy burgh commanded visits from American presidents and future presidents, such as William McKinley, Teddy Roosevelt, William Taft, Calvin Coolidge, and Herbert Hoover. Teddy Roosevelt stopped over at the Frick mansion for lunch and took a nap in the upper room. William McKinley had dinner at Westinghouse's "Solitude." Pittsburgh's East End was the home of U.S. Senator Philander Knox, who often joined in the weekly poker game at Frick's mansion. The game included the Carnegie brothers and the Mellon brothers. These eight blocks had enough major art pieces to rival any European museum. It was here that Westinghouse conceived of the AC power grid; Tom Carnegie persuaded his brother to get into the steel business; and Heinz created his "57 varieties." Its famous Hotel Schenley was the corporate gathering place of some of the world's greatest industrialists, politicians, bankers, art collectors, and philanthropists. The neighborhood was the first to use natural gas, the first to have a telephone switching station, the first to be electrified, and the first to have a gas station. In 1905, the neighborhood had more telephones, automobiles, and dollars per capita than any other community in the world.

The East End of Pittsburgh made an impression on reporter Theodore Dreiser: "Never in my life was the vast gap which divides the rich from the poor in America so vividly and forcefully brought home to me.... Never did the mere possession of wealth impress me so keenly.... Even the street lamps were of a better design than elsewhere." It was truly the center of opulent wealth of the Victorian era. Besides the more famous names mentioned, other millionaires abounded. Frick's closest neighbors were the Mellon brothers, Andrew and Richard, George Westinghouse, and H.J. Heinz.

There was Thomas Armstrong, the founder of Armstrong Cork, and sons. Philander Knox, who would be a U.S. Senator and Attorney General under President McKinley, lived there. Teddy Roosevelt was a neighbor, as well as Thomas Howe, a banking and copper magnate, who served two terms as a U.S. Senator from the Whig Party. Andrew Carnegie's mother lived on the southern edge of the neighborhood, as well as Tom Carnegie in the 1880s. Carnegie's partners and their sons were numerous in the neighborhood over the years. Some of these partners were Francis Lovejoy, Latham Abbott, Lawrence Phipps, Henry Curry, George Lauder (Carnegie's cousin), Alexander Peacock, Daniel Clemson, and the Borntraeger brothers, William and Carl. Other industrialists who lived in the neighborhood included George Mesta, founder of Mesta Machine Company; Jacob Vandergrift, partner of Rockefeller in Standard Oil; Thomas Mellon, founder of Mellon Banks; Charles Lockhart, co-founder of Standard Oil with Rockefeller; Alfred Hunt, founder of ALCOA Aluminum; Sylvester Mar-

Frick's mansion "Clayton" as it looks today (from Frick Collection).

vin, founder of National Biscuit Company (Nabisco); James McCrea, president of the Pennsylvania Railroad; Robert Pitcairn, vice-president of Pennsylvania Railroad and industrial investor; Oswald Werner, developer of dry cleaning; Willis McCook, co-founder of Pittsburgh Steel; Wallace Rowe, another co-founder of Pittsburgh Steel; Alexander King, glass magnate; Henry Hillard, president of Alcania; Henry Laughlin, Jones and Laughlin Steel; Alexander Bradley, stove manufacturer; Benjamin Thaw, railroad magnate; James Guffey, oil and gas magnate; Julian Kennedy, world furnace expert; George Macbeth, founder of Macbeth-Evans Glass; Daniel Clemson, a Carnegie partner; Benjamin and Thomas Bakewell, of Pittsburgh's famous glassmaking family; Thomas Messler, president of the New York and Erie Railroad; Lillian Russell, national theater star; and Joseph Woodwell, hardware baron and artist. Others included Durbin Horne, president of Joseph Horne Department Store; Alexander Moore, newspaper baron (as well as Ambassador to Spain); James McClelland, famous homeopathic physician; Arthur Braun, publisher and banker; Thomas Howe, president of the Exchange National Bank of Pittsburgh; George Berry, president of Citizen's National Bank; Rueben Miller, president of Fidelity Trust Company; August Succop, banking executive; and bank president John Holmes.

In the 1880s and 1890s, the East End was a tight-knit neighborhood. Sundays were days of picnics and walks. Frick often met with the Mellon brothers and Joseph Woodwell to discuss art. Early Sunday morning they would meet in Frick's library, and later in the day they moved to Woodwell's home studio. On Saturdays, Frick often walked over to his friend and lawyer Philander Knox's house. Mrs. Frick often walked in the gardens of H.J. Heinz. There were many neighborhood flower shows in which the Fricks participated. Often Frick would offer a small prize for the best flower. The Westinghouses were best known for their informal dinner parties. Westinghouse often invited his neighbors to dine with a visiting scientist or artist. The period from 1880 to 1895 was the peak of these informal days. As the close of the century neared, many of the neighbors had summer and winter homes elsewhere.

George Westinghouse's home, known as "Solitude" (courtesy Carnegie Library of Pittsburgh).

East Liberty, as the area was also known, was about six miles from downtown Pittsburgh. The importance of these men assured mail was delivered several times a day. Telegram offices and telephones came to the area in the 1860s and 1870s. The first telephone in Allegheny County was installed at the East Liberty home of Thomas David (president of the local telegraph company) in 1877. H.J. Heinz was one of the first to use a telephone for his business in 1879. Frick added several phones to Clayton in 1883. Pittsburgh's first telephone switching station was built in East Liberty and manned by operators twenty-four hours a day. The area had a special flag station for the Pennsylvania Railroad, which allowed men like George Westinghouse to take the daily train to his factories east of Pittsburgh in the Turtle Creek Valley. The Fifth Avenue Car System and Citizens Passenger Railways serviced East Liberty in the 1870s. They were both horse-drawn trolley systems. Many of the neighbors invested in Westinghouse's Pittsburgh Traction Company, which installed a new cable car system in 1889; but the first trolley line was that of Citizens Traction Company. Frick was an investment partner in the company with the Republican machine boss Christopher Magee. The cable car was the first "rapid" transit system, reducing the hour-and-a-half trip to Pittsburgh to one hour. In 1890, an electric trolley cutting the commute time to Pittsburgh to 30 minutes serviced the area. George Westinghouse had also installed an experimental electric trolley around his mansion. The Pennsylvania Railroad had its only long-distance nonstop train, the Pittsburgher and the Iron City Express, which went direct from the East End to the New York financial district.

Frick, the Mellon brothers, and the Ferguson brothers had started a personal investment in East End land in the 1880s. The Oakland district was the first East End section that was developed. Another individual investor was Pittsburgh's Republican boss Christopher Magee and his cousin (and city director) Edward Bigelow. Magee and Bigelow were able to purchase a huge piece of Oakland land owned by Mary Schenley, who was the granddaughter of Pittsburgh's first industrialist and capitalist James O'Hara. O'Hara had purchased the land prior to the Revolutionary War. Magee used the land to develop a park, modeled after New York's

Central Park, hiring the son of Central Park designer Fredrick Law Olmsted, Jr. Schenley Park included a race track, a man-made lake, a band shell, and endless carriage paths. Magee's park was followed by Andrew Carnegie's decision to build his museum in Oakland. This development quickly increased the property values for Frick, the Mellons, and many of Frick's East End neighbors.

These neighbors had difficult schedules and auxiliary homes elsewhere, such as New York. Many such as Philander Knox, Joseph Woodwell, Benjamin Thaw, and Robert Pitcairn were members of the South Fork Fishing and Hunting Club. Henry Clay Frick was one of the founders of the Schenley Riding Club and participated in races at their track on Brunots Island. In 1899, H.J. Heinz was introduced to a new game: golf. In 1899, Pittsburgh's first golf course was built in the East End's Homewood neighborhood. Belmar Golf Course was a six-hole course, and as a result, H.J. Heinz preferred a six-hole game his whole life. In the late 1890s, Frick was also introduced to golf. Frick would see H.J. Heinz often at Belmar, but Frick preferred the 18-hole game. He loved to play for a $1.00 a hole, and on the 17th hole, it was "double or quits." Most of the neighborhood, including Frick, belonged to the Oakmont and Pittsburgh Country Clubs. Pittsburgh Country Club was on Beechwood Avenue, and Frick remained a member until his death. Frick also used the Pittsburgh Country Club for business entertaining. As he got older, Frick would have some very distinguished golf partners, such as President William Taft, and he played on the world's greatest courses. He appears to have played almost daily in his later years. Frick also loved winter golf trips to Palm Beach. Frick became known for his outstanding golf clothes. He used Purple Dot Bramble golf balls imported from London and monogrammed his balls using a Simplex ball marker.

Frick and Howard Heinz also became interested in automobiles, as the first races were held in nearby Schenley Park.

George Westinghouse (courtesy Carnegie Library of Pittsburgh).

Heinz Residence, Pittsburgh, Pa.

The H.J. Heinz residence Greenlawn, in 1900 (courtesy Carnegie Library of Pittsburgh).

Howard Heinz would also become an attendee and racer at Schenley Park. It was a neighborhood of greenhouses. The greenhouses supported some personal plant experiments as well as plants from around the world, inspired by the nearby Phipps Conservatory, which had opened to the public in 1899. The Phipps Conservatory was considered the second largest in the world. H.J. Heinz opened his conservatory to the public. Heinz had over ten greenhouses where he was testing new vegetables and flowers. Heinz's fall chrysanthemum show became a favorite with the people of Pittsburgh. In 1915, he put much of the grounds into wartime victory gardens. Frick had his own conservatory as part of Clayton and took up the hobby of raising orchids and other flowers. It was a lifelong hobby he shared with his wife, and Frick also was happy to take visitors through the conservatory. Often there was an informal competition between neighbors. Frick opened his conservatory to the public in 1915. In New York, he also entered flower shows and financially supported them. Frick was also known for raising mushrooms. He became a charter member of the International Garden Club in 1914.

H.J. Heinz was within a block of Frick, and his mansion became a public attraction. Heinz continued to expand his "Greenlawn" mansion in the late 1890s with a billiard room, conservatory, bowling alley, tennis court, additional greenhouses, an expanded library, and an expanded museum. Eventually, his mansion would have nine greenhouses. Heinz's sisters, Mary and Henrietta, lived there and acted as hostesses for Heinz. Like Frick, Heinz had trees brought in from the world over, including cuttings from the Vatican. In 1897, Heinz added a pedigreed St. Bernard dog known as "Homewood Don." (Dogs were extremely popular in the neighborhood. Helen Frick had a dog named "Fido.") Heinz's private museum on the fourth floor had caught the imagination of the local and national press in 1897 and was opened on a limited basis. Heinz had hired Professor Samuel Harper, a local scientist, to maintain and catalog the museum. The collections included the pre–Indian mound people of the Pittsburgh area, a collection of footwear from around the world, carved ivories, oriental rugs, a complete armor collection, art pieces, and countless curios. Heinz's eclectic assortment was much different from the classic art museum of Clayton. Heinz loved to collect, and his passion took him in many different directions. Heinz often took his salesmen through the museum, as well as hundreds of social guests and local school children.

The East End was one of America's first true suburbs. These beautiful mansions were in a rural setting. A deep wooded ravine cut by Nine-Mile Run ran several miles from the back of Clayton to the Monongahela River (today it is still a nature preserve known as Frick Park). Not far away was the hilly nature preserve known as Highland Park. Highland Park was a 436-acre park created in 1889 with the help of William Flinn. Frick Park and Schenley Park featured popular horse-riding paths. Helen Frick was fond of riding her mare called "Patricia" on these wooded trails. Even the mansion owners such as H.J. Heinz brought in large trees to plant on their grounds, keeping the rural nature of the area to this day. The Fricks loved to picnic in nearby Swissvale alongside the Monongahela. More than anyone in the family, Helen Frick came to love walking in the woods and the neighborhood. Childs, who developed his love for nature in the wooded ravines, left for Princeton in 1901. Henry Clay Frick was spending more time in New York, where United States Steel was headquartered. Like many of his neighbors, he owned his own railroad car, the *Westmoreland*, on the Pennsylvania Railroad, allowing him to go to New York in luxury and take the family on vacation. Henry had rented an apartment in New York's Sherry's Hotel; the family often vacationed at the Breakers Hotel in Palm Beach, Florida.

Frick also built a summer home at Eagle Rock on Boston's North Shore (Pride's Crossing was the mailing address). Neighbors included William Taft, Henry Cabot Lodge, Louis Comfort Tiffany, Theodore Roosevelt, Justice Oliver Wendell Holmes, and Philander Knox's summer home. Helen, however, preferred Clayton to these other homes, since it seemed to pull the family back to Pittsburgh. Frick's Eagle Rock home was not far from President Taft's summer home, and Taft and Frick became good friends. Both Frick and Taft were conserva-

The Mellon family estate in 1900 (courtesy Carnegie Library of Pittsburgh).

tive Republicans opposed to Roosevelt's progressive wing. Taft and Frick also shared a friend and golf partner in department store king John Wanamaker. They were members of the exclusive Myopia Hunt Club. The Myopia had the nation's first polo field for Childs Frick to learn the game, and one of the most famous golf courses, having hosted the U.S. Open in 1898, 1901, 1905, and 1908. Frick would golf with Taft and take part in his famous "automobile parties." They also competed in the Myopia Club's horse shows, in which Frick often won medals for his horses. At Eagle Rock, one of Frick's first visitors was George Westinghouse and his wife, who had a summer home in the Berkshires.

Frick and his neighbors drew many of the world's most powerful men to this Pittsburgh suburb. Presidents, princes, artists, politicians, and scientists came routinely to visit the residents of Pittsburgh's East End. Frick's neighborhood had a constant stream of famous scientists for dinner, such as Nikola Tesla, Lord Kelvin, and Benjamin Lamme. Many presidents, before, during, and after their presidencies, including Grover Cleveland, William McKinley, Teddy Roosevelt, Warren Harding, William Howard Taft, Herbert Hoover, and Calvin Coolidge made stops at the neighborhood; but probably the most famous visit was that of Teddy Roosevelt to Clayton in 1902. The affair was on the Fourth of July and included the U.S. Marine Corps Band. The guests were some of Pittsburgh's top businessmen. Frick sat at the head of the table with Roosevelt to the right and friend and Attorney General Philander Knox on the left. Others included

Henry W. Oliver (steel "aristocrat"), Andrew Mellon, George Laughlin (steel "aristocrat"), James McCrea (president of the Pennsylvania Railroad), General John P. Penny, George Oliver, George Cortelyou (president's secretary), John Wylie, James Brown, Charles Speer, Calvin Wells (president of the Pittsburgh Forge), Henry Porter (Pittsburgh locomotive manufacturer), William McConway (iron manufacturer), W.C. Latin, John Urie, Albert Barr (Pittsburgh editor), J.O. Brown (banker), J.O. Jones (military guard, Sheridan troop), and Albert Logan.[1] After lunch, a number of Pittsburgh businessmen stopped by. Over 600 American Beauty roses were used in the rooms, as well as special Frick-grown orchids. Twelve waiters served a luncheon from New York's Waldorf Astoria Hotel. The lunch consisted of salmon mayonnaise, melon, tomato aspic, sweetbreads, fillet of beef, roast duck, new potatoes, pickles, asparagus, peas, and cheese. The dessert was ice cream, cake, coffee, and fruit. After lunch, Roosevelt

Andrew Mellon (courtesy Carnegie Library of Pittsburgh).

took a nap in the guest room. In addition, tents in the back were used to serve the troops. That evening Roosevelt would head for the Schenley Hotel in Oakland for a large dinner meeting. While a major contributor to Roosevelt, Frick was not a huge fan, but he would be involved with Roosevelt in a number of future trust cases as well as being an envoy for J.P. Morgan. The visit was the occasion for Roosevelt, who had become president after the assassination of William McKinley in the fall of 1901, to try to win over Frick.

Frick had given Roosevelt a Frits Thaulow painting known as *Smoky City*. It was obviously a symbol of the industrial might of Pittsburgh. Roosevelt needed to calm the concerns of Pittsburgh industrialists, as his rhetoric about trust-busting heated up. Roosevelt had kept Frick's neighbor Philander Knox as attorney general to help calm the industrialists. Roosevelt would also need Frick's support to win in 1904, so the visit was to build an alliance and a relationship, which both men would draw on in the future. While young Childs may have been a fan of President McKinley, it was Helen who took to Roosevelt more than her father. Martha Frick Symington Sanger suggests that it was Roosevelt's environmental policies that inspired Helen to ask her father to establish Frick Park as a wilderness perverse.[2]

Frick, however, never warmed up to Roosevelt, calling him the "damned cowboy." He did realize that Roosevelt was the only Republican for 1904. After Roosevelt became president with the 1901 assassination of McKinley, Roosevelt went after some big trusts, which worried capitalists like Frick. Philander Knox, attorney general and Frick's friend, convinced Frick that Roosevelt's actions were necessary. Frick, however, had deep philosophical differences with Roosevelt and the progressive wing of the Republican Party. There was a lot of concern over Roosevelt's pushing of the legal case against Morgan's railroad trust. Another concern had been Roosevelt's jumping into the anthracite coal strike and forcing the owners to settle. Frick became a financial supporter of Roosevelt in 1904, donating $50,000, while board members Morgan and Rogers each donated $150,000. Philander Knox's remaining in the position of attorney general was probably a requirement of Frick's support. Frick actively supported Roosevelt in financial circles but had many doubts. However, after Roosevelt's victory, Morgan and Frick thought Roosevelt owed them. Frick would, of course, call in the marker; but before that, Roosevelt appointed Frick to the popular Isthmian Canal Commission.

In 1857, the Thomas Mellon home was the first in Pittsburgh to have running water. The East End was one of the first neighborhoods in the world to have natural gas and then electric lightning, thanks to Frick's neighbor, George Westinghouse. Westinghouse hired geologists to explore the grounds at Solitude near Thomas Boulevard. By the end of 1883, Westinghouse had started to drill for natural gas on his property. He beamed with enthusiasm and spent nights designing drilling tools to amuse himself. He encouraged the drilling crew and spent hours talking and taking notes on drilling. One night the well came in with a major explosion, and a hurricane-like hiss disturbed the once peaceful residential neighborhood. To test the well, it was lit, producing a huge column of bright light that could be seen for many miles: "The gas lamps of the city dwindled to little points of light, and persons in the street not less than a mile away were able to read distinctly the finest newspaper print by the light of the gigantic natural flambeau on the heights of Solitude." The Pittsburgh fire department had to be summoned to hose down the mansion to prevent it from burning. The tremendous pressure at the wellhead was obvious, and the first step was to design and make a stopcock to cap the well. Westinghouse handled this task personally, as the neighborhood awaited some relief. By 1885, Westinghouse was supplying Pittsburgh's industry natural gas and the East End's gas lighting. Westinghouse owned the Philadelphia Gas Company that supplied the East End, and Frick served as a director. Westinghouse converted the homes of his neighbors H.J. Heinz and Frick to natural gas first. Frick's home

was converted to natural gas in 1884, and then to electric, again with the help of George Westinghouse, in 1890.

The neighborhood got electric service in 1886 with the formation of the East End Electric Light Company. East End was the first residential neighborhood in the world to be
electrified. The company started as a direct current arc company for East End street lighting.
In 1887 it converted to the Westinghouse system of alternating current. The new alternating
current generating station on Penn Avenue was the world's largest in 1887, servicing a nine-
mile circuit. This distribution area was considered a limit for alternating current, but it was
much better than the Edison direct current system, which required a power station every two
city blocks. By 1889, Johnstown, which was almost 100 miles away, was being supplied from
the station. The houses of George Westinghouse, Herman Westinghouse (George's brother),
and Henry Frick Clay were the first on the circuit. These houses had electrical power prior
to the White House. While George and Frick were neighbors, Herman's house was four miles
away in Edgewood. The company used 1,000 volts of pressure to distribute power and then
stepped it down to 110 volts for incandescent lighting; however, to reach Herman's house in
Edgewood required a pressure of 2,000 volts. Allegheny County Light Company took over
the East End in 1896.

Another technology that developed in Pittsburgh's East was the automobile. The East
End would foretell of the American automobile-linked suburbs. Frick's neighbor and son of
H.J. Heinz, Howard Heinz, had the first car in Pittsburgh at his East End mansion. It was an
imported 1898 Panhard-Levassor with a German Daimler engine. The Heinz car reached a
speed of forty miles an hour, and became known by East End residents as the "Red Devil";
today it can be seen in the Frick Museum at Clayton. H.J. Heinz preferred his chauffeured
Pierce Arrow. Frick had taken his first auto trip in a Mercedes while in France in 1904. Frick's
purchase of a Mercedes in 1904 made it one of Pittsburgh's earliest cars. Frick had it shipped
over, but could not find a driver, so he had to import a French chauffeur. East End neighbor
Thomas Hartley had two Stanley Steamers and an electric car in 1902. East End neighbors
Louis and Charles Clarke started the Autocar Company in 1897. They produced a small car
called the "Pittsburgher." The Clarke brothers first patented the spark plug, later selling the
rights to Champion.

In the early 1900s, the East End had an unbelievable array of steamers, diesel, electric,
and gasoline cars. The first automobile club in Pennsylvania known as the Wilkinsburg Automobile Club, was formed in the East End in 1905. The Wilkinsburg Club arranged horseless
carriage caravans to "tour" weekly. Beechwood Boulevard was used for short races in the first
years of the century and had to be rebuilt in 1903 by Fredrick Olmstead. By 1906, there were
3,000 cars in Pittsburgh, and 2,000 of them were in the East End. Not surprisingly, Pittsburgh's
first traffic light was at Penn and Highland Avenues in the East End. Thomas Hartley (of the
Vandergrift family) was one of the nation's most famous auto enthusiasts, with steamers,
electrics, and gas-driven autos. There were 12 dealerships in the East End in 1906, two of them
selling all-electric cars. For a brief period from 1898 to 1905, Pittsburgh became the "Motor
City" with 20 car makers, including the Penn, the Keystone, the Brush, and the Artzberger.
Pittsburgh Motor Company opened in 1907 in the East End to fix and manufacture electric
cars, and George Westinghouse was a minor investor. Because of the demand in 1906 and
before Henry Ford opened his first assembly-line operation, Ford Motor had a small hand-
assembly operation in the neighborhood. George Westinghouse, Frick's neighbor, had one of
the nation's first electric cars but preferred the railroad to car trips. Frick was one of the first
of the Pittsburgh capitalists to fully embrace the automobile. In 1907, Frick took an automobile tour of Europe. Gulf Oil of Pittsburgh built the first drive-through gas station in Pittsburgh's East End.

The East End was full of beautiful churches, parks, and other amenities. The most famous church was the East Liberty Presbyterian Church, known as the "cathedral of capitalism," which dated back to some of the founding families of Pittsburgh, such as the Negleys. The original building at Highland and Penn Avenues goes back to 1819. East Liberty Church was the church of the Mellon family and a long line of Pittsburgh industrialists including George Westinghouse and H.J. Heinz. Frick was never a regular churchgoer, but he preferred the ritual of Calvary Episcopal Church, as well as its active social outreach programs such as the Kingsley Association. Calvary Episcopal was redesigned in 1906 by a donation from Frick. It's a beautiful Gothic church with a 220-foot spire. Mrs. Frick requested a special gift of eleven bronze bells, which took over a year to design and cast. East Liberty had the beautiful Highland, Schenley, and Frick Parks on its borders. In 1898, political boss and Frick business partner Christopher Magee opened a zoological garden, and later opened a zoo at Highland Park. The zoo was one of the delights of Childs Frick. The Carnegie Museum and Art Institute was also in the East End, and another of Childs's delights. The world's first collection of huge dinosaurs not far from Clayton clearly inspired his career in paleontology. In addition, the Natural History Museum housed many of then–Colonel Teddy Roosevelt's big game trophies. Years later, stuffed animals from the safaris of both Roosevelt and Childs would be exhibited together.

Frick had become active in the commercial development of Pittsburgh's East End and Oakland area with entrepreneur Franklin Nicola, who believed in the future of Oakland as a cultural center for the Pittsburgh area. Nicola formed Bellefield Company to develop the Oakland area. Nicola was able to enlist Frick as an investor as well as Andrew Carnegie, George Westinghouse, H.J. Heinz, and Andrew Mellon. The first project was a first-class hotel, the Hotel Schenley. H.J. Heinz and United States Steel would move their annual company meetings to the Hotel Schenley. Built in 1898, the Hotel Schenley would have guests such as William Howard Taft and Teddy Roosevelt. The Hotel Schenley would be the corporate and conference hotel for Pittsburgh's great corporations such as Westinghouse Electric, Jones and Laughlin Steel, H.J. Heinz, Westinghouse Air Brake, and Carnegie Steel. Known as the "Waldorf of Pittsburgh," it was the host to the "Millionaire's Dinner" that hailed the formation of United States Steel on January 9, 1901. The dinner assembled over 89 millionaires in one room, something that had never occurred before in the history of the world. Carnegie built his new museum across the street, and a few blocks further down, Carnegie Institute of Technology (now Carnegie Mellon University). The Veterans of Foreign Wars (VFW) was organized at the Schenley Hotel in 1914. The hotel register includes such names as Babe Ruth, Ty Cobb, and Roger Hornsby. Today the Hotel Schenley is the part of the University of Pittsburgh (William Pitt Union). Bellefield Company is considered to be one of the first real estate development companies. In 1909, Bellefield Company developed Forbes Field, the home of the Pittsburgh Pirates. Forbes Field would be the first of the nation's "baseball palaces," and was soon followed by stadiums in Chicago, New York, Cleveland, and Boston. Also in 1909, the University of Pittsburgh moved its Cathedral of Learning from the north side to "Frick Acres" in the East End. Bellefield Company was behind most of the campus development. Bellefield also was responsible for Soldiers and Sailors Hall, Carnegie Institute of Technology, the Carnegie Museum and Library, the Pittsburgh Athletic Association, and the Masonic Temple.

Pittsburgh's East End, particularly Oakland, had become the cultural center and included some outstanding schools. Shadyside Academy was built in 1883 to be a college preparatory high school for the sons of East End's wealthy and famous, such as Childs Frick. For the daughters, there was Pennsylvania Female College, which is now Chatham College. Pennsylvania Female College became a pioneer in offering hard science degrees to women, having the money to equip large biological and chemical laboratories. Frick had belief in the education of women and was a donor to the Pennsylvania Female College. Both schools reaped the rewards of being in the world's wealthiest suburb with guest speakers such as President William Howard Taft. Of course, in neighboring Oakland, Carnegie Tech was built in 1905.

Frick had started his move to New York City with the formation of United States Steel in 1901, as United States Steel headquarters were moved to New York. Still, Frick loved Pittsburgh, as did his daughter Helen, and the move was a slow one. More motivation came in the sulfurous smoky atmosphere of Pittsburgh. Mill dust was everywhere, and the sulfur in the air was highly corrosive. The atmosphere's attack on his beloved paintings became obvious. Frick had been planning for years to build an art museum on or near Gunn's Hill, which over looked the great Homestead Works. In 1905, Frick leased a Vanderbilt mansion on New York's Fifth Avenue. It was considered one of America's most beautiful homes. It had been the house a young struggling Frick had visited on his way to Europe and had never forgotten. Frick moved about half of his paintings from Clayton to New York. The move appeared to affect Helen the most.

Frick would always remain a legal resident of Pennsylvania and maintained an office in the Frick Building. Helen had a deep love of Clayton and often wanted to return. In fact, it would be Helen who returned later in life to maintain Clayton until her death in 1984. Helen continued her high school education in New York but refused to have a debutante party there. She clashed with her father by wanting to use the beautiful art gallery of their Fifth Avenue home as a backdrop for socializing. Frick would relent and allow for a Clayton party. The neighborhood was happy to see the Fricks for this beautiful party. A twenty-two-member group from the Pittsburgh Orchestra played on the porch. Frick had been an original and major supporter of the orchestra. As was typical, flowers were everywhere, many grown in the Frick greenhouse.

Like Hollywood of today, the East End would have its sex scandals and national crime cases. One of Helen Frick's best friends and neighbor was Henrietta Thaw, the daughter of railroad and coal magnate Benjamin Thaw. It was Henrietta's uncle who would make the headlines in the O.J. Simpson–type trial of the 1900s. Harry was a notorious playboy known for destroying cafes and riding a horse up the steps of the exclusive New York Club. In 1905 Harry Kendall Thaw (son of William Thaw) married a chorus girl, Evelyn Nesbit, who had been in relationships with architect Stanford White and actor John Barrymore. Harry took his wife to the New York Theater in 1906, and seeing her old boyfriend there, he casually went over and shot him. What followed was the most sensational trial ever held in America. Thaw's mother hired America's most famous lawyer, Delphin Michael Delmas, for $100,000, as the case turned into a racy scandal. The trial descended into stories of immorality, sex parties, torture, child molestation, and drugs on a scale never heard of in America. America's newspapers followed every detail, and it was the first time sex was discussed in an American open court. While the trial was in New York, Mrs. Thaw was pulling the strings from Pittsburgh's East End and bringing the limelight to the neighborhood. Mrs. Thaw allegedly paid Evelyn $200,000 to testify for her husband. The first trial ended in a hung jury; the second found Harry Thaw not guilty, but committed him to an asylum. The Thaws helped him escape to Canada, and a third trial after the second verdict was voided found him not guilty and sane. He returned to Pittsburgh to a hero's welcome, only to be convicted two years later of whipping a young boy in a hotel room.

By 1900, the East End residents had developed "Pittsburgh chapters" in New York and Florida. Residents such as Benjamin Thaw and Louis Clarke were early developers of Florida's Palm Beach in the 1890s. Clarke bought the "Coconut Grove House" hotel there. East Enders such as Frick, Knox, Thaw, Clarke, and Harvey went there for the winter season and spring break of Washington's Birthday. A lot of the old South Fork club members found their way to the new Florida resort. Frick loved the golf there, which involved many friendly wagers. Frick also loved the fishing for sheephead and bluefish. Mrs. Frick was particularly fond of the tea and card parties, which resembled her Thursday parties. In winter of 1904, the Fricks took one of their longer trips to Palm Beach, enjoying more of the ten-week season. The Palm Beach rich centered their spring break around the week of Washington's Birthday. There were week-long parties and one of the earliest Pro-Am golf events.

19. New York and the Panic of 1907

The move to New York in 1905 was in many ways the achievement of Frick's second lifetime goal. Frick had achieved his goal of becoming a millionaire by age thirty; shortly afterward, he and Andrew Mellon had visited the Vanderbilt mansion on their way to Europe. Frick would dream ever since of having such a mansion and art collection. He was now moving into the very mansion that had inspired him in 1880. Frick had signed a ten-year lease with Vanderbilt. Always a shrewd negotiator, Frick did get Vanderbilt to foot the bill for an expensive remodeling for Frick's personal tastes. Actually, Frick's increased activity with United States Steel left him no choice but to move to New York. And as the nation's leading capitalist on numerous boards, he found that New York made the ideal location. He maintained a full staff of seven at Clayton for the family's many visits. Frick still had extensive real estate and business ties in Pittsburgh. Some other ties were cut in 1905 with the death of his mother in Wooster, Ohio, and the graduation of Childs from Princeton. To a large degree, he may have been as cold as many believed him to be, but his heart was in Pittsburgh. Years earlier, he had anticipated a physical break with Pittsburgh by commissioning a cenotaph for the Frick plot in Homewood Cemetery behind Clayton. The cenotaph was of Westerly pink granite quarried in Rhode Island and was designed by Chicago architect and Frick Building designer Daniel Burnham. Burnham was also the designer of the Chicago World's Fair and Washington, D.C.'s, Union Station. The cenotaph weighed 47 tons and required a twenty-two-horse wagon to deliver it from the railroad station. Many believed the cenotaph was symbolic of his heart's being in Pittsburgh. The Frick plot was a 4,200-square-foot lot that could hold 125 graves. It had an original cost of $10,185 in 1892.

The period from 1900 to 1905 saw Frick's personal assets approach $70 million, putting him in the top twenty wealthiest in America, if not the world. Quiet and most often without publicity, Frick continued giving, and on a faster pace. In the hometown of his parents, Wooster, Ohio, he donated a library building for Wooster College, but declined to have it named after him. In 1905, the Allegheny Observatory lacked half the funds needed for completion. While men such as Carnegie had made headlines for their giving, Frick was happy to give the funds ($35,000) to his old friend John Brashear without any publicity. After the observatory was complete, Frick supplied another $15,000 to assure schoolchildren and parents could be admitted free on evenings. Frick himself had an interest in astronomy because of its use in industry. The Allegheny Observatory's main source of revenue after donations was a contract to provide the Pennsylvania Railroad with the correct standard time, which was used to regulate railroad time, by telegraphing the time based on the observatory clock to railroad stations. This early application of the observatory helped Frick become interested in astronomy. Frick had also donated and upgraded an observatory for the residents of Westmoreland County. Impressed with the education of Childs, Frick was a major donor to Princeton University. By 1903, he had given nearly $100,000 for Princeton's Colonial Club and a gymnasium, all without any fanfare. In 1905, Frick donated $100,000 to the American Academy of Arts in Rome. The academy donation was at the request of the famous artist Augustus Saint-Gaudens. Maybe with a bit of remorse, Frick built a park in Homestead for children to play in. It is also believed by many that Frick donated a Steinway piano to the

Homestead Library at a possible cost of $80,000.[1] The long list of his giving included many children's agencies, hospitals, the Salvation Army, houses for the homeless, the YMCA, the YWCA, homes for children, churches, and schools.

Frick seemed to miss the active involvement in United States Steel between 1901 and 1905, but he increased his personal investing with Andrew Mellon. He even increased his involvement with local politics. The Pittsburgh Republican machine tried to draft him for a run for U.S. Senator in 1902, but Frick wanted nothing to do with active politics. Frick remained a behind-the-scenes major supporter of the Republican Party. In 1906, Frick and Andrew Mellon purchased the Democrat paper, the *Pittsburgh Leader*, and turned it Republican. Frick's concern was more on the national level. He had business dealings with the city machine but really was not active in the political details. Frick divided his time between New York and Pittsburgh through the 1901–1905 period. He was pulled more toward United States Steel headquarters in New York. Family ties had slowly been cut in Pennsylvania and Ohio. His father had died in 1888. His brother Aaron was committed to Massillon State Mental Hospital in 1900. His mother died in October of 1905. Business and friends still pulled him to Pittsburgh often. Adelaide still had family in Pittsburgh, and Helen was emotionally anchored to Clayton, which Frick would staff until his death.

The faltering of United States Steel in the early years drew Frick into efforts to solve the problem. As Frick moved into more active United States Steel management after Charles Schwab resigned in 1903, he had to deal with the basic issue of the finance problem of the company. The dividend-paying common stock was backed by "blue sky." This fact was made public in 1916 in a corporate history:

> It has been admitted that a large part of the Steel Corporation's original capital was water. Just how much was water will never be decided. Herbert Knox Smith, Commissioner of Corporations under President Roosevelt, estimated that substantially half of the corporation's total issue of securities was not based on any tangible property assets. Other critics have gone further, while some have placed the amount of overcapitalization at a lower figure.[2]

Both Morgan and Frick realized the truth. In the early years, Frick had slowly sold all his common stock, realizing it lacked value. Morgan, who had profited by the overcapitalization, was well aware of the problem but wanted to keep it from the public. Initially, Morgan had convinced Frick that face had to be saved; but by 1905, dividends were suspended for two years on common stock. Frick made the necessary adjustments in capitalization, and to many, he might well have saved United States Steel.

The year 1905 was representative of the situation that industrialists, capitalists, and the country found themselves in. Times had been good since the end of the Panic of 1893 in 1896, but dark clouds were gathering. The booming stock market had covered the lack of capitalization in many of the mergers. The economic expansion was showing signs of extravagance. The merger mania had brought in the progressive government of Teddy Roosevelt, initiating the trust-busting era. Newspapers were full of scandals in all areas of society. Spending was over the top in all areas, but for the country, these were truly the "best of times and the worst of times." In Pittsburgh, the steel mills were running full out, and in New York the stock market was booming. United States Steel stock hit $50 per share. U.S. steel production had jumped an amazing one million tons in 1905 (3,192,347 in 1905 versus 2,137,347 in 1904). Steel production would peak in 1906 at 3,791,459 tons. Frick had made the painful adjustment of suspending a common share dividend in 1904 and 1905 to reinvest in the company and strengthen its financial picture by the end of 1905. Frick was brilliant in taking action in an up market, making United States Steel strong for the coming downturn. America's focus, however, appeared to be on the lives of the rich and famous, and the soaring stock market.

Frick represented less than a handful who realized United States Steel had been formed out of blue sky. The common share dividend was being paid out of future profits and was unsustainable. Frick had slowly sold his common shares from 1901 to 1905. Morgan was watching the stock price and felt the dividend was necessary. The Morgan trusts before United States Steel had used dividends to prop up stock prices. Morgan had not fooled everyone. Only a few months after the formation of United States Steel, Edward S. Meade in the *Journal of Economics* correctly laid out the problem that Frick was more concerned with than the other executives. Meade calculated that the dividend on common should be suspended to allow for capital improvement.[3] Meade was concerned about the lack of capital for improvements, but few took Meade's analysis to heart. Frick's new position on the finance committee changed that direction, and United States Steel started to pour capital into the operation instead of paying dividends. As Frick rebuilt infrastructure, new problems surfaced. In addition, the stock market was facing the end of its great bull run. The year 1905 was marked more by scandals than financial news. The parties, scandals, and overspending filled the nation's newspapers.

On January 31, 1905, the greatest ball of the Gilded Age would occur. It was the infamous ball of James Hazen Hyde at New York's Sherry's Hotel (where Frick had an apartment from 1900 to 1905). James Hyde was the young heir of the insurance fortune built by his father. The twenty-eight-year-old James had become the major stockholder and director of the Equitable Life Assurance Society. The Equitable at the time was one of America's largest insurance companies, with over 300,000 policyholders and over a billon dollars in force. At the time, insurance companies were the major investors in Wall Street, and Equitable was a major holder of railroad stocks. Equitable Life had a significant number of offices in Pittsburgh's Frick Building. Frick sat on the board, but he rarely attended meetings, seeing it as an honorary position. Young James had taken over but lacked any real business sense or even the work ethic of his father. Frick had been an outside director since 1901 but had little, if any, dealings with the company. The Hyde Ball would soon change all of that. The costume ball would have over 600 guests and even encouraged full press coverage.

The guests were predominantly America's "old money" such as the Astors, Belmonts, Depews, and Vanderbilts. A young Franklin D. Roosevelt represented his old New York family. Frick and most of the Pittsburgh capitalists were not there. J.P. Morgan and Elbert Gary also were absent. The Hyde Ball lasted from 6 P.M. to 7 A.M., during which time three meals were served. The menu was French, as was the entertainment. The total bill was around $200,000. It was considered the greatest ball of the Glided Age.[4] Several stories quickly started to circulate that Hyde had used Equitable money for the party. The result was an uproar at the Equitable Board meeting. The Board of Directors selected Henry Clay Frick to head up an investigatory committee. Initially, some policyholders feared that the issue might be covered up. The result showed the character of Frick as a tough and ethical businessman. Frick dug deep into the whole issue of corporate affairs, going over cash balances, salaries, and compensation dating back to 1900. Frick found a long history of mismanagement and misuse of corporate funds. Frick had always argued that parties and even personal giving should never be supported by corporate funds. The recommendation was to fire Hyde and ask for some payback, as well as to demand a state investigation. The report highlighted corporate corruption, as well as Frick's dislike for business parties and other entertainment expenses.

When the board hesitated on the implementation of the report, Frick walked out, stating: "I will no longer sit on the same board with that young man."[5] Frick dropped off the boards of Franklin National Bank and Commercial Trust so as not to be on boards with Hyde. Hyde did resign, as the state announced an investigation, and he took a thirty-five-year vacation to France. The newspaper reports in his home state reached the desk of President Teddy Roosevelt, who launched a federal investigation. These investigations supported Frick's conclusion. Frick and Roosevelt agreed that Frick's neighbor and friend, George Westinghouse, should be put on the new board to restore public confidence in the insurance industry. Grover Cleveland, former president of the United States, joined Westinghouse. For Frick's part, he demonstrated that he was above the big-business scandals of the period.

Scandal also touched United States Steel in 1905 as President William Corey's weaknesses made headlines. In Corey's case, it was wine and women on a publicly conspicuous level. While his wife remained in Pittsburgh, Corey made headlines with his partying and girlfriends. His affair with a New York chorus girl, Mabelle Gilman, made the paper almost daily, even in Pittsburgh. Workers at Homestead called the works "Mabelle Gilman Works," and it is rumored that Corey wanted it changed officially.[6] The Thaw trial was in the headlines at the same time, making matters much worse. The affair resulted in Mrs. Corey's going to Reno, accompanied by her Braddock girlfriend Mrs. Charles Schwab, for a divorce and a $3 million settlement. James Gayley, vice-president of United States Steel and another of the "Boys of Braddock," was involved in a divorce as well, but Gayley decided to resign quietly. For Judge Gary, this was another nightmare. An informal meeting was held at the Duquesne Club in Pittsburgh with Frick, J.P. Morgan, and H. Rogers on what should be done about the "Corey problem." There was little that could be done. Corey would make matters worse in late 1908 with an extravagant headline detailing his wedding to Mabelle Gilman, which cost over a half million dollars ($5 million plus today), which is huge even by today's standards. The wedding was held at New York's Gotham Hotel with crowds being roped off and held back by police. The wedding breakfast was $5,000, the flowers $6,000, and $200,000 for the honeymoon. This was in contrast to Corey's first wedding in Braddock, which cost five dollars in total. The tasteless wedding was enough for Gary, and he forced Corey to resign while on his honeymoon. Interestingly, as the "Boys of Braddock" dug their own holes with Morgan and Gary, they often turned to Frick for help. Corey had tried to gain the support of Frick, but Frick consoled him that resignation would be best for all. With Gayley, Dickson, and Dinkey having retired earlier, Gary had finally purged United States Steel headquarters of the "Boys of Braddock" and the "sons of Carnegie."

Even with the scandals, United States Steel moved forward, expanding and improving its operations. Frick seems to have led the changes in United States Steel that enabled it to become a true corporation. Prior to Frick's seating on the Finance Committee, United States Steel didn't even have a strategic plan. Strategic planning and committee organization had always been the strength of the Frick approach. In 1905, the Finance Committee issued the following statement: "The subject matter for formulating a comprehensive plan for the future development of all the properties in which the United States Steel Corporation is interested, *considered as a unit*, was referred to a special committee to be appointed by the chairman of the Board for consideration and report."[7] One result of the special committee was the proposal of a Chicago super mill (the future Gary Works). This works would be fully integrated, with docks for iron ore, blast furnaces, open hearths, breakdown mills (blooming and plate), and finishing mills to produce rails, plates, bars, and structural steel. The plant would be huge with four blast furnaces and twenty-four state-of-the-art open hearths. Similarly, a new state-of-the-art coal mine in Fayette County, Pennsylvania, was also underway. The new Traves-kyn mine would have electric lights, a full ventilation system, electric locomotives, and an independent telephone system. Again, the man most responsible for the super mill was Henry Clay Frick.

Frick's return to an active role in United States Steel made him the power behind the throne. Frick was the driving force behind United States Steel's strategic expansion. Frick clearly had become Gary's key advisor, wielding strategic power even though George Perkins was chair of the Finance Committee. The man whom Gary went to first for advice was Henry

Clay Frick, not Corey or Perkins. In January of 1907, when political pressure had mounted for a steel mill to be built in Duluth, the special committee to study it consisted of Gary, Corey, Perkins, and Frick. It became clear to President Corey and his United States Steel vice-presidents that after Gary, Frick was the most powerful man in United States Steel. On a strategic level, no one understood the steel industry better than Henry Clay Frick. While not a technology expert, Frick had an aggregate view that others lacked. Furthermore, few had the investment and finance experience of Frick. Anytime Gary faced a major question, a committee was formed, and Frick was on it. Maybe just as important, Gary and Frick had grown to be friends; and Gary, like most other associates, trusted Frick's confidentiality in delicate matters. The use of committees, of course, had been a technique of Frick's corporate management style.

By early 1907, the great expansion and prosperity that had started with the McKinley administration had run its course. The Panic of 1907 began in the summer of that year with a stock market downturn. That very summer both Gary and Frick were in Paris on an automobile tour of Europe. They returned to find a shaky stock market in August. In addition, financial scandals had rocked a number of important insurance and financial companies. In October, the stock market started falling rapidly, and the Dow Jones average would lose 25 percent by month's end. The situation had reached crisis stage with little hope of stabilization. While the New York exchanges struggled, regional stock markets such as Pittsburgh closed for lack of liquidity. Interest rates were spiraling out of control as stock prices plummeted day after day. It was becoming clear that this panic was more serious than the "Rich Man's Panic" of 1903. It would also be much different from the great Panic of 1893. This time the currency problem had international roots. Currency problems in Europe had already started a wave of gold hoarding. Even world markets such as Japan had a currency shortage. At the time only a few Americans realized what was taking place in the world's financial centers. Soon insurance and trust companies found themselves unable to get credit. Without credit, financial operations froze, and insiders at the stock exchange drove stock prices down. The Pittsburgh steel mills were still running flat out, the Pittsburgh smoke was thick with prosperity, and overtime was available to any worker. To the Pittsburgh steelworkers, things seemed normal. By now, however, the word was slowly getting out. The New York bankers were starting to worry.

October 13 was considered a lucky day by Morgan, and he was clearly preparing for the opportunities that might arise from a financial panic. Morgan, who had been in England earlier in the year on an art-collecting trip, may have consulted with the Archbishop of Canterbury, which he often did for "mystical" signs. On October 13, Morgan was at a church convention in Virginia, and Teddy Roosevelt was hunting bear in Louisiana. Frick had been in touch with Morgan, realizing the problem was mounting. Frick was one of several called to Morgan's library at Thirty-Sixth Street and Madison Avenue to take the helm as Morgan returned. On October 14, 1907, the stock of United Copper fell from $62 a share to $15. The stock loss forced owner F.A. Heinze to pull money from his Butte, Montana, savings and loan, which affected a chain of banks. Nine banks pooled together to aid in the United Copper problems, but it was too late. Then a run started on Knickerbocker Trust Company because of its president Charles Barney's close relationship with F.A. Heinze. Depositors withdrew over eight million dollars in less than four hours. On Friday, October 18, the run reached a point at which all backers pulled out, thereby assuring the company's failure. J.P. Morgan had his own copper interests and allowed his competitor to fail. The stock market saw a number of companies go under that Friday in addition to United Copper Company. The weekend added to the tension as stories of bank failures hit the nation's press. In Pittsburgh, as the stock market closed, rumors spread that Westinghouse Electric could not meet a call on its loans. The debt was over $40 million for Westinghouse Electric alone, although Westinghouse Electric had just reported record profits. It was a short-term issue, which would not be a problem with today's Federal Reserve. The immediate danger at the time was that the banks would call in short-term money market loans, which was typical of financial panics before the Federal Reserve. Four million dollars in cash would be needed by midweek just to keep the financial markets from freezing up. Thursday had been payday in the Turtle Creek Valley and Westinghouse met it, but Westinghouse would have to reduce the payroll Monday to get all the cash possible. George Westinghouse had left for New York to look for help from the New York banks after Mellon Bank had refused to help. In New York, Westinghouse's primary banker, August Belmont, refused, and Morgan controlled the others. Morgan also controlled General Electric, which was Westinghouse Electric's biggest competitor.

On Monday morning, October 21, the city of Pittsburgh braced for the arrival of the New York financial tidal wave. At the mills, there were only rumors of some problem in New York, but by afternoon, word had hit the city that payrolls around town would be affected, including those of the booming mills of Carnegie Steel Division of United States Steel. Ernest Heinrichs, Westinghouse's public relations man, described the mood in the Westinghouse Building on October 21: "An atmosphere of ominous oppression [is] pervading the offices. Conversations were carried on in whispers. Everybody seemed to have a feeling of fearful expectancy, as if some dangerous catastrophe was about to descend on the factories of Pittsburgh. Although nobody appeared to have any idea what was going to happen." The same feeling existed at Carnegie Steel Headquarters. Cash calls would quickly become canceled orders and layoffs for Pittsburgh's industries. All morning Carnegie Steel had been taking order cancellations, and the mounting problems lived up to the term "panic." The monthly profits of United States Steel reflected the plunge in orders: profits were $17.05 million in October, $10.47 million in November, and $5 million in December. Tuesday morning the news came by telegraph that Knickerbocker had failed, which meant the banks would be calling in loans. Again, America's banker, J.P. Morgan, stood on the sidelines, except to assure cash for United States Steel operations. Only Morgan was in a position to decide the course of this panic.

Interestingly, J.P. Morgan's refusal to aid Knickerbocker on October 22 caused the panic to proceed, but now Morgan could direct its path. Morgan chose to organize aid for Trust Company of America. Westinghouse was again the target of press articles, claiming poor management. Morgan, of course, had great influence in the press. Edison Electric was part of the Morgan electrical trust and had everything to gain from Westinghouse's problems. The panic provided another opportunity for Morgan to see a competitor, this time Westinghouse Electric, fail. Westinghouse could find no help in the local papers either. With Morgan's takeover of Carnegie Steel in 1901, Pittsburgh's press followed the lead of the Morgan-controlled New York press. Besides the press, Westinghouse was an outsider to the Scotch-Irish bankers, who controlled the city's financiers such as Andrew Mellon. They met briefly with Judge Reed at the Duquesne Club, hoping that he might act as a bridge. Reed had been Carnegie's chief lawyer and had worked with Morgan to negotiate the formation of United States Steel. Westinghouse's old friend and now Mellon Bank lawyer, Judge Reed would try heroically to pull together Pittsburgh bankers to help. On October 23, the Pittsburgh stock exchange was forced to close, which crippled Pittsburgh's banks. It's not clear if Frick realized his neighbor's company was about to tank. It does seem likely that Frick knew Mellon would not help, and Morgan wanted Westinghouse Electric to fail. Westinghouse had always been vocal about his dislike of bankers.

By now J.P. Morgan was in his library, directing events. Morgan's library was the nerve center of the crisis, and Henry Clay Frick was with him most of the time. The panic had hit the streets, with bank depositors pulling their money, since in those days there was no protection of bank savings. The Panic of 1907 was different from earlier crises because of its speed. Some creative individuals earned as much as $10 a day to wait in bank lines as depositors tried to salvage other parts of their life savings. The drawdown on bank reverses caused banks to call in loans from big and small companies. In Boston, retailers had "panic prices" to help generate cash. Morgan held day and night meetings in his library as he moved to take control of the panic. Morgan even forced the banks to issue scrip in lieu of cash to keep the banking system afloat. Lacking any government regulation, the public and the government looked to Morgan as their savior. It was an image promoted by the *New York Times*, as Morgan controlled most of their debt. The president of the United States at the time had no way to influence financial markets. Even Teddy Roosevelt had no choice but to ally himself with Morgan. Morgan's European connections promoted the image as well. Europe was also near collapse, and renowned banker Lord Rothschild called Morgan, the world's greatest financier. Morgan was informally in charge of the nation's money supply; Roosevelt and Congress could only watch as the nation spiraled into depression. Morgan controlled not only the nation's press and banks, but most of its major corporations. J.P. Morgan & Company officers served as directors in 114 corporations with a capitalization of $22.5 billion, compared to the total capitalization of $26.5 billion for all of the New York Stock Exchange. New York bankers were said to be hourly coming and going at Morgan's library. Morgan was able to stall the panic in October by putting into a bank alliance to save the market. Still, many companies remained only days away from collapse, and Morgan was the only one who could save them.

Morgan had no interest in saving Westinghouse or Heinze, who had refused to join his trusts. Morgan could now strengthen his many trusts. This was his overall strategic approach, which awaited only the opportunity to activate. Furthermore, Westinghouse had soundly defeated Morgan, Edison, and General Electric in the "war of the currents." Westinghouse Electric was thus left to fail. It is interesting that there is no record of Frick's efforts, if any, to help his friend Westinghouse. Morgan and the New York banks, however, had a deep dislike of Westinghouse, who often rebuffed them in good times. President Roosevelt sent his secretary of the treasury to ask for help to prevent a full collapse. The meeting with Frick and others on the situation went all through the night, which was typical of Morgan's "library meetings." The Morgan meeting resulted in a move to stabilize the nation's banks, while also picking some industrial plums as part of the harvest. Frick and the United States Steel Company moved to purchase Tennessee Coal and Iron.

In a short period, the steel industry was hit hard, with 175 out of 314 blast furnaces closing by 1908. Tennessee Coal and Iron was insignificant in terms of national production. In 1907, TC&I accounted for a mere 1 percent of steel production, which served a niche in the Southern rail business. Tennessee Coal and Iron had pioneered the use of open-hearth steel in rails, and it was gaining in popularity. Frick had studied the possibility of taking over TC&I, but felt it to be inefficient and overcapitalized. In addition, TC&I was producing rails for about $3 a ton more than United States Steel plants, even though they were using cheap black labor and free state convict labor. Gary also was more interested in putting state-of-the-art equipment in the Indiana plant than in purchasing Tennessee Coal and Iron. Morgan was the architect of this deal, believing TC&I's regional position would pay off. Morgan was interested in besting John "Bet-a-Million" Gates, who was looking to merge TC&I with Republic Iron and Steel. The merger of TC&I and Republic would have created a major competitor of United States Steel with 34 blast furnaces and 25 mills.

Tennessee Coal and Iron was rich in mineral rights, including massive Southern iron ore reverses. Many believed the Superior iron ore was running out, although neither Frick nor Gary believed so. Morgan continued to push for a deal, while the United States Steel Financial Committee hesitated. As TC&I stock continued to decline along with their New

York brokerage house, Moore & Schley, the opportunity arose for a financial deal that would deliver TC&I at a cheap price. Moore & Schley creditors were holding TC&I stock as collateral for Moore & Schley loans. In addition, if Moore & Schley were to fail, the market would tank again. It was November 2, 1907, a Saturday, and the rumors were that the market would crash Monday if Morgan didn't jump in with aid. Morgan got the United States Steel finance committee to agree, but the concern from Gary was that Roosevelt would file an antitrust case if they moved forward. Morgan knew he was holding all the cards, but he sent Gary and Frick to meet with the president.

Late Sunday, Frick got the Pennsylvania Railroad to provide a locomotive and his Pullman car, the *Westmoreland*. As a director of the railroad, Frick could pull the necessary strings. He and Gary got to Washington by 8 A.M. and met the president over breakfast. Roosevelt had little choice, believing the nation's markets to be near collapse. Frick and Gary got Roosevelt's approval to move ahead. Years later in his autobiography Roosevelt used the following justification:

> It was necessary for me to decide on the instant, before the Stock Exchange opened, for the situation in New York was such that every hour might be vital.... From the best information at my disposal, I believe that the addition of the Tennessee Coal and Iron property would only increase the proportion of the Steel Company's holdings by about four percent.... It offered the only chance for arresting the panic, and it did arrest the panic.[8]

Morgan had won. In addition, Morgan's saving of the brokerages was hailed in the popular press as a miracle, and Morgan was a savior.

In fact, most populists and Republicans of the time suspected that Morgan had caused the panic to take over companies such as Westinghouse Electric. Wisconsin's populist Senator Robert La Follette stated in 1907 that Morgan and his associates "deliberately brought on the late panic, to serve their own ends."[9] John Moody charged that Morgan and associates stopped the panic by "taking a few dollars out of one pocket and putting millions into another." Upton Sinclair used the panic as a basis for his novel *The Money Changers*, to illustrate Morgan's ruthlessness. In the novel, a Morgan-like character orchestrates a financial crisis for private gain while destroying ordinary people across the nation.[10] The Senate committee, after investigating the panic for years, concluded Morgan had taken advantage of the situation. Congress believed that United States Steel paid a mere $30 million for a $90 million company, although Frick never believed it. The $30 million represented 35 times earnings, which hardly seems like a deal. United States Steel did invest another $24 million in the next four years to upgrade the operation. The market share of both ingot and finished steel products actually declined after the TC&I deal.

Teddy Roosevelt testified in 1909, no longer as president, that he had given tacit approval to Morgan and Frick to proceed for the good of the country. The testimony took the energy out of the investigation. At the end of November 1907, Frick tried to push Roosevelt for more favors. In particular, Frick wanted the antitrust case against Standard Oil be dropped, but this time Roosevelt refused.[11] Frick was extremely upset with Roosevelt over this and his antitrust policies in general. Later the next month, however, Frick and his wife were special guests at a White House dinner. Still, he never believed that Roosevelt was a true Republican, and he lamented the passing of the McKinley administration. Frick wanted to purge the Republican Party of the liberals and progressives. Frick continued to work in the party to elect more conservative Republicans. Frick and Morgan would support William Taft in 1912, which forced Roosevelt out. For Morgan, however, politics was not philosophical. Morgan cared little about who was president as long as he could be bought. In retrospect, too much was made of the antitrust issues. United States Steel's market share declined and competition increased. Judge Gary, for his part, was a progressive Republican, probably seeing it as enhancing his public image. Another result of the investigations into Morgan's role in 1907 was the signing of the Federal Reserve Act by Democratic President Woodrow Wilson in an effort to free the government from the House of Morgan in future financial emergencies.

Another part of the landscape during the Panic of 1907 was the famous "Gary Dinners" held in New York with the heads of all major steel companies. With the TC&I takeover, Morgan was in no position to pursue further takeovers. Gary moved to ease cutthroat competition during the deep recession that followed the liquidity crash. The first large formal dinner was November 20, 1907, at the Waldorf Astoria in New York. Frick gave only tacit support for these dinners, and accepted cooperation because there was no more to gain in the short run by competition. Frick, however, preferred his own network of industry ties, which were extensive, confidential, and knowledgeable. Frick could use his networks for a type of "cooperative advantage." Also, Frick never liked to deal with large conferences, preferring the small luncheon group. Too much has been made of these dinners, although they did evolve into the American Iron and Steel Institute. The idea to resist price cutting in a recession was smart business for all the companies involved. Prices held, but United States Steel was forced to close eight major finishing plants. The dinners continued quarterly into 1909 as the recession deepened. The United States Steel workforce was cut from 210,000 in 1907 to 165,000 in 1908 as the recession continued.

Besides the Panic of 1907, United States Steel and its Pittsburgh mills faced the results of a major social analysis known as the "Pittsburgh Survey," which had been funded and supported by the Chamber of Commerce and Pittsburgh's new Democratic reform mayor, George Guthrie. Neighbor H.J. Heinz and Frick's close friend Benjamin Thaw helped fund the project. As a major real estate holder and a major Pittsburgh social donor, Frick supported the survey as well. The results were eye-opening. The survey's director noted: "Pittsburgh is not merely a scapegoat city. It is capital of a district representative of the untrammeled industrial development, but a district which, for richer, for poorer, in sickness and in health, for vigor, waste, and optimism, is rampantly American."[12] The horrific report that followed was made public in 1909, and profiled water pollution, air pollution, living conditions, industrial accidents, and wage issues for the Pittsburgh area's 1.6 million immigrants. United States Steel's executives were clearly moved by the facts. Alva Dinkey, who was manager of Homestead Works, said the report was an epiphany similar to Lincoln's seeing the abuse of the slaves in his youth. United States Steel executives, including Frick, became important partners in finding solutions to the city's problems. Even Carnegie in Scotland aided in programs to improve the lives of his old employees.

Another reaction to the Pittsburgh Survey was the further development of cultural and educational institutions. Most of this was in the development of the Oakland section of the city by real estate developers such as Frank Nicola and Henry Clay Frick. Frick and Nicola would propose the Pittsburgh Athletic Association to 40 Duquesne Club members in 1908; by the end of the year it had 1500 members. While aimed at the wealthy, it was an attempt to combine sound mind and body as part of the Oakland cultural district. The Pittsburgh Athletic Association was part of a huge expansion of the Oakland cultural district. Nicola and Frick now owned all the land in Oakland, upon which the University of Pittsburgh stands. Oakland, with its expansive parks, clubs, Forbes Field Baseball Park, Carnegie Museum, University of Pittsburgh, Carnegie Institute of Technology, theaters, art galleries, and beautiful architecture, was a center for all Pittsburghers. After Nicola, Frick was the major real estate holder in the Oakland district.

By 1909, the country and the corporations had emerged from recession. The Finance Committee, with George Perkins as committee chairman, Gary as United States Steel CEO, and Frick as the senior member, continued to manage United States Steel. Gary was every bit as opposed to organized labor as Frick, but Gary saw paternalism as an alternative. Conditions under Gary had only improved slightly, but President Corey and his right-hand man William Dickson pushed for a sweeping number of changes in 1909. Dickson led the charge, wanting the elimination of Sunday work and the twelve-hour day. A Bureau of Labor study of the steel industry suggested that in 1910, 51 percent of workers worked twelve-hour days, 43 percent worked seven days a week routinely, and 29 percent of the workers worked seven days regularly.[13] Dickson did win a major reduction in Sunday work, but the Finance Committee maintained the twelve-hour day. In 1912, the committee moved to a six-day week but retained the option of the twelve-hour day as necessary. Frick and the Finance Committee had for years opposed union demands but were open to corporate initiated proposals. Frick's only real issue was with organized labor, not the length of the working day or the improvement of working conditions. Frick maintained that unions had no rights. It was not Gary or the Finance Committee that pushed the end of Sunday work, but two of the "Boys of Braddock," President Corey and William Dickson. It had been an internal struggle that Gary gave in to and, as always, publicized to his advantage. The internal struggle had, however, highlighted the problems with Corey. Corey's vice-president Dickson was considered a crusading nuisance who was uncontrollable. Gary and Frick had come to believe it was time for both Corey and Dickson to leave.

Frick and Gary grew closer over the years and generally were consistent in their views. While George Perkins was chair of the Finance Committee, Frick was clearly the wealthiest and most powerful member. Frick's network and interlocking directorships in banking, mining, railroads, and shipping made him the true heart of American industry in general. Frick clearly enjoyed this status; he had the power but was free of day-to-day responsibilities at United States Steel. Frick was richer and more powerful than even J.P. Morgan, but he posed no threat to Gary because Frick wasn't tied down by daily duties. In 1911, both Frick and Gary believed the time had come to remove Corey as president of United States Steel. Frick believed that the Carnegie element needed to be purged from top management if United States Steel was to develop its own culture and legacy. The Carnegie managers and old Illinois Steel managers had held up the cultural evolution of United States Steel for a decade. Frick wanted the position of president to be eliminated. As chairman of the Finance Committee, Gary could deal directly with the division presidents. The structure was similar to that which Frick had implemented in the later days of Carnegie Steel. On viewing the organization chart today, any management student would conclude that the office of a United States Steel president was redundant and unnecessary. Frick saw the problem as structural while Gary saw it as one of personalities. In either case Corey and Dickson had to go. Under pressure, Corey and Dickson resigned at the end of 1911. It appears that Gary's first choice to replace Corey was Eugene Buffington, who was president of Illinois Steel. Frick believed this would only reinforce the Carnegie/Illinois fault in the overall organization. A compromise decision allowed James Farrell to become president of United States Steel. Farrell had been working on international sales for American Steel and Wire Division and had an extensive background in sales. Frick agreed that sales, not operations, was the needed background to perform as United States Steel president. Farrell quickly became a friend of Frick, and Frick became more comfortable dealing with the position of president.

Frick's strategic position at United States Steel allowed him the freedom to pursue his art collecting and other interests. He started a relationship with the famous art dealer Duveen. In 1911, Frick made national headlines by paying $500,000 — and outbidding the Louvre — for a Thomas Gainsborough painting, *Frances Duncombe*.[14] The same article noted the purchase of George Romney's *Lady Milnes*. That same year he purchased Diego Velazquez's *King Philip IV of Spain* for $400,000. While 1911 was a major collecting year, publicity was never part of

Frick's collecting and was clearly the work of Duveen. The same year Frick added another by one of his favorite painters, Johannes Vermeer's *The Officer and Laughing Girl* ($175,000). Publicity became more favorable as Helen's Christmas parties for poor children were being noted in the press. In 1911, Helen had 75 children at the mansion for Christmas Day with gifts, food, and play. It was a tradition she continued and was reminiscent of her work with her mother in helping poor children in Pittsburgh. In 1913, Helen held the Christmas party at Clayton for 100 poor Pittsburgh children. Over the years, Frick's image was being softened by the press, but in some quarters, Homestead would continue to haunt him.

20. Final Years, 1910–1919

Henry Clay Frick had become America's elder capitalist, serving on the boards of America's most powerful companies. No single person in the United States so perfectly reflected industrial America and Big Business. He was a central figure in the Republican Party and a strong patriot as America approached the war. Frick quietly give millions anonymously to schools, children's projects, and hospitals. His personal net worth was over $70 million; by comparison, Rockefeller was worth about $200 million, Carnegie $400 million, and J.P. Morgan about $50 million. Frick's yearly income was around $4 million, which was second after Rockefeller's $5 million in 1918.[1] Frick was the key member of the United States Steel ruling Finance Committee, a director of the Pennsylvania Railroad, Pittsburgh's biggest owner of real estate, and the elder statesman of the Republican Party. Frick's restructuring of United States Steel's Finance Committee was to be his career highlight. The first success of the Finance Committee was Gary Works, which cost $100 million. It would have eight batteries of 70 coke by-product ovens, eight blast furnaces, 56 open hearths, a billet mill, a plate mill, a rail mill, five merchant mills, and an axle plant. Its harbor unloaded ore at 1,250 tons an hour.

Frick's United States Steel Financial Committee remained a major force in the development of investments such as Gary Works and equipment upgrades. Much has been made of Frick's seeming opposition to the new technology of by-product coke making. The choice, however, appears to have been a decision to run out beehive oven production in Connellsville. In 1908 when the first rectangular oven was built, Frick Coke had 24,071 beehive ovens in operation. The by-product coke oven captured chemicals and gases for other applications, which the beehive oven pumped into the environment. Frick served on a special committee on coal as well. By-product ovens were selected for Gary Works, where Illinois lower grade coal could be utilized and the by-product coke gas could be used to heat the new open-hearth furnaces. Connellsville was too distant from United States Steel's Monongahela Valley open hearths to supply heating coke gas. In retrospect, Frick managed the beehive/by-product oven balance at United States Steel with amazing financial sense. While Frick had personally not invested in the new technology, his best friend Andrew Mellon had, and owned the rights to Heinrich Koppers's by-product oven. In steel technology, Frick forced improvements, but they were always based on accounting numbers. H.C. Frick Division of United States Steel was a pioneer in automated coke drawing machines in 1906, and that decision was made using cost accounting methods. Frick, who had originally questioned the Tennessee Coal & Iron purchase, led a modernization plan for the Tennessee melt shop. In addition to new furnaces, better practices were brought in from other United States Steel plants. These new open hearths tripled the capacity and made superior quality steel. Frick's technology approach was much more complex than Carnegie's old rule of always applying new technology as it became available.

Frick's personal giving increased from 1907 on, as he remained very much active at United States Steel. He gave a matching donation of $200,000 for the YWCA and $100,000 for the Metropolitan Opera. One of Frick's favorite causes remained education, a passion that went back to his grandfather Overholt. Frick's style of Pittsburgh capitalism could appear to be greedy, but that is part of capitalism. The only possible justification for the sort of capitalism that allowed the wealth of the Gilded Age is that it is open to all. Education remained the key part of class mobility and the open gate to prosperity. One of Frick's efforts was to raise the level of grade school education in Pittsburgh. He created a fund of $250,000 for the betterment of Pittsburgh grade schools. Initially, he requested that he remain anonymous. In 1916, Frick gave another $250,000 to the fund, and left it $5 million in his will. Frick appointed friend and astronomer John Brashear to head up the commission. Brashear (known as "Uncle John" in Pittsburgh) said after years of commission work: "I feel free to say that the splendid gift of Henry Clay Frick for the betterment of public schools of Pittsburgh has done more good, more effective work than any endowment ever given for education, be it college, university, or public schools."[2] The main focus of the commission had for years been the improvement of teachers. Frick requested that the commission be a mix of educators, judges, and engineers. Brasher headed the commission with Pittsburgh educator George Gerwig as treasurer. John Porter of Fisher Oil and Judge Miller were also members. In the 1920s, Helen Frick became a member of the commission. As with all his donations, Frick attached no strings. Frick also continued his numerous smaller, but still significant donations to children's homes and hospitals. In 1915, Frick anonymously gave $2.5 million to the Massachusetts Institute of Technology.[3] He made a second donation of a new X-ray machine to Mercy Hospital in Pittsburgh (about a $40,000 machine). It was now clear an X-ray machine would have not only saved his daughter Martha's life, but that of assassinated president and friend William McKinley. McKinley was shot at the 1901 World's Fair, which had an X-ray on exhibit that was never used on McKinley.

Frick continued to make trips to Europe for collecting and relaxation. In early 1912, Frick and family (Adelaide and Helen) made an extensive four-month European trip, which also included a visit to Egypt. His friend J. Horace Harding, an art collector and financial advisor, accompanied them. Harding was a partner of J.P. Morgan and Frick's New York neighbor. They had become friends because of their shared interests in art and flowers. They also served on a number of boards including the Tobacco Products Corporation. J. Horace Harding would become a director of the Frick Collection after Henry Clay's death. The party also included Helen's friend Frances Dixon and Egyptologist George Reisner of Harvard. Frick had recently helped fund Reisner's explorations, and Reisner would be an excellent guide for the family. J.P. Morgan was also on a collecting and business trip in Europe, and they would meet briefly. The tour included Rome, the Vatican, and Pompeii. From Helen's memory, this was one of the most enjoyable of the family trips. Certainly, pictures suggest it was a fun trip for all. The trip home had been booked on the *Titanic*, but Frick canceled. Two reasons have been given: One is that Adelaide's sprained ankle delayed the party[4]; the other is that Helen feared the ship's eventual sinking.[5] The suite of rooms (B-52, B-54, and B-56) was transferred to J.P. Morgan, who also canceled. The Hardings took over the suites, but they too canceled. Eventually, the shipping line's director, J. Bruce Ismay, took the suite and would perish in the sinking.

Part of the excitement of the 1912 trip for Frick and family was to make purchases for their new mansion in New York. Frick purchased two paintings of the Venetian Renaissance master Paulo Veronese. In 1912, Frick paid $200,000 for Knoedeler & Company to purchase *The Choice between Virtue and Vice* and *Wisdom and Strength*. As the house progressed, Frick hired two interior decorators. For the first floor and areas that might become a museum, he hired Sir Charles Allom, the decorator of Buckingham Palace and Hastings. On the ground floor, Allom designed a small gallery (today's Enamel Room) to highlight the newly acquired Veroneses. For the second floor and areas of family living, Frick hired Elsie de Wolfe. Elsie de Wolfe was an actress turned decorator with some of the Gilded Age's most famous clients, including the Vanderbilts, the Morgans, the Duke and Duchess of Windsor, Stanford White, and Oscar Wilde. Frick had his hands full trying to control costs with these two, but he monitored them closely. Frick made a shorter 1913 trip to Europe to collect more and play golf. While in Paris on a golf outing, Elsie suggested he stop at the personal home of the late Richard Wallace (of the Wallace London collection). At the Wallace home, he was able to purchase some antique furniture. Frick also called on Durveen to coordinate the furniture with the art.

Frick may have wished he had been on the *Titanic* as they returned to a congressional investigation of United States Steel in August of 1912. In October of 1911, the Justice Department had filed suit, requesting that United States Steel and its eight subsidiaries be declared an illegal monopoly. The Democrats and progressive Republicans had made gains in Congress, and this Stanley Committee became the national inquisitor of United States Steel. The Stanley Committee went into working conditions, pay scales, and operational decisions of United States Steel. Frick had little tolerance for politicians pointing the finger at business. The Committee called 402 witnesses and recorded 12,151 pages of testimony. It was a true political witch hunt. The Committee found United States Steel in violation of ethics in the Tennessee Coal & Iron purchase, in interlocking directorships, in the Gary Dinners, in stock and bond manipulation, and in dealings with the unions. All the directors of United States Steel, including Frick, had been called to testify. The Republicans held off action. The reports linked trusts, so-called robber barons, and Republican administrations in the public's mind and became a real threat to the Republican hold on the White House and Senate. It did result in the Democrats taking the White House and an antitrust suit against United States Steel. The company eventually won in the Supreme Court in 1915, and United States Steel became an accepted part of America. The appeal lasted until 1920, but it settled the issue for good. Frick, for his part, would work behind the scenes to build the Republican Party and the acceptance of vertical integration trusts. Frick's effort would prepare America for World War I, and the massive contribution of United States Steel in the war. Frick's hand on the Finance Committee assured aggressive investment prior to the war.

The election of Democrat Woodrow Wilson in 1912 was a disaster on the level of the *Titanic* for Frick. Wilson represented everything politically that Frick opposed. Wilson was an internationalist and anti-tariff. Wilson took Progressivism to a new level. With the Democrats in charge, the tariff reduction was assured. Since tariffs were the main source of income for the government, another source would be needed. That would be the 16th Amendment, allowing an income tax. The anti-tariff Democrat Congress had passed an income tax in 1894, but the Supreme Court had struck it down, requiring a constitutional amendment. The progressive trust-busting era had set the stage for a tax on the rich. The income tax was to focus only on those making $500,000 or more, which at the time was less than 1 percent of the population. The rate was to be 1 to 7 percent. Riding the anti-business sentiment of the time, the amendment moved quickly in 1913. The federal income tax would affect so few that the amendment found populist support at the time. The high living and corporate corruption had cemented a populist movement against wealthy businessmen. Frick never really publicly opposed the income tax and probably was more upset with the tariff reductions. Frick would have supported a temporary tax to armor America, but this new income tax was a targeted tax at a handful of Americans to reduce tariffs. Frick, however, realized that giving the government the power to tax income would lead to an expansion of the definition of who was "rich." Frick would once again become involved in politics and the rebuilding of the Republican Party.

The Frick family seemed to enjoy new directions in the decade of the 1910s. Childs was now a budding scientist, and Frick financed South African and east African expeditions to collect African mammals for the Carnegie Museum of Natural History and birds for the Smithsonian. Many of Childs's specimens remain important museum specimens at Carnegie

Museum of Natural History and the American Museum of Natural History even today. In 1916 Childs became a trustee of the American Museum of Natural History. Some of his large mammals are displayed with those of Teddy Roosevelt in Pittsburgh. At the Carnegie Museum there was a pair of black rhinoceroses, one shot by Colonel Theodore Roosevelt and one shot by Childs. The Pittsburgh collection includes zebras, giraffes, wart hogs, African buffaloes, antelopes, and Buxton's koodoos, all shot by Childs. Childs was named an honorary curator of mammals at the Carnegie Institute. At the American Museum, Childs founded the Frick laboratory. Childs also helped finance the paleontology department at the University of California at Berkeley as well as adding a major fossil collection. Childs had little interest in business, politics, or even art. At the time, polo was Childs's major passion. Helen, however, reflected her father's interests. Teddy Roosevelt's Progressives had drawn Helen into politics. She often argued with her father over Roosevelt's polices. Helen had little interest in the parties of the rich and found pleasure in social issues of the day. Helen took up the cause of poor working girls in the textile mills of Massachusetts. The approach was a combination of help and self-help she had learned from her mother and father's work with Kingsley House in Pittsburgh. Her first project was a type of summer camp that had been used by Kingsley for poor girls from textile mill families. Frick supported Helen and encouraged her work.

Helen Frick, like her father, believed strongly in a labor republic where men and women could rise to their highest potential. Helen prepared well for her summer camp project by consulting with family friend and Kingsley House founder George Hodges. She studied settlement houses such as the Sarah Heinz House in Pittsburgh and the South End Settlement House in Boston. Helen, like her father, believed in the bootstrap gospel of self-improvement. It was a philosophy based on rugged individualism and a total rejection of socialism, which, in her view, included trade unionism. Frick's Kingsley House had been a leading voice in helping boys and girls work their way out of poverty. Helen's experiment at Eagle Rock became a permanent farm home for the girls, known as the Iron Rail. It was a true piece of clean living for these poor girls, who formed their own clubs known as "True Blue Clubs." Frick purchased a thirty-seven-acre farm as a permanent camp. This is a side of Frick that for decades was hidden from the public. Frick's donations were quiet, while Carnegie made even his smallest giving the subject of front-page headlines.

One of the important events in Frick's life was the construction of his permanent home in New York. When Frick took up residency in New York at 640 Fifth Avenue in 1906, he also purchased the site of the Lenox Library on Ninety-first Street and Fifth Avenue (what would become One East Seventieth Street and the present site of the Frick Collection). He wanted to build but had to wait for the New York Library to take over the book collection, which took till 1912. Helen Frick relished the wait, as she wanted her beloved Clayton to be the family center. Frick, however, needed to be in New York with his extensive corporate board duties, including the United States Steel Board, which was headquartered in the city. Finally, in 1912, he started the work of demolishing the Lenox Library. Construction and the move took over two years. He clearly envisioned that this mansion would ultimately become a future art museum along the lines of the Wallace Collection in London. To that end, he hired the firm of Carrere and Hastings, who had designed the New York Public Library.

One East Seventieth Street had the cold look of a museum versus the homelike nature of Clayton. Even with Helen's opposition, Frick and Adelaide were consumed by the move. Working with art dealers Knoedler and Durveen, and interior decorators Allom and Wolfe, Frick was often in the middle of arguments over decorations and price. This house, however, was a true labor of love for Frick. Adelaide also became involved, visiting the suite daily and suggesting changes. The struggle for Henry Clay Frick was the dual nature of the building. In the end, it probably was more museum than house. Frick added recreation space in the basement, which included a billiards table, and built a pine and maple bowling alley. Several sources believe this basement room was used for Masonic lodge meetings. One New York reporter recently described Frick and his mansion:

> Accordingly, Henry Frick in 1913 began building a magnificent limestone temple 20 blocks to Carnegie's south. It cost $5 million, which showed Carnegie a thing or two; but it was never a home so much as it was a great vaulted hall suitable for display of Frick's $50 million collection, a palace that would endure forever, Frick's permanent testament to his own passage through this life, a monument for all the ages no less than Tutankhamen's tomb. The Fricks actually lived in this grim mausoleum for a few years, which the old man spent wandering the cold and silent corridors, smoking a cigar, gazing raptly at his priceless pieces for hours on end.[6]

Certainly, Helen Clay Frick agreed with the coldness of the description, preferring to live out her life at Clayton in her later years.

Childs Frick married Frances Shoemaker Dixon of Baltimore in 1913. Henry Clay Frick purchased a Georgian mansion in Roslyn, New York, which had been owned by poet William Bryant. The estate cost $550,000. The couple lived there over 50 years and named the estate "Clayton." In addition, Frick had handed Childs's wife a $2 million check as a wedding gift. In many ways, Childs represented the sons that Pittsburgh capitalists feared the most, and the sons that most Pittsburgh capitalists had. Shortly after the wedding Frick tried to involve Childs in his real estate and local businesses in Pittsburgh. Childs served briefly on the Mellon Bank board but had little aptitude for business. Childs seemed happy to play the social role of the rich son, and he had built an extensive social network from his days at Princeton. Childs traveled the country on the polo circuit of the rich and famous. Childs also showed little interest in Republican Party affairs as well. Childs did share with his father a love of golf. Frick was a demanding father and was clearly disappointed in his son's lack of interest in business affairs.

Childs also showed little interest in helping in the war. Childs was a licensed pilot, and it was hoped he might join the air corps, but he didn't enlist. Helen, on the other hand, was actively involved in the war effort from the beginning. She worked with the Red Cross and toured the front lines. She also worked as a nurse in operating rooms. She lined up Red Cross tours. Helen became America's front-line volunteer, helping soldiers and the children of war-torn Europe. This period seems to have led to a feud between father and son. Frick's relationship with Childs seemed to have resulted in a change in his will. Frick made Helen heir to the family business and empire. Part of the reason was that Helen was the only one capable of managing her father's dream of an art museum. Helen was every bit her father's "son," interested in art, active in Republican causes, and good at business. Helen was even favored over his wife, who seemed crippled by depression and not likely to maintain the family business or manage his massive art collection. Frick did support Childs's scientific pursuits and interests. Childs would ultimately become a paleontologist of note. He specialized in the fossils of early mammals, and was an expert on the evolution of the American camels. Childs added things like a polo practice field, lighted tennis courts, and swimming pools to his New York "Clayton." During this period of stress with his father, Childs moved the family to California as he worked with the University of California. Frick seemed clearly disappointed that Childs refused to get involved in the war effort.

Both Frick's and Helen's war donations continued long after the war. Helen ran a four-story department store under the Goodwill wing of the Red Cross. She asked the wealthy of New York to donate jewels, furniture, paintings, antiques, etc., for sale to generate money for wounded soldiers. Friends like Duveen and Knoedler donated paintings. In the first three months, Helen generated $34,000.[7] Frick himself donated $10,000 of Cartier jewels anonymously.[8] The store ultimately raised over $50,000 to help wounded veterans. Frick teamed up with Gary to personally donate some of the world's first fully armored trucks to the New York National Guard at a cost of over $100,000. This was a type of giving not done by Andrew Carnegie; it was giving without engraved memorials. It was giving from the heart. Frick was always anonymous, while Carnegie's total giving was a public scorecard covered by the press. Often Carnegie's total was compared to the running total of Rockefeller in the press.

Another important donation for Frick would be the McKinley Memorial and Presidential Library in Niles, Ohio. Joseph Butler, steelmaker and friend of William McKinley, had started this drive to honor the slain President McKinley at his hometown. President Taft passed a bill in early 1911 for the memorial, but another $100,000 would be collected from the public. Butler had hoped to get a major donation from the Carnegie Library Foundation, but paperwork had stalled the effort. On September 30, 1914, Butler met Frick at Clayton to discuss the memorial. Butler was astonished when Frick wrote a personal check for $50,000. The only stipulation was that his name not be part of the name of the library. Frick would continue to give more over the next few years, including a gift of 1,000 books. By contrast, Carnegie would demand that the community supply the books for his libraries. In appreciation of Frick's generosity, Butler commissioned John Massey Rhind to create a bronze bust of Frick, which to this day remains in a prominent position at the circulation desk of the library. Frick's original check, with Martha's likeness, remains part of the memorial's permanent collection. The memorial was a 232-foot-by-136-foot marble monument with two wings. Butler added bronze busts of donors, which amounted to a true pantheon of American industrialists such as Frick and his Pittsburgh East End neighbors. Carnegie refused to donate directly, but the Carnegie Veterans Association did. A Carnegie bronze bust is in the Pantheon, but Frick would have the prominent seat of Jupiter at the memorial.

Frick's art collection increased dramatically with the acquisition of Morgan's collection. In 1914, the Frick family moved into their New York mansion at One East Seventieth Street, which he intended to be a living museum. The design of the mansion included not only Frick's architects but art "Dealer King" Joseph Duveen. Frick passed over architects Osterling and D.H. Burnham, selecting Thomas Hastings, the designer of the New York Public Library. Frick, the perfectionist and amateur architect, could be extremely hard for architects to work with. Adelaide could also be demanding, but things moved smoothly with the New York mansion. While Frick spent time with the architecture, Adelaide spent most of her time on the decorations. For his part, Joseph Duveen would bring paintings and place them in various locations for Frick's approval. Frick was extremely stressed by the move from their rented Vanderbilt house, and the end result was a crippling attack of inflammatory rheumatism. The attack was crippling for weeks, and in retrospect, appears to have seriously damaged his heart. Frick struggled through the forced imprisonment with his cigars, paintings, and the loving care of his daughter.

In her excellent study of Frick and his art, Martha Frick Symington Sanger points out that Frick brought Martha's memory to their new home. Frick purchased a George Romney portrait of *Lady Hamilton*, which bore a striking resemblance to Martha holding her dog Brownie. He also put another Martha in the bedroom, Thomas Lawrence's *Miss Louisa Murray*, in addition to other paintings throughout the house that invoked memories of Martha. Sanger reports that Helen, fighting for her father's love, even had a miniature of Martha redone to add Helen as her twin sister.[9] After an argument with her brother Childs, Helen changed her name to Helen Clay Frick (dropping the Childs). Just as fascinating was Frick's selection of pictures that reminded him of industry and Pittsburgh, such as Francisco de Goya's *The Forge*. Part of Frick's heart remained in Pittsburgh. Frick also continued to remain active as Pittsburgh's major real estate developer. In 1914, Frick sold a large piece of land in downtown Pittsburgh at a price of $1.4 million. The very same day, Frick purchased 10,000 acres of prime coal land in Greene County. Henry Clay Eldowney, who was a director and president of Union Trust, acted as Frick's banker and broker. Most of these large transactions were brokered through the Union Trust Company, of which Frick remained a director. Frick maintained a full office in Pittsburgh as well as a fully staffed one at Clayton.

Frick continued his real estate investments and land investments in Pittsburgh until his death in 1919. In 1916, he constructed the Union Trust Building on Grant Street in downtown Pittsburgh. The Union Trust Building was designed by Fredrick J. Osterling and was originally known as the Union Arcade. An earlier office building, of which Frick had been part owner with the Mellons, was the Union Trust Company Building (First Union Trust Building) on Fourth Avenue. This 1916 Grant Street building was originally built to be a shopping arcade with 238 stores and 817 offices. It was a Flemish-Gothic design modeled after the famous Municipal Hall at Louvain, Belgium. It had beautiful terra-cotta dormers, chapel-like towers, and a stained-glass dome. It remains today on the National Register of Historic Places. The cost was $1,497,000. Many headlines were created over Frick's disappointment with Osterling. Frick had always been a perfectionist and had argued with Osterling over the original renovation of Clayton. The bigger sin with Frick, though, was to fall behind schedule. Frick refused to pay Osterling for his services, which resulted in a very public lawsuit. Ultimately, Osterling won the suit, but many believe it destroyed his career. Frick was a key node in the network of the Pittsburgh rich through his banking ties.

Frick made a collecting trip to Europe in the spring of 1914 and returned stricken with rheumatism, which laid him up for months. However, he bounced back. From 1914 to his death was a very productive period in the quality and quantity of his art collecting. He added such treasures as Van Dyck's *Paola Adorno* (at a cost of $400,000), Gainsborough's *The Mall* (at a cost of $300,000), and Giovanni Bellini's *St. Francis in the Desert* (at a cost of $250,000). Although in his mid-sixties, Frick seemed almost to become more involved in the steel industry from 1914 through 1918. He regularly attended the United States Steel finance committee meetings and often chaired them. He served on many special committees looking at an expansion. Frick was considered an elder statesman of the industry, and he had many friends running key companies throughout the industry. Rockefeller controlled the western steel and mining giant Colorado Fuel & Iron. Rockefeller had often turned to Frick for advice, and Frick's personal friend Frank Hearne had been made president of Colorado Fuel & Iron on Frick's advice. He even once again had been talking to Charles Schwab at Bethlehem Steel. With Morgan dead, Frick was also America's premier capitalist, with heavy investments in the railroads and serving on many boards.

After the death of J.P. Morgan in 1915, Jack Morgan realized only $20 million in assets, with the balance of J.P.'s wealth being tied up in illiquid art treasures. Interestingly, Frick's worth in 1915 was around $70 million, most of which was in liquid assets. The Morgan art collection was brokered through Joseph Duveen in 1915. Frick paid $1.25 million for Jean-Honore Fragonard's panels *The Progress of Love*. Duveen had originally purchased the panels for J.P. Morgan's London home. Frick purchased Morgan's Chinese porcelains valued at $3 million.[10] A few months later, with Duveen's involvement, Frick added Morgan's extensive collection of Renaissance bronzes. Frick purchased to decorate his new home. It was said that Morgan made catalogues, and Frick made rooms. The press hailed Frick as Morgan's heir in the collecting of museum-grade art. However, more so than Morgan, Frick was a knowledgeable collector and art historian. Morgan saw art as an investment, while Frick found true pleasure in art. Frick also bought a substantial amount of art from Knoedler's Gallery, including El Greco's *St. Jerome*, Bellini's *St. Francis in the Desert*, Rembrandt's *Polish Rider* ($300,000) and Vermeer's *Officer and Laughing Girl* ($175,000). Duveen added some additional pieces for Frick's bedroom in Degas's *Rehearsal*, El Greco's *Purification*, and Carriere's *Motherhood*.

Vermeer had become one of Frick's favorites. His last purchase, and said to be his favorite, was the Vermeer's *Mistress and Maid*, which Duveen brokered for Frick at a cost of $290,000. Lover of art or not, Frick no doubt noticed that his Vermeers had seen the most appreciation in value of all his paintings. He bought his first Vermeer, *Girl Interrupted at Her Music*, for a mere $26,000 in 1901, and his third Vermeer, *Woman Holding a Balance*, for $175,000 in 1914.

Frick's many business ties and interlocking directorships became the focus of the liberal progressive movement. Interlocking directorships, which J.P. Morgan had used so successfully, were viewed as monopolistic by the progressives. Morgan and Frick had always argued their advantages of cooperation and improved efficiencies, but abuses had also been extensive for years. The Democrats passed the Clayton Act in 1914 to restrict collusion between the railroads and manufacturing. Frick had often used his ties to improve coordination between the two, playing by the rules as they existed at the time. With all his dealings and directorships, Frick was never involved in a hint of illegal or even unethical behavior. Frick was forced to resign several directorships, but he remained on the United States Steel board and that of the Pennsylvania Railroad. Frick only became more interested in the long-run success of the Republican Party.

The war in Europe had created a boom in American steel. It appears that Frick was involved in suggesting a second steel trust in 1915.[11] Clearly, after years of review, no one knew the steel industry better than Frick. Part of the motivation for a second trust was to supply Europe. The rumored trust would have centered on three companies: Bethlehem Steel, Jones & Laughlin Steel, and Colorado Fuel & Iron. Schwab, once again friendly with Frick, had built Bethlehem into a major competitor of United States Steel. Rockefeller controlled Colorado Fuel & Iron, the sleeping giant of the west, and Frick had many friends at Colorado Fuel. Cambria Steel was also involved, with strong ties to Frick through William Donner and the Pennsylvania Railroad. Frick was also a stockholder in Cambria Steel. Frick had suggested that United States Steel purchase Jones & Laughlin in Pittsburgh a few years earlier. The owners of Jones & Laughlin had been part of Pittsburgh's Pig Iron Aristocracy, which Frick had always been socially close to; and Benjamin Jones was part of Frick's Duquesne Club luncheon group. Other companies rumored to be involved were Crucible Steel, Lackawanna Steel, and Youngtown Sheet and Tube. While nothing came of the rumor, it had Frick's fingerprints all over it. Frick had studied and maintained files on all steel companies, and these were companies that Frick had always graded highly. The scope of this possible trust was huge, and would have required a financier on the scale of Frick. While the merger never happened, a smaller merger of Midvale Steel did, which was headed by Carnegie's "Boys of Braddock," Corey, Dinkey, and Dickson. Midvale was far from a second trust, but it was a major arms producer.

Frick remained active in Pittsburgh's civic development as he had with business. His commitment to the city was significant, being its largest real estate owner. He remained active in the development of Pittsburgh's East End. In November of 1916, Frick planned a citywide celebration of its distinguished astronomer John Brashear. The Union Club became the center of this public 75th birthday anniversary of Brashear. Behind the scenes, Frick had been a major donor for the Allegheny Observatory. Frick's William Penn Hotel was completed a few months prior in downtown Pittsburgh. Much more than Carnegie, Frick was tied to Pittsburgh.

Frick held onto his resentment for Carnegie tightly, never missing an opportunity to needle him. The final battle between Frick and Carnegie would be on the political front. Frick was the main supporter behind the "conservative internationalists" of former President Taft and Henry Cabot Lodge (Eagle Rock neighbors of Frick) in 1914, while Carnegie was the main supporter of President Wilson's "Progressive internationalists."[12] In 1915, Carnegie send a letter to the editor of the *Pittsburgh Dispatch* detailing the position of the Progressive internationalists: "Our beloved Republic has no enemies in the world; neither personal nor national.... She needs no increase in army or navy.... Our Republic has nothing to fear." Frick saw things much differently. The Progressive internationalists started to talk of a world alliance, which after the war would become the proposed League of Nations. The leader of the new Democrat progressives was President Woodrow Wilson. Frick was a true nationalist, believing strongly in American exceptionalism, rejecting the premises of internationalism. Frick was a hardliner on "America first." He had always opposed "free trade" capitalists such as Carnegie and J.P. Morgan. He was willing to lose international business for the sake of his country. This characteristic appears traceable back to his German-American roots, his *McGuffey Reader* education, and his belief in McKinley's protectionism. He differed from men like J.P. Morgan, who made money from foreign trade and were not constrained by patriotism.

When the United States declared war in 1917, Frick wrote President Wilson, a Democrat he opposed, that he would give his full support. Frick would prove his patriotism over his belief in capitalism. The government had been negotiating with United States Steel and Gary over the price of armor. United States Steel's price was too high and the government could not come to agreement with any other steel companies. All companies were holding at a price of 4.25 cents a pound. President Wilson asked that Frick be contacted in his name to get the industry costs. At the president's request, Frick revealed it to be 2.5 cents per pound, and the government negotiated a price of 3.25 cents a pound. The president's representative said Frick had told him his consultation would be held in strict confidence, to which Frick responded: "I should prefer that it be kept that way. I should be criticized no doubt, and perhaps rightly. But if I had wished to dodge, I should not have answered at all. I am always responsible for what I say and you may tell the President that, if the accuracy of my figures should be questioned in any such way as might embarrass him, he need not hesitate to ask me to prove them openly."[13]

Frick proved to be a patriot in giving and business. Frick and the Finance Committee invested in a 110-inch mill at Homestead to produce armor. United States Steel expanded at Gary and increased its overall shipbuilding capacity. Frick stood against many calls to nationalize the industry, and he proved that the company could put country ahead of self-interest. The nationalization of the railroads had led to the destruction of its infrastructure, and Frick had always seen it as a violation of company property rights. Frick remained true to his belief in capitalism. The railroads were literally run into the ground for lack of investment. On the other hand, United States Steel invested over $303 million into its plants during the war. The company moved into new endeavors such as shipbuilding, and most of these investments became unprofitable after the war. The company outproduced the whole country of Germany, supplying the government with steel below market value. United States Steel purchased $124 million in Liberty Bonds, and Frick personally purchased over $5 million of them. He made the largest Liberty Bond purchase of $1.5 million in the name of the city of Pittsburgh. He gave generously to a number of charities for wounded soldiers, including $300,000 to the Belgian Relief Fund. Frick donated land and a house for soldiers and sailors to relax on Pittsburgh's Fifth Avenue. As a pure capitalist, Frick was willing to pay taxes for the war but noted his dislike for income-based tax. We can see this in a letter to friend Senator Philander Knox: "I thoroughly believe that those of us who stay at home and take our ease should willingly pay any taxes that may be assessed to carry on the war, although, I have to confess that the present disposition seems to be to impose unfairly upon those who are supposed to have large incomes."[14] Such a strong belief in capitalistic principles was often not popular and commonly misunderstood. Another demonstration of his strong beliefs was seen when he gave his mansion to French Marshall Joffre on a 1917 mission to the United States, only to be angered when his hero kissed union leader Samuel Gompers on the cheeks.

When Frick heard the mayor of New York had refused to build a viewing stand for disabled veterans to see a military parade, he built a covered viewing stand for 500 disabled soldiers and fed them. He donated personally a number of fully armored trucks and cars. Frick poured millions more into Helen's war projects and the Red Cross. The full record is not complete, but biographer George Harvey reported a substantial reduction in Frick's net worth during the war. Frick also gave his personal time as well, speaking to and thanking employees in the service. He was just as active in assuring that the company recognized its veterans. Frick's die-hard capitalism was always American capitalism in his mind. Personally, Frick demonstrated disapproval of German goods, refusing to buy German. He supported many ethnic opposition groups such as the Italian Roman Legion of America.

Frick opposed even most fellow capitalists who saw the world only as a market to be conquered. Frick had showed himself a true patriot with his heavy investment in war bonds and the financial support of Helen's Red Cross efforts. It is believed that Frick purchased more Liberty Bonds than anyone else in America. When the railroads were nationalized for the war effort, Frick sold his private rail car and used public transportation to travel. Similarly, he sold his shipbuilding interests for a profit prior to nationalization, but turned the profit over to the United States War Treasury. He gave money to a number of war charities to help maimed soldiers. Frick was one of a few influential Americans who opposed the League of Nations, opposing progressives in both parties over the matter. The Wilson administration viewed this world body as a means of preventing future wars, but men like Frick saw it as a threat to America. Senators Philander Knox and Henry Cabot Lodge led the Republican opposition, as they saw it as a move toward internationalism. Frick had always been a nationalist; even in business he had little interest in foreign trade. The opposing Republicans became known as the "Irreconcilables." The Democrats and Wilson mounted a nationwide campaign, and Andrew Carnegie joined in on the side on the League. Carnegie's support could have only strengthened Frick's opposition. Frick was also in opposition to many old Morgan partners, whose railroads made money from foreign trade. He spoke out often that companies should not profit from war. The Republican Party eventually took up the cause against the League for the 1920 presidential election.

One of Frick's final imprints on the nation was his alleged involvement in the selection of Warren Harding as the Republican candidate for president in 1920. Frick had first met Senator Harding at a Pittsburgh Chamber of Commerce meeting in 1916 and had noted, "He looks like fine presidential timber."[15] Frick's opposition to the League of Nations had taken on an unusual vigor for a political issue, and Harding was in Frick's camp against the League. Many New York businessmen were supporting the Democratic pro–League view. Even the Morgan camp was split on the issue. These businessmen saw it as a way to increase their foreign trade, but the League would financially be backed by the United States. Frick held a private dinner in 1919 that included George Perkins (United States Steel and J.P. Morgan Company), Dan Hanna (son of Senator Mark Hanna), Ambrose Monell of International Nickel, George Whelan (head of United Cigar), Henry Sinclair (Sinclair Oil), A.A. Sprague (Chicago Wholesaler), George Harvey, and others.[16] The dinner was the source of a major fund to defeat the League of Nations, and many believed it picked Warren Harding as the Republican candidate. Sinclair was assigned the job of building a campaign chest to defeat the League. The fund was believed to be over $3 million. Frick was considered the largest contributor, but the list was long, including Charles Schwab, George Westinghouse, H.H. Westinghouse, John Rockefeller, Andrew Mellon, Walter Chrysler, Harry Sinclair, and many others. Harding won a landslide victory in 1920. President Harding would ultimately name Andrew Mellon his secretary of Treasury and George Harvey to Ambassador to Great Britain, further supporting the link to Frick.

From 1907 to his death, Frick had the financial leadership of the Republican Party. Carnegie had really started his break with the party during the Spanish-American War in the McKinley Administration. In his retirement, Carnegie turned into a liberal internationalist. Carnegie became a popular witness before Congress, pushing an anti-business series of laws, beginning in 1907. Carnegie actively opposed the steel tariffs in retirement after these tariffs had made him a wealthy man. Frick and Gary charged Carnegie publicly with hypocrisy. Frick had always maintained the importance of tariffs, although he recommended not increasing them in the boom from 1898 to 1905. In 1908, at Roosevelt's' request, Carnegie testified before Congress on the demand placed on the laborers and environment by the coal companies. Carnegie seemed to oppose anything Frick, the steel industry, and the Republican Party wanted. Carnegie was a major supporter of the League of Nations and Woodrow Wilson. Carnegie believed he was a superior being, having succeeded in the survival of the fittest. He took on the role of philosopher. Frick never saw himself as anything other than a capitalist. Carnegie's behavior certainly gave credence to the claim that most managers preferred to deal with Frick because they always knew where he stood. For all his money, Frick was an average American in his outlook on life and his living of it.

Frick's last year was extremely active. He continued to sit on the United States Steel board and his railroad boards. He continued the national fight against the League of Nations. His art collection grew, and he continued to spend late nights with the paintings. He continued purchases, adding an Indian rug by seventeenth-century Taj Mahal builder Shan Jahan for $39,050. This was a handmade rug, which may have taken 30 years to make. He found great happiness in visits from his grandchildren. He also loved to telephone them daily. The grandchildren had become a major part of his life. There was Adelaide (4 years old), Frances (3 three old), Martha (2 years old), and his namesake Henry Clay, born in 1919. Henry Clay II was born on October 18, around the time that Frick's health started its final decline. Heart failure would bring the end, but during the last few weeks of his life, he was a very sick man.

Family reminiscences of Frick's final months are of a much different man from that of history. Frick remained a businessman to the end, but he also remained the family man lost to history books. Sanger noted:

> Frick's joy in the granddaughters was boundless, and so was his pride.... As grandfather, Henry Clay Frick played leapfrog with the children and, with great amounts of laughter, slid down the sliding board at Eagle Rock with them, landing, as his biographer Harvey noted, "with an awful bump." At the end of the day, he often sat on Eagle Rock's piazza and let the children climb into his lap. As they rested their heads against his chest in pretense of sleep, he would sit motionless until the children became restless and wriggled away.[17]

He still enjoyed an automobile ride or a trip to the club. He even talked of taking an airplane ride, which he never did, but one of his descendants, Stephen Frick, would pilot the space shuttle *Atlantis* in 2002.

One of the last trips Henry Clay Frick made was with Andrew Mellon to the McKinley Memorial in Niles, Ohio, in October of 1919. They traveled in Frick's Rolls-Royce Silver Ghost from Pittsburgh. This monument to capitalists and McKinley Republicans was one of the few places where Frick's bust was prominently displayed, a testimonial to Frick's belief in American capitalism and republicanism. Teddy Roosevelt had died earlier in the year, ending the progressive wing of the party that Frick had worked hard against. H.J. Heinz, Frick's neighbor and one of Roosevelt's biggest financial supporters, had also died. Frick and Mellon found solace in the memories of the McKinley administration (1896 to 1901). Of course, Carnegie was gone as well, having died in August. In the memorial's 44 bronzes busts, Frick could see his life. The busts included friends and neighbors such as Philander Knox, George Westinghouse, and Andrew Mellon. There were busts of many of his Duquesne Club lunch club members, such as Benjamin Jones, Frank Buhl, and Henry Oliver. There were busts of the business associates who shaped his career, such as Andrew Carnegie, Elbert Gary, Marcus Hanna, James Farrell, and John Gates. Finally, the presidents he had known personally, such as William McKinley, Teddy Roosevelt, Howard Taft, and future president Warren Harding, were commemorated in the busts and marble columns. This monument was a tribute to Frick's golden years as much as to President William McKinley.

Certainly, the bust of Carnegie given by the Carnegie Veterans Association would have invoked a more recent memory. In the spring, a Carnegie messenger had arrived with an invitation to meet and put old differences behind them. Frick's terse answer was, "Tell Mr. Carnegie I'll see him in hell, where we are both going." Some say Frick's response was added to.[18] Frick never showed any remorse or even admission of guilt for Homestead, and while he may have believed Carnegie was going to hell, it is doubtful that Frick was counting on such a trip.

The Niles trip would be a day of remembering with Andrew Mellon, his closest and oldest friend. They shared a love of art, Pittsburgh real estate, and investing. They shared a philanthropic interest in the University of Pittsburgh. They still were the owners of Overholt Distillery, their first joint investment, which was worth over $3 million in 1919. Overholt had a special contract to produce whiskey for medicinal purposes, and Frick had been hoarding carloads of whiskey at Eagle Rock. They both had been active in selling and giving away whiskey prior to Prohibition, which became law in January 1920.

On October 24, 1919, Frick attended an American Iron and Steel Institute dinner at the Hotel Commodore. Frick had not been active in the institute, which had evolved out of the "Gary Dinners," but this evening was to honor King Albert of Belgium. King Albert had joined forces with the United States and allowed Allied armies to attack through Belgium. The day before, Frick had held a reception for the king in Pittsburgh. This dinner was the last public event of Henry Clay Frick. At the time, Frick appeared healthy, but he had had a long history of quick downturns.

By November of 1919, at age sixty-nine, Frick was once again struggling with his health. He started the month with a small luncheon celebrating the defeat of the League of Nations. He appeared to have developed a case of laryngitis on November 3, which deteriorated into something more serious by November 10. Frick tried to continue business from East Seventieth Street. He was blessed to have both his wife and daughter Helen caring for him. His wife Adelaide, however, was limited in her help, as she continued to struggle with depression. Helen readily took on the role of caretaker. Frick tried to keep a normal schedule, including political meetings, business meetings, art dealings, and time with the grandchildren, but by November 14, he was bedridden. He still smoked his cigars and spent nights with his paintings. He lunched at the club and played cards with Helen. At the club, he still liked to gamble on cards as well. Never a heavy drinker, Frick still enjoyed a glass of whiskey at a meeting or time of relaxation. His personal giving continued with a gift of $10,000 to St. Bartholomew's Church in Manhattan. He was suffering from a cold and a flare-up of his inflammatory rheumatism. With badly swollen joints, getting around became difficult; but he still took chauffeured car rides to get out. He preferred the couch in his library to his bed. By Thanksgiving, Frick was fully bedridden. Death came on December 2, with the portrait of *Miss Louisa Murray* (resembling Martha) and Romney's *Lady Hamilton* in his sight.

There was a short funeral service the next day in New York for close friends and business associates. The main funeral was to be at Clayton in Pittsburgh. The Pennsylvania Railroad's Iron City Express, with Frick's car, the *Westmoreland*, took Frick's corpse to Pittsburgh. Elbert Gary, James Farrell, William Moore, and George Harvey were three of fifteen pallbearers to load the coffin on the train. The Iron City Express made symbolic stops at Harrisburg,

Altoona, Cresson Springs, and Johnstown. The casket was opened again at Clayton for a small viewing of Pittsburgh friends. The Reverend Van Etten of Calvary Episcopal Church gave services at Clayton. The burial took place at nearby Homewood Cemetery. Pallbearers included Andrew Mellon, Richard Mellon, Philander Knox, and Asa Childs. At the cemetery, Frick was reunited with Martha and his infant son. The copper-lined casket was surrounded in 200 cubic feet of concrete to protect against graverobbers. Andrew Mellon was the executor of the estate.

Frick's net worth at his death was estimated to be $143 million.[19] The actual number was later reduced to $77,230,392, with the paintings appraised at $13,000,000.[20] Frick left an amazing five-sixths of it to charity. Frick's estimated giving during his life was just as amazing, consisting of $60 million, very little of which was publicly marked or attributed to Frick![21] The estate taxes of $10,000,000 set a new record. After Uncle Sam, Helen was the main benefactor. Helen received around $5 million direct in cash and stocks. Adelaide received about $6 million. Helen, however, received $12 million in Pittsburgh real estate and another $1 million for maintenance. Other related real estate shares to Helen were valued at $6 million. Helen also got control of $2.5 million for her charities. Frick probably realized that Adelaide was incapable of managing money. Martha Frick Symington Sanger noted that under Pennsylvania law, Adelaide could have settled for as much as 34 percent of the estate.[22] Childs Frick and his wife got about $1,000,000 with a life interest in $2,000,000. Nephews, nieces, and cousins received $50,000 each. The art collection was assessed at $13 million in 1920 and was finally settled at $30 million in 1931. The estimated value in 1948 was $50 million.

The residual estate was divided into shares and varied with market price. In 1923 prices,[23] the amounts included $7,200,000 to Princeton, $2,400,000 each to Harvard and Massachusetts Institute of Technology. The Pittsburgh Educational Commission, which he had started, received $2,400,000. The bequest to the City of Pittsburgh for Frick Park was $2,000,000. Mercy Hospital in Pittsburgh got $1,500,000. The Lying-In Hospital in New York received $720,000. The following Pittsburgh hospitals and organizations each received $240,000: Children's Hospital, Allegheny General, Home for the Friendless, Pittsburgh Free Hospital, Pittsburgh Newsboy Home, Kinsley House, Western Pennsylvania Hospital, YWCA, Uniontown Hospital, Braddock Hospital, Cottages State Hospital, Mount Pleasant Hospital, Westmoreland Hospital, and Homestead Hospital. Frick's legacy would be the Homestead Strike, his philanthropy and art; but just as important, he left a legacy of a Pittsburgh capitalist.

21. Pittsburgh Capitalism

Pittsburgh's East End was much different from New York's Fifth Avenue. Pittsburgh was the home of the working rich. There were few parties, such as those of the Vanderbilts and Hydes in New York. They had mostly risen from the lower class to the upper class through hard work. The neighborhood of the East End was one of many contrasts as well as similarities. They were charter Republicans coming from early Whig roots. Mostly Scotch-Irish and German, they were mostly Presbyterians. Few had a college education; most had been trained on the *McGuffey Readers* in one-room schoolhouses. They traveled widely, and many had extensive foreign operations, but they were fiercely nationalistic. With the exception of Carnegie, they made no claim of aristocratic rights or God-given royalty or being part of a plan of Providence. Nation trumped capitalism, but they were deeply committed to the philosophy of capitalism. In that context they were protectionists, but they believed in a fair playing field. Frick had often advised Presidents McKinley and Roosevelt that iron tariffs were adequate in the 1890s. Most collected art, and all were philanthropic. While many maintained homes in New York as well, they loved Pittsburgh, often more than Pittsburgh loved them.

These Pittsburgh capitalists were working capitalists far different from their rich brothers in New York. They had come not from wealth, but almost all had been poor. Men like Frick, Heinz, and Westinghouse worked and invested in their companies. Yes, Frick personally collected art, but money also flowed freely into new plants that created jobs. Shortly after the Homestead Strike, Reverend Thomas Boyle wrote of Carnegie and Frick: "There is one thing with both these men that ought to be recognized by all workingmen — and that is, instead of employing their capital for merely speculative purposes, they invest it where it will not only bring return to them, but where it will afford employment of thousands of workingmen. Capital is not the enemy of labor when it is used that the wage earners are constantly employed."[1] This was why so many Pittsburghers respected them and their wealth. It was also why the socialists had found few roots in Pittsburgh factories and steel mills. Work was hard and dangerous, but it paid well. Immigrants found the money and work they had not known in Europe.

While part of the "400" wealthiest, Pittsburgh capitalists were not considered equal to the New York bluebloods such as the Astors, Vanderbilts, Roosevelts, Morgans, and Goulds. Carnegie had been the most accepted, probably because he was the richest American; and Carnegie truly wanted to be part of this leisure class. The term "Four Hundred" came from the Astor family guest lists, which were based on the belief that there were only four hundred people in America worth inviting. Frick often appeared on the guest list but rarely attended large parties. One example of the mindset difference between New York and Pittsburgh capitalists is seen in Helen Clay's twenty-fifth birthday party at Eagle Rock. The party of 500 guests was to feature dancing and John Philip Sousa's band. Frick, probably with the encouragement of Helen, invited most of the North Shore townspeople, not realizing the uproar it would cause. North Shore Society refused to mingle with mere townspeople. The uproar made both New York and Pittsburgh papers. Many balked at attending, and the response required Frick to split the party into two separate groups. Frick himself made no public statement about the well-publicized party.

Frick was also the most representative of the Pittsburgh capitalists. Frick was wealthy and lived extremely well, but he was never over the top in wild spending. Frick's schedule of work was tough and included little in the way of parties like those of the New York wealthy. Frick worked hard and his family enjoyed the fruits of his success. This is one thing that Carnegie and Frick were together on. Lesser men such as Charles Schwab, "Bet-a-Million" Gates, and William Corey were personally destroyed by money, and these men made the headlines. Their excesses destroyed their families and put a whole class of capitalists in a bad light. Frick's strong stand against the abuses and uses of policyholder money at Equitable showed he had little tolerance for such spending. Frick had a code of ethics about proper business dealings that went back to his Mennonite roots. Frick was tough and hard, but he was honest and straightforward in his dealings. He hated the business politics of personal destruction, avoiding the press and preferring to always deal head-on in business duels. A *New York Times* editorial on Frick's death summarized his ethics: "Mr. Frick belonged to a race of creators of industry and graspers of industrial opportunity, playing the game as fairly as they understood it and as it was played in their time."[2] Fair play had been drilled in the psyche of these Pittsburgh capitalists in grade school. Pittsburgh capitalists had earned their money by producing goods, not stock deals.

The policies of Carnegie and Frick often frustrated lesser partners because of their reinvestment philosophy. They believed in pouring profits back into the business. They built new plants, added the latest technology, and used new equipment. Usually in good years Carnegie put 25 percent into dividends for the partners, but most of the profits were reinvested. Such aggressive investing assured that Carnegie Steel would stay on top. Carnegie Steel policies were adopted by neighbors George Westinghouse and H.J. Heinz in their industries. In fairness, reinvestment was more of a Carnegie policy than an absolute Frick policy. Personally Frick was an investor, not the spender that New York capitalists were. Frick did, however, believe in the replacement of men with machines, which he accelerated after breaking the union. The investment in machinery worked an unusual bit of capitalistic magic. As costs were driven down, a massive expansion of market resulted, creating more jobs and even wage increases. Of course, profits grew at a much faster rate.

Still, Pittsburgh capitalists did not hide from the belief that one should be allowed to make as much as possible. Honest accumulation of wealth was considered a basic right to the Scotch-Irish settlers who fled Europe over property rights. They didn't deny that greed was a force in capitalism. They believed that as long as everyone had the opportunity to obtain wealth, capitalism was fair. The Pittsburgh capitalists, unlike the wealthy of New York, had mostly first-generation rags-to-riches wealth. When many of them moved to New York, they found it hard to mix with second-, third-, and fourth-generation wealth. They did not see themselves as American aristocrats. They worried about their own second generation being corrupted by wealth. Their companies were known by the ability of the employees to rise as far as possible. Educational degrees gave their managers little advantage; all was based on performance. Their charitable giving, such as Frick to educational causes and Carnegie to his many libraries, focused on keeping the gate open to all. For whatever reason, their giving back distinguished them from old-line wealth. Their giving was in a time when there was no income tax or income tax benefit for giving. They were ethical under the rules of the time. Frick, in particular, had always had little tolerance for those who did not play by the rules.

One common factor of these Pittsburgh capitalists is that most, like Frick, grew up on the *McGuffey Readers*. Henry Clay Frick long remembered his struggle in the 1850s to memorize the McGuffey poem "Twinkle, Twinkle, Little Star." The *McGuffey Readers* began early to reinforce individual property rights, the need to give to the poor, the importance of saving, Christian principles, an appreciation for the classics, and American exceptionalism. It explains the heroic admiration of Napoleon by so many of them. Napoleonic stories were common in the *Readers*. The *McGuffey Readers* used by the Scotch-Irish in western Pennsylvania promoted fundamental rights that led to America's embracing capitalism, but placed charity far ahead of making money. McGuffey's capitalism was far from the Darwinian concept of survival of the fittest, so popular at the time. McGuffey felt the right of property was at the core of America, but with that right came with a duty — the duty of property owners to help and care for the less fortunate. In fact, McGuffey spends a disproportionate amount of effort on the duties of capitalists to the poor. McGuffey did not use Christianity to justify or promote capitalism but to modify the very soul of capitalism. The Scotch-Irish McGuffey approach helped temper the root individual greed of capitalism into charity to the community. The measure of a capitalist was not how much that was made but how much was given.

Property and the right of property ownership constituted another fundamental western principle in the *McGuffey Readers*. The Romans called it *meum et tuum* or "that is yours and this is mine," a concept reiterated in the *McGuffey Readers*. The Scotch-Irish, including the McGuffey family, had emigrated to own a piece of low-taxed land of the kind that had been denied them in Scotland. Property rights were fundamental to the Scots-Irish and the western frontier. Many early Germans came to America because inheritance laws diluted family land ownership. The Irish immigrants had their land taken from them in Ireland. Land had been the motivator of the great western migration of East-Coast Americans. The right to own property had priority over everything in the Western psyche. Without the right of property, there can be no capitalism. Scottish philosopher Henry Kames put it this way in 1748: "It is a principle of the law of nature and essential to the well-being of society that men be secured in their possession honestly acquired." Scottish economist and Kames follower Adam Smith argued all laws and government flow from the right of property. The right of property was the argument most often used against union activity. It explains why strikes often found little support in Scotch-Irish western Pennsylvania. The Scotch-Irish were anti-union to the bone, and Pittsburgh-style capitalism was a reflection of these hard Scotch-Irish principles. In the 1920s, the Scotch-Irish capitalist Henry Ford would create a living memorial to McGuffey's principles at Greenfield Village.

Politically, the Pittsburgh capitalists were Republicans and mainly descendents of Whig Party families. They were strong supporters of protectionism, as were their workers in the mills. While Republicans, they would revolt against the Republican city machine in the early 1900s. Generally, they were McKinley Republicans who were cautious about the progressiveness of Teddy Roosevelt. They supported the early Republican values of Lincoln. Most were sons of abolitionists and temperance supporters. Most were Scotch-Irish or German Protestants. Presbyterianism was the religion of the majority. They opposed the union concepts of racism and limited membership. They believed unions to be an extension of European socialism. They did have some weaknesses in that they lost touch with their roots. They often saw the workforce in its aggregate as a cost of production. They tended to be too accounting-based, putting property rights on a higher level than human rights. Many were blinded by their own wealth, and many were eventually corrupted by it.

Pittsburgh capitalists were not only Republicans but also the heart of the protectionist movement, which made them the avowed enemy of even conservative Democrats such as Grover Cleveland. Tariffs played a key role in the politics of the Homestead Strike in 1892, which could be seen in the questions asked during the Senate investigation. The tariff could also be seen in the press and political treatment of the bloodier Pullman Strike of 1894 in Chicago. The Pullman Strike began in the summer of that year, while Democrat Grover Cleveland was president, and the Democrats controlled Congress. The strike was over a 25 percent pay reduction. As the strike progressed, strikebreakers were brought in. Cleveland used 6,000 federal troops, in addition to 3,100 police and 5,000 deputy marshals. A federal injunction was used for the first time to end the strike. Eventually, 12 workers were killed and over a hundred wounded. Property damage went over $340,000 and included the loss of 500 rail cars. With the Democrats in charge, the strike offered no political advantage for the Democrats to attack tariffs. The Pullman Strike never became a political football like the Homestead Strike.

Pittsburgh capitalists shared the Whig-Republican view of wage labor as a starting point. Most came from the supporters of Henry Clay and the Whig Party. They believed that social mobility would take care of the wage earners' struggles. Property rights were a fundamental freedom to these Whig descendants. Labor historian Eric Foner summarized this original Republican view of Abe Lincoln: "The interests of labor and capital were identical, because equality of opportunity in American society generated a social mobility which assured that today's laborer would be tomorrow's capitalist."[3] Pittsburgh capitalists believed this because they had risen from the ranks of wage earners. Unfortunately, they never fully appreciated that their very economic success had distorted the path of rapid upward mobility. Still, they realized correctly that economic growth would mean growth of the middle class. This belief had deep roots going back to the early Pittsburgh Federalists and Whigs. Many still see Frick's view and methods as unique, when in fact they were very representative of the Pittsburgh capitalists as well as much of the Pittsburgh middle class. Their belief in the American dream and mobility rang true because they had entered the workforce on the beginning of a great boom that swept many into upper-level jobs quickly. They believed that wage earners were a type of temporary or transitory class and even attributed long years in the wage-earning class to laziness. They didn't understand unions that seemed to reinforce a permanent wage-earner class. Sadly, they failed to perceive that a profound economic change had taken place with full industrialization. Their experiences of early times clouded their view of the impact of industrialization on the American laborer and immigrant as well as their view of the individual laborer. Upward mobility was still there, but it was a narrower and a slower path than they had known. To a large degree, they had lived in a very special window of opportunity at the start of America's industrialization.

Another shared concept of all businessmen of the time was a hatred of the union movement. It was hatred based in fear. The story is often told that the hatred was a means to underpay and abuse the working class. The real root of the dislike of unions was a matter first of control, then of property rights. Loss of control, as seen in the socialist movement, was a real fear in businessmen of the day. It was not opposition to wage increases. Socialists took the other extreme, portraying capitalists as treating labor as a mere manufacturing expense, like raw material costs. In fact, Christian capitalists such as H.J. Heinz, George Westinghouse, and John Wanamaker gave much in benefits, pension, medical care, and housing. Frick was far from unique in his hatred of unions. Frick's methodology was different and left him more open to criticism and less lovable to the press. It must be understood that from 1870 to 1920 was a period of experimentation for both capitalism and socialism. Europe had drawn very clear conclusions while America was searching for its own path. The result was a very different type of capitalism and unionization from those of Europe.

Pittsburgh capitalism was always nationalistic, which is a bit different from the capitalism of today. It centered on stiff tariffs to protect domestic industries. The Pittsburgh capitalists chose to bring cheap labor to American factories rather than send the factories to the cheap labor in other countries. It was a philosophy that placed American industry first. Frick became the main advisor to Congress and to William McKinley on the fairness and balance of tariff rates. Frick, more than Carnegie, had made protectionism a Republican policy; in fact, Carnegie was slowly being converted to internationalism. Frick believed manufacturing was fundamental to American-style capitalism. It was a principle Frick would not vary on. Frick opposed J.P. Morgan, who believed in free-trade internationalism as a banker and transportation mogul. In 1894, in an effort to appease the Democratic administration of Grover Cleveland, Carnegie wrote a letter to the *New York Tribune* supporting the reduction of the 1890 McKinley tariffs (the Wilson Tariff Bill of 1894).[4] It was the first of many breaks in tariff philosophy by Carnegie. Frick was angered by Carnegie's willingness to trade capitalistic principles for political favors. Carnegie pulled his support of the second McKinley presidential campaign of 1900, which again Frick saw as critical.

In many ways, Frick set the example for capitalism during war. Frick saw capitalism as an ally of the government during war. He opposed wartime nationalization of industries and pointed out the problems of a nationalized railroad system during World War I. Frick believed and personally demonstrated that industry should make sacrifices during war, but a minimum profit should be allowed for maintenance and upgrading of the equipment. He rightfully pointed out the degraded condition of the railroads after nationalization. Frick and his neighbors such as H.J. Heinz proved to be major purchasers of war bonds to support the capitalistic approach to war. United States Steel's behavior during the war was exemplary due, in some part, to Frick's role on the Finance Committee. United States Steel's contribution to the war was truly amazing, producing more steel than the combined output of the Central Powers of Germany and the Austro-Hungarian Empire. United States Steel invested heavily in equipment for government production. United States Steel expanded at Gary and Homestead for the specific needs of government. The company would produce a record 23.4 million tons of steel in 1916, employing over 268,000 workers. United States Steel also made record profits, but it invested heavily in war applications, which proved to have little market after the end of the war. United States Steel even started to build a major plant on Pittsburgh's Neville Island only to have the government cut orders with the end of the war.

While these capitalists had common philosophies and beliefs, they were diverse in their methodology, even within a few blocks of Frick's house. They were traditional Victorian capitalists in their opposition of unions, which they viewed as an extension of European socialism. The approach to the problems of labor varied from paternal capitalism and welfare capitalism to the stern resistance of Henry Clay Frick. The problem, to some degree, is what is often called "sense making," or the ability to fully comprehend the workplace they owned. These capitalists could be grouped as operations men or financiers— men like H.J. Heinz and George Westinghouse were operations managers. These two loved to go daily to the plants and factories. They interacted with the employees, often circumventing formal channels in the organization to address an employee problem. They tended to favor a paternal approach to their employees. For Westinghouse and Heinz, their weakness was finance. H.J. Heinz suffered a bankruptcy and Westinghouse lost Westinghouse Electric because of this weakness; but they had a better sense of the employee's world. Frick, Mellon, and Carnegie proved to be geniuses at finance and investment, but they lacked the common touch in dealing with their employees. Workers were viewed in the abstract as part of the labor factor. The abstraction allowed them to be Christians at the level of their own view, but their actions created a much different world from that of their workers. They were often blinded by their own success, believing that hard work alone would result in certain success. They had lost the heart of a worker and, some would argue, their own souls.

What Frick failed to understand was the real roadblocks to the workers' ability to acquire property. The threats to the worker's capability to earn money, though it was still far better than that of Europeans, were real and significant. Many of these difficulties for the worker remain today. The base 270-day year was not the average. In economic downturns, a worker commonly worked fewer than 100 days in the mill. The long hours were less of a problem than the fear of not working every week. An injury or disability would crush a family as well. The focus, even today, remains the wage rate; but the uncertainties are just as important. Even in the paternal organizations of H.J. Heinz and George Westinghouse, loyalty and obedience were demanded. Still, men like Frick were not intrinsically evil, but they were far removed from their workers' struggles. To better understand their psyche, one needs to try to understand them as human, not as devils.

A more balanced view to understand the problem of abstraction for these capitalists is to treat it more as a sin of omission. Frick does not represent raw evil, but the more common evil we all deal with. Money blinds as much as it corrupts, and this is why we see such a dichotomy between the personal and business lives of these Pittsburgh capitalists. In reality, they suffered the same blindness as the union master craftsman who was paid ten times as much as the laborer, and banned the immigrant laborer from joining the union. What seemed common to both the laborer and capitalist was the desire to make money and acquire property. The pursuit of this basic desire had been limited in Europe by one's class.

The influx of Slavic and Hungarian coal miners by Frick and others had created a new work environment. Replacing the skilled miner with immigrant miners had reduced the rate per ton of coal mined to almost subsistence levels. These Hungarian families tended to operate as a family economic unit. They sub-rented housing units, planted large gardens, and shared the work. Wives and sometimes children started to accompany their husbands into the mines; while they were not paid directly, the number of tons mined increased, and the workers' pay along with it. The practice became widespread with immigrant miners. Injuries increased and many union groups opposed the practice.

Early on, Carnegie developed what would become known as paternal feudalism or welfare capitalism. Critics argue that it was a dependency fostered by the company. The birth of Carnegie's welfare capitalism may well have started at Edgar Thomson Works in 1883. In that same year, the non-union employees accepted a wage cut. The willingness to help in downturns impressed Carnegie. In turn, Carnegie posted a notice that the company would supply employees coal at one to two cents a bushel below market price.[5] Furthermore, for one month, the employee's house payment was reduced 25 percent. Jones and Carnegie helped finance a worker's cooperative store to reduce the price of groceries and dry goods. Such incentives were developed by Carnegie's progressive manager, Bill Jones. Jones had convinced Carnegie that such benefits helped stabilize the workforce and increase morale at a small cost. These types of payments hardly affected the cost per ton of steel, which Carnegie followed daily. The program helped Edgar Thomson Works avoid the union violence of the decade and became a long-term benefit. Carnegie employees would get coal at cost for heating, and company housing was made available. Frick applied similar programs at the mines.

Bill Jones often had to create these welfare-type innovations to balance the wage cuts of his boss with the hardships of the men he directly managed. Jones had argued and won with Carnegie over the eight-hour day versus the twelve-hour day. Frick similarly had a district manager in Thomas Lynch, who was as progressive as Jones. Lynch developed contests for the best home gardens. He used crews to help maintain town utilities and streets. Lynch supplied money for community events and activities. Lynch and Jones were the important linking pins between the company and the employee. These creative middle managers compensated for the remoteness of their bosses from the working environment. Without these company benefits, the mills and mines could have approached the organization of a prison camp, which many critics maintained it was. Jones and Lynch lived with the men and took it upon themselves personally to help. Their approach was paternal.

Carnegie's welfare capitalism was different from the paternal capitalism of Elbert Gary, George Westinghouse, George Pullman, and H.J. Heinz. Carnegie saw his role as a designated distributor of wealth. He believed he knew best what was needed by society. His gifts of libraries were honestly based on a desire to help, but it was *his* idea, not the worker's, that what the worker needed was libraries. The paternal capitalists looked at superior working conditions and worker aid, with necessities being more important than cultural gifts. It is clear that Carnegie's thousands of libraries did much good, but many argue they were built on the backs of the workers. Gary's approach was more correctly seen as paternal capitalism aimed directly at the worker's daily life. Frick viewed capitalism as purely economic and giving as purely personal. Frick saw Carnegie's approach as a type of corporate socialism. Frick's giving was aimed at the poor, helpless, and needy; but it was at the personal level. Frick hated Carnegie's habit of using the company for much of his giving. Frick had even less tolerance for the public nature of Carnegie's giving. Carnegie made his giving into a type of public competition, which was not typical of most Pittsburgh capitalists. In any case, with the Pittsburgh capitalist, there always was a giving part. Frick's personal approach was more typical of the Pittsburgh capitalists than that of Carnegie. Men like H.J. Heinz, Charles Schwab, and George Westinghouse also gave quietly.

Carnegie's idea of philanthropic capitalism as a balance had its weak points as well. Biographer Peter Krass offered the following analysis:

> Consider that to support a typical six-member family unit (children and grandparents included) and stay debt free in 1886, a man had to earn $600; but many of the hundred men at Edgar Thomson were making less than $400. An investigation by the Senate Committee on Labor and Education several years earlier had confirmed that the average workingman couldn't afford a decent maintenance of their families. Supposing an additional $200 was given to every laborer, bringing everyone close to or above the $600 mark, it would have cost Carnegie $360,000 or just 12 percent of his $2.9 million in profits. (Meanwhile, Carnegie committed over $350,000 to library and hospital donations in the early 1880s.) Life could have been immeasurably better for these oppressed mules, but wasn't reality in the steel industry.[6]

Westinghouse often said the best philanthropy was to give a worker a good paying job.

Actually, Frick's model of large corporations ended the great era of philanthropic capitalism of such icons as Carnegie, Frick, Rockefeller, and Schwab. Progressives forced corporations to take on more paternal giving, moving towards employee benefits. Westinghouse and Heinz, both considered saints by labor, had pioneered the idea of German paternalism, where profits were given more directly to the worker's environment versus redirecting profits through owner philanthropy. These capitalists added health and insurance benefits. Gary tried to apply this as well. Once some balance was achieved and corporations replaced all-powerful individual owners, there was less motivation for philanthropy on the scale of Andrew Carnegie. In a world of income taxes and progressivism, personal giving became personal again, which is how Frick and most other Pittsburgh capitalists had always seen it. Paternalism had many positive points, but workers still served at the pleasure of management. This is the point that Frick failed to appreciate; and with Frick's temper and hardheadedness, he himself would have been the type of worker most threatened. Labor would have to protect its rights through the evolution of industrial unions.

22. The Labor Republic

While the worker republic envisioned in the 1870s and the utopian crafts model has disappeared, much of the old system survives to this day in the trades. Frick correctly foresaw the inability of the crafts union model to fit into industrial America. However, Frick offered no real alternative to the worker. The path to American industrial unionism was difficult, slow, and filled with setbacks. Today's American model for unionism is unique because of its early roots in the worker republic's owning or controlling the means of production. The worker republic had been the vision of European craftsmen in the early 1800s, including some of Frick's own early descendants. Such a vision had developed in the German crafts city of Lancaster and early Pittsburgh. The worker republic also left its mark on American capitalism. Until the arrival of Pittsburgh Bessemer Steel Company, even Homestead was a worker's republic. Early glass companies in Homestead and Pittsburgh had been modeled on the worker republic. Glass company owners such as Charles Bryce managed finance and sales, while skilled craftsmen handled the production. The master craftsman made most of the operating decisions, including hiring, payroll, manufacturing processes, scheduling, and worker advancement. It was an industrialized craft guild system.

One of the struggles was between industrialization and its production demands with the guild system. Early on, it appeared that the guild system could be adapted to the industrial requirements. The glass industry that dominated Pittsburgh in the 1850s had successfully modified the partnership between capital and labor to achieve a more quantity-oriented approach. Even iron puddling was modified to fit a guild model, but in both cases the production rates were low and the use of machines limited. Civil War production remained under the crafts guild system, but things were beginning to change. The steam engine was starting to supply energy to automate operations. The conversion to machines changed the nature and need for skilled nature. This was a revolutionary change that had not been seen in the workplace prior to the late 1700s. It had been the automated loom that sent the first shock waves of industrialization in Europe. It had been this type of automation in the weaving industry that had forced Frick's great-grandfather and Carnegie's own father to emigrate to America. Interestingly, Frick's ancestors adapted to the new economy, while Carnegie's father died a broken man from the automation of his craft. Carnegie noted in his autobiography:

> The change from hand-loom to steam-loom weaving was disastrous to our family. My father did not recognize the impending revolution and was struggling under the old system. His looms sank greatly in value, and it became necessary for that power which never failed in any emergency — my mother — to step forward and endeavor to repair the family fortune.[1]

Carnegie was well aware that a real revolution was under way, but no one could foresee the ultimate end. It would not be the socialism that Frick feared or the crafts utopia that labor envisioned. The "end" would be a hard-fought path of transitions. Labor and capital would have to literally fight it out as in any revolution. American industrial unionism would be far different from that of Europe. The collectivism of European socialism was not suited for American-style democracy and its belief in property rights. Neither complete owner nor worker control would work in America. Furthermore, the American nation had to come to grips with the privileging of industrialism over Jefferson's agrarian utopia. Just as complex was the nation's struggle with slave labor. It would not be an easy adjustment.

The revolutionary period of the 1840s in Europe had caused the crafts guilds to be banned. In addition, socialism was on the rise and a more radical approach was evolving in Germany. In the 1840s, many German craftsmen had gone to France to learn their trades, but France followed the German approach in the late 1840s. German craftsmen looked next to the United States. German weavers, locksmiths, tailors, shoemakers, cigar makers, brewers, bakers, and others headed for America. By 1855, Germans dominated the trades in New York City, but they also labored in sweatshops. The German socialists, however, followed the crafts to America. The craftsmen wanted control of the production, which is what they had in the first half of the 1800s in America. In the 1850s, the flood of Irish and Germans continued, but in the case of the Germans, the diversity of the immigrants increased. Prior to 1848, the German immigrants were known as "Grays" versus the later "Greens." The forty-eighters and after were a very different group. First, more German Catholics came as the focus of religious persecution changed in the German states. Another change was the immigration of the middle class and artisans. These "Greens" tended to be Democrats because of the nativists in the Republican Party. The ironworkers, glassblowers, glass gatherers, puddlers, and other crafts unionists were "Grays" and Republicans.

The American unions had the same infrastructure of the old European guilds. The only difference was that they functioned as "operatives." The manufacturing company contracted the crafts master, such as a puddler or miner, to do the work. The master used his own group of apprentices and workers. The crafts master set the production quality and quantity produced. The master was paid and he, in turn, paid his team. The crafts guild became a "lodge" under the crafts union model. The American model underwent much evolution from 1850 to 1875. Technology was changing rapidly, and with it, the workplace. America was also shifting to a consumer society that caused demand to heat up. The craftsmen had to speed up from the leisurely pace of the 1700s. Furthermore, competition was forcing a change in the pricing of product. No longer did the craftsmen set the price for their handiwork. The craftsmen were trying to adapt to the new pace of capitalism. Men like Frick were also trying to create a new model of manufacturing capitalism.

The crafts union model had another disadvantage in that the master craftsman was a subcontractor and business owner. The crafts union was, therefore, a supplier in the manufacturing chain. When the steel market took a downturn and the price per ton went down, the supply chain would then be asked to reduce their cost for supply to the steel mill. The miner craftsman was, in fact, paid on tons of coal mined or tons of coke made. Wages, therefore, became an integral part of the product cost and pricing structure. To the corporate owner, the scale reduction seemed to be less of a wage cut than tied directly to a human being. From a public relations standpoint, such a wage reduction could be spun as a business-to-business pricing issue. The laborer's wages were actually decided by the union lodge in the 1870s. The manufacturer paid the master craftsman, who in turn paid his crew. Initially, non-apprentice laborers fared no better under union craftsmen than directly under the owners.

The Amalgamated crafts model was an effort to extend the guild model into the industrial age. It was a struggle for control over the operations' decision-making. At Amalgamated mills such as Homestead, the master workers controlled all of the decision making, which today resides with management. Hiring was done by the union lodge and was based on nationality and personal connections. Working hours and worker organization were under the control of the master crafts worker. The master craftsman, who contracted a tonnage pay with the company, set the wages of most laborers on the crew. The glass houses and iron plants of the 1850s in Pittsburgh reflected this true labor republic. By the 1870s, Carnegie's industrial giant mill at Braddock and Frick's large coal mines were challenging the labor republic. In turn, the owners were competing with each other for lower costs and higher productivity. Andrew Kloman and a syndicate of Pig Iron Aristocrats formed a company to challenge Carnegie. The company, known as Pittsburgh Bessemer Steel, started to built its mill at Homestead in 1879. Kloman, an original Carnegie partner, was a believer in rolling as a craft. Kloman had been an ironmonger and roller in Germany. Kloman had built a reputation of craftsmanship in his original Pittsburgh forge shop. He embraced the Amalgamated Union to help his venture gain the immediate expertise in rolling steel rails. Within a year, some of the other syndicate members challenged the union control of the workplace, forcing a strike in 1882. Ultimately, it led to Kloman's failure, and Carnegie bought the mill in 1883. Carnegie had planned from the start to end the control of the crafts union.

The records of Lodge No. 11 of the Rollers, Roughers, Catchers, and Hookers Union at Columbus Rolling Mill Company illustrate the crafts union model of the 1870s. The following union record is from a six-week strike over wages for the skilled rolling mill employees.[2] The work of rolling iron meant passing iron back and forth through a set of different-sized rolls. The bar had to be caught and then passed over to the other side to pass through another set of rolls. This passing, catching, and hooking was done a couple of dozen of times as the bar was reduced to proper size. The crew had a hierarchical scale based on the old guild system of work. The highest pay went to the highest skill level, which generally correlated to the oldest on the rolling crew. This was the head or master roller, who coordinated all phases of work through the lodge. The company offered to pay $1.13 a ton, which had to be divided up. The top workers (rollers) would get 19.5 cents a ton. The roller was, in effect, the crew boss or master craftsman, or the manager. The operation in 1876 was really subcontracted by the company to the master roller with the head roller being paid for the tonnage produced; he in turn usually paid other skilled crew members. Under this particular lodge, the general laborers (buggymen) were paid by the roller. Technically, each of the skill levels, including apprentices, was a separate craft. Today a supervisory foreman would be in management. Being at the next highest skill level in the crew, the rougher would get 10 cents per ton. The catchers were next at 9 cents per ton, and the hookers got 5 cents a ton. In reality, the catchers and hookers required some skill, but not the level of most craftsmen. A laborer on the crew might get as little as 2 cents a ton. In this case 13.5 cents a ton was allotted for laborers. It was a very complex system of labor, skills, and control, which did not truly reflect the process, but imposed a crafts system. The lodge also decided how many "heats" they would work in a day.

After the loss of another strike by the Brotherhood of Iron Heaters, Rollers, and Roughers, the workers of the whole mill had to unite. The Amalgamated Association of Iron and Steel Workers united all the mill workers into a union, with the puddlers, rollers, heaters, and nailers having a lodge based on the craft. The roller lodge still had the rollers, roughers, catchers, and hookers. The lodge model did evolve to a more streamlined system in the 1890s, where it was under the overall craft of roller. The roughers, catchers, and hookers eventually became unskilled laborers but were paid an ascending hourly pay scale. Today the passing and catching would be done automatically, and one operator would do the work of a 13- to 15-man crew. The operator is still known as a roller, and in union mills this is still one of the highest-paid positions, with the highest hourly wage plus a tonnage bonus. The roller, for the most part, has some limited supervisory authority but remains responsible for the workmanship.

The evolution of such a rolling crew was slow and often painful. In the mines, Frick started the practice of putting a company man in a supervisory position of foreman ("pusher") along with the master. Frick wisely had started the policy of selecting foremen from the ranks of skilled workers, which eased the transition to the new system. Technology often replaced skilled positions in the chain between 1880 and 1930, pushing the union and management into more general work positions. New equipment usually switched unskilled operators for skilled workers. After the Strike of 1892, the effect on employment at Homestead was amazing, with a 25 percent reduction in the workforce. The company took advantage of union policy of not allowing unskilled membership and put these men under the supervision of the foreman. The arrangement increased the power of the foreman over the master crafts worker because of the crew coordination. Unskilled company labor was paid by the hour versus tonnage. The master craftsmen had originally supplied the tools and equipment for the crew, such as picks, shovels, and lanterns in the mining industry. As the company started to supply tools and equipment again, the foreman, as part of management, became more integral to the overall operation. "Work Rules" replaced the full control of the production process by the crafts union.

One result of the change in infrastructure and control after the Homestead Strike of 1892 can be seen in the Homestead Open Hearth Department. The open-hearth department proved less resistant to Frick's new supervisory system. In 1905, Frick's new structure was evident. In 1892, there was a master craftsman-melter in charge of each furnace. The melter was paid $6.00 a day and had a First Helper making $5.00 a day. The melter controlled the whole furnace crew and the pace and quality of the furnace operation. Things had changed by 1905, when a melter-foreman (management) managed the operation of three open-hearth furnaces at a salary of $9.00 per day. Each furnace still had a union First Helper at $5.00 per day. The average wage actually increased slightly from $2.70 a day to $2.77 a day. While there was a $4.00 a day savings in top wages, the real cost saving was in management control and productivity. Control had always been at the heart of the struggle with the Amalgamated union throughout the industry. This is the same structure Frick had achieved in the coal mines in the 1880s. In retrospect, it would likely be the result of industrialization, and it was unfortunate that lives had to be lost in the process.

Eventually, by the 1920s, the industrial model had replaced the crafts model, but some of the old infrastructure still exists to this day. The old crafts model still holds in some trade unions such as electricians. The hierarchical structure still exists, but the pay is per hour, with the top job often paying four to five times the lowest, plus a tonnage bonus. Other than the trades, the apprentice system has been replaced by seniority, pay being by seniority, although some new work system companies are again looking at "pay for skills." The foreman or front line manager to this day is often paid less than the skilled union laborer. Of course, the issue of union membership and pay had been an internal struggle in the union movement. The Amalgamated stood at odds with the Knights of Labor. The Knights of Labor offered broad membership to all workers in a graded type of pay system, which was still hierarchical. The Knights recognized that the end of the crafts system was at hand, although they appeared to have been slightly ahead of the curve. They were even willing to accept a wider application of hourly rates. The Knights had even found acceptance with some of Carnegie's managers, since they had little interest in fighting over control of the process or establishing complex work rules. A simple demand for the universal eight-hour day was their core work rule issue.

Frick would have nothing to do with the Amalgamated because of its grip on the functioning of the workplace. He was a little more tolerant of the Knights, but he was concerned about socialists' infiltration of the union. The Knights believed in political activism, which, in fact, had made the union popular with socialists and anarchists. The "Father of American Unionism," Samuel Gompers, opposed the political action of the unions that the socialists wanted. In fact, the socialists were able to force Gompers out of the union movement temporarily. Gompers believed in a non-political approach. Gompers and his American Federated Labor Union were cutting a middle path between the Knights and Amalgamated.

Gompers had even refused to help the Amalgamated in the 1901 strike against United States Steel. In 1910, Gompers denounced United States Steel as soulless and tried to help the Amalgamated; but it was too late, and the Amalgamated accepted the open-shop requirement of United States Steel. Gompers made a failed run to support the closed-shop union policy in Great Lakes Shipping, which was the main subsidiary of big steel. Again the seed of failure in the shipping industry was the inability of the Amalgamated to accept unskilled workers. Gompers realized, as did the Knights, that the unskilled had to be brought into the union movement. In the long run, Gomper's union model would most reflect American unionism, but Gompers would never win the blessing of Frick.

The rise of technology and unskilled labor doomed the union's hierarchical system. The Amalgamated defeat at Homestead in 1892 marked the beginning of the end of steel unionization by the Amalgamated and steel unions in general. The Amalgamated union continued to have strengths in the finishing operations of United States Steel, but their national power was gone. Its own rules against unskilled labor had doomed it more than any capitalist opposition. The unions' greatest defeats were often rooted in their lack of solidarity. The miners were the first to realize the change and adapted to it by accepting unskilled labor. The miners centered on solidarity, creating the power base needed in strikes. The miners' union became a serious force almost fifty years before that of the steelworkers. While men like Frick and Carnegie had accelerated the death of the Amalgamated, it came about as a result of a combination of the end of crafts production, union bias, industrial size, technology, and the rise of unskilled labor that served the final blow. Crafts production was incapable of supplying the growth of the market, which in turn required highly automated production levels.

Another factor in the changing labor picture was the rise of the common laborer, which was directly related to technology. For example, the Bessemer converter basically eliminated the skilled steel puddler. Handling systems eliminated the specialty roller. Coke ovens eliminated colliers. Rolling technology eliminated hookers and catchers. Common laborers now made steel, as opposed to craftsmen. The automated glass bottle machine eliminated the skilled glass blowers and replaced them with an hourly paid machine operator. The crafts unions adapted where possible, made new arrangements where possible, but still declined. The loss of skilled craftsmen was irreversible. At another level, the master craftsman was replaced by the modern foreman. Even common laborers were needed less than before. The electric crane was said to have eliminated 300 workers at Homestead in the 1890s, and in general between 1892 and 1897, over 2,900 jobs, or 25 percent, were lost to technology and automation.[3] The main movement and cost reduction, however, was the replacement of skilled labor by unskilled. An iron mill in 1877 had about 20 percent common laborers in the operation. Ten years later in 1887, a Carnegie steel mill had about 35 percent common laborers. The skilled-to-unskilled labor ratio continued to decrease at a similar rate through the 1890s. By 1900, most manufacturing had 60 percent unskilled labor. The crafts unions had held to the old crafts guild standard that refused to represent unskilled workers and machine operators, and this would be the main contributing factor to their end.

The rise of Judge Gary to president of United States Steel was hailed as a new era for labor, but in fact, conditions changed little. Gary hated unions, as did Frick and Carnegie. What was different was that Gary expanded the paternal approaches to counter the unions. He offered a softer approach, but things were not significantly changed in the mill. Gary's vision of a labor republic evolved around the idea of employee ownership in the form of equity holding. The actual plan was the brainchild of Morgan's partner, George Perkins, who was the first chairman of the Finance Committee. Frick showed some hesitation, but the plan had few drawbacks. Gary embraced the new plan, and it was implemented in 1902. The plan was open to all United States Steel employees. Employees would be able to purchase stock routinely at prices below market value. For ease of purchase, an installment plan was available. Employees would receive the normal common share dividend plus a $5 a share annual bonus. The average price from 1901 to 1905 was $30 a share with a high of $55 and a low of $8. The dividend was around 2 to 3 percent (2 percent was the target). With the bonus, the return averaged 10 to 15 percent. The plan had mixed results. In the first year, the plan gained 13,000 subscribers, but most of these were the higher-paid employees. Charles Schwab was a major subscriber. By 1911, the plan reached 30,000, or about 15 percent, of all employees. The income level of the average steelworker could not support the program. An unskilled worker made from $1.65 an hour to $2.00 a day. Frick had actually been supportive of the stock program.

One of the most overlooked points about Frick was his ability to learn and change. Initially, Frick had concerns about Judge Gary's liberal policies. Frick and Gary became very respectful of each other, and Frick in particular learned from Gary. Years later Gary would say:

> The Corporation at the beginning decided upon policies which, in several respects, were somewhat different from those which had been previously pursued in the management of large business affairs. Therefore, during the early period of Mr. Frick's connection with the Corporation he was somewhat doubtful in regard to some policies adopted, but was quick to appreciate the reasons presented and readily became a strong supporter of all including the idea that large corporations should openly recognize their obligations to others.[4]

In general, however, the policies of United States Steel were not revolutionary.

In 1907, one of the nation's largest-ever social and civic surveys was performed on living conditions in the Pittsburgh area. Homestead of 1907 was very different from that of 1892. Unskilled labor had increased from about 32 percent in 1892 to 58 percent in 1907. The common laborer who had made 75 cents to $1.00 a day in 1892 now made $1.65 a day. The average wage was around $2.50 a day. The native-born American was dominant in 1892, but in 1907 over 58 percent of the workforce were immigrant laborers. The majority were Slavs, which included a large array of Eastern Europeans. Immigrants continued to pour in, since the wages were 3 to 4 times higher than wages in Europe. The average wage in Europe was around 30 cents a day. A steel roller in Eastern Europe made 39 cents a day. Life in Homestead was far from improved, but due to a very strange opportunity, Slavs progressed in society. The average stay in the industrial mill ghetto was less than a generation. The Slavs demonstrated creativity and capitalism on a level equal to that of Carnegie and Frick. In the end, it was the immigrant workers themselves who saved capitalism. They saved and bought homes and businesses. They formed fraternal organizations to fill insurance needs. The community formed its own social safety net. Even in the most difficult environments, these immigrant steelworkers found more hope in the American dream than the socialism of Europe.

As might have been expected with the defeat of the Amalgamated crafts union in 1892, the wages of the highest-paid crafts jobs did decline from 1892 to 1907. The decline was a combination of technology, management structure, and tonnage rate reduction. A roller wage rate of $11.09 a day in 1892 compared to $7.38 a day in 1907. A heater made $5.65 a day in 1892 and $4.98 a day in 1907. Melters made $6.00 a day in 1892 and $5.00 a day in 1907. Lower-paid skilled workers showed an increase, however; in the open-hearth department, the wage was $2.00 a day in 1892 and $2.70 a day in 1907.[5] The non-unionized common labor had increased from $1.00 a day to $1.65 a day. The numbers pretty much show what Frick had predicted. Wages were still well above the national average.

The foreman had improved to a daily wage of around $3.00 a day and the general foreman around $6.00 a day. While the Amalgamated Union had disappeared at Homestead, the hierarchical pay scale still existed. The following daily wages were in place:

Rollers	$7.00–$8.00 a day
Roller assistants	$4.00
Heater	$5.00
Inspectors	$2.30
Common Laborer	$1.65

The average family budget for a mill laborer per week in 1907 included $1.88 for rent, $4.16 for food, 38 cents for fuel, and 94 cents for clothing. Other weekly costs included 70 cents for insurance, 20 cents a week for liquor, and 10 cents a week for medicine. Workers

A Homestead alley in 1900 (courtesy Carnegie Library of Pittsburgh).

still raised chickens and pigs in the streets of Homestead, and made homemade wine and distilled liquor.

Interestingly, one major improvement in the steelworker diet — increased protein and lower food costs—came as a side benefit of reduced steel-making costs for tin plate. Tin plate allowed for the introduction of canned beans and soups by Pittsburgher and Frick neighbor, H.J. Heinz. Heinz adjusted his product to the economic downturn created by the Panic of 1893 by adding canned baked beans in 1895 and cream of tomato soup in 1897. Baked beans offered high protein at a very low price, and Heinz advertised to exploit that fact. Baked beans became a staple of the Pittsburgh mill worker. Heinz put in an automated canning line for his baked beans, pushing the price down from 15 cents a can to 10 cents by 1905. The beans were baked and put automatically in cans with tomato sauce. A mill worker could take a tin can to work and heat it quickly for lunch. Baked beans dramatically reduced the cost of packing a lunch, and eliminated preparation time for the struggling steelworker housewife or daughter, who was often working to supplement the family income at an H.J. Heinz factory. The price of pickles, a mainstay of dinner and supper at the time, had dropped significantly with Heinz's assembly production in 1907. Heinz also introduced high-protein peanut butter in 1909, and mill worker sales made H.J. Heinz the largest peanut butter manufacturer in the world.

Housewives showed exceptional skill in stretching the food budget, and scorned the housekeeping classes offered by the company as too theoretical. Foods for breakfast might include eggs (28 cents a dozen from a small business egg man), bacon (7 cents a pound), bread

Homestead in 1902 (courtesy Carnegie Library of Pittsburgh).

(5 cents a loaf), coffee (14 cents a pound), and jelly (homemade). Some fruits might be included for breakfast in the summer months. Dinner (now known as lunch) included things like soup (homemade or Heinz tomato at 10 cents a can), bread, beans (10 cents a large can), stew (from leftovers), and milk (8 cents a pail). Supper included beef (8 cents a pound), potatoes (40 cents a bushel), pickles, beans, coffee (14 cents a pound), and assorted garden vegetables. Often families ran small businesses to sell jellies, horseradish, mustard, pickles, and other home garden products. This is how a young H.J. Heinz got started in a worker neighborhood not far from Homestead, where rent in a two-room apartment was around $8 a month.

Amazingly, many of these families found a way to save 50 cents a week over expenses. The family did this with gardens, by taking in sub-renters, and through other family members' incomes. Generally, wives added to the family budget by sewing and doing laundry. Daughters and wives often worked at the H.J. Heinz plant for $1 a day. Women could also work in the light assembly plants of Westinghouse and earn a bit more. Women were forbidden to work in the steel mills, but Heinz and Westinghouse actually catered to women, with 60 percent of their workforce being women. Women at the Heinz plant got free health care. The majority of immigrant families took in renters, turning a profit at times by crowding four to six people in a single room. The housewife also offered meals and laundry to the renters, again making a small profit. Rent of a six-room house for the higher-paid workers was about $40 a month. A four-room rented house without plumbing was around $16 a month. Single workers could sign on to a boarding house for $40 a month. For this, a worker got a bed in a dorm-type room and two meals a day. One of the meals was a packed dinner pail for work. Laundry was also included with rent.

The worker's biggest fear remained the loss of work. The real problem facing the worker and his family was not wage rates per se or working conditions, but recession. The recession of 1907–1908 caused a 21 percent cut in the workforce and a 10 percent to 30 percent cut in wage rates. Those lucky enough to stay working were working 2 days a week instead of 6 or 7 days. These downturns created havoc in family budgets. The Republican Party for years had offered the "full dinner pail" by imposing high tariffs on foreign product. This is why in 1907, "Most of Pittsburgh steel workers vote the Republican ticket, because they see no immediate hopes of success through the Workingmen's party; but they are ready to accept any political theory that promises something worthwhile for labor."[6] Any disruption of work created a crisis for a family. The dark smoke-filled skies were a symbol of prosperity to these families.

The immigrant workers lacked benefits over the years but formed fraternal and beneficial organizations to cover sickness leave, disability, and death benefits. The initiation fees were around $2 and the monthly dues about 60 cents. For this a worker got a death benefit of about $1,000 and disability of $1,000. Sick leave cost about $5 a week. In addition, Andrew Carnegie created a retirement fund for Carnegie Steel Division workers. After 18 years' service, a laborer would get a pension of $8.38 a month. In 1910, United States Steel put in an accidental insurance plan for employees. In the end, the capitalist spirit of these steelworkers improved their own lot more than their employers did. Benefits and wages improved from the time of the Homestead Strike, but working conditions were still a problem with Judge Gary.

In many ways, Gary's approach was an extension of Carnegie's paternal capitalism. It was welfare capitalism, but Gary's had a softer and more caring face. In fact, Gary opposed unionization, the eight-hour day, and the six-day workweek. In the great Steel Strike of 1919, Gary held firm against unionization and the elimination of the twelve-hour day. In this case, it was the effort of the American Federation of Labor to organize United States Steel. Gary stonewalled the strike and broke the union movement. The three-month walkout was 90 percent effective except for Homestead Works and the works of the Monongahela Valley. Gary's own words in reviewing the 1919 Strike echoed those of Frick in 1892: "The workman, if he belongs to a labor union, becomes the industrial slave of the union. He has no power of initiative or opportunity to apply his natural mental and physical capacity.... The natural and certain effects of labor unionism are expressed by three words: inefficiency, high costs."[7] Frick believed in the cold application of capitalism, but as many noted, he was honest in his opinions and everyone knew were he stood. A steel labor historian noted on Gary: "Gary, far more sensitive to public opinion, recognized the need to appease the demands for reform. He always spoke respectfully of workers and their rights and professed a concern for their well-being. The welfare capitalist program that he adopted aimed chiefly at warding off and dampening down criticism, and as might be expected, impressed reformers more than he did laborers."[8]

Still, the Strike of 1919 was every bit as violent and oppressive as Homestead. Further, Gary had publicly called out union leader Samuel Gompers prior to the strike at the 1919 October meeting of the American Iron and Steel Institute with: "It will be observed that the strike is not the result of any claim by any workmen for higher wages or better treatment nor for any reason except the desire and effort on the part of union leaders to unionize the iron and steel industry."[9] Gary was clear that he planned to break this unionization effort, and he called on the whole industry to stand united against the union. The 1919 strike was nationwide, and deaths numbered 20 with hundreds more beaten and wounded. Armed guards and federal troops were used and plants turned into forts. Strikebreakers were brought in on a large scale; in particular, 40,000 blacks were employed as strikebreakers. This was a major influx of blacks into the industry. There was much property damage. Yet Gary escaped the hatred often directed at Frick in 1892.

Thanks to an excellent propaganda machine at United States Steel, history has deemed Gary labor-friendly. Yet at Homestead, labor-management relations were not improved under Gary. Gary had not moderated on the twelve-hour day or recognition of the union, the main issues after wages in the Homestead Strike. Even more telling is that the use of company spies actually increased substantially under Gary. The Pittsburgh Survey of 1907 told a story that was similar to the Soviet Union of the twentieth century. Workers would meet in secret to talk about any work issue. There was a fear of any strangers in the town. Spies were part of daily life.

In 1907 the emphasis changed from structure and wage rates to working conditions and life in the Pittsburgh mill towns. Frick's neighbor, H.J. Heinz, also led a small group of businessmen, along with reform Mayor George Guthrie, to have a social analysis of conditions in Pittsburgh. With support of Benjamin Thaw and others (including Frick), Heinz contributed to have a nonprofit New York company do the survey. Frick had given his support because he was Pittsburgh's largest owner of real estate and had become a progressive in the area of community development. The "Pittsburgh Survey" was a unique experiment in social analysis and remains today a rare source of data about early industrial America. The idea was not popular (but reluctantly accepted) with most heavy industry capitalists, who were well aware of the poor working conditions. Those conditions would be a stark contrast to their mansions. The Pittsburgh Chamber hoped that such a study would help with their efforts to get pollution control. Pittsburgh offered a major opportunity to look at American industry and life. It was the fifth largest city in the United States and the center of American industry in 1907. The survey would cover a six-county area that accounted for most of America's steel and iron production, with special emphasis on the infamous mill town of Homestead. The steel industry had brought massive numbers of immigrants to the area of over 1.6 million. Of that population, over 60 percent were foreign-born or children of foreign-born. It was also a city of contrasts, with more millionaires than any other American city and a huge cultural district. Kellogg could have added complex as well. Labor was searching for its identity.

Unions (crafts and trade), socialists, capitalists, government, progressives, and political parties were trying to influence the direction of labor.

The survey did wake the conscience of many industrialists, including Frick. Two steel executives whom Heinz had worked with on civic committees were particularly touched. These were William Dickson, then first vice-president of United States Steel, and Alva Dinkey, the plant manager of the vast Homestead Steel Works, which came under heavy criticism. Dickson was clearly moved by the survey, professing that it changed his life and likening it to Abe Lincoln seeing the abuse of slaves as a youth and resolving to destroy slavery. Dickson moved to improve hours and working conditions throughout United States Steel Corporation and continued the quest throughout the steel industry for 30 years. Dickson would become a passionate labor reformer for the rest of his life, and an admirer of H.J. Heinz. The survey touched another steel executive, Charles Schwab, who implemented reforms at Bethlehem Steel. Even the retired Andrew Carnegie was moved reading it, and established a fund for workers' pensions and insurance for his old employees. For his part, Frick became involved in smoke abatement and flood control. Frick had always been active with the Chamber of Commerce, and in 1908 (the two-hundredth anniversary of the city) Frick donated $1,000 of the $10,000 needed for a large celebration. The survey changed not only Pittsburgh, but also the nation.

Homestead was a tale of two cities in 1907–1915, but as a whole, it fared about the same under Gary's United States Steel. The slums had actually increased under United States Steel as immigrants and blacks poured into the city. In any Pittsburgh area mill town, the slums were the region "below the tracks," referring to the flood plain from the river to the railroad tracks. The Homestead slums were rows of wooden boarding houses lining dirt streets. Doors were one to two feet off the ground level because of flooding. Hogs and chickens ran wild. There was little sewage service or running water. The row houses had "courts," which were public toilets and had running water. A court would service 100 to 200 people. The spring floods usually destroyed everything on ground level. In Homestead, the slum was known as the First Ward (Lower Homestead) and was the port of entry for new immigrants. About half of the town's population was crowded into the First Ward. The Ward was a town of its own with cheap boarding houses, hotels, and saloons. A worker could get a cheap bed in a dorm room for $3 a month. Food and laundry might run $2 a week. For single men, the idea was to live as cheaply as possible, saving for the future. At one point there were over fifty saloons in the Ward. The Pittsburgh Survey found a mix of Lithuanian, Polish, Russian, Hungarian, and 24 dialects of Slavic. As bad as the slums were, the average stay in the slums was brief. Immigrants learned skilled trades, earning more and "moving up the hill." Single men saved money to return to Europe or move up the hill. One estimate is from 1908 to 1910, for every 100 Eastern European immigrants coming in, forty-four returned to Europe.[10] The Eastern Europeans were noted for their habitual savings. Some became saloon owners or store owners but moved their residences further up the hill. They often paid for more family members to immigrate to America. After earning some money and getting citizenship, many moved on to other American cities. The company, the YMCA, and churches all offered classes in citizenship to help the immigrants' progress.

In 1907, Gary and United States Steel had a "model" housing project for 250 families. The neighborhood was in Munhall next to Homestead and was "above the tracks." Frick supported such a project, having been one of the earliest employers in the mining industry to supply company housing. In fact, Carnegie Steel had an employee housing loan benefit going back to 1884. These Homestead houses were for unskilled labor families. They rented for around $11 a month, although this could be adjusted to wage rate. These houses had five rooms, including a kitchen and bathroom. Electric lighting was available for $1.50 a month.

There were also some rows of houses available with four rooms, no electric lights, and no running water for $8.50 a month. Critics viewed company housing as pure paternalism or welfare capitalism, but this was much different from the European paternalism model. Mill workers who came to stay found ways to save and clawed their way up the hill. The company actually had a savings and loan program even in the 1890s. A worker could buy a small "cottage" for $150 to $300 down and a monthly payment of $17 to $20 a month. Home ownership was something unknown in the mill towns of Europe, and became a major factor in the labor republic of America. In many ways, the mill workers became capitalists themselves, saving and investing. In addition, they subleased, thereby becoming landlords; they created their own insurance companies and opened an array of small businesses.

Still, the mill slums below the tracks would remain the port of entry for thousands of immigrant steelworkers into the 1930s. In 1919, Reverend Adelbert Kazincy, a Catholic priest from Braddock's St. Michael Church, described slum mill housing to a Senate committee: "Two rooms, as a rule, are the headquarters of the workers. The lower part is a kitchen and the upstairs a living room, if you can call it such, and the sleeping room for the family. Sometimes they have boarders and sometimes there are four or five in a room."[11] There is no question that the face of capitalism was harsh in the early 1900s. The good news was the stay in the slums remained well under a generation. Many of the grandsons of the 1919 strike became doctors, lawyers, small business owners, and engineers.

The city of Homestead fared a bit better than the individual workers. The Carnegie Library was opened in 1898, and was a massive community center. It was an imposing Renaissance brick fortress, considered at the time to be the largest free library in the world. The main floor had a 20,000-volume library, a 1,000-seat auditorium, a 36-foot-by-68-foot swimming pool, a billiards room, clubrooms, and bowling alleys. The second floor had a basketball court, running track, and exercise room. The library offered a wide variety of lectures and classes for the improvement of the worker. To a large degree, Homestead was propped up by the capitalists to show that workers could pull themselves up. All floors were embellished in rich Gilded Age accessories of ivory, marble, and oak. Frick added a beautiful park and Schwab added a technical school. United States Steel used the experience of Frick and Schwab to donate to churches and community centers, which were a stabilizing factor in the workforce.

While Frick's poor treatment of labor has been exaggerated, so has Gary's good treatment. Gary was every bit as anti-union as Frick, resisting unionization efforts in 1907, 1914, and 1919. Frick commented to Gary in 1914: "You had done your country a great and lasting service. I was glad to see you said that you would not treat with Gompers or with any other Union leaders who come to you as Union men, and that there would be no compromise — That's the stuff!"[12] These issues in 1907, 1914, and 1919 were essentially over the same issues that led to the Homestead Strike of 1892, chief among them the recognition of the union as the bargaining agent. It was always more about control than money per se. Gary resisted the organizing efforts of Samuel Gompers of the American Federated Labor Union, which took a more moderate approach than the early Amalgamated unions. Gompers, in particular, attacked United States Steel for its common use of the 12-hour day. Gompers did offer the workers full representation, as his union was considered a trade union versus a crafts union. A United States Steel Finance Committee subcommittee suggested about 25 percent of the workforce worked a 12-hour shift in 1912. It was 60 percent among the highly-paid employees of the blast furnaces, open hearths, and rolling mills. Elimination of the 12-hour day had public support, but both the steel manager and steelworker alike opposed it. In 1914, Gompers lacked the infrastructure to mount a successful strike against United States Steel. The individual steelworker stood to lose a third of his take-home pay. United States Steel estimated it would take an increase of 60,000 employees and increase production costs 15 percent.[13] The estimated cost would be over $4 million a year. Of course, this overlooked the productivity increases claimed by Bill Jones of Edgar Thomson Works in 1887.

Still, even Bill Jones hated the idea of unions. Frick was supported by the other capitalists, with the possible exception of William Dickson, in his resistance to unions among the steel masters. Even Corey, who went on to form an idealistic worker utopia at Midvale Steel, supported Frick and Gary in his opposition to unions. In his 1911 retirement speech, Corey summarized these aggregate feelings:

> If there has been any one subject which I been intensively interested, it is that of what I am pleased to call "free labor" as against so-called "union labor." The company in which I passed my early years of my business life had to face this question many times, and decided once and for all in 1892 that however beautiful in theory, as a matter of practical operation the intervention of any third party between a company and its employees could not be tolerated. No sane man will question the abstract right of the workmen to organize. It is a "condition," however, and not theory that confronts us. Until organized labor has demonstrated its ability to deal with economic problems in an enlightened and progressive spirit, and abandons its reactionary attitude, as indicated by its pernicious practices of restriction of output, dead level of wages regardless of efficiency, and the closed shop, we must deal with it as an hindrance to progress and steadfastly refuse to be hampered by its unreasonable demands.[14]

Gary or Frick could not have said it better. The approach does seem a bit self-serving; however, like Bill Jones, these men did find ways in their own minds to improve the nature of work.

Schwab's problem with the union was also part of Frick's: that, it destroyed ambition. Schwab defined his view in a 1901 testimony before Congress: "Under the labor-union system all members are reduced to a dead level of equality, and the wage scale largely is determined by the worth and capability of the cheapest workman, instead of the most capable and highest priced. This narrows opportunity, dulls ambition and gives no man a chance to rise."[15] Again Gary and Frick would heartily agree. What Frick, Schwab, and Gary were blinded to was the potential of the owners to abuse the workers. In many cases, the owners even used the union as an excuse not to improve conditions. In the long run, the union, like government regulation, would be needed as part of a system of checks and balances.

With Frick's support, Gary designed a major safety program at United States Steel in the 1910s. The safety program was a major investment of $400,000 in 1910 and $750,000 in 1916. The safety program, however, made good economic sense, with a rapid payback through reduced insurance and related medical costs. The safety program was a positive step, but it hardly addressed the overall problems of labor. The real problem with Frick, Carnegie, Gary, Schwab, Corey, and others is that they offered no alternative to the union other than a trust in the benevolence of the owners. Frick and most of these capitalists had been laborers, but they showed amazing blindness to the struggle of laborers at their factories. They had lost touch with their roots. They feared wealth would ruin their sons and daughters not realizing it had ruined *them*. They were not alone. Crafts unions had exhibited an elitist approach of their own, banning immigrants and unskilled laborers. Labor leaders of the time did not know how to deal with the breakdown of the crafts system with industrialization. The union had to develop the principle of solidarity. The workers were often at odds with the union movement over matters such as the 12-hour day. The government had no answers either. McKinley's labor-management political alliance broke down with the increase in size of the trusts, leaving politicians at a loss as to what to do. The workers themselves were torn with racism and their own type of class structure. Probably, the only real lights in the gloom of the period were Carnegie's plant manager, Bill Jones, in the 1880s and the union movement's Samuel Gompers, but again lasting solutions could not be built around any individual. The solution would, like the end of slavery, come slowly through many struggles.

Another roadblock to the evolution of the steelworkers' union was World War I, which created major labor shortages. The war had cut off immigration just as production had to be raised to new levels. United States Steel reacted by moving blacks into laborer positions and promoting unskilled immigrant labor into skilled positions. Recruiting stations for Pittsburgh plants were set up in Virginia, and for Chicago plants, the recruiting centers were in Mississippi and Louisiana. The war had actually improved upward mobility for Slav and Hungarian immigrants. The gap in union solidarity between the skilled and unskilled workers actually increased, which again weakened the union movement. Wages for the unskilled actually doubled as the mill tried to hold on to black laborers. Blacks actually tended to be more geographically and horizontally mobile than the immigrants. Turnover rate was as high as 50 percent. The problem of acceptance of the black workers was again with the older employees, who bordered on racist. Homestead again barely avoided a race riot in 1917.[16] Blacks numbered as high as 15 percent of United States Steel's Pittsburgh workforce up to 4,000 in 1917. Most of these blacks had started years prior as scabs; some even had roots to the Homestead Strike of 1892. Social ills such as segregation quickly arose. The internal union problems once again became a weakness. Still, after the war the union would once again mount a challenge in 1919.

Gary and United States Steel were complete victors in the Steel Strike of 1919 as Frick had been in 1892. The Strike of 1919 addressed the same issues as 1892 — union recognition, wages, and the eight-hour day. Like Frick in 1892, Gary refused to negotiate with the labor leader or his union, in this case, Samuel Gompers and the American Federation of Labor. The 1919 strike was national in scope, and at its peak reached 350,000 steelworkers on strike. The main issue turned out to be open shop versus closed shop, which required union representation. It is estimated that 90 percent of immigrant workers were involved, but the AFL was still basically organized around the crafts. The 1919 strike, at least, saw solidarity among the workforce. The union represented all ranks and levels. There was still violence, and twenty steelworkers died. Public reaction was mixed, as it had been in 1892. Support in the Pittsburgh district was weak. Interestingly, Frick's pick of Republican President Harding would put the final pressure on the United States Steel Finance Committee to establish the eight-hour day in 1923.

The dream of the original Homesteaders of a labor republic would never be realized, nor would Frick's dream of a union-free workplace. The shorter day and better working conditions did evolve through the many struggles. Employee benefits arose from some of the original paternalism of men such as Gary, Carnegie, Westinghouse, Heinz, and Dickson. It wasn't until the union dropped the crafts structure that it gained the necessary infrastructure to take on United States Steel. In 1936, eight presidents of the AFL–affiliated unions in heavy industry formed the Committee for Industrial Organization (CIO). The Committee was headed by John Lewis of the United Mine Workers, which had been the most successful industrial union. Within a year, the Steel Workers Organizing Committee (SWOC) was founded. On January 1, 1937, United States Steel accepted a one-year contract with the SWOC that included union recognition, the 40-hour work week, time and a half for overtime, holiday pay, a week's vacation and a $5 a day wage. Other industrialists saw United States Steel as selling out, and a national strike against the other companies raged in 1937. The strike reached a peak at Republic Steel's South Chicago Plant with 10 workers killed (seven shot in the back) and over fifty wounded by the police in one day, with a total of sixteen dead overall. Other plants in Ohio had men killed as well. It was this bloody strike (far bloodier than Homestead) that ended in the acceptance of the United Steel Workers union throughout the steel industry. Thus, in 1937, the first industrial union was fully developed.

The dream of the crafts union was not fully destroyed by technology or big corporations. The purest crafts, such as bricklaying, carpentry, and plumbing, did survive in the crafts system union. Even some new technology craftsmen, such as electricians, organized under a crafts system. In the construction and building industry today, one sees a workplace closely related to the old crafts lodges of the Amalgamated. And in these industries, the struggle between skilled and unskilled laborers and labor control of the workplace continues. In general, the struggle for open shops versus closed shops, one of the major premises of the Homestead Strike, continues to this very day. The battleground has moved to state and federal legislatures with right-to-work laws. Even the unionization process is again being debated, with the secret ballot issue at the forefront.

23. An Organizational Genius

Frick's corporate view brought Carnegie's various plants and operations together as a corporate operating unit. He tied plants together via a corporate railroad. Frick took vertical integration to its logical conclusion, adding railroads, limestone, iron ore mines, and shipping. He coordinated management between operating divisions, taking the company to more productivity gains. From 1892 to 1900, Carnegie Steel production went from 878,000 tons to 2,870,000 tons. Profits went from $4 million in 1892 to $40 million in 1900. Never before had an organization achieved such results. Frick also realized that the age of Carnegie's competitive advantage, survival of the fittest, and social Darwinism, was changing. Frick shared the vision of banker J.P. Morgan in that cooperation brought greater profits. The age of trusts was beginning. Bringing companies together was the expertise of Frick versus that of Carnegie, who preferred to beat competitors into submission. Frick had brought Duquesne Works, H.C. Frick Coke, and iron mines into the mix. No one in the Carnegie organization had the expertise of Frick in finance and investment. It was easy for Frick to buy into Morgan's idea of great industrial trusts. Morgan believed competition resulted in waste from so much time, money, and resources being consumed in competitive struggle.

Frick was the first CEO of a large American corporation, or at least the first CEO who had not been a founder. Frick learned much from the paternal founder, Andrew Carnegie, but he also developed a new role in business, the corporate executive. The CEO managed as a leader responsible to a corporate board. Clearly, Frick lacked the people skills of Bill Jones, Charles Schwab, and even Carnegie, but Frick more than anyone was the father of the modern corporation. Carnegie had grown his steel company with motivational genius, but it was Frick who enabled it to become the United States Steel Corporation. Frick mastered the necessary organization and communication networks needed to run a large corporation. People knew what Frick wanted and where he was coming from. Carnegie ran the business as an autocrat, like many founders and owners, while Frick ran it as a businessman. Carnegie was a paternal manager, while Frick was an organizational manager. For all his impersonal mannerisms, Frick was better suited to manage the huge corporation. It is unlikely that Carnegie could have been as successful in managing the massive corporation of United States Steel. Carnegie had a simple organizational view: he defined a mission of the most cost efficient steel company, hired highly motivated young managers, motivated them with stock and ownership, and have all report their efforts direct to him. Carnegie's "Board of Managers" was really a type of kingly court to supply measured advice when asked.

Frick had early on believed that a corporation would be the best framework for Carnegie Steel. Interestingly, Carnegie claimed his partners helped balance the management and opposed incorporation on that basis. In a letter to Frick, Carnegie noted: "Don't want anything to do with a corporation as long as I am in business— Partnership is only thing — no one man can manage well — every one needs the companionships of equals in business."[1] Of course, Carnegie seemed to exclude himself from this concept. In fact, a partnership with Carnegie in the majority allowed him to rule. A corporation would have formally limited Carnegie's ability to run Carnegie Steel. In effect, though Carnegie's collection of gifted and highly motivated managers made the system work, Carnegie Steel was an autocratic corporation.

Carnegie ran Carnegie Steel with all managers basically reporting to him. Carnegie saw no need for infrastructure and often short-circuited it. He loved to read the different views of his managers and then question them on the facts. Carnegie also loved to second-guess and override decisions. His style could frustrate many types of managers. Carnegie assigned secretaries, who took meeting minutes, to his key managers. The minutes were then sent to Carnegie in Pittsburgh or Scotland. Carnegie would send back his written "thoughts on minutes." Whenever Carnegie was in New York, a weekly report from all his superintendents was to be on his desk Monday morning. As Carnegie spent more time in Scotland, he demanded even more in the minutes. For the Board of Managers, he demanded that individual votes be recorded in the minutes. He even went as far as to have the reason for each vote recorded.[2] This became more important to Carnegie as Frick became more independent as a general manager. The managers under Carnegie would meet infrequently to discuss key issues among themselves, but Frick tried to foster more sharing versus the sort of inter-department competition Carnegie favored.

This over-control was Carnegie's weakness, and Frick's organizational integration was his strength in building a corporation. Frick formalized meetings and reports. It necessitated that every superintendent had a male secretary. Superintendents often would meet on Saturdays once a month with their managers to go over the week and make the written report to Carnegie. Carnegie's type of over-managing is one of the limiting factors often in the growth of American companies. Frick mandated the Board of Managers meet every Tuesday over lunch. Superintendents were to meet every Saturday at noon. Frick asked that this meeting include all department and ancillary operations. Frick would ultimately bring this highly effective reporting system into the corporate system and chain of command. Frick eliminated internal competition, which had plagued Carnegie's organizations for years, since he realized that success depended on internal cooperation. Frick proved brilliant at adopting the strengths of the organization and modifying the weaknesses. He transformed the Carnegie system into a corporate structure and created an organizational revolution. The transition from a company to a corporation requires a special individual who is as critical as the company founder, and Frick was to play that role. In the late 1890s and early 1900s, a new breed of corporate managers arose to make these transitions. Men like Howard Heinz at H.J. Heinz performed these critical transitions. Frick, however, was again unique in that he was not part of the founder's family.

In key events such as the Homestead Strike, Carnegie managed with letters and telegrams to managers and partners. He respected no chain of command. Often Carnegie would ask the same question to different managers to try to discern the truth. Carnegie could be harsh in his responses and had a low tolerance for major failures. Carnegie also required absolute loyalty. Carnegie's routine of going to Scotland for part of the year actually helped the company to grow. When Carnegie was in his Pittsburgh office, he often required managers to attend weekly. In the late 1870s and early 1880s, Carnegie received a daily report and often wanted his managers to hand-deliver it in the evening. In the 1880s, this practice angered Carnegie's brilliant plant manager, who had to make a ten-mile trolley or carriage ride from Braddock to Pittsburgh. Jones assigned a messenger in Charles Schwab.[3] As the company grew under Frick's management, Frick tried to filter these endless reports to Carnegie and tried for a single corporate report. Frick would often make humorous comments about these notes at meetings. Under Carnegie, these operating meetings and reports were for Carnegie's information rather than improving the functioning of the company.

Like all transitions, it was a struggle for Frick. Many of the partners favored Frick's style and respected his business expertise over that of Carnegie. Frick's banking, financial, and investment expertise clearly stood out. Frick and Carnegie often had competing sources of information. For example, at Homestead, Carnegie counted on Schwab and Corey, while Frick heard from Leishman and Lovejoy. This is not uncommon in such transitions, and Frick handled it extremely well. He was generally slow to anger with Carnegie's meddling. Frick was very aware of the situation and built structure around the problems. Carnegie's approach often restricted his managers because they wanted to please him. Frick, on the other hand, allowed his managers more latitude to act while getting feedback in a much more organized manner. Similarly, Carnegie's objectives were not clear at times, while Frick made his objectives part of the organization. Frick had grown up with the corporation, and while Carnegie founded the seed company, it is doubtful Carnegie could have successfully managed the huge United States Steel Corporation.

Frick also represented a more restrained management style. Frick, unlike Carnegie, was not interested in scapegoats or blame, but in problem solving. Frick refused to go public with problems or internal matters, while Carnegie used them as a carrot and stick. While tough and temperamental, Frick refrained from backstabbing and gossip. He earned a type of trust that Carnegie could not. Frick knew how to keep communications confidential. Frick was rarely liked on a personal level, but found great respect on a business level. As the "Boys of Braddock" dug their own holes at United States Steel, they often came to Frick for advice, knowing they could trust him.

While Carnegie was autocratic in his decision-making, Frick used his organization to make decisions, and this heralded the corporate approach of today. Frick, when making a decision, would assign an individual to study and report. This approach resulted in the highly successful Union Railway and the purchase of Duquesne Works. Frick improved on the idea by using a study committee to look at key decisions. When Jay Moore approached Frick in 1898 about selling land to Moore at Conneaut for blast furnaces, Frick assigned his furnace expert, James Gayley, to a study committee. Frick asked the committee to answer the question: "Can we afford to sell land for the use of two furnaces without interfering with our own operations at Conneaut?"[4] This committee approach to decision-making was new in the 1890s. Most companies were autocratic, and Carnegie managed like a king with a court of partners. Carnegie made the decisions, but Frick was not afraid to use corporate expertise to make the best decision. This corporate decision-making was the root of Frick's success. Another Frick study had correctly foreseen the site of Sparrows Point, Maryland, as a seaport integrated mill, although Carnegie refused to hear of it. Charles Schwab at Bethlehem Steel would build the nation's largest integrated mill there. Frick's organizational methodology was always his true genius.

Carnegie's decision-making was based on bringing in knowledgeable partners from the operating ranks such as Schwab, Gayley, and Peacock. The only problem was that it was a court of advisors: the king made the decision. This approach worked well when Carnegie Steel was in the entrepreneurial and growth phase. It allowed Carnegie to move fast and not get bogged down in debates. It came with high risk and Carnegie himself often got stuck on his own indecisiveness. Frick's committee or study approach slowed things down, but it had become a necessary step in organizations of such size. It increased the precision and accuracy of the decision, and reduced the risk of a big mistake. Corporate or multi-plant management created a new type of executive who was removed from actual plant operations, and hands-on knowledge was reduced. In the 1890s, Frick was in charge of huge diversified mills at Braddock, Homestead, and Duquesne, as well as Union Railway, coke plants, and a dozen smaller finishing operations. Purchasing operations were being done on a scale never seen in the history of the world. The combined tonnage of materials transported exceeded that of all of American industry. The partnership was the combination of the world's largest transportation, steel, and coke companies. Processing on orders often had to be coordinated through several plants. This was beyond the control of one man or even a group of men. Many of Carnegie's boys disliked the distribution of control among departments and committees; they preferred the autocratic control.

To Schwab's horror, United States Steel was modeled after Frick's organizational setup. Robert Hessen summarized Schwab's disappointment with United States Steel Corporation's bylaws:

> Schwab was not satisfied with his position in the corporate hierarchy. He expected that he would have undivided authority—that he could be "an autocrat." He believed that his experience as a "practical steelman" should have given him preeminence over men whose training or background had been in law or finance. Yet the U.S. Steel Corporation's structure was deliberately arranged so that no one individual could have undisputed authority. It was to be a business whose policies were made by committees of experts

Henry Clay Frick in his 50s (courtesy Carnegie Library of Pittsburgh).

in the areas of finance and operations. These committees, in turn, were subordinate to the Board of Directors. Ultimate power rested with the board, whose twenty-four members, meeting monthly, were responsible for electing the officers of the corporation, the members of the Executive and Finance committee, and the officers of the subsidiary companies within the subsidiary companies within the corporation.[5]

Carnegie men were trained to be autocrats with their underlings, and loyal lieutenants of their superiors. Committee structure was foreign to them.

In fairness, the committee system at United States Steel had its failures. It was slow to develop new technologies because of the committee system.[6] Part of the problem was that Frick preferred to use three-man committees and the individual project manager, whereas United States Steel tended to use too-large committees like those in Rockefeller's Standard Oil. Frick, like Carnegie, didn't believe in pioneering, and the committee system was also not good at it. In the early days of United States Steel, the corporation was behind in structural steel production. This was a growth market, as America was building skyscrapers and bridges. The United States Steel mills were at a technological disadvantage to those of Jones & Laughlin and Bethlehem Steel. United States Steel failed to get the needed equipment through the committee system. Frick, however, did try to buy Jones & Laughlin for $30 million but was turned down. Technology for Frick was a financial problem as much as an operating one. He had never built a coke oven but ended up running over 10,000. Frick saw advancing technology as the role of entrepreneurs, not large corporations. He would buy the technology once it was fully proven. Frick's view seems to have been proven over the years, that is, large corporations are inefficient at developing technology, and it is work done best by entrepreneurs. While the corporate committee system lacked entrepreneurial drive, it made up for it in process enhancement.

Frick's committee approach was particularly well suited for the transition years of United

States Steel, which in 1901 was an amalgamation of factories that had functioned as separate units for years. The committee system did lend itself to process improvement through information sharing. Besides the infrastructure committees, technical and department committees were formed to share operating practices and improvements. There were committees for the open hearths, blast furnaces, blooming mills, rolling mills, wire production, sheet production, and many others. These quarterly operating committees brought operating department managers together to share improvements and solve problems. Gary estimated a 10 percent savings by committees comparing practices. It was, however, a struggle for the old Carnegie managers. Committees tended to be well grounded in cost accounting. Once technology was proven, Carnegie moved rapidly to install it. Frick's committee approach slowed this; in fact, H.C. Frick Company was one of the last to convert to by-product coke furnaces, deciding to run out the beehives until they were unprofitable. When Frick became the key member of the Finance Committee, he further improved the committee system. Frick designed special committees or project teams of diversified knowledge to tackle special jobs. The special committee on Gary Works suggested, planned, and implemented the building in less than a year. This special committee reported directly to the decision maker, which was the practice Frick had used at Carnegie Steel. The special committee approach allowed for faster work inside the corporate model. This type of matrix management is common today, but was new to large corporations of Frick's day.

Frick and United States Steel's management was quick to adopt the scientific management practices of Fredrick Taylor. These analysis-driven, cost-based principles came into direct conflict with the "drive system" of Carnegie and Schwab. Taylor himself described the Carnegie/Schwab system thus: "Each department in command of a separate individual, who ... is allowed to use practically whatever methods of managing the men he sees fit, the only check upon this man being that if he fails to make good in earning money, at the end of the year his head comes off. Under his plan you will necessarily have, in the same works, several kinds of management."[7] There was no question that the committee style reduced corporate pressure on managers.

As revolutionary as Frick's approach was to the top of the organization, it was even more revolutionary at the bottom. The most overlooked reason for Frick's struggle with the unions was his quest to put management at the level of base decisions. The crafts coal miner system required the subcontracting of hundreds of mining groups. These master miners often were wasteful internally. Frick had fought for the development of a foreman to coordinate strategic goals of the company. Ultimately, he was able to bring the workers under the supervision of a foreman. The efficiency and success of the foreman at planning and coordination made it a natural for application in Carnegie Steel. The Amalgamated Union of Carnegie Steel was also a crafts union and had resisted the use of company foremen. One of the consequences of the Homestead Strike was the strengthening of the foreman position. Frick's efforts after the strike to hire replacements showed him that the employment and human resources function needed to be a department.

The size of Homestead created the need for other department-level managers. Frick's struggle with Carnegie's "tonnage driven" men pointed to the need for production planning and quality control. Carnegie's goal and singular management style created huge bottlenecks in large corporations. Every manager was out to set a tonnage record in his area, picking orders that could increase tonnage throughput. This was often at the expense of other operating departments, other customers, and the overall corporation. Frick was one of the first to see and correct this weakness in Carnegie Steel. Frick realized that large corporations had other conflicts such as quality and product requirements. Frick used a type of product manager to coordinate products such as armor through the operations. Carnegie was blind to these weaknesses, viewing the company as his little enterprise. Frick allowed Carnegie Steel to transition from a "family" company to a large corporation and become a model for American business. Frick saw that a corporation was more than a large company; it was an entity of its own. Corporations required a new system for command and control. Frick's friend Philander Knox even brought the Frick system to the State Department. Knox, as Secretary of State, reorganized the department on a divisional basis, and developed a merit bonus system.

More so than any position, Frick created the model for a corporate executive. Frick had a basic knowledge of business's accounting level, that of credits and debits, as well as front-line operating experience at the mines. He, like Carnegie, loved the science of cost accounting. He had built a company from the bottom up, as had Carnegie. Frick's finance and investment experience was beyond that of even Carnegie. This unique combination of accounting, operating, and finance helped to define the skill set for future executives. Frick also had the correct temperament for an executive. An executive, more than other managers, needs to delegate tasks and study conflicting views. An executive walks a tightrope of needing to understand the operation and needing to stand back and look at it. The executive moves from the tactical life of an operating manager to the strategic one of a corporate manager. Frick learned that decisions must to be considered in their total effect on the whole organization. Unfortunately, Frick brought coldness to the corporate position, which seems to have been an early model for executives as well. The cold, calculating approach is what men like Rockefeller admired in Frick. This approach, of course, showed its weakness when dealing with unions and other managers. Charles Schwab found a way to merge the best of Frick and Carnegie in his management style.

More than anyone, Frick argued for cooperation within the old Carnegie partnership. Carnegie's style of promoting competition did have a weakness: cooperation between departments and plants was reduced as superintendents fought for new and better records to report to Carnegie. Carnegie Steel had grown into a mix of mills, which needed coordination more than competition. The bigger problem would always be the giant operation at Homestead. After the Homestead strike and the armor issue, Frick brought in D.R. Dillon to act as a corporate troubleshooter. Dillon had experience at Union Mills and Beaver Falls. His role would be to review every department and make recommendations on efficiency, whether human or mechanical. Dillon served several purposes. As a "Carnegie" insider, his review would have some credibility. Dillon's review served notice that his goals and his power were on a level with Carnegie's. The timing was right, since Schwab, who normally could count on going directly to Carnegie, was in a bit of a weakened position after the armor scandal. Schwab was forced to become a loyal lieutenant, although he never personally took to Frick. Schwab learned from Frick the corporate view, which served him well in later life as president of United States Steel and Bethlehem Steel.

Carnegie had created a simplified mission of cutting costs, boosting throughput time, and increasing production. This simplistic mission served Carnegie well in the building of Carnegie Steel. Carnegie believed he knew how to make steel and cared little for government or customer imposed specifications. Carnegie's philosophy led to the prominence of tonnage men such as Bill Jones, Charles Schwab, and the Boys of Braddock. The huge Homestead works was the first sign of a problem. The market for things like high-quality steel had changed to one that required staff functions such as quality control. The Carnegie tonnage system had problems integrating other priorities such as quality and delivery. Corey, for example, "whose chief interest was in making tonnage records rather than in making deliveries to the customers in accordance with contracts ... would leaf through order books, tearing out those orders on which his department could roll the largest quantity of steel possible. Paying little or no attention to promised delivery dates."[8] The result was a plethora of missed deliveries. The logic of rolling large orders for large customers was disappearing. Customers were increasing in number and they deserved attention.

Frick proved his ability to organize and set customer-oriented production after the armor scandal review by Dillon. Frick's organization did come through with the making of better armor at Homestead, and Homestead armor would be credited with America's victory in the Spanish-American War in 1898. Some limited armor plates were produced to arm the Navy in 1897. Admiral Dewey and the Homestead-armored American fleet engaged the Spanish at Manila Bay on May 1, 1998. Within five hours every Spanish ship was sunk and 381 Spaniards killed. The victory was a triumph of America's might, with American steel-armored ships cutting down the Spanish wooden ones. On May 19, the other Spanish fleet reached Santiago, Cuba. Here the Americans blockaded them as they prepared to mount a land attack on Cuba. The American troops landed on June 30 and proceeded on two fronts. The Americans quickly won two battles, and Teddy Roosevelt (who had just resigned as Secretary of the Navy) and his volunteers the "Rough Riders" made a name for themselves. The Spanish fleet, sensing defeat, made a run for it on July 3. The American fleet quickly engaged and destroyed every Spanish ship, killing 474 Spanish. The Spanish Army surrendered on July 17 in Cuba, followed by Guam Island and Wake Island in the Pacific. Insurgents took Manila in late July and the war was over. Homestead's 110-inch plate mill was bathed in fame. Frick wanted to move forward with the production of true nickel steel armor, believing it would be a very large and profitable market.

The problem of missed deliveries became obvious to Dillon in his review. Dillon reported to Frick that poor quality had a secondary effect of missed deliveries. The tonnage managers of Braddock, like Corey, were single-minded. In addition, meeting customer orders would require coordination between departments on a new level. An order needed to be pulled and managed through the operation. The result was the development of something very different. It was the beginning of the "shipping and order department" that would be known today as "production planning." Frick brought in Hampden Tener to act as coordinator of customer deliveries. Tener had great organizational planning skills and started a series of weekly planning meetings to coordinate departments and rolling mills with the customer deliveries. Unfortunately, Frick underestimated the organizational resistance of the Schwab and the "Boys." Tener was in what we call today a staff position and lacked the authority over the powerful mill superintendents. It was no surprise that Tener had a nervous breakdown. Frick and Schwab worked together for a better solution. Still, as long as Carnegie was in the picture, many men like Schwab had two masters, but Frick was gaining authority in the organization to achieve results.

William Dickson, who had been serving as Tener's assistant, was made head of the shipping and order department. Dickson was the perfect man to make things work. He was considered one of the new and younger "Boys of Braddock," although he had come up through the clerical side of the business. Dickson was another Duff's College-trained accountant, which Frick saw as a plus. Dickson had family ties to Corey and the Mellon family, which had old ties to Frick. Dickson's father had been a partner of the Coreys and Mellons in Braddock coal mining. Dickson lived in Swissvale, across the Monongahela River from Homestead. He used a small rowboat to get to work in Homestead. Dickson, who had labored at low levels in the mill before moving into the clerical side, was the perfect fit for the evolving corporation. Like Frick, he had taken accounting courses at Duff's College and took readily to Frick's cost accounting style. Dickson worked with the mill superintendents to "compromise between mill efficiency and contract obligations."[9] Dickson would evolve into one of the steel industry's most unusual managers, pioneering production planning, safety programs, employee relations, profit-sharing, and union recognition.

24. A Final Look

After years of research into Henry Clay Frick, one is left at the beginning. Just who was Frick really? The bias of the press after 1889 makes it difficult to test any thesis. Carnegie's public relations machine has remolded history to make Frick all that was wrong in the steel and coal industry. Frick never answered critics in private or public. He avoided the press and the printing of personal stories. The personal depression following the death of his daughter Martha and the Homestead Strike caused him to withdraw even further. The Carnegie Veterans' Association, which existed to promote the legend of Carnegie Steel, continued into the 1930s to color Frick's legacy. Most of the Carnegie Veterans never understood Frick. The popular Charles Schwab summarized Frick to an interviewer in the 1930s: "No man on earth could get close to him or fathom him.... He seemed more like a machine, without emotion or impulses. Absolutely cold-blooded. He had good foresight and was an excellent bargainer.... His assets were that he was a thinking machine, methodical as a comptometer, accurate, cutting straight to the point ... the most methodical thinking machine I have ever known."[1] John D. Rockefeller said he had the soul of a bookkeeper. He seemed to earn money like many pursue athletic awards. After Homestead, the unions looked upon him as a murderer and even a monster, but Homestead took on its own political mythology. Often Frick's charity, philanthropy, and achievements were footnoted by his involvement at Homestead by the press.

Homestead was a true political football. It was far from America's bloodiest strike; in fact, mine strikes within 100 miles of Homestead were bloodier but received less than a paragraph of newspaper print. The union at Homestead represented only a handful of the best-paid workers at the works. Homestead, unlike other strikes, had a press and publicity buildup to it, as politicians saw it as an opportunity to promote various issues. The tariff was one of the underlying issues. Homestead offered the Democrats an opportunity to make inroads into the Republican labor vote. Frick, Carnegie, and others made plenty of mistakes, although Frick's have been highlighted. Frick's stands were too strong and this cornered him. The theme had been developed in the press months ahead of time, and the details were made to fit. Frick lacked the people skills to negotiate with union leaders, and that was a problem. His set of beliefs about unions was shared by most managers of the time. It was a hardness born of the times, not in Frick the man. Even the best of managers such as Bill Jones, Charles Schwab, George Westinghouse, and H.J. Heinz cared little for unions of the time. Still, Frick's hardness created the conditions for the worst to happen. Frick was not an operations manager but would find his voice as a corporate executive.

The Homestead Strike, an active Carnegie public relations machine, and Frick's own shyness and coldness have molded much of Frick's legacy with the public. The famous business writer, B.C. Forbes, explained in 1917: "Frick is imperfectly understood, largely because he has had neither faculty nor inclination for the bringing of himself and his achievements to public notice."[2] Even Frick's giving approached that of Carnegie, but lacked the publicity of Carnegie's. Frick's hatred of unions was typical of most Victorian managers, and most average Americans were split between favorable and unfavorable views about unions. The Carnegie effort to blame Frick for Homestead has been successful, but Carnegie is just as much to blame. As late as 1914, Carnegie was trying to personally rewrite history by enlisting William

Dickson to write a favorable history of the Frick feud.[3] The Carnegie Veterans' Association, which excluded Frick, would meet into the 1930s and remained a powerful Carnegie spin machine. On Frick's death, Carnegie loyalist William Dickson and Secretary of the Carnegie Veterans wrote this stinging comment:

> A man I never admired. He was a cold taskmaster and was primarily responsible for the twelve-hour day and the seven-day week in the Carnegie Steel Company and United States Steel Mills. He will no doubt leave a large fortune. In my opinion the manner in which a man makes his money is more important to his fellows than the manner in which he disposes of it. He debased his fellow men in acquiring of his money.[4]

In fact, both the twelve-hour day and seven-day week were always industry-wide, not unique to United States Steel or Frick. Dickson would later say about the same for Carnegie: "The methods by which it was acquired were not so commendable, especially his attitude toward labor, as shown by the twelve-hour day and seven-day week in his mills."

In retrospect, Carnegie and Frick both blundered at Homestead. Frick's approach to Homestead would have been taken by most Victorian managers, who were strongly anti-union. Even the American public at the time was anti-union (especially the crafts unions); this was particularly true of German immigrants. Frick must be seen as a man of the times. Most business leaders, liberal and conservative, not only respected Frick but also believed him to be ethical. Frick avoided attacking opponents in the press or personally. Frick saw himself as a capitalist knight, and battles were on the field, not in the castle. Frick even moderated his views on unionization under the guidance of Judge Gary. Still, labor would never relent on their view of him as a type of capitalistic monster, and he became the poster child for union oppression by capitalists. But in reality, the Frick model of labor-capital relationships remains to this day, though both the nature of the union and management attitudes have evolved.

Strikes today remain a type of serious game that have the potential for violence. The labor-capital relationship in a democracy is a necessary argument over money. In 1904, Schwab said it best: "It has always seemed to me a curious thing that people should talk about 'conflict' between capital and labor. There is no conflict. It is human nature to want money. Capital wants money, so does labor. Where you see men, either as individuals or in groups, wanting more money, that's not conflict. The interests are identical."[5] Schwab and Frick were right that in a democracy capitalists and laborers share a mutual interest. The only difference today is that both sides are a little more responsible. Government's role has expanded to that of mediator. This is much different from socialist countries, where the relationship is a struggle on the level of good and evil. In many ways, writers at the time of the Homestead Strike elevated it to the level of such a battle between good and evil.

As a representation of evil, Frick could easily be accepted if it were not for his family and personal life. It is here that we seem to have a Jekyll and Hyde. He had a personal side that didn't match the caricature of an industrial monster. He was not the freespending party-goer like many of the beloved "robber barons." He seemed to live as a simple family provider, but on a much wealthier scale. Life consisted of work and family, and money was merely the measure of success in work and providing the best possible life for his family. He was a loving father and family man, who felt the suffering of his young daughter. He was a man who was touched by the suffering of children throughout his life, regardless of their status or nationality. Every donation he gave to charity was written on a check that had the image of his lost daughter.[6] He preferred to work hard and return home, eat a family dinner, play with the kids, study business for the next day, and go to bed early. Frick gave to charity anonymously, according to a Victorian code of giving. Martha Frick Symington Sanger has done a wonderful job in looking for Frick's soul in his life's passion of collecting paintings. For Frick his legacy was his art collection, and therefore, it must tell us much about the man. Certainly, the love of his daughter and the pain of her loss are reflected in his art, even to the untrained analyst.

To view Frick as a cold tyrant and enemy of the little guy would also be a mistake, even though his charity and philosophy may seem misguided. While many said he never did enough for the strikers of Homestead, his record of those who died on management's side was much different. He often helped the families of his fallen management employees. These were the deaths that no one remembered. In 1894, a gang of strikers killed his chief engineer, Joe Paddock. In 1916, Frick wrote a letter to the president of United States Steel to hire Paddock's son: "The son of Mr. J.H. Paddock, who was formerly in the employ of Frick Coke Company and lost his life during the strike in the coke region many years ago in defending the property of the Company. I should like very much if you could place him somewhere. He will tell you what he is fitted for and what he would like."[7] He continued to help the social efforts of his old friend Father Lambing in the coal fields.

In the workplace, he hired without discrimination, though he did so, many argue, for the wrong reasons. He moved Hungarians and Slavs into permanent jobs based on their willingness to work at a time when Hungarians, Slavs, and blacks were banned from entrance into the union based on their ethnicity. The union would not even allow them to be common day laborers. Frick was one of the first to move Irish Catholics into mining management. The price of labor was his only guide. In business, he was tough but always fair and above board. In a 1905 article about Frick's being selected to clean up the mess at the Equitable Life Assurance Society, the following was said about him:

> Mr. Frick is scrupulously honest. He would not pick a man's pocket nor attack a safe with jimmy or nitro-glycerin. He plays the game of business fair; if loaded dice are permissible, why, he didn't make the rules. If some have been burned as he sped through the milky way of money getting, it was not his will.... Business is his passion, floriculture his pleasure and the family his pride. With the first he permits nothing to interfere; he is inexorable. Withal, he is suave and of kindly manner, repressing his feelings usually, though sometimes exulting immeasurably over the driving of a particularly profitable bargain.[8]

So what can be added to the descriptions of so many? Frick personally was a workaholic and an overachiever. In many ways, men like Carnegie and J.P. Morgan exploited these weaknesses of Frick. He had only one measure of success and progress towards his goals, and that was money. Still, even with his expensive collecting, he did not care for opulence. Fame and public approval meant nothing to him. He was more driven than ruthless. His problem with unions was more an issue of control than money. He was a true believer in American capitalism and a nationalist. Capitalism was not a political philosophy, as it was for Carnegie, but an economic way of life. Frick never tried to justify capitalism on a spiritual level, as did Carnegie. Frick saw it as the preferred economic policy. While extremely private in his religious views, Frick saw his wealth as a blessing from God for hard work, whereas Carnegie saw wealth as a Darwinian personal triumph.

As a pure capitalist and businessman, Frick had many supporters and few detractors. Over the years, Carnegie had nothing but praise and depended on his investment and organizational advice. Schwab, who disliked Frick's cold approach, felt he was a man who could be trusted, as did several American presidents. When the Carnegie boys got in trouble in United States Steel, they often went to Frick for advice. They could trust Frick and expect confidentiality. What was entrusted to Frick stayed with Frick. Frick came to respect Gary, and Gary respected Frick. Morgan had the utmost respect for Frick, as did John D. Rockefeller. Frick was always tough, but he played by the rules, as they existed at the time. When unethical behavior was involved, as with Hyde in the Equitable case, Frick took a strong stand. He never went to the press to use the politics of personal destruction. His coldness and shyness allowed him to avoid participating in gossip and was part of the trust many found in him.

Frick was best described as the quintessential capitalist, and to a large degree, Frick defined the very nature of American capitalism. Frick made his money through stock, bonds, and real estate investments. His biggest investments were in railroads, banks, coal companies, steel companies, and Pittsburgh real estate. More than any other capitalist, Frick expounded and defended property rights, which is the root of capitalism. He had a deep hatred of the very concept of socialism. He saw almost no role for government except for the most meager regulation. Frick even opposed any type of government takeover during wartime. As to business, he saw no limit in its size, believing, like J.P. Morgan, that efficiency was gained through size and cooperation. Frick served on over thirty corporate boards, though these were reduced by the Clayton Act, which limited interlocking directorships between the railroads and manufacturing. Frick, who saw nothing wrong with cooperative deals between companies, fought hard against such legislation by the progressives. He had fought antitrust legislation for decades. In Frick's defense, he was one of the more responsible board members of the period. In wartime Frick showed patriotism beyond any desire to profit.

Frick never saw himself as anything other than a capitalist. He saw his generous giving as a personal responsibility that he had learned in the *McGuffey Readers* of his youth. He did not see giving as necessary or a requirement of capitalism. Gary eulogized Frick on his death: "He was unusually generous in his benefactions, contributing hundreds of thousands, and even millions, for the benefit of others, although his liberality was but little known. He disliked publicity and abhorred ostentation."[9] His views on unions and labor were typical of most American industrialists of the time. His cold demeanor led him into problems early in his career. Homestead was one of those mistakes; but Frick, while regretting the loss of life, never regretted his position against the Amalgamated Union. He never tried to explain himself in the press. He was hardheaded and tough in business, but in his personal life he was big-hearted. He always played by the rules in his business dealing, and enemies admired him for that. He was a private family man who lived well but was not drawn to the spectacle of Gilded Age parties and spending. The lifelong defense of him by his daughter was a testimony to his being a loving father. He believed that capitalism was a natural part of America, but his capitalism ended at the American shore. He put America and American industry above foreign involvement.

Frick's role in the formation, structure, and growth of United States Steel is clearly understated by history. Henry Clay Frick was the link pin that closed the deal between Morgan and Rockefeller in the formation of United States Steel. Frick's meeting with Morgan in 1905 was the critical event that saved the corporation from internal and financial collapse. Frick, more than Morgan, Gary, Schwab, or others, left his signature of the infrastructure of America's first super corporation. Frick created a model for the corporate executives, production planning departments, committee management, and corporate cooperation.

Frick's strongest belief after American capitalism was the need for education for all. Most of his giving was for education. With education, Frick believed it should be inspirational versus merely steeped in facts. This had been his own experience with the *McGuffey Readers*. In a letter to Princeton in 1916 he stated:

> The fact that the college system is being called into question is an indication of some inherent weakness in it; and I have long felt myself in agreement with William George Jordan, the author of *Mental Training, a Remedy for Education*, who, in this and other writings, holds that the weakness of our whole system of education, including that given in colleges, is based on information, not inspiration.[10]

Yet, Frick never put any strings on his giving, nor did he try to force his views on anyone through charity.

Finally, the aspect of Frick the patriot cannot be overlooked. His giving and personal sacrifice during the war were amazing. He poured millions into the war effort and into helping wounded soldiers. He donated ambulances and armored cars to the army. He was proud of his daughter Helen's efforts as a nurse and volunteer. Frick opposed any profiteering during the war. Where other capitalists twisted the arms of their workers to buy war bonds, Frick led by example, purchasing millions in bonds. Frick was active in bringing the price of steel down to help the war effort. He gave money to honor the memory of soldiers from his birthplace of Westmoreland County. Biographer Harvey noted: "In point of fact, the appraisal of Mr. Frick's estate following his death showed that his fortune shrank many millions between the beginning and the ending of the war of the United States against the Central Powers of Europe."[11]

Frick exhibited the complexities in all of us. He had biases, fears, soft spots, and passions. He made mistakes. He lived well but demonstrated a responsibility in the use of his wealth. Wealth did not corrupt him. He loved his family, friends, and country. Very few men have given so much of their wealth to good causes. To the end, it is best to give him the benefit of the doubt, as his hometown paper did on his death:

> The name of Henry Clay Frick stands very near the top of the list of builders of America.... He worked long hours. His conception of life he expressed in terms of work. The difference between him and many thousands of other men ... was that as he labored he dreamed. The humdrum years of his modest toil were illumined by the light that has led every great doer of the world's work. His dreams took the form and substance in vast structures of steel, in long lines of rails, in roaring furnaces fed by an improved fuel, in one of the most notable art collections the world ever saw. There are some things that Frick did that other men would have done otherwise or left undone. But, as a great constructive personality his name is destined to perpetuated in the amazing annals of America's material development.[12]

Chapter Notes

A Technical Note

1. Jules Verne, *Begum's Millions* (Middletown: Wesleyan University Press, 2005), pp. 56–57.

Introduction

1. Samuel A. Schreiner Jr., *Henry Clay Frick: The Gospel of Greed* (New York: St. Martin's, 1995).
2. Mammon is the devil of greed, one of the seven deadly sins.
3. *New York Times*, October 4, 1915.
4. Thomas Cochran and William Miller, *The Age of Enterprise* (New York: Harper & Row, 1942), p. 12.
5. David McCullough, *The Johnstown Flood* (New York: Touchstone, 1968), p. 256.
6. Martha Frick Symington Sanger, *Henry Clay Frick: An Intimate Portrait* (New York: Abbeville, 1998).

Chapter 1

1. George Harvey, *Henry Clay Frick: The Man* (Privately printed, 1938).
2. Charles F. Jenkins, *Guide to Historic Germantown* (Germantown Historical Society, 1904).
3. Carl Bridenbaugh, *The Colonial Craftsman* (New York: Dover, 1990), p. 119.
4. Herbert Casson, *The Romance of Steel: The Story of a Thousand Millionaires* (New York: A.S. Barnes, 1907).

Chapter 2

1. Harvey, *Henry Clay Frick*.
2. Mary O'Hara, "My Father, Henry Clay Frick, by Helen Clay Frick," *Pittsburgh Press*, August 1959.
3. Lewis Mumford, *Techniques and Civilization* (New York: Harvest, 1962), p. 23.
4. Also called Harry, a common nickname for Henry.

Chapter 3

1. Carmen DiCiccio, *Coal and Coke in Pennsylvania* (Harrisburg: Pennsylvania Historical Commission, 1996), p. 19.
2. Anthracite coal was also known as mineral coke.

Chapter 4

1. Kenneth Warren, *Triumphant Capitalism* (Pittsburgh: University of Pittsburgh Press, 1996), p. 12.

2. David Cannadine, *Mellon: An American Life* (New York: Alfred A. Knopf, 2006), p.28
3. Henry Oliver Evans, *Iron Pioneer: Henry W. Oliver* (New York: E.P. Dutton, 1942), p. 123.
4. Dod or Dodd is a Scotch nickname for George, which Carnegie used.
5. Andrew Carnegie, *The Autobiography of Andrew Carnegie* (Boston: Northeastern University Press, 1986), p. 211.
6. "Defender of a Memory," *New York Times*, May 26, 1967.
7. Harvey, p. 69.

Chapter 5

1. Paul Krause, *The Battle for Homestead 1880–1892* (Pittsburgh: University of Pittsburgh Press, 1992), p. 103.
2. Joseph Rayback, *The History of American Labor* (New York: Macmillan, 1959), p. 135.
3. Krause, p. 158.

Chapter 6

1. McCullough, p. 61.
2. B.J. Hendrick, *The Life of Andrew Carnegie* (New York: Doubleday, 1932).
3. Warren, p. 26.
4. *Pittsburgh Gazette*, December 16, 1881, p. 4.
5. Letter, Andrew Carnegie to H.C. Frick, January 6, 1882, Carnegie Papers.
6. Letter, Andrew Carnegie to Robert Garrett, December 28, 1881, Carnegie Papers; Warren.
7. Krause, p. 175.
8. Sanger, p. 87.

Chapter 7

1. Robert C. Alberts, *Good Provider* (Boston: Houghton Mifflin, 1973), p. 63.
2. David Nasaw, *Andrew Carnegie* (New York: Penguin Press, 2006), p. 248.
3. Sanger, p. 89.
4. Harvey, p. 80.
5. Dan Rottenberg, *In The Kingdom of Coal* (New York: Routledge, 2003), p. 77.
6. Lane S. Hart, *Annual Report of the Secretary of Internal Affairs* (Harrisburg: State of Pennsylvania, 1884), pp. 337–338.
7. Ibid.
8. Sanger, p. 91.

Chapter 8

1. Joanne Reitano, *The Tariff Question in the Glided Age* (University Park: Pennsylvania State University Press, 1994), p. 76.
2. Andrew Carnegie, "An Employer's View of the Labor Question," *Forum Magazine* (April 1886), p. 20.
3. Ibid.
4. DiCiccio, p. 81.
5. Krause, p. 217.
6. Krause, p. 222.
7. *National Labor Tribune*, April 14, 1888.
8. John Fitch, *The Steel Worker* (Pittsburgh: University of Pittsburgh Press, 1989), p. 117.
9. Mark Summers, *Party Games* (Chapel Hill: University of North Carolina Press, 2004), p. 217.

Chapter 9

1. In 1917 Helen changed her name to Helen Clay Frick.
2. Joseph Frazier Wall, *Andrew Carnegie* (Pittsburgh: University of Pittsburgh Press, 1970), p. 497.
3. Krause, p. 266.
4. Nasaw, p. 341.
5. Harvey, p. 99.
6. *Social Mirror of Pittsburgh*, 1888, Digital Collection-Historic Pittsburgh.
7. McCullough, p. 87.
8. McCullough, p. 259.

Chapter 10

1. Nasaw, p. 371.
2. Krause, p. 269.
3. Wall, p. 499.
4. Letter Andrew Carnegie to H.C. Frick, December 31, 1890, Henry Clay Frick Papers, University of Pittsburgh, Box 3, Folder 1.
5. Nasaw, p. 389.
6. Warren, p. 73.
7. Sanger, p. 138.
8. W. Martin, *Pittsburgh Post*, November 27, 1898.

Chapter 11

1. Krause, p. 289.
2. William McKinley, " The Value of Protection," *The North American Review* 150, no. 403 (June 1890): pp. 747–48.
3. David Brody, *Steelworkers in America: The Nonunion Era* (New York: Harper Torchbooks, 1960), p. 51.
4. Krause, p. 291.
5. Letters, Carnegie to Henry Clay Frick, June 10 and 28, 1892, William Martin Papers, Archives of Industrial Society, University of Pittsburgh Library.

Chapter 12

1. Arthur G. Burgoyne, *The Homestead Strike of 1892* (Pittsburgh: Rawsthorne, 1893).
2. Interview of Frick, *Pittsburgh Post*, July 8, 1892.

3. *Pittsburgh Post*, July 8, 1892.
4. Les Standiford, *Meet You in Hell: Andrew Carnegie, Henry Clay Frick, and the Bitter Partnership that Transformed America* (New York: Crown, 2003), p. 117.
5. Richard Sheppard, "Homestead Steel Strike of 1892," *Susquehanna* (February 1988).
6. Wall, p. 354.
7. Krause, p. 291.
8. Gerald Eggert, *Steelmasters and Labor Reform 1886–1923* (Pittsburgh: University of Pittsburgh Press, 1981), p. 13.
9. James H. Bridge, *The Inside History of the Carnegie Steel Company* (New York: Aldine, 1903), pp. 201–202.

Chapter 13

1. Schreiner, p. 73.
2. Krause, p. 279.
3. Edward Slavishak, *Bodies of Work* (Durham: Duke University Press, 2008), p. 65.
4. Letter, H. O'Donnell to W. Reid, July 16, 1892, *Journal of Political Economy* 2, p. 385.
5. Standiford, p. 213.
6. Cannadine, p. 106.
7. Sanger, p. 199.
8. Schreiner, p. 102.
9. Standiford, p. 214.
10. John Conway, "America's Workmen," *The Catholic World* 56 (January 1893).
11. Charles Calhoun, *Benjamin Harrison* (New York: Times Books, 2005), p. 147.
12. *New York Times*, February 10, 1890.
13. *Pittsburgh Dispatch*, October 25, 1892.
14. *New York Times*, October 30, 1892.
15. Robert Hesson, *Steel Titan* (New York: Oxford Press, 1975), p. 40.
16. Burgoyne, p. 75.
17. Nasaw, p. 426.
18. Carroll Wright, "National Amalgamated Association of Iron, Steel, and Tin Workers," *The Quarterly Journal of Economics* (November 1901).
19. Harvey, p. 177.
20. Casson, p. 138.
21. *Pittsburgh Post Gazette*, June 28, 1992, p. C-1.
22. Bridge, p. 233.
23. Ron Chernow, *Titan: The Life of John D. Rockefeller* (New York: Vintage, 2004), p. 334.
24. Thomas Boyle, "A. Carnegie and H.C. Frick," *The Independent*, January 19, 1893.
25. Letter, Andrew Carnegie to George Lauder, July 17, 1892, Andrew Carnegie Papers, Library of Congress, Volume 17, #3111.
26. Both Dickson's and Corey's fathers had been partners with Thomas Mellon in the coal business.

Chapter 14

1. Quentin Skrabec, *William McKinley: Apostle of Protectionism* (New York: Algora, 2008), p. 111.
2. Letter, McKinley to M. Hanna et al., March 14, 1893, McKinley Papers, Canton, Ohio.

3. *Pittsburgh Press*, December 9, 1892.
4. Stefan Lorant, *Pittsburgh: The Story of an American City* (Garden City: Doubleday, 1964), p. 551.
5. Often called "Harry"; Harry was a common nickname for Henry.
6. Bridge, p. 259.
7. Evans, p. 210.

Chapter 15

1. William Corey was the son of James Corey of Braddock. James Corey was the coal business partner of Thomas Mellon, who first recognized Frick's skills.
2. Hesson, p. 44.
3. Warren, p. 154.
4. Letter, Carnegie to William Whitney, February 1887, Whitney Papers, Library of Congress, Vol. 41, #7649.
5. Warren, p. 157.
6. Telegram, Henry Phipps to Andrew Carnegie, December 22, 1894, Volume 29, Andrew Carnegie Papers, Library of Congress.
7. Letter, Andrew Carnegie to John Leishman, January 4, 1896. Andrew Carnegie Papers, Library of Congress, Volume 35.
8. Harvey, p. 335.
9. Sanger, *Helen Clay Frick*, p. 94.
10. Letter, Andrew Carnegie to Carnegie Steel, May 16, 1895. Andrew Carnegie Papers, Library of Congress Volume 31.
11. Richard Mancke, "Iron Ore and Steel: A Case Study of the Economic Causes and Consequences of Vertical Integration," *The Journal of Industrial Economics* 20, no. 3 (July 1972).

Chapter 16

1. Warren, *Triumphant Capitalism*, p. 229.
2. *Report on Conditions of Employment in the Iron and Steel Industry*, vol. 3 (Washington, D.C.: U.S. Bureau of Labor, 1911).
3. Harvey, p. 295.
4. Warren, p. 229.
5. Carnegie Steel Board Meeting Minutes, March 4, 1899, Volume 63, Andrew Carnegie Papers, Library of Congress.
6. Tarbell, p. 98.
7. Tarbell, p. 107.
8. Wall, p. 725.
9. Hendrick interview, Volume 256, Andrew Carnegie Papers, Library of Congress.
10. Wall, p. 733.
11. Letter, Andrew Carnegie to Dod Lauder, November 25, 1899, Volume 70, Andrew Carnegie Papers, Library of Congress.
12. Hendrick Interview, February 16, 1928, Volume 239, Andrew Carnegie Papers, Library of Congress.
13. Letter (minutes), Andrew Carnegie to Carnegie Steel board of managers, August 23, 1898, Andrew Carnegie Papers, Library of Congress.

14. Stewart Holbrook, *Iron Brew* (New York: Macmillan, 1939), p. 256.

Chapter 17

1. John Winkler, *Morgan the Magnificent* (Babson Park: Spear & Staff, 1950), p. 202.
2. Carnegie Board Minutes, Andrew Carnegie to Charles Schwab, July 7, 1900, Andrew Carnegie Papers, Library of Congress.
3. Vincent Carosso, *The Morgans: Private International Bankers* (Cambridge: Harvard University Press, 1987), p. 467.
4. Thomas Kessner, *Capital City* (New York: Simon & Schuster, 2003), p. 303.
5. Casson, p. 191.
6. Ida Tarbell, *The Life of Elbert H. Gary: The Story of Steel* (New York: D. Appleton, 1925), p. 110.
7. Ron Chernow, *The House of Morgan* (New York: Grove, 1990), p. 82.
8. Hesson, p. 114.
9. Hesson, p. 116.
10. Schreiner, p. 183.
11. Wall, p. 788.
12. Tarbell, p. 257.
13. Brody, p. 19.
14. Holbrook, p. 260.
15. Rayback, p. 218.
16. *Daily Picayune*, September 13, 1901, p. 7.
17. Cannadine, p. 163.
18. Andrew W. Mellon Papers, 1902, National Gallery of Art, Washington, D.C.
19. Frick Collection, University of Pittsburgh, Box 1 and Folder 1.
20. Casson, p. 237.
21. "When Frick Protested and Morgan Wept," *Current Opinion* 62, no. 3 (March 1917): p. 174.
22. Warren, p. 303.
23. Warren, p. 58.
24. Frick Collection, University of Pittsburgh, Box 1, File 5.
25. *New York Times*, October 15, 1903.

Chapter 18

1. *Pittsburgh Times*, July 4, 1902.
2. Martha Frick Symington Sanger, *Helen Clay Frick* (Pittsburgh: University of Pittsburgh Press, 2008), p. 83.

Chapter 19

1. Maria Sciullo, "Play it, Henry Frick?," *Pittsburgh Post-Gazette*, March 13, 2008.
2. Arundel Cotter, *The Authentic History of the United States Steel Corporation* (New York: Moody Magazine, 1916), p. 29.
3. Edward S. Meade, "The Genesis of the United States Steel Corporation," *Journal of Economics* 15, no. 4 (August 1901): p. 517.
4. Patricia Beard, *After the Ball* (New York: HarperCollins, 2003), p. 178.

5. Schreiner, p. 34.
6. Holbrook, p. 280
7. Warren, *Big Steel*, p. 39.
8. Theodore Roosevelt, *The Autobiography of Theodore Roosevelt* (New York: Scribner's, 1958), p. 245.
9. Jean Strouse, *Morgan: American Financier* (New York: Harper Perennial, 2000), p. 589.
10. Ibid.
11. Harvey, p. 309.
12. Roy Lubove, *Twentieth Century Pittsburgh* (New York: John Wiley, 1969), p. 9.
13. Memoirs of William Dickson, William Brown Dickson Papers, Pennsylvania State University Library, University Park.
14. *New York Times*, June 13, 1911.

Chapter 20

1. *New York Times*, February 10, 1921.
2. Harvey, p. 348.
3. *New York Times*, March 15, 1915.
4. *Chicago Record-Herald*, Friday, February 19, 1912, p. 3.
5. Sanger, *Helen Clay Frick*, p. 83.
6. Jay Meader, "Henry Clay Frick American Sepulchral," *New York Daily News*, February 25, 1999.
7. *New York Herald*, March 3, 1919.
8. Sanger, *Henry Clay Frick*, p. 478.
9. Sanger, *Helen Clay Frick*, p. 94.
10. Chernow, *House of Morgan*, p. 173.
11. "Says Steel Trust is to Have Rival," *New York Times*, July 26, 1915.
12. Paul Boyer, ed., *The Oxford Guide to American History* (Oxford: Oxford University Press, 2001) p. 435.
13. Harvey, p. 322.
14. Harvey, p. 318.
15. Harvey, p. 363.
16. Ferdinand Lundberg, *America's Sixty Families* (New York: Citadel Press, 1938).
17. Harvey, p. 370.
18. Charles McCollester, ed., *Fighter with a Heart* (Pittsburgh: University of Pittsburgh, 1992), p. 221.
19. *New York Times*, December 3, 1919, p. 1.
20. *New York Times*, February 3, 1922.
21. Lorant, p. 558.
22. Sanger, *Henry Clay Frick*, p. 413.
23. *New York Times*, March 3, 1923.

Chapter 21

1. Thomas Boyle, "A. Carnegie and H.C. Frick," *The Independent*, January 19, 1893, vol. 43.
2. Editorial, *New York Times*, December 3, 1919.
3. Eric Foner, *Free Soil, Free Labor, Free Men* (Oxford: Oxford University Press, 1995), p. 20.
4. *New York Tribune*, January 5, 1894.
5. Fitch, p. 193.
6. Krause, p. 219.

Chapter 22

1. Carnegie, *Autobiography*, p. 17.
2. David Montgomery, *The Fall of the House of Labor* (Cambridge: Cambridge University Press, 1987), p. 9–11.
3. Curtis Miner, *Homestead: The Story of a Steel Town* (Pittsburgh: Western Pennsylvania Historical Society, 1989), p. 14.
4. Warren, p. 306.
5. Fitch, pp. 154–160.
6. Fitch, p. 235.
7. Colston Warne, *The Steel Strike of 1919* (Lexington: D.C. Heath, 1963), p. 29.
8. Eggert, p. 171.
9. *Year Book of the American Iron and Steel Institute*, 1919.
10. Brody, p. 106.
11. Warne, p. 61.
12. Sanger, *Henry Clay Frick*, p. 383.
13. Tarbell, p. 294.
14. Warren, p. 114.
15. *Report of the Industrial Commission*, 57th Congress, Document 76, 1901.
16. Brody, p. 187.

Chapter 23

1. Letter, Andrew Carnegie to H.C. Frick, January 1, 1894, Frick Papers, University of Pittsburgh, box 4, folder 1.
2. Letter, Andrew Carnegie to Francis Lovejoy, February 25, 1895. Andrew Carnegie Papers, Library of Congress, Volume 30.
3. *Personality Magazine* 45 (December 1927).
4. Minutes of Carnegie Steel Board of Managers, December 13, 1898, Volume 32, Andrew Carnegie Papers, Library of Congress.
5. Hesson, p. 125.
6. Warren, p. 86.
7. Hesson, p. 167.
8. Eggert, p. 23.
9. Ibid.

Chapter 24

1. Rottenberg, p. 67.
2. "When Frick Protested and Morgan Wept," *Current Opinion* 62, no. 3 (March 1917): p. 174.
3. Eggert, p. 88.
4. Eggert, p. 164.
5. Fredric Quiver, "Connellsville Coal and Coke" (Washington, D.C.: National Parks Service, 1991), p. 43.
6. Editor, "A Great Steelmaster," *Outlook*, December 17, 1919, p. 490.
7. Letter, Henry Clay Frick to Farrell, January 31, 1916.
8. Ray Mayhew, "Henry Clay Frick," *Leslie's Monthly Magazine* 60, no. 3 (July 1905).
9. *New York Times*, December 3, 1919.
10. Harvey, p. 369.
11. Harvey, p. 324.
12. *Uniontown Herald*, December 5, 1919.

Bibliography

Archival Sources

Alexander Holley Papers, National Museum of American History, Washington, D.C.

Andrew Carnegie Papers, Library of Congress.

Andrew Mellon Papers, National Gallery of Art, Washington, D.C.

Carnegie Library Oakland, Pennsylvania Room.

Frick Papers and Frick Collection, University of Pittsburgh.

George Perkins Papers, Michigan State University Library.

Mellon Bank Papers, Historical Society of Western Pennsylvania.

President William McKinley Papers, Presidential McKinley Memorial Library, Canton, Ohio.

Terrence V. Powderly Papers, Catholic University of America, Washington, D.C.

Thomas Lynch Papers, University of Pittsburgh at Greensburg.

Thomas Mellon Papers, National Gallery of Art, Washington, D.C.

William Dickson Papers, The Pennsylvania State University Library.

William Martin Papers, Archives of Industrial Society, University of Pittsburgh Library.

William Whitney Papers, Library of Congress.

Books

Alberts, Robert C. *Good Provider.* Boston: Houghton Mifflin, 1973.

Barron, C.W. *They Told Barron.* New York: Harper, 1930.

Beard, Patricia. *After the Ball.* New York: HarperCollins, 2003.

Berkman, Alexander. *Prison Memoirs of an Anarchist.* New York: Schocken, 1970.

Boyer, Paul, ed. *The Oxford Guide to American History.* Oxford: Oxford University Press, 2001.

Bridenbaugh, Carl. *The Colonial Craftsman.* New York: Dover, 1990.

Bridge, James. *The Inside History of the Carnegie Steel Company.* New York: Aldine, 1903.

Brody, David. *Steelworkers in America: The Nonunion Era.* New York: Harper Torchbooks, 1960.

Burgoyne, Arthur G. *The Homestead Strike of 1892.* Pittsburgh: Rawsthorne, 1893.

Burnley, J. *Millionaires and Kings of Enterprise.* Philadelphia: Lippincott, 1901.

Butler, Joseph. *Fifty Years of Iron and Steel.* Cleveland: Penton, 1917.

Byington, M. *Homestead: The Households of a Mill Town, Pittsburgh Survey.* New York: Russell Sage Foundation, 1910.

Calhoun, Charles. *Benjamin Harrison.* New York: Times Books, 2005.

Cannadine, David. *Mellon: An American Life.* New York: Alfred A. Knopf, 2006.

Carnegie, Andrew. *The Autobiography of Andrew Carnegie.* Boston: Northeastern University Press, 1986.

Carosso, Vincent. *The Morgans: Private International Bankers.* Cambridge: Harvard University Press, 1987.

Casson, Herbert. *The Romance of Steel: The Story of a Thousand Millionaires.* New York: A.S. Barnes, 1907.

Chernow, Ron. *The House of Morgan.* New York: Grove, 1990.

_____. *Titan: The Life of John D. Rockefeller.* New York: Vintage Books, 2004.

Cochran, Thomas, and William Miller. *The Age of Enterprise.* New York: Harper & Row, 1942.

Corey, J.B. *Memoir of J.B. Corey.* Pittsburgh: Pittsburgh Printing, 1914.

Cotter, Arundel. *The Authentic History of the United States Steel Corporation.* New York: Moody Magazine, 1916.

DiCiccio, Carmen. *Coal and Coke in Pennsylvania.* Harrisburg: Pennsylvania Historical and Museum Commission, 1996.

Doherty, Donald. *Pittsburgh's Shadyside.* Chicago: Arcadia, 2008.

Eggert, Gerald. *Steelmasters and Labor Reform 1886–1923.* Pittsburgh: University of Pittsburgh Press, 1981.

Evans, Henry Oliver. *Iron Pioneer: Henry W. Oliver.* New York: E.P. Dutton, 1942.

Fisher, Douglas. *Steel Serves the Nation.* Pittsburgh: United States Steel, 1951.

Fitch, John. *The Steel Worker.* Pittsburgh: University of Pittsburgh Press, 1989.

Foner, Eric. *Free Soil, Free Labor, Free Men.* Oxford: Oxford University Press, 1995.

Garraty, J. *Right Hand Man: The Life of George Perkins.* New York: Harper, 1957.

Goldman, Emma. *Living My Life.* New York: Dover, 1970.

Hart, Lane S. *Annual Report of the Secretary of Internal Affairs.* Harrisburg: State of Pennsylvania, 1884.

Harvey, George. *Henry Clay Frick: The Man.* Privately printed, 1938.

Havighurst, Walter. *Vein of Iron.* Cleveland: World, 1958.

Hendrick, B.J. *The Life of Andrew Carnegie.* New York: Doubleday, 1932.

Hersh, Burton. *The Mellon Family.* New York: William Morrow, 1978.

Hesson, Robert. *Steel Titan.* New York: Oxford Press, 1975.

Holbrook, Stewart. *Iron Brew*. New York: Macmillan, 1939.

Jenkins, Charles F. *Guide to Historic Germantown*. Germantown Historical Society, 1904.

Kellogg, Paul, ed. *The Pittsburgh Survey*. 6 vols. New York: Survey Associates, 1908–1914.

Kessner, Thomas. *Capital City*. New York: Simon & Schuster, 2003.

Krause, Paul. *The Battle for Homestead, 1880–1892*. Pittsburgh: University of Pittsburgh Press, 1992.

Lorant, Stefan. *Pittsburgh: The Story of an American City*. Garden City: Doubleday, 1964.

Lubove, Roy. *Twentieth Century Pittsburgh*. New York: John Wiley, 1969.

Lundberg, Ferdinand. *America's Sixty Families*. New York: Citadel, 1938.

Mancke, Richard. "Iron Ore and Steel: A Case Study of the Economic Causes and Consequences of Vertical Integration." *The Journal of Industrial Economics* 20, no. 3 (July 1972).

McCollester, Charles, ed. *Fighter with a Heart*. Pittsburgh: University of Pittsburgh Press, 1992.

McCullough, David. *The Johnstown Flood*. New York: Touchstone, 1968.

Meade, Edward. "The Genesis of the United States Steel Corporation." *Journal of Economics* 15, no. 4 (August 1901).

Meader, Jay. "Henry Clay Frick, American Sepulchral." *New York Daily News*, February 25, 1999.

Mellon, Thomas. *Thomas Mellon and His Times*. Pittsburgh: University of Pittsburgh Press, 1994.

Miles, Lisa. *Remembering Allegheny City*. Pittsburgh: Pennsylvania Historical Commission, 2007.

Miner, Curtis. *Homestead: The Story of a Steel Town*. Pittsburgh: Western Pennsylvania Historical Society, 1989.

Montgomery, David. *Beyond Equality: Labor and the Radical Republicans*. Urbana: University of Illinois Press, 1981.

_____. *The Fall of the House of Labor*. Cambridge: Cambridge University Press, 1987.

Morgan, H. Wayne. *From Hayes to McKinley: National Party Politics*. Syracuse: Syracuse University Press, 1969.

_____. *William McKinley and His America*. Syracuse: Syracuse University Press, 1962.

Mumford, Lewis. *Techniques and Civilization*. New York: Harvest, 1962.

Nasaw, David. *Andrew Carnegie*. New York: Penguin, 2006.

Nelson, Ralph. *Merger Movements in American Industry 1895–1956*. Princeton: Princeton University Press, 1959.

O'Hara, Mary. "My Father, Henry Clay Frick, by Helen Clay Frick." *Pittsburgh Press*, August 1959.

Rayback, Joseph. *The History of American Labor*. New York: Macmillan, 1961.

Reitano, Joanne. *The Tariff Question in the Glided Age*. University Park: Pennsylvania State University Press, 1994.

Report on Conditions of Employment in the Iron and Steel Industry, vol. 3. Washington, D.C.: U.S. Bureau of Labor, 1911.

Ripley, W. *Trusts, Pools, and Corporations*. New York: Ginn, 1905.

Roosevelt, Theodore. *The Autobiography of Theodore Roosevelt*. New York: Scribner's, 1958.

Root, Waverly, and Richard de Rochemont. *Eating in America: A History*. New York: Echo, 1981.

Rottenberg, Dan. *In The Kingdom of Coal*. New York: Routledge, 2003.

Sanger, Martha Frick Symington. *Henry Clay Frick: An Intimate Portrait*. New York: Abbeville, 1998.

_____. *Helen Clay Frick*. Pittsburgh: University of Pittsburgh Press, 2008.

Schlereth, Thomas. *Victorian America*. New York: Harper Perennial, 1991.

Schreiner, Samuel A. Jr. *Henry Clay Frick: The Gospel of Greed*. New York: St. Martin's, 1995.

Scoville, Warren. *Revolution in Glassmaking*. Cambridge: Harvard University Press, 1948.

Sheppard, Murial. *Cloud by Day*. Pittsburgh: University of Pittsburgh Press, 1991.

Sheppard, Richard. "Homestead Steel Strike of 1892." *Susquehanna* (February 1988).

Skrabec, Quentin. *George Westinghouse: Gentle Genius*. New York: Algora, 2007.

_____. *The Metallurgic Age*. Jefferson, NC: McFarland, 2006.

_____. *Michael Owens and the Glass Industry*. Gretna, LA: Pelican, 2007.

_____. *William McKinley: Apostle of Protectionism*. New York: Algora, 2008.

Slavishak, Edward. *Bodies of Work: Civic Display and Labor in Industrial Pittsburgh*. Durham: Duke University Press, 2008.

Standiford, Les. *Meet You in Hell: Andrew Carnegie, Henry Clay Frick, and the Bitter Partnership that Transformed America*. New York: Crown, 2003.

Strouse, Jean. *Morgan: American Financier*. New York: Harper Perennial, 2000.

Summers, Mark. *Party Games*. Chapel Hill: University of North Carolina Press, 2004.

Taft, Philip. *Organized Labor in American History*. New York: Harper & Row, 1964.

Tarbell, Ida. *The Life of Elbert H. Gary: The Story of Steel*. New York: D. Appleton, 1925.

Timmons, Bascom. *Portrait of an American: Charles G. Dawes*. New York: Henry Holt, 1963.

Verne, Jules. *Begum's Millions*. Middletown: Wesleyan University Press, 2005.

Wall, Joseph Frazier. *Andrew Carnegie*. New York: Oxford University Press, 1970.

Warne, Colston. *The Steel Strike of 1919*. Lexington: D.C. Heath, 1963.

Warren, Kenneth. *Triumphant Capitalism*. Pittsburgh: University of Pittsburgh Press, 1996.

Watkins, Elizabeth. "Heinz Varieties on Six Continents." *Western Pennsylvania History* 82 (1999).

Welch, Robert. *The Presidencies of Grover Cleveland*. Lawrence: University of Kansas Press, 1988.

Wiley, Harvey. *An Autobiography*. Indianapolis: Bobbs-Merrill, 1930.

Winkler, John. *Morgan the Magnificent*. Babson Park: Spear & Staff, 1950.

Wright, Carroll. "National Amalgamated Association of Iron, Steel, and Tin Workers." *The Quarterly Journal of Economics* (November 1901).

Zieger, Robert. *Republicans and Labor*. Lexington: University of Kentucky Press, 1969.

Index